Translated Texts for Historians

300–800 AD is the time of late antiquity and the early middle ages: the transformation of the classical world, the beginnings of Europe and of Islam, and the evolution of Byzantium. TTH makes available sources from a range of languages, including Greek, Latin, Syriac, Coptic, Arabic, Georgian, Gothic and Armenian. Each volume provides an expert scholarly translation, with an introduction setting texts and authors in context, and with notes on content, interpretation and debates.

Editorial Committee
Phil Booth, St Peter's College, Oxford
Sebastian Brock, Oriental Institute, University of Oxford
Averil Cameron, Keble College, Oxford
Marios Costambeys, University of Liverpool
Carlotta Dionisotti, King's College, London
Peter Heather, King's College, London
Robert Hoyland, Institute for Study of the Ancient World,
        New York University
William E. Klingshirn, The Catholic University of America
Michael Lapidge, Clare College, Cambridge
Neil McLynn, Corpus Christi College, Oxford
Richard Price, Royal Holloway, University of London
Claudia Rapp, Institut für Byzantinistik und Neogräzistik,
        Universität Wien
Judith Ryder, University of Oxford
Raymond Van Dam, University of Michigan
Yuhan Vevaina, Oriental Institute, University of Oxford
Michael Whitby, University of Birmingham
Ian Wood, University of Leeds

General Editors
Gillian Clark, University of Bristol
Mark Humphries, Swansea University
Mary Whitby, University of Oxford

I0593111

For full details of **Translated Texts for Historians**, including prices and ordering information, please contact: Liverpool University Press, 4 Cambridge Street, Liverpool, L69 7ZU, UK (*Tel* +44-[0]151-794 2233. Email janet.mcdermott@liverpool.ac.uk, http://www.liverpooluniversitypress.co.uk).

Translated Texts for Historians
Volume 76

Sidonius Apollinaris Complete Poems

Translated with commentary by
ROGER GREEN

Liverpool
University
Press

First published 2022
Liverpool University Press
4 Cambridge Street
Liverpool, L69 7ZU

This paperback edition published 2024

British Library Cataloguing-in-Publication Data
A British Library CIP Record is available.

ISBN 978-1-80034-859-2 (hardback)
ISBN 978-1-80085-997-5 (paperback)

Typeset by Carnegie Book Production, Lancaster

CONTENTS

ACKNOWLEDGEMENTS

I wish to thank Mary Whitby, editor of *Translated Texts for Historians*, Mark Humphries for invaluable help at earlier stages of my research and more recently for his learned correction and polishing, Clare Litt and other staff of Liverpool University Press; and Tom Brown, Jill Harries, Luke Houghton, Gavin Kelly, Lawrence Keppie, Jesús Hernández Lobato, Costas Panayotakis and Joop van Waarden for their help with various points.

ABBREVIATIONS

Amm.	Ammianus Marcellinus
c.	*carmen* (poem)
c.m.	*carmina minora*
Chron. Gall.	*Chronicon Gallense*
ep.	*epistula* (letter)
John Ant.	John of Antioch
OCD⁴	*Oxford Classical Dictionary*, fourth edition
OLD	*Oxford Latin Dictionary*
Ovid, *M.*	Ovid, *Metamorphoses*
Pan. Lat.	*Panegyrici Latini*
Pliny, *NH*	Pliny the Elder, *Natural History*
PLRE	*Prosopography of the Later Roman Empire*
RE	Pauly-Wissowa, *Realencyclopädie der classischen Altertumswissenschaft*
S.	Sidonius Apollinaris
TLL	*Thesaurus Linguae Latinae*
Vergil, *A.*	Vergil, *Aeneid*
Vergil, *E.*	Vergil, *Eclogues*
Vergil, *G.*	Vergil, *Georgics*

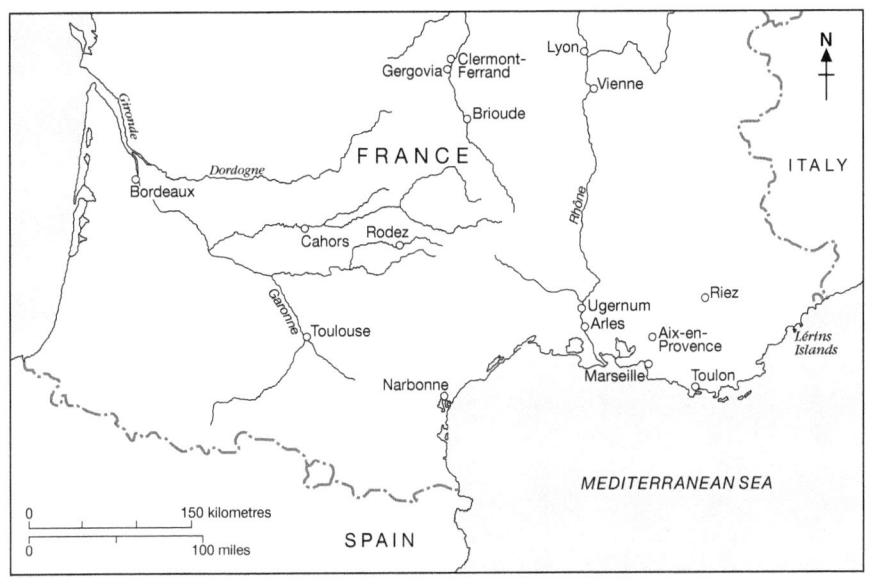

The Gaul of Sidonius

INTRODUCTION TO
THE POEMS OF SIDONIUS APOLLINARIS

1. SIDONIUS: HIS LIFE AND BACKGROUND

Sidonius Apollinaris – the second of these names is less commonly used today, as is a third name, Sollius, which he uses in two poems (*c.* 9.15.1 and *c.* 23.28) – lived in the mid-fifth century AD, and spent almost all of his life in Gaul; the exceptions that we know of, relatively short though very significant, were visits to Rome. Born in about 430,[1] he lived until at least 480, perhaps beyond 485.[2] He lived at a critical time in the history of Gaul, as shown for the early fifth century by the fragile nature of its boundaries and coastal areas, the presence of Goths and invaders of other peoples and their armies and the general inability of imperial Roman authority to check usurpers or subdue warlords in the Western half of the empire. By the time Sidonius grew old and died, a king of the Visigoths exercised power over most of Gaul, and was able to ignore weak puppet emperors and the voice of the church; Sidonius was actually imprisoned and exiled late in life. Living in central and south-eastern Gaul, Sidonius was a witness of these developments and a major player in many of them. According to the historian Gregory of Tours, writing a century later, who refers to Sidonius frequently (albeit sometimes in an anecdotal way), he was 'a man of most noble birth in terms of secular honours, and one of the leading senators of Gaul'.[3]

---

1 The date of his birth, 5 November, is known (*c.* 20.1/2), but the year 432 given by Stevens (1933/79), 1 is too precise, as he acknowledges in his note 3. The evidence for this date is in the passage quoted below from *Ep.* 8.6.5. See also Harries (1994), 36, n. 1.

2 As stated by Stevens (1933/79), xiv, and argued by him in Appendix G, 211–12, between 480 and 490. Sidonius's successor Aprunculus died relatively young in 490.

3 Gregory of Tours, *Histories* 2. 21, as translated by L. Thorpe, *Gregory of Tours: History of the Franks* (Harmondsworth, 1974). He would in fact be a senator 'from his cradle' (Stevens (1933/79), 1; Gregory is thinking of the holding of elevated office. Summary with references in *PLRE* 2.115–18, Apollinaris 6, at 116.

2. SIDONIUS'S MOTHER AND FATHER

Relatively little is known about his mother and father, and their names are not known for certain.[4] His mother's standing is implicitly illustrated by one of Sidonius's letters (his many letters, unlike most of the poems, were from later life), which is written to a kinsman named Avitus[5] and states that their mothers were united by a very close tie of kindred blood (they may in fact have been sisters). The name of the mother of Sidonius, and also her exact lineage, are not fully clear, but the absence of this detail is certainly not a sign of alienation. In general, the under-representation of women's names in Gallo-Roman society is a noticeable fact.[6] It is speculated by Mathisen that at some time, if his father died in middle age, Sidonius lived with her in Clermont in the Auvergne.[7] The same letter shows in its general references to schools, sports and state services that Sidonius's upbringing and that of his kinsman were typical of that of a young aristocrat.

The high nobility of his father and other ancestors seems to be attested by a jovial and mildly sarcastic letter (*Ep.* 1.3.1, here I follow Anderson's translation), of uncertain context and date, in which Sidonius speaks of distinctions[8] that were attained 'by my father, my father-in-law, my grandfather, and my great grandfather' – these consisted, apparently, of 'distinctions of praetorian and city prefectures and masterships at court and in the army'. In another letter (*Ep.* 5.9.2) he recalls that his father had been a tribune and notary (*tribunus et notarius*), or secretary, under the emperor Honorius (395–423), a relatively humble office that was a frequent step to higher service in the state.[9] His father is clearly described

---

4 *PLRE* 2.1220, Anonymus 6.

5 *Ep.* 3.1.1. *PLRE* 2. 94–5, Avitus 1. This is not, of course, the emperor.

6 Mathisen (2020), 40–1.

7 Mathisen (2020), 60.

8 On the offices mentioned here, see the later section (10) on political nomenclature. As Anderson's note on the passage makes clear, each ancestor mentioned did not hold all these distinctions.

9 Jones (1973), 574: 'By the middle of the fifth century there were apparently a large number of wealthy men who bore the title of tribune and notary in the Western parts, but only thirty who were in active attendance at court' (with n. 21 on page 1235 for examples). Presumably at some stage the appellation of 'notary' had been elevated by the addition of the older and more august name of tribune. See further Hans Teitler, Notarii *and* Exceptores: *An enquiry into the role and significance of shorthand writers in the imperial and ecclesiastical bureaucracy pf the Roman empire (from the Early Principate to c. 450 AD)* (Amsterdam, 1985).

as praetorian prefect of Gaul in a very illuminating letter (*Ep.* 8.6.5) that deserves fuller analysis. Here Sidonius tells us that as a young man hardly emerged from boyhood he accompanied his father to Arles (this was in January 449), where as praetorian prefect his father presided over the delegations of the Gallic provinces to the annual council, namely the council of Goths and Romans instituted after the settlement of the Goths in Aquitaine (418).[10] His father, without making a formal inauguration of the new consul Astyrius[11] – this was outside his power – was celebrating his entry to the consulship and making it widely known in Gaul, no doubt with his own emphases.[12]

Anderson is surely wrong to refer to the meeting just described as simply a 'trivial incident which gave him much pleasure' (1936, Introduction, xxxv). In fact the passage perhaps tells us as much about the young Sidonius as about the assembly that he reports. He was impressed (*Ep.* 8.6.5–6) not just by his father's authority at this gathering and by the consul's robe and formal chair – items about which he later wrote in his poems – but also by the fact that in the crowd, where he could mingle with officials and others, he was 'next to those who were next to the consul'. He knew his place, certainly, but the ceremony, the hierarchy and the formal pretence of modesty by a speaker (he calls it the 'prologue' of modesty [nice phrase])[13] made a strong impression and may have moved him towards a possible career in politics. In this same episode he shows his appreciation of a panegyric delivered in honour of the said consul that was very effective, with 'not a single word that I did not admire' (*Ep.* 8.6.8). We may note that he himself showed no inclination to the military side, though he later wrote about battles with gusto and in gory detail. And, unlike the young Avitus (the emperor) that he will portray (*c.* 7.218–24), he shows no particular interest in the Goths as potential friends or allies at this stage.

10 On this institution and its importance see Matthews (1975), 334–8, citing G. Haenel, *Corpus Legum* (1857), 1171 (p. 238) ; for commentary, see esp. J. Zeller, *Westdeutsche Zeitschrift* 24 [1905], 1–19). In this case the agenda of the council also included distribution of 'largesse' (this shows the Roman viewpoint, no doubt) and the scrutiny of a new law from Valentinian III.

11 For the consul's previous military career, cf. (the chronicler) Hydatius 117 [125, Mommsen], date 441; cf. *PLRE* 2.174–5, Fl. Astyrius.

12 This fascinating letter is referred to again in section 10 of this introduction.

13 On this feature, prominent in the panegyrics for Anthemius and Majorian, see Béranger (1948).

His father's father Apollinaris, who had been praetorian prefect in the early fifth century,[14] is mentioned by Sidonius in a piece of verse within a letter (*Ep.* 3.12.5)[15] where he describes an inscription in verse to commemorate his grandfather that he wrote to replace the one that had been vandalised. Sidonius mentions in this inscription (this was the greatest of his honours) that this grandfather was the first of his line to give up pagan worship and be baptised (lines 13–16). In another letter (*Ep.* 5.9.1) he states that Apollinaris, and his other grandfather Rusticus,[16] had abhorred the usurpers Constantine (407–11) and Jovinus (411–13). Apollinaris was mooted by Anderson as the name of Sidonius' father; the name Alcimus has now also been suggested.[17]

3. SIDONIUS AND PAPIANILLA

Sidonius married Papianilla, the daughter of Eparchius Avitus, probably at some time before Avitus became emperor (July 455).[18] Two other Papianillas are attested, one being the wife of Tonantius Ferreolus in *c.* 24.34–8;[19] the other is certainly an unrelated person. Part of the dowry received by Sidonius was the family property on lake Aydat, at Avitacum, which he describes carefully and lovingly in *Ep.* 2.2; this, he says, became his preferred home (*Ep.* 2.2.3), and was dearer than the one that he inherited, near Lyon. Avitacum is also referred to by Sidonius in *c.* 17, where he thanks his friend Ommatius for helping him (lines 19–20), perhaps with the actual move, but more probably with the process of settling in, through his love and the grace of Christ.[20] We know of four children (the birthday of one of

14 *PLRE* 2.113, Apollinaris 1.
15 There are some sixteen examples of this in the letters.
16 *PLRE* 2.965, Rusticus 9.
17 By Anderson (1965), II. 422, n. 1, and Mathisen (2020), 57, respectively.
18 In *c.* 23.430, looking back over Avitus's brief reign, Sidonius speaks of 'the court of my wife's father'.
19 The possibility of a relationship between her and Sidonius's wife is discussed by Harries (1994), 34 and n. 30. See also Santelia (2002) on lines 37–40 of poem 24. In *Ep.* 2.9.3, the kitchens and other delights of the two parties (Sidonius had relations with both, and enjoyed the hospitality of both) are jokingly compared. The third Papianilla belongs to the mid-sixth century; her murder is mentioned in Gregory of Tours, *History of the Franks*, 3. 36.
20 Stevens (1933/1979), 189–95 (Appendix B) fully discussed the claims of Aydat to be this home of Sidonius, and the location has been generally accepted by the influential Loyen (1960) among others. The position of Avitacum has been more elusive.

them is referred to in *c.* 17.1–3),[21] of whom three were daughters: Severiana (*Ep.* 2.12.2), who at the time suffered from severe and persistent coughing, leading to fever; Roscia (*Ep.* 5.16.5), then being nurtured by grandmother and aunts; and Alcima, who acted as patron of a church at Clermont (Gregory of Tours, *Glory of the Martyrs* 64) and later became involved in a plot against Theoderic I, who exiled her (Gregory of Tours, *Histories* 3.12; *PLRE* 2.54). There were no twins, as was inferred by Mommsen from *c.* 17.3 (see the note of Anderson [1980], 1. 254) and repeated by Stevens in a long note on pp. 84–5, importing unnecessary difficulties. The son with whom according to *Ep.* 4.12.2 Sidonius read the comic poet Terence (see below [p. 8]) had the family name of Apollinaris; references to him in the letters are frequent and he later became bishop of Clermont in his own right in 515, but died four months later (*PLRE* 2.114, Apollinaris 3).

4. THE EDUCATION OF SIDONIUS

It is likely that the education that Sidonius received was divided in the traditional way between elementary teaching (possibly at home), and then the school of the *grammaticus* and the school of the *rhetor*.[22] He will have learnt first, from a young age, what was termed 'grammar', in which acquiring the basic skills of reading simple texts was the main aim; and then, when older, the skills of rhetoric and effective public speaking. These skills were generally taught by the exercises of *suasoria* (which is a deliberative speech 'advocating a course of action') and *controversia* ('a speech in character on one side of a fictional law case').[23] At both levels the works of classical poets could play a large part, as appropriate, and the young Sidonius will have met stories and episodes of the classical poets he would later know so well.[24]

That he studied rhetoric (and perhaps 'grammar' too) in Arles seems very likely. His father, as praetorian prefect of Gaul, lived in or near the

21 Kelly (Kelly and van Waarden [2020], 173) mentions the possibility that, supposing she had married young, the birthday mentioned might be Papianilla's.

22 One should not understand by 'school' a purpose-built structure: cf. OCD[4], education, Roman, p. 490.

23 These definitions derive from OCD[4].

24 The standard work on ancient education is Marrou (1956). For Sidonius in particular, see Stevens (1933/1979), 1–18, and, more sensitively, Harries (1994), 47 and 107. Green (1985) considers teaching arrangements within the large Gallic city of Bordeaux.

city, and two of his son's later friends, Probus and Magnus Felix, lived in
Narbo,[25] much nearer to Arles than to Lyon or Clermont, the other possible
locations for Sidonous' education. A teacher of philosophy (among other
things, no doubt) named Eusebius, of whom Sidonius speaks quite warmly
in *Ep.* 4.1.3, may well have operated in Arles.[26] (There is, incidentally,
no evidence, *pace* Stevens (p. 7), that he flogged his students). Modern
discussions of the teaching of ancient rhetoric, and some ancient ones,
have often lamented that debate and mock-pleading followed the same old
topics, which were (to judge from some of the evidence from much earlier),
lacking in relevance or genuine excitement. But against this one can set the
picture, albeit written somewhat later in his life, that Sidonius gives of how,
under the leadership of Probus, the friend and fellow-student mentioned
above, the house of Eusebius, like 'a mint of various studies', provided
an environment that showed what could be learned by the intelligent
(*Ep.* 4.1.2): Probus demonstrated, among other things, 'the loftiness of the
epic poet, the truthfulness of a historian, the raillery of the satirist, the
fun of the epigrammatist, and the excitement that would gain applause for
the panegyrist'.[27] Sidonius has a vivid memory of the possibilities in such
sessions – a world away from the dry-as-dust dogmatic rules and classifi-
cations that still continued in the footsteps, or at least under the names, of
masters such as Quintilian.[28]

The outstanding orator Cicero (also a theorist of note) was perhaps
not a great influence on Sidonius. In his quick account of the youth and
upbringing of the emperor Avitus (*c.* 7.174–5) he briefly mentions that
his mind was moulded by the 'thunder' of Cicero, which is, for Sidonius,
fundamental and an important part of an emperor's function. Later, in the
panegyric for Anthemius, Cicero, 'the consul from Arpinum' (mention of
his consulship directs attention to his triumph over Catiline)[29] is said to
offer 'help for speaking' (*c.* 2.186): that is to say, he was a model for any
public speaker (not this emperor in particular). In *c.* 23.145–6, the only
other place in the poems where Cicero is mentioned, he is fitted into a

---

25 Sidonius describes himself as a schoolmate of Felix at *c.* 9.330–1; for Probus see below.
26 The evidence is briefly given in Harries (1994), 47, n. 37.
27 The Latin word is *plausibile*, which means 'liable or able to win applause' in rhetorical
contexts, and certainly not 'plausible'.
28 The great teacher of oratory Quintilian is mentioned by Sidonius in *c.* 2.191 and
c. 9.317, and in *Ep.* 5.10.3 is praised for his pungency.
29 In the year of his consulship (63 BC) Cicero denounced Catiline in many speeches as
a conspirator against the state and had him executed.

line of writers outstanding in eloquence. In the letters of Sidonius he is mentioned from time to time as a paragon of oratory, or for the occasional semi-proverbial phrase or allusion, in a rather perfunctory way. In the school context, perhaps, Cicero did not have a high profile or leave a strong impression on Sidonius. It is interesting that in places where Sidonius lists Latin prose authors Cicero is not prominent (*c.* 23.145–69), where the prose writers Varro, Tacitus and Petronius have more lines, as potentially more interesting authors; and in the quirky poem *c.* 9, which lists themes that he will not allude to in his reply,[30] he is absent. There is, moreover, little in the poems on the life and career of Cicero; Demosthenes, his Greek counterpart, gets more attention in *c.* 2.186–8 and *c.* 23.136–44.

Reference has just been made to what I call 'listing', a notable feature of Sidonius's writing. The passage of the Anthemius panegyric just cited began with a remarkable list of his boyhood attention to the so called Seven Sages and other philosophers, followed by a list of literary luminaries in lines 182–92. Here Sidonius refers to the Latin prose authors Livy, Sallust, Varro, Quintilian and Tacitus, adding that Anthemius was accustomed to range through them (182–3). In the poem in praise of his friend Consentius (*c.* 23) there is a comparable list, in which (145–57), after the Seven Sages and numerous Greek writers, come the 'masters of Latin eloquence': Cicero, Livy, Vergil, Terence, Plautus, Varro, Sallust, Tacitus and Petronius (145–67).[31] It would be ridiculous to suggest that Sidonius thought that Anthemius and Consentius senior had read or even browsed all these, or might read them. Nor is Sidonius claiming to be familiar with them himself; but the lists do seem to show a fascination with such writers, and even their mere names, that may date from the years of his early education, which planted aspirations eventually to read more.

Where or when Sidonius acquired a knowledge of Greek can only be guessed. There is little possibility that he read any of the Greek authors that he names in the above-mentioned lists; he does not claim this in any way, and some are very abstruse, perhaps unavailable at the time.[32] (Plausible verbal allusions to Greek writers have not come to light, as they have in some cases in the lighter poems of Ausonius, a century earlier).[33]

---

30 For a survey of this poem see below, and the notes in the commentary.

31 Interestingly, Petronius replaces Quintilian, if *c.* 2 was written before *c.* 23. He may have read Petronius quite recently. See my note on *c.* 23.155–8.

32 See Green (1990) for a survey of Greek texts known in Late Roman Gaul.

33 See Green (1991), *Index Rerum* s.v. 'Greek; lost epigrams'.

But we have Sidonius's own report (*Ep.* 4.12.1–2) that he and his son were reading a play of Terence (*Mother-in-law*) with help from a copy of the Greek comic poet Menander's play *Epitrepontes* (now usually rendered as 'Arbitration').[34] (Their reading was unfortunately interrupted by a domestic slave who arrived with a hangdog look and a disturbing message.)[35]

It cannot be divined whether he read the Bible from a Greek version or one of the Latin translations available; it is perhaps unlikely that the Bible was read at school in either Greek or Latin. It should be inferred from various pieces of evidence in his poems that he was a Christian in early life.[36] His remarkable poem addressed to Faustus of Riez (*c.* 16; date uncertain) is an adaptation of the classical genre of epicising encomium to Christian praise, based on private reading and public worship, but probably not schooling.

5. THE CAREER OF SIDONIUS, POETIC AND POLITICAL

Up to the death of Avitus

From early 449, when we saw Sidonius and his father in Arles, to the second half of the year 455 (above, section 2), there is no direct or indirect information about Sidonius's activities or his aims, political or otherwise. At some point he gained the title of *tribunus et notarius* ('tribune and secretary'); this was a relatively minor post suitable for a young aristocrat (in the words of *PLRE* 2.117) and also a platform for an eventual political career, as it gave entry to the senate.[37] It was at this point, on or very close to 1 January 456, that he delivered at Rome a panegyric of the new emperor, Eparchius Avitus. He had been proclaimed the following year in Gaul, and Sidonius was probably one of the party sent ahead to Rome to prepare for his formal presentation there.[38] But his reign was brief: before the end of the year he had been defeated and deposed by the general Ricimer; he was made a bishop, but died soon afterwards. The death of

---

34 Sidonius tells us that for once he was 'following his natural inclination and oblivious of his (Christian) profession'.
35 Treated in the commentary of Amherdt (2001), who inclines to the dating 470–4.
36 See *c.* 22.218, *c.* 13.16 and probably *c.* 9.179–80.
37 On this rank see Jones (1966), 203, and Jones (1973), 574 and 1235.
38 *PLRE* 2.196–8, Avitus 5.

Avitus was a harsh shock, especially if he had hoped to build a career on the writing and delivering of panegyrics, like the poet Claudian, who was a *tribunus et notarius* at the court of Honorius fifty years before, and whose works Sidonius read at some stage with care and enthusiasm;[39] and his death will have confirmed, or perhaps created, his opinion that Gaul and Gauls had long been neglected by the emperors based in Italy (*c.* 7.537–43, *c.* 5.354–7).[40] He did, however, have a significant and tangible trophy, and memorial, of his support of Avitus, one that he prized throughout his life: the statue of him, Sidonius, set up in the Forum of Trajan in Rome,[41] from which time, as he records with pride in a poem in one of his last letters, 'Nerva Traianus (he means the forum of Trajan, who was to many the greatest of all Roman emperors) beheld my statue, with my titles, for all time'.[42]

Majorian

Sidonius was obliged to find new patronage, necessarily imperial patronage or an avenue to it, and there is no sign that he changed his career plans when Majorian, complicit with Ricimer in the defeat and deposition of Avitus at the battle of Placentia, was acclaimed emperor in April 457.[43] With the power of Avitus broken (he died in late 456 or early 457) Sidonius transferred his allegiance to Majorian, and the panegyric of Majorian (*c.* 5) followed at the end of year 458, eighteen months after the panegyric of Avitus. It could have been in that interval that Sidonius signals that he had a new patron, namely Petrus, to whom, evidently a poet of similar inclinations, he wrote elegant epigrams and from whom also, no doubt, he tactfully sought advice.[44] There is also (*c.* 4) a short poem, written presumably not long after Placentia (in which Sidonius may have fought in some capacity, though this is not known), directly addressed to Majorian, in which he deferentially asks for pardon and compares his situation to that of the classical poets Vergil and Horace, defeated and impoverished in wars against Octavian (the future Augustus), but poetically talented.

---

39 Claudian was studied deeply and productively by Cameron (1970).
40 He put these comments into the mouths of others, respectively a Gallo-Roman nobleman and Rome herself.
41 Chenault (2012).
42 *Ep.* 9.16, 25–8. The dismissive comments in *c.* 8.7–8 are purely mock modesty.
43 *Chron. Gall.* 511 (the Gallic Chronicle up to the year 511), no. 628.
44 *PLRE* 2.866, Petrus 10.

Majorian is addressed there in full formal nomenclature, as in the panegyric to him (*c.* 5).[45]

Much is uncertain about the political situation that led to the Majorian panegyric, but it is highly likely that Petrus was strongly involved in the arrangements for the expedition which took Majorian, a large army and many of his staff from Ravenna, Majorian's seat of government, to Lyon. Petrus had apparently made an earlier visit, freeing the city from the enemy (perhaps Burgundians in revolt against Rome);[46] given that Sidonius was a native of Lyon or the nearby region, Petrus will have thought Sidonius the ideal man for the job. Sidonius duly obliged: travelling with the army (so we are led to believe), he delivered this, his second panegyric, to Majorian, stressing his military successes in recent years (Europe shouted 'bravo', line 8), his full legitimacy as emperor (this was not the official inauguration, as the celebration in Rome was for Avitus) and his future plans for meeting the Vandal threat.

Most importantly, perhaps, the panegyric is also a plea to the emperor for aid for Lyon, a heartfelt plea for the rehabilitation of the city and countryside after recent suffering. Sidonius appears among his countrymen as their committed and powerful advocate, and, what is more, one reassuringly close to the emperor, a patron who could intimately say to him, 'I recognise that smile of yours, a smile that ... heralded mercy' (*c.* 5.598–9). The same impression, almost one of intimacy, is present in a much shorter poem, *c.* 13, which is addressed to Majorian (he was then, presumably, in Lyon); with remarkable wit but also in suppliant mode Sidonius there pleads for some kind of remission of tax for himself and restoration in general for his fellow-citizens.

From a slightly later time (probably 461, after the emperor's ignominious return from Spain after his failed naval expedition against the Vandals, but before his capture and execution by Ricimer in the same year), there is a fascinating account of a banquet for various courtiers held in the emperor's quarters at Arles in *Ep.* 1.11.10–13, at which Sidonius reports the conversations in some detail. As talk went on, the emperor suddenly addressed Sidonius, calling him *comes*, and perhaps deliberately referring to his rank, or even awarding it there and then, but not simply

---

45 The titles of Majorian are given at the head of his poem as Lord and Emperor, Caesar, Valerius Maiorianus, Caesar Augustus. In the panegyric (*c.* 5) the title is similar.

46 There are interesting discussions of this point in Mathisen (1979b) and Loyen (1960), 180 n. 96.

using the word colloquially as 'my friend'.[47] Sidonius leaves the point open, as perhaps Majorian himself had done. Whether we have an imperial pun or even an imperial error, Sidonius will have been very pleased both by the title and also, on that occasion, by the discomfiture of a slanderous enemy, who had falsely accused him of writing an offensive satire that Majorian wished to investigate.[48] Sidonius refers to this matter again at the end of *c.* 12, by which time he can safely make it a joke. He will have been disappointed by Majorian's sudden disappearance from the scene a little later.

Severus and standstill

Almost nothing is known of Sidonius's activities in the immediately following years, but he remained productively (if not politically) engaged in poetry of various kinds under the next emperor, Libius Severus, who acceded late in 461. It is unlikely that he was encouraged or stimulated in any way by Severus, whose profile is one of the flattest of any Roman emperor and was certainly not an attractive subject for panegyric or even shorter poetry. Stevens called him a phantom emperor.[49] He had been proclaimed by Ricimer in November 461 but not recognised by Leo, the Eastern emperor (Jordanes, *Roman Matters* 335–6). Evidence of interaction between Sidonius and Ricimer, in itself unlikely, is limited to the assumption, accepted by Loyen ([1960] 174), that Sidonius was somehow persuaded or obliged by Ricimer, 'le terrible patrice', to state that Libius died naturally (*c.* 2.317–18).[50] There is no evidence that Sidonius was so influenced. It is true that Sidonius defends Ricimer's efforts to repel Geiseric the Vandal (*c.* 2.352–7) and that he praises Ricimer (*c.* 2.483) in the context of his forthcoming marriage to the daughter of Anthemius: that is part and parcel of the panegyric he undertook (see below).

During the four years of Severus's reign Sidonius remained actively engaged in poetry of various kinds, albeit not emperor-facing. Many of his poems can be seen to date from the decade 461–70, but accuracy is elusive. Five of them are *epithalamia* ('wedding poems'); there are two pairs of

---

47 The point hinges on the fact that the word in question, *comes*, may be 'friend', but also 'companion', denoting a rank of some standing, for which see Jones (1966), 379–80.

48 For this matter see Stevens (1933/1879), 52–6; Harries (1994), 93–6.

49 Stevens (1933/1979), 88.

50 Loyen (1960), 174.

these (each has a preface). The fifth is strictly not an *epithalamium* but an explanation to a friend why his request for one is being turned down: technically speaking a *recusatio*.[51] That these compositions might all date from the early 460s[52] need not be significant: Sidonius was not conducting a marriage agency, and probably not seeking a niche for his talent, but rather obliging friends. There are also from this period five epigrams, some referring to his home Avitacum, perhaps new at the time (mentioned above, p. 5). The letter–poem to Bishop Faustus of Riez, mentioned above as a notable Christian departure or experiment, cannot be dated; perhaps Faustus laid down the bishopric in 462.[53] Attempts to date the already mentioned remarkable poem of Felix have been unfruitful, and, like *c.* 24, will be mentioned again. Poem 23 was written after Theoderic II, king of the Visigoths, acquired Narbo and before his death in 466/7.[54]

Anthemius and aftermath

But before long (though it might have seemed a long time to Sidonius) his prospects for a longer work of poetry improved. While engaged in some confidential contacts between Arvernum, his *patria*, and Rome (in the new situation created by the belligerence of Euric, king of the Visigoths)[55] he was invited to make a speech on the first day of January 468 in honour of the new emperor Anthemius, proclaimed emperor by the eastern emperor Leo in April of the previous year and then escorted with a large army to Italy.[56] This invitation came from Basilius, a man of high seniority (consul in 463 and twice praetorian prefect of Italy),[57] who was chosen after careful discussion and eventual compromise as a man of discretion and authority (*Ep.* 1.9.3–5). Basilius advised Sidonius that if he agreed to 'exercise his old Muse' (*Ep.* 1.9.6) in this way he would receive help and support at the time of delivery and, at a later

---

51 The technical term *recusatio* covers giving of excuses, declining or objecting, but is not often equivalent in a literary context to 'refusal'.

52 As in the dating by Kelly in Kelly and van Waarden (2020), 171–2.

53 Line 6 suggests that he is currently bishop, and the duties mentioned in lines 116–125 are those of a bishop.

54 There is a useful tabulation of likely dates or time-spans of these poems in Kelly and van Waarden (2020), 174.

55 As king of the Visigoths, he succeeded his brother Theoderic II in 466.

56 *PLRE* 2.96–8, Anthemius 3, gives numerous references.

57 *PLRE* 2.216–17, Basilius 11.

stage, personal recognition and help with fulfilling his own aims. With the eager agreement of Sidonius, Basilius duly arranged with the consul in Rome that Sidonius should hold the office of Prefect of the City for the coming year 468.[58]

The prefect of the city, who took the grade of *vir illustrissimus* ('most illustrious man'), had wide and powerful responsibilities, particularly in the administration of justice, within Rome and for a considerable distance beyond it; he was also responsible for the supply of corn and wine to the city and, with his staff, for keeping public order. He was, moreover, president of senate for the year concerned. The office was considered the peak of a senatorial career[59] and, after an apparently trouble-free year, Sidonius had good reason to believe that he had gained some recognition for Arvernum and Gaul and added to the distinction of his forefathers. It was at about this time, perhaps, that he gained the title of 'patrician'. He mentions it to Papianilla in a letter (*Ep.* 5.16.4), which seems to be an announcement not of their own news but of her brother's; he notes that as they themselves had moved from being praefectorian to patrician with heaven's help so her brother's family, currently patrician, might one day become consular.

In 469–71 Sidonius became bishop of Clermont[60] and in the following years faced the varied and demanding tasks of a bishop, but also the strong hostility of Euric, who at one point went so far as to exile him.[61] In a letter apparently dating to the end of the 470s (*Ep.* 9.12.1–2), he avers that twelve years earlier he had in particular renounced the pleasurable exercise of writing in verse, in case it compromised his devotion to serious matters; to that decision there were but a few apparent exceptions. The recent publication of a hitherto unknown version of Sidonius's epitaph makes it possible to reconsider the date of 479 for Sidonius's death, if the twelve years are reckoned inclusively from his last major work, the panegyric of Anthemius; but the matter remains unclear.[62]

---

58 For this important office see Jones (1973), 380, 385–6; and on the urban prefecture in general Chastagnol (1960).

59 OCD⁴ *praefectus urbi*.

60 In 469 according to Anderson (1936), xlii. Details of the process are uncertain.

61 Stevens (1933/1979), 162–3, and Harries (1994), 238–9.

62 Furbetta (2015), and Kelly and van Waarden (2020), 189.

6. THE POEMS AND THEIR ARRANGEMENT

The poems may be considered in two parts,[63] one consisting of Sidonius's three panegyrics together with some closely associated shorter poems (these are poems 1, 3, 4, 6, 8), the other of a very varied series of sixteen generally lighter poems (9–24). The order of the panegyrics is not chronological, and the position of *c.* 2 has sometimes caused surprise; but, as argued above, the panegyric for Anthemius and its preface probably take the front position because they were written at the zenith of Sidonius's power and fame, notwithstanding their relative brevity.[64] The panegyrics to Majorian (*c.* 5) and Avitus (*c.* 7), each with a preface preceding it, follow in reverse chronological order, Avitus being the earlier. It may be that poems 3–5 were published as a group, as Kelly suggests,[65] and poems 6–8 naturally hang together in topic and probably date.

The remainder of the collection contains poems that are very diverse, not least in length.[66] Some are epigrams; on the other hand, poem 9 has 346 lines and poem 23 510 lines, hardly less than *c.* 2, which has 543 lines. 'Shorter poems' has become a common designation for this section, but is best avoided. Leaving aside the long poem 9 for the time being, the first part (10–15) consists mainly of epithalamia, 10 and 11, 14 (the poem shares its numeral with a prose letter) and 15. As mentioned already, poem 12 has something to do with epithalamia; Sidonius was asked to write one. Poem 13 is a surprise in its context, being a plea to Majorian, when probably in Lyon, for remission of tax. Perhaps it owes its place here to chronology, if other data were known to Sidonius or a compiler, though no such person is attested. Poems 12 and 13 have nothing in common with each other (it seems), except perhaps their date. Poem 16 is the Christian poem mentioned above, a letter-poem to bishop Faustus. Poems 17–21 are all short epigrams, to Ommatius (also known from Poem 11), to his brother-in-law Ecdicius, and perhaps to others. Two longer poems (22 and 23) follow, respectively entitled *Burgus* or 'the castle' and 'to Consentius'.

---

63 The short portions of poetry within some of the letters are not included here, because closely attached to the letters in which they occur.

64 See also Kelly and van Waarden (2020), 170, with a different argument.

65 Kelly and van Waarden (2020), 169–70.

66 There were no other, now lost, poems that we know of. See Kelly and van Waarden (2020), 18 and n. 35 for a summary of evidence and views, and also Consolino (2020), 360, n. 95.

The final poem, given various modern titles since its composition, gives detailed instructions to a book he is sending on a journey to friends who live in various country places. Among them is a Felix, the same Felix to whom poem 9 was written; the book is told to deposit itself in his father's excellent library. Nothing suggests a pivotal link with poem 9; he was a good and lasting friend of Sidonius, but no more.

This collection, on the grounds of its arrangement and other factors, has been seen as consciously constructed, even perhaps, whether partly or wholly, by Sidonius; but the case is not strong. The similarity between the first and last of these poems (9 and 24) goes no further than the name of Felix, and other features of the question must now be examined.

In poem 9, according to the first part of Sidonius' reply to him, Felix had asked Sidonius to provide him with some poetry; Sidonius's retort is to ask why he wants thoughtless and youthful scribblings, the 'trifles' written by Sidonius in his early youth. He is, modestly, turning away the request (of which nothing else can be gleaned), as if he had said 'you surely don't really want my youthful rubbish?' According to various scholars[67] this phrase functions as a dedication of the sixteen poems written at various times. There is nothing here to suggest that any of the sixteen deserves the description 'trifles', and such disparagement of his current and recent poetry, even on a small scale, is lacking. The unsuitability of the word *nugae* ('trifles') to *c.* 16, to bishop Faustus, for example, is obvious, and neither does it match the carefully written *epithalamia* or the poem 'To Consentius' (*c.* 23), which is virtually a panegyric. There is a certain similarity to the first poem of Catullus,[68] who asks himself who should be the recipient of his useless poems (this is not the problem that Sidonius expresses), but the varied content of the Catullan collection (especially if Catullus is referring to all or even some of the poems transmitted) makes it unlikely that the *nugae* (not uncommonly used as a self-debasing term) of Catullus are an influence on Sidonius or a guide to the purpose of his collection.

It is not of course impossible that Sidonius was instrumental in putting together the sixteen poems, with or without the help of friends. There are, as the above analysis shows, some indications of grouping or matching of poems, but no obvious sign of planning above the ordinary. The date is usually taken as 469, so that all is done and dusted by the time of the beginning of his

---

67 Notably Schetter (1994) and Santelia (2002), 18–19. See also Loyen (1960), xxx–xxxi.
68 Catullus's first poem begins (lines 1–4) 'Whom do I give a neat new book …? to you, Cornelius, for you always thought my trifles some good' (trans. Guy Lee, adjusted).

life and work as bishop;[69] but, according to Kelly, 'one could easily imagine a unitary publication of the *Carmina minora* [the 'shorter poems'] as we have them at any point from about 462 or 463 onward'.[70] Perhaps they were assembled quietly and carefully, in good order, over the 460s.

7. THE MANUSCRIPT TRADITION OF
THE POEMS OF SIDONIUS: A NOTE

There is a rich manuscript tradition for the poems of Sidonius, with over one hundred manuscripts, mainly medieval. Printed editions begin in the late fifteenth century (the first edition actually has no date), and were gradually refined, or at least changed, as new manuscripts were found and read. After the *editio princeps* just mentioned there is a fine edition by Giovanni Battista that dates from the late fifteenth century (Bologna, 1498), presenting the letters as well as the poems. Furbetta's evaluation of the whole work is that it is 'highly accomplished'.[71] Among the earliest texts of Sidonius with commentary are those of Savaron (1599 and 1609) and Sirmond (1614 and 1652), which are still worth consulting, though they were soon overtaken, and used, by many others.[72] A recent study of the manuscript tradition (2020)[73] notes the importance of three critical editions, those of Lüetjohann (1887), Mohr (1895) and Loyen (1960, for the poems). (A critical edition is one based on an appraisal of the interrelationships of manuscript texts, using various kinds of evidence, including the copying of another text, or shared omissions, or palpable shared errors or corruptions.) Anderson (1936 and reprints: these are unchanged) was the beneficiary of a fairly settled text, close to those of Lüetjohann and the more succinct one of Mohr. The base text used for this translation and commentary is Anderson's; my few divergences from it are noted in a short appendix. Some of these divergences are due to emendations of his that have been judged unhelpful (these were first published in Anderson [1934]), though that is not to say that further emendation (in its sense of removal and replacement of errors) may not be necessary for future readers and scholars.

---

69 Harries (1994), 6–7, among others.
70 Kelly and van Waarden (2020), 176.
71 Furbetta (2020), 543–7, at 547.
72 Some of these are noted in Green (2020), 608–27.
73 Dolveck (2020), 479–512.

8. THIS TRANSLATION

In this verse translation, which may be the first such one into English, I have set out to provide a version at least as accurate, precise, clear, and readable as those of Anderson (1980) and Loyen (1960, in French). I have kept as closely as possible to the original numbering of the lines, without which the book's teaching purpose would be much reduced, complicating quick access to references made in modern literature and needed in discussion. To try to reproduce Sidonius at the closely verbal level, word for word, would have been clumsy and misleading, but I have not forgotten the original in any way. As for particular issues of the translator's art, the occasional English archaism may appear here (these are actually less frequent in Sidonius than sometimes thought). Sometimes a typically Sidonian choice of an impressive word (whether for its length, or perhaps its rarity) has been emulated, or matched elsewhere. The condensed or artistic arrangement of five or six short words in a single line (I call it 'listing') cried out for imitation if at all possible. Various kinds of wordplay characterise Sidonius (and irritated Anderson, at least those of the weak 'new/old' variety): his wordplay is often alliterative, and the jingle *ponte ponto* (*c.* 23.44: 'bridge and sea') has become 'bridge and brine', for once in the footsteps of Anderson. A constant challenge to the translator is the common situation where a noun and its adjective are in different lines, or where the object of the sentence precedes a transitive verb, generally an anomaly in English (though Hernández Lobato has tackled the difficulty in his interesting Spanish version).[74] Personal names have been rendered closely; and names of plants and flowers have been carefully treated. Long sentences in metre (in similes, for example) can be quite a challenge, but I have not neglected them, especially as many clothe carefully crafted descriptions or similes. A glossary has been provided in the appendix to help with the large number of words, mainly adjectives, relating to places mentioned in the text, including rivers and mountains – Sidonius likes to provide exotic colour from various places, both inside and outside the empire's boundaries, and often mentions geopolitical régimes of long ago.

This commentary does not include a glossary or list or any kind of formal tabulation of passages from Latin authors who wrote before Sidonius that may have influenced his choice of words or phrases.

---

74 Hernández Lobato (2015). See also Green (2020), 624–5.

Since the massive work of Geisler[75] countless more suggestions have been made in books, commentaries and articles, with varying attention to their aptness and significance, and the intertextuality. To gather these offerings together, even online, with any degree of comment and discussion is out of the question, except perhaps for a single work. Such an inventory would certainly include a wide range of classical Latin poets and indeed prose writers too. The line-by-line notes in this the present edition offer a relatively small though carefully selected selection, with my comments.[76]

The favourite authors of Sidonius – those whom he seems to recollect most often – are Vergil, writing in the later first century BC, under the wing of the emperor Augustus, and Claudian, who wrote at the court of the emperor Honorius in the late fourth century and early fifth. Others certainly deserve attention: Ovid and Statius are also apparent, the former for passing allusions to narratives in the *Metamorphoses*, the latter for various elegant features from his epics on Thebes and on Achilles, useful in places for the diverse narratives of the panegyrist. But various others, particularly Horace, Juvenal, and Martial, have a claim; he does not always write in the high style.

The presence of Vergil is very clear right from one of his early poems (*c.* 4), with its evocation of the young shepherd poet Tityrus of the first *Eclogue* and hints that Sidonius could well become a court poet in due course, and (*c.* 6) his subsequent poem the *Georgics*, recalling its patron Maecenas and Sidonius's new situation. In general Vergil supplies Sidonius, as he did for many Latin poets, with a treasury of elegant and memorable phrases; moreover, Sidonius is able to use Vergilian intertexts to present a picture of Rome's history, exploiting against present demorali-sation the growth of a determined Rome. When personified Rome speaks in *c.* 7.87 she faithfully echoes a passage straight from a prayer of Aeneas to Apollo ('I have entered many seas ...') at *Aeneid* 6.59, to stiffen resolve. Elsewhere evocations of Republican Rome's struggle against Carthage and her eventual victories are made in various references to the barbarian Geiseric, currently lording it over the African city. Outside politics, there is an attractive poem of Sidonius often known as the envoi (*c.* 24), apparently a farewell to local friends. When praising a friend and relative,

---

75 Geisler in Lüetjohann (1887), 384–416.
76 On wider questions relating to intertextuality the apposite words of Kelly in Kelly and van Waarden (2020), 733–4, should be noted.

Apollinaris,[77] the poet recalls a sumptuous picture from the *Georgics*,[78] as it were bringing the best of Italian husbandry to a charming poem set in the Cevennes.

The poet Claudian produced almost thirty hexameter poems in the epic style, congratulating and praising leaders of his time and supporting their policies against political and military foes. He also wrote many poems, collected under the title of Shorter Poems (as already remarked),[79] on matters of commonplace interest such as the formation of crystal, or that strange bird the Phoenix; there is also an epithalamium by him, and an unfinished mythical epic, 'On the seizure of Proserpina'. Sidonius knew them all, we may assume, and was a keen reader, showing many signs of his familiarity, though he tends not to favour Claudianic high points, such as we have seen in his use of Vergil. Often he chooses to focus on the same heroes of ancient Rome as Claudian (for example, Cocles or Scaevola). He sometimes follows Claudian in the choice of themes (for example, the use of a lament by Rome against Gildo – who had recently taken control of the province Africa – at Claudian, *c.* 15; compare the lament by Africa in Sidonius that interrupts the ceremony at *c.* 5.53 and takes up much of that poem). Both poets make the commonplace point that Africa is a third of the known world (Sidonius *c.* 5.56 and Claudian *c.* 15.161), and there are numerous verbal similarities.

The degree of Sidonius's dependence on Claudian has been greatly exaggerated, and attacked in some surprising ways (for which Geisler [1887], who chronicles similarities clearly and without comment, is not to be blamed: his endeavour was the done thing in the late nineteenth century. He cannot be reproached for not asking, say, whether a similarity between the two poets is cogent or accidental.) The laments of critics such as F. J. E. Raby, mourning in the early twentieth century the 'death' of the ancient poets, were influential. Too often it is clear that past scholars have vied to find colourful language to attract attention to 'borrowings' or other supposed faults; one such, rather surprisingly, is the editor W. B. Anderson, who seems to have hated his poet because of a dislike (that word is too weak; for reasons he seldom gives, he hated it) of his style. As if sitting on Raby's shoulders, the acclaimed critic Alan Cameron (1970) made a whipping-boy of Sidonius, and tended to turn away flaws in Claudian by

---

77 24. 51–74 (significantly longer than the other notices in this poem).
78 Vergil, *Georgics* 4. 125–48.
79 See section 4, above.

insisting that at least he was better than Sidonius.[80] At one point he breaks into an otherwise calm discussion by irrelevantly denouncing Sidonius as being 'in so many other respects Claudian's monotonously servile ape'. It has been too easy to trace or imagine other flaws in Sidonius; for example, since he gave his first panegyric when young he was to some critics a 'callow youth', and so his opinions on political or other matters can be disregarded en bloc. Small wonder that a recent historian recalls approaching him as a bête noir.[81] It is to be hoped that my own small book, and others, will be successful in presenting a better picture of the life and works of this fascinating writer.

Finally, a note on poetic metres, and the challenges they present. Three different metres are used by Sidonius (and are a major source of the attractiveness of his poetry): firstly, the hexameter (six Latin feet), which (secondly) forms with the pentameter (five feet) the so-called elegiac couplet; and, thirdly, the hendecasyllabic metre (eleven syllables).[82] In my translation, using not metres based on the nature of syllables ('heavy' or 'light') but stress-based metres where the stress of the component words is determinative, I have differentiated the metres of Sidonius accordingly: for hexameter poems I use lines of fourteen syllables (with the option of an added non-stressed syllable at the end), and I replicate the other two metres with twelve-syllable lines.

9. SIDONIUS ON THE BARBARIANS

I give here a short outline, based on the poems and panegyrics of Sidonius, of the effects on the Western Roman empire (and on Sidonius and his family) of the invasions and inroads of peoples collectively known then, and now to modern scholars, as barbarians. It will also be a quick survey of Sidonius's presentation of the severe problems that ensued, as an orator and commentator from central Gaul with strong loyalties to persons involved in government and to Rome and her empire.

The notion of 'barbarian' was pervasive in Greco-Roman society of the ancient world, no longer related to foreign speech as it clearly had been by the Greeks but broadened out to make a distinction of fundamental

---

80   Cameron (1970), 288.
81   MacGeorge (2002), 1.
82   These are described humorously by Sidonius in *c.* 23.2–7, as poets often do.

importance.[83] In Roman society it means 'foreigner' (that is, not Greek or Roman) and may carry overtones of ignorance and cruelty (as often exploited in comedy and oratory, for example). Sidonius in the poems uses the word *barbarus* some twelve times; there are two uses of the collective noun *barbaries*, which suggests the concentrated might of numerous peoples.

In the fourth century, and long before, Romans were well aware of frontier problems: the need to manage or deter invasions or movements of peoples was a major element of the reforms of the emperors Diocletian (284–305) and Constantine (306–337), and problems on the coasts of north-eastern Gaul, which were to be apparently severe in the time of Sidonius, had been addressed in the late third century by Carausius, for some time the self-appointed emperor in Britain (286–93).[84]

The crossing of the Rhine, whether freezing or not, on the last day of the year 406 by a combination of Vandals, Alans and Sueves, gathered together at Mainz, opened the way for large numbers to enter Gaul and create havoc. Once in Roman territory they continued their different paths: the Vandals, at least in one branch, crossed into Spain (409), eventually passed on to Africa (429), and took Carthage (439); the Sueves and Alans, or some contingents of them, are later attested mainly in Spain, but also remain in or return to Gaul. The subsequent plundering and devastation by these and other peoples preceded a decade (at least) of many-sided turbulence, which has left its mark in poetry as well as various chronicles.[85] The settlement, pacification and provisioning of the barbarian invaders was for many years a slow and fitful process; their need for land and corn had to be somehow met, whatever the season. No less worrying (more worrying, perhaps, to the western Roman government centred on Italy), there were in these years numerous usurpers (that is, self-styled emperors, not formally appointed), all of them with unofficial armies. The Constantius whom the young Avitus met was indeed, as Sidonius put it (*c.* 7.210–11), 'the most powerful of the leaders', who overcame at least two or three usurpers in Gaul. He was soon appointed emperor, formally chosen by command of Honorius, the official (but frequently ineffective) emperor (395–423, when he died in faraway Ravenna).[86]

83 See among others, Cartledge (1993).
84 Aurelius Victor, *On the Caesars*, 39. 20.
85 Roberts (1992), 97–106.
86 For Constantius III, see *PLRE* 2.321–5, Constantius 16. On Honorius' reign, see McEvoy (2013), 153–220.

One of the achievements of the abovementioned Flavius Constantius was to negotiate a resettlement of Goths, who had been warring in Spain against Alans and a branch of the Vandals in the Garonne valley, with the agreement of their king Wallia,[87] in the years 416–18. It is no coincidence that in these years (the exact date is still not agreed) there was an important initiative from the emperor Honorius that produced a remarkable development in Romano-Gothic relations and government. This is the Gallic Council of the Seven Provinces,[88] revived and redesigned as a forum to meet regularly in Arles for discussing issues arising from the settlement of the Goths. An important source of information about this, mentioned and analysed above in section 2, is the letter in which Sidonius reminisces and gives his impressions from perhaps two decades beforehand (*Ep.* 8.6.5). It is possible, indeed, that certain discussions or transactions made in that body are presented by Sidonius in the panegyric of Avitus more dramatically in other ways; this could be the context of his appearance before Constantius mentioned above, and seems to be the forum of the decision to nominate and declare Avitus as emperor (*c.* 7.571–5) or the meeting shortly before.

This assembly was well planned and well organised, a serious instrument to meet real needs on both sides: justice and peace-keeping, and observance of the treaties, of course for both sides; corn and subsidies for the Goths, a frequent need, and peace and security for Roman landholders and travellers in southern Gaul. Arles was a significant commercial centre, with good communications.[89] On the Roman side, we know that it was well staffed – with assessors,[90] secretaries and formal agendas – and there was careful monitoring of attendance, with heavy penalties for default. It is naturally difficult to estimate its overall effectiveness. Matthews (1975: 336–7) suspects that justice was often rough and ready and that some areas, liable to 'endemic disaffection' at the best of times, were at best 'intermittently governed'; it may be that the visit of a headstrong, no-nonsense Roman general such as Litorius (see below) was more appropriate. How

---

87 Wallia (Vallia) is mentioned by Sidonius in *c.* 2.363 and the following lines (emphasising his victory over the Vandals), and also *c.* 5.268. Also the chronicle Hydatius 52 [60] Mommsen.

88 They were Narbonensis, Lugdunensis, Aquitania (three provinces) and Belgica (two provinces).

89 As noted by Matthews (1975), 334–5.

90 In *Ep.* 1.3.3 Sidonius emphasises the importance of the office of assessor. See also Jones (1973), 141, on the prestige involved.

long its influence lasted in more peaceable times and societies can only be guessed; Sidonius seems to have a clear and happy memory of his young impressions, twenty or so years after the council's institution, though often in his letters his memories may be idealised and his style artificially mellow.

The Council was a notable attempt to conciliate Gothic and Gallo-Roman interests, but many resorted (and always had) to less formal and peaceful methods of settling major differences or achieving powerful ambitions. This is the time *par excellence* of the 'warlord' – a convenient generalising term[91] that emphasises the leader's belligerence but leaves his rank, in political terms, unclear (though pressure could be applied to weak emperors to regularise the situation and grant formal nomenclature). Noting the difference between emperors of the third and fourth centuries, who had led their armies in the field and cultivated the respect and loyalty of their men, MacGeorge notes that this 'sea-change' gave high-ranking imperial officers opportunities to exploit and develop their status.[92] Such an arrangement was fostered by the Roman practice, followed since at least Theodosius,[93] of enrolling, on the basis of a treaty, fighting men as 'federates' (*foederati*), or the appointing of *bucellarii* (bodyguards, or 'minders'). Having to fight for pay and provisioning gave enhanced motivation for leader and soldier alike.[94]

What follows is based mainly on the military career of Avitus, from poem 7, his panegyric. This began with service in the army of Aetius, a Roman general who might be called a warlord – he had his own armies and followed his own initiatives – but was ultimately acknowledged as the most powerful person in the state[95] until his unexpected execution, or assassination, by Valentinian III in 454. The young Avitus joined up with Aetius because, according to *c.* 7.230, Aetius was 'expert in Scythian warfare' – that is, their modes of fighting (perhaps these included cavalry) – and generally supreme in warfare (231). In the wars fought at the time (*c.* 7.233–5) against minor German groups who were unsettled by the nearby Burgundians and consequently threatened the Alpine frontier adjacent to Gaul, Sidonius notes that in the forces opposing the Romans

91 MacGeorge (2002), 2.
92 MacGeorge (2002), 5.
93 Jones (1973), 157–60.
94 The emperor Majorian (*c.* 5) was no such warlord (as noted by MacGeorge 2002, 6).
95 Jordanes, *Getica* 191; Cassiodorus, *Variae* 1. 4. 11. For details of his career: *PLRE* 2.21–9, Aetius 7.

there were Heruls, Huns, Franks, Sarmatians, Salians (also known as Salian Franks) and Gelonians. He attributes to each of these contingents a different weapon or a particular physical superiority and, as a climax, a fortitude when wounded; but all were surpassed by the Roman army (or even, since Sidonius does sometimes exaggerate, by the troops under Avitus alone). One cannot believe that their various ways of fighting are exactly reproduced here, even if the material came to Sidonius from Avitus himself, which is possible; rather, Sidonius has set himself a task in artistic arrangement, as he likes to do (as in *c.* 7.74–5, 80). How large these barbarian forces were, there is no way of knowing; probably small.

Elsewhere Roman armies did not have it all their own way. Sidonius speaks of Gaul being buffeted by 'varied tempests of war' (*c.* 7.215), of which one consequence was that a friend of Avitus was taken hostage by the Goths (a common practice, made to guarantee the peace) and Avitus, not a hostage himself, subsequently visited the Gothic capital at Toulouse and attracted the notice and friendship of the Gothic king Theoderic I (*c.* 7.215–33). In a different context, the young Aetius had once been required to serve as a hostage of the Goth chieftain Alaric for three years.[96] Aetius later (in 423–5) exploited a relationship with the Huns that derived from an embassy on which he served, and used the mass of Roman gold entrusted to him for diplomatic purposes by the usurper John to obtain Hunnic soldiery to be used in Italy; and their infantry and cavalry would constitute an important part of the armies he led after this. He won victories over Goths (near Arles, 430, and again in 438) and Franks (432), making peace with them. If Avitus was fighting with Aetius in these battles, Sidonius does not mention it.

An episode from about 439 illustrates the tensions and indeed hatreds that the use of barbarian armies could create. A substantial part of his cavalry was lent by Aetius to the (high-ranking) Roman general Litorius who was sent to subdue the Aremoricans in north-west Gaul, and their various allies; Litorius was victorious, but, as they returned through central Gaul to Narbonne, part of the Huns completely lost their discipline and gave themselves to wild plundering of towns in their path – one of which happened to be Arvernum, the home town of Avitus. Greatly enraged by the killing of a servant of his, Avitus took full vengeance, in a passage carefully written up as an epic confrontation – but in so doing he had in fact attacked a part of the Roman

---

96 Gregory of Tours, *Histories* II. 8; for the dating, Clover (1971), 56–8.

army itself.[97] Litorius, perhaps unaware, hurried on to attack Gothic forces at Toulouse (in 439), together with his Huns, and raise the siege of Narbonne begun by the Goths three years before. This siege – indeed the very sight of Huns near his walls, according to Sidonius – infuriated the Gothic king Theoderic, and his anger, like his plans for territorial expansion, knew no bounds. Nothing shows better than these two years how the mutual hatred of Hun and Goth dominated mid-fifth-century Gaul. In the preparations before the potentially crucial battle of the Catalaunian Plains (*c.* 7.320–35) against Attila and his barbarian confederacy in 451 Aetius makes a woefully over-confident forecast of the unity of his own Huns and the Gothic armies, almost causing the battle to be lost.

Finally, a few words may usefully be added about the geographical terms 'Scythia' and 'Scythians', those supposed to live there or to see it as their homeland; these are mentioned some twenty times in the poems. As usual in antiquity, this vast region north of the Black Sea is roughly defined, but not bounded, by rivers: the familiar Danube and the Don, and the Hypanis, due north. Romans under Majorian fight in both areas (*c.* 5.113). In the same very broad area, located in what is known today as the Crimea, are the partly mythical and savage Taurians, mentioned for their cruel religion. An example of the soldiers enlisted by Majorian is the 'Tanaitic drinker of the Scythian water' (*c.* 11.97). The mountain range of the Caucasus is also part of Sidonius's mental map of Scythia and his conception of it; it is severely, bitterly, cold.

The inhabitants of the region (all those mentioned are men) have temperaments that are correspondingly tough and hardy, indeed violent. The Vandal leader Geiseric was supposedly from the region of the Tanais, being described by Sidonius (*c.* 23.257) as 'the Tanaitic rebel': that is, an insurgent after arriving from the far north (his actual birthplace is not attested) in southern Europe and Africa, with a temperament to match (Jordanes, *Getica* 168). The enemy of Avitus in *c.* 7.280 is described by him as being 'nurtured beneath the Scythian Bear'. There are at least two men in the poems who call themselves Scythians: one is the anonymous soldier climbing the Alps with his hard task-master Majorian, who complains that he had met no cold as bad as this in Roman service (*c.* 5.518) and, though a Scyth, could not cope with the cold (*c.* 5.530); the other the Gothic king who is supporting Avitus, who speaks modestly of his 'Scythian ways' which the poetry of Vergil, as taught by Avitus, had softened (*c.* 7.495–8).

97 Harries (1994), 75. For Litorius, see *PLRE* 2.684–5.

The appellation 'Scythian' is in fact used of certain tribes from time to time (though not consistently). At *c.* 5.219 the enemy whose apparent celebrations of a wedding in north eastern Gaul were attacked, while their choirs sang, by the young Majorian and his army are denoted as Scythians. These are Goths or Franks, who may have had more threat than it appears, but were not out-and-out fighters as Scythians could be. Secondly, the political body that strongly supports the claims of Avitus to the purple is referred to by Sidonius as *Scythicus senatus* ('Scythian senate') in *c.* 7.403, surprisingly: their clothing may be crude, but their support for the Gallo-Roman Avitus is strong. The whole episode of Avitus's rise to power – a Gallo-Roman assisted by the barbarian – is thus neatly encapsulated.

10. A NOTE ON POLITICAL NOMENCLATURE IN LATE ANTIQUITY

I add here a short section on the nomenclature of the main offices of the empire in the fifth century. There are many new names, and the old ones had changed considerably. The *consulship* (dating to the very beginnings of Rome) had retained its glamour; it was still an honour to give one's name to the year, albeit now with a colleague from, or agreeable to, the Eastern half of the empire, and to be clothed in the dignity of a *trabea* or official cloak, as often mentioned by Sidonius. By contrast, the responsibilities of the *quaestor* had changed, so that he is now (since Constantine) a legal officer and also spokesperson of the emperor. When Sidonius refers to the *quaestor* of former times (*c.* 5.122–4) this is to illuminate the contemporary term *numerarius* (though he never uses this word) or controller of public finances. On the other hand, the ancient offices of *aediles, praetors* and *tribunes* (as opposed to those known as 'tribunes and notaries': see p. 9 above) have not much changed, as far as can be seen from the rare mentions of them (Jones [1966], 274).

In the panegyrics of Sidonius military posts are very prominent, almost part and parcel of gaining the imperial power (which is also known as 'the purple' [*purpura*] or 'kingly rule' [*regnum*]). (Emperors may be said to 'rule', but are never/very seldom? called 'kings'.) Military posts are the master of infantry and cavalry (*peditumque equitumque magister*; the office may be expressed as 'both services' (*utramque militiam* or *utrique militiae*) with simply *magister* ('commander in chief'), as in *c.* 5.378. When Sidonius refers to the man who guides the *scrinia sacra* (that is, 'imperial' archives, *c.* 5.564), he means the *magister epistularum* (this term would not scan). The holder of the office of prefect may be *praefectus*, the rank being in full *praefectus praetorio* (that is 'praetorian prefect'), usually with an indication of his sphere of authority (such as 'the East', 'the Gauls', Italy) (the term *praetorium* goes back to the headquarters of a Roman camp). Within the ranks of the senatorial order senators were classed on the basis of offices held as 'illustrious' or 'honourable' (*spectabilis*) or, perhaps most commonly, 'very distinguished' (*clarissimus*). At the top of the tree (excepting the emperor himself, who is usually called *Augustus*) is the patrician (*patricius*); usually this is an honour issuing from, and combined with, military leadership.

Translation and commentary

Poem 1
Preface to the Panegyric given for
the Emperor Anthemius, consul for the second time

In this preface S. imagines a lively party held by the gods to celebrate
the primacy of Jupiter, but with the neutral concept of 'nature' replacing
the violent agency sometimes attributed to Jupiter in ousting Saturn in
versions of the myth. The motley reverence of the worshippers, the poet
included, is allegorised as a manifold celebration of Anthemius, with a
tactful compliment in the word 'youthful' in the first line. As explained
below, the name Victor can no longer be read in lines 25–8.

When Nature placed the youthful Jupiter above the stars[1]
  and the new god began his ancient sovereignty,
The gods vied with each other to give reverence to their god
  and in their differing ways sang out the same 'bravo'.[2]
Mars with his ringing trumpet paid tribute to his father,   5
  and with its thunderous din lauded his thunderbolts;
the Arcadian and the Archer God played on the tuneful strings,
  one more skilful to thrum the guitar, one on the lyre,
and the chorus of the Castalides added various acclaim
  with songs, with reeds, with thumb and finger, voice, and foot;   10
but after the heaven-dwellers the new god is also said
  to have endured the feeble song of demigods.

---

1 There is no mention here of any of the aggression by Jupiter found in some versions of
this mythical event, in which he attacked Saturn, for no good reason, like a usurper or indeed
one of the belligerent emperors of the early 450s. The myth is important in the (differing)
accounts by the poet Vergil in his *Aeneid* (*A.* 7. 48–9, *A.* 8. 319–20). The vaguer 'nature' of
S. leaves the matter open. Calling Jupiter 'youthful' here could be seen as a compliment to
Anthemius.
2 The word here translated 'bravo' (*sophos*) – it originally meant 'clever' or 'well done'
– is used also in *c.* 5.8, of the general Majorian, and in *Ep.* 1. 9. 7, where it describes public
reactions to S. himself.

Then Dryads joining up with Fauns, Mimallones with Satyrs,
  a rustic company, gave voice to a charming song.
Those hemlock-reed singers, the Pans, left lofty Maenalus,   15
  and after so much lyre the raucous pipes pleased Jove.
Among them Chiron, dancing to the sonorous strings, twisted
  his lumbering horse's limbs with verve and elegance.
Half-man, he justified their attention , and earned the applause,
  in spite of a tendency in song to give a neigh.[3]   20
Thus a sacred offering was made by the tongues of rich and poor,
  and the highlight of that ceremonial was song.
So I, O Caesar, greatest hope of this our age, after
  our great leaders make this small offering of incense,
boldly singing in the presence of the learned teacher who[4]   25
  is used to speak with the tongue of Phoebus, or with yours;
who although he is your quaestor in your everlasting court[5]
  will everlastingly be my own master too.[6]
So, emperor, let offerings from varied tongues praise you,
  for you make of our hearts new temples for your praises.   30

---

3 For this joke see also *c.* 14.29–30. Chiron is a centaur who combines the figures and
minds of both person and animal.

4 At this point the name Victor has appeared heretofore in all editions of S., but as argued
by Kelly (2018 and 2020) it has no manuscript support. There is therefore no name for the
quaestor who is mentioned; this official is now anonymous, and the details given in PLRE
2.1158–9 not applicable. See Notes on the text used. The learned or 'well taught' teacher has
not been identified.

5 Phoebus gives speech to a poet; a quaestor is among other things the mouthpiece of the
emperor, like the one mentioned in c. 5.569–71. See further the general introduction, section 10.

6 The imperial court, and often its members, are conventionally described in Late
Antiquity as 'everlasting'; S. playfully applies the word to his own relationship to the person
he is praising.

Poem 2
Panegyric of Anthemius

INTRODUCTION

In a letter to his friend Heronius (*Ep.* 1.9) Sidonius tells how he was asked during an informal conversation in Rome to consider composing and then delivering, at what seems very short notice, a panegyric of the emperor Anthemius when he took his consulship on 1 January 468. Doing so, he was told, would advance many of his own plans and concerns, and S. was duly, with the emperor's agreement, appointed Prefect of the City for that year. The attainment of that important rank may have persuaded him (he does not pretend inability or make excuses), but he was arguably the obvious candidate to give the speech, although he had not exercised that particular Muse for almost ten years, since giving his panegyric for Majorian in late 458. The speech for Anthemius as we have it shows little sign of haste; he had informed himself of the emperor's earlier life and family connections, and shows awareness of the political issues. To speak again before the senate, as he had done in 456, in a more stressful situation, held no terrors for him, to judge from the evidence of the abovementioned letter.

Anthemius had been proclaimed Augustus on 12 April 467, when, with the support of emperor Leo, emperor in the East, and with no obvious rival, he had marched to Rome. There had been an interregnum (in the West) since the death of the previous emperor, Libius Severus, in November 465. Once S. has told the senators that all bodies of the state urgently want Anthemius, the sensitive matter of Eastern influence is broached early on in the speech. With Leo now involved, a government of two will make the state more perfectly one (line 29), and there is a less audacious paradox in the image of lines 66–7.

Panegyrics in the ancient world followed a regular schema, the main topics being arranged in a careful order. In poem 23, in praise of his friend Consentius (this is not a public panegyric), S. pretended to ask (32–6) whether an honorand's parents or his birthplace should come first, and following normal practice chose the latter course. So here the city of

Constantinople is described before his family, distinguished though that was, and with it the Thracian hinterland, which raises men toughened since birth, the backbone (it is implied) of a strong army. The focus switches (30–63) to the city's position, its prosperity, its temperate climate, its buildings. Is a point being made when he says that the cement used for the city's expansion is said to have come from Puteoli in Italy?

The honorand's father was Procopius; this man's wife, the mother of Anthemius, is not mentioned, only her father Anthemius (whose distinguished career is passed over). The baby's gleaming cradle promised imperial power, as did the flames in his hair; there were numerous omens from nature and from historical figures. Surrounded at home by weaponry and armour, the young Anthemius became intensely keen on warfare, playing with his father's weapons and helmet, and later hunting. At no stage, it seems, did his education suffer; there are almost fifty lines giving a panorama, or bibliography, of thinkers and authors, both Greek and Latin, ranging from Thales to Tacitus; this list is actually a development (assuming it was later in date) of passages in poem 23.101–69 and in the briefer 15.42–50, where the Seven Sages are enumerated, with their supposed words of wisdom.

After marriage (194–6), to the emperor Marcian's daughter, who chose him (not, then, the reverse), Anthemius sought military experience on Rome's vital Danube frontier; this was followed by high office at Rome (205–9). Later, when Marcian died, we are told that Anthemius, though already popular, had no desire to be emperor, and S. insists that the marriage with the daughter of the deceased was irrelevant to his eventual fortune. S. now chooses (224–6) to relate the triumphs of Anthemius in Illyricum, in an extended tableau of the kind that he favours. The devastation by the Ostrogoth Valimir, the damage done by a renegade general on his side, the stress of a city (Serdica) under siege, and the fight with rampaging Huns, whom, like many Roman writers of Late Antiquity, he describes carefully and in some detail, together provide a full (and exciting) display of his ability.

With the death of Libius Severus in 465 (he died naturally, according to S, but not all have believed him) the narrative moves onto a fully mythological plane; the characters are Oenotria – that is, Italy (mentioned in Vergil, she has a small speaking part in Claudian) – the river Tiber, Rome and Aurora (or Dawn), their appearances all finely described. Oenotria is greatly concerned about Rome; going to visit Tiber, she outlines what she wants for Rome and what Rome should do (that is, essentially, to put off her pride); she also complains on Rome's behalf of Fortune's choices of leader. S. here modifies strongly political complaints made in his two earlier panegyrics – and of the problems caused by the Vandal, using his navy in a way that even Ricimer (who will be prominent at the end of the panegyric) cannot successfully counter. Tiber goes to Rome, finding her impressively accoutred in martial garb (as in *c.* 5.13–32), who then flies to the distant region where, in scenes of perpetual spring and exquisite vegetation, Aurora lives. Needlessly, it seems, Rome makes a long and rather aggressive speech: it describes, no less, the many military victories and her creation of provinces in the eastern regions, claiming, amazingly, that all this was done on behalf of the East. Aurora, submissive when Rome arrived, and unfazed by this long tirade, grants Anthemius to Rome, and a bride (Alypia, daughter of Anthemius) to Ricimer. Finally, mindful of the small boat in which, he, as poet, sails, S. takes refuge from the winds that drive it, hiding any forebodings that he may have had about these two. Meanwhile the new emperor must turn to the duty of liberating slaves, in the traditional manner, an effective diminuendo.

Synopsis

1–12 Address to Anthemius and Janus

13–29 The need for Anthemius to be emperor, and the widespread support for him; the attitude of Leo, Eastern emperor.

30–67 The land of the Thracians and (46–67) the city of Constantinople, its climate and its growth in size; the two 'halves' of the empire equalised.

68–93 Procopius, father of Anthemius, who negotiates peace with Persian leaders (75–88), and (89–93) wins subsequent honours.

94–133 Procopius marries the daughter of the noble Anthemius (senior) ; the birth, with omens, of the future emperor.

134–55 The boy's love of playing with military equipment; his skill in riding.

156–92 His education in philosophical texts.

193–209 His military activity in the Danubian provinces, and subsequent high office.

210–22 Sidonius assesses Anthemius's prospects for becoming emperor.

223–71 War in Illyricum after its devastation by the Ostrogoth Valamir (223–34), and war against Huns, who are described (243–71).

272–306 The relief of the siege of Serdica; the treachery of his colleague and its punishment by Anthemius.

307–17 Apollo and the Muses are invoked to tell the story of how, after the death of the emperor Severus, Anthemius became emperor with support of two realms.

318–31 The goddess Oenotria, her attire described in some detail, goes to visit the river Tiber.

332–86 Oenotria complains of Rome's weakness, and explains the problems.

387–406 Tiber delivers the message to Rome, and Rome (391–406) prepares for a long journey to the east.

407–35 The home of Aurora (Dawn), and the appearance of Aurora herself, are described.

436–515 Rome makes a long and impassioned speech to Aurora, ending with the request for Anthemius to be her ruler (478–82), and for his daughter to be wedded to the Roman general Ricimer (483–503).

515–21 Aurora reminds Rome that in the distant past she sent Memnon to fight for them.

522–36 The two parties are united by Concord, and the poet rejoices that the new emperor is in many ways superior to many of the great names of Roman history.

537–48 The poet looks forward to further consulships that he may one day celebrate in his verse; for now Anthemius must attend to the traditional ceremony of manumitting captives.

TRANSLATION

Take up, Augustus, your *fasces*[1] second in number and
import;[2] aglow with the weight of gold upon your *trabea*,[3]
as an old consul open the new year, and without disdain

---

1 The *fasces* were a bundle of rods carried before a magistrate, a sign of his legitimate authority and power (*c.* 5.6, *c.* 7.8).

2 The Latin word *secundus* means 'favourable' as well as 'second', and this meaning is certainly present here: the situation was auspicious and important. Anthemius had been consul in 455, 'old' in line 3 contrasting rhetorically with 'new'.

3 The *trabea*, a consular garment, embroidered in gold as remarked here. For a good description see Dewar (1996), 64–6.

be enrolled once more in the Fasti.[4] Although with diadem[5]
upon your hair you stride exalted, and a Tyrian cloak[6]   5
enshrouds your shoulders, may the purpled gown[7] of the consuls
delight you more. Recurrent consuls have always been rare.[8]
And you, Janus,[9] to whom a yearly laurel wreath is owed,
banish your sloth and bind with any foliage your hair
and do not fear the newly appeared light of this emperor,   10
or think that the world's elements are being torn apart.
Nature is not changing: today's sun again came from the East.

This is the one, leaders,[10] demanded by Roman courage
and by your love, to whom our state, like a ship engulfed by storms,
lacking a pilot, has brought in her broken hulk, to be   15
better controlled and guided by a respectable captain,
so that she need no longer fear tempests, or you, pirate.[11]
The countryman in prayer, the federates[12] with their consent,
the camps with trumpets, the senate with cheers, have all sought you,

4 The *fasti* were a chronological list of magistrates, of which the consular ones were of
prime importance. S. refers to others from time to time, somewhat vaguely.

5 The diadem of Late Antiquity, part of the imperial regalia, has been described as a
'purple band fitted with jewels and pearls' (OCD[4]). As in *c.* 7.13, it is not foregrounded; the
ceremony of the new year focuses on the consulship.

6 The cloak or cape (Latin *chlamys*) was more crimson in colour (the dye is 'Tyrian'). In
the *Historia Augusta* (of the late fourth century AD), the same distinction between crimson
cloak and the simpler toga is mentioned, with the author preferring the latter as imperial garb
(Gallienus 16.4). S. gently alludes to this debate, fitting his point to the consular setting.

7 This, the *picta toga*, is the embroidered toga, equivalent to the abovementioned *trabea*.

8 It is broadly true that repeated consulships were rare, but there were notable exceptions
– Marius in the Republic and more recently the mid-fifth-century general Aetius, and many
emperors. S. makes this rarity a special reason to prefer the consular dress.

9 Janus was 'god of door and gate at Rome' (OCD[4]), and by extension the new year, when
he received special honour, as in *c.* 7.11.

10 By 'leaders', the listening senators are addressed, as in *c.* 7.8.

11 The typically Sidonian feature of apostrophe, used as if addressing someone or
something not present, may be a way of alluding to pirates in general, but the main point is
a particular allusion to Geiseric, the Vandal leader settled in Carthage. He is referred to in
various ways in this poem and poem 5, and never (actually) named; not because the Latin
word is difficult in metre but because of the poet's strong distaste for him.

12 By federates are meant contingents of various kinds from allied barbarian populations.
Their consent was certainly not required, at least formally, for such a decision.

the tribes have marked you with their votes,[13] your colleague has sent you 20
to us, and power to you; in your support there are as many
voices as the whole world contains. We were all alarmed, I admit,
that your good colleague might not like to refer to your wishes[14]
what was the public wish. Will future ages believe this?
To ensure that you, emperor, had total power over us   25
full power over yourself was not allowed to you. You outdo,
Leo Augustus,[15] the accomplishments of those before you:
one who orders someone to rule is above all regal power;
your state can only be more unified, as made from two.

Hail, summit of sceptres, queen of the East, Rome of your world,[16]   30
and, now that you have sent to me a sovereign set to rule,

13 The tribes into which Roman citizens were divided had long ago been excluded from
voting, let alone required to record their choices, as is apparently implied here.
14 There was widespread concern, S. claims (cf. *c.* 5.9 for similar language) that
Anthemius's 'good colleague' Leo might prefer not to consult Anthemius, in case he gave
a modest or diffident reply (cf. *c.* 5.9, and note) that might complicate the desired transition
of power. By calling Leo 'good' he takes care to avoid any hint or imputation of insincerity
on Leo's part. It is, S. claims, a sign of Leo's greatness (unparalleled, lines 27–8) that he
can command a man who has total power (25); this is most unusual, as S. implies with the
trite question of line 24. The Roman state ('your' is plural) is surely strengthened thereby
(lines 28–9). The fact that Anthemius has as it were followed orders is glossed over as
S. turns to exalted praise of Constantinople and the East, and praises the assumed unity
of the two. For discussion of the particular circumstances, see the introduction to this
poem.
15 The emperor Leo, emperor in the East 457–74 (*PLRE* 2.663–4), is mentioned by name
for the first time, with his title Augustus. S. implies that his predecessors had done nothing
of equal significance; that is not surprising perhaps, since they gave recognition or legitimation rather than orders, and the turnover of emperors in the West in the years 450–7 was
unusually speedy, with Avitus in fact neither recognised nor condemned (Mathisen [1991],
233–4). On Leo in general, see the brief sketch by A. D. Lee in Cameron, Ward-Perkins and
Whitby (2000), 45–9.
16 The address to Constantinople begins with three resounding and unusual titles,
conveying high praise. The city is complimented as the summit of sceptres (that is, 'the
highest power'; but the secondary meaning 'mainstay' or 'pillar' may also be conveyed).
The title of 'queen of the East' is unusual in its scope (the idea of a female head of state is not
in itself unusual, and Rome is addressed as queen in 432 below). As 'Rome of your world',
Constantinople is implicitly as powerful and important in the East as Rome is in the West;
and in this sense she is a 'new Rome' (Grig and Kelly [2012]; a work of many useful essays).
The poet is highly respectful, but not submissive.

to be revered not only by the Quirite of the East;[17]
abode of empire, but more valuable because you are
clearly the mother of empire. Supporting Rhodope
and Haemus, yours is the land of Thrace, prolific in heroes.   35
Here babies are welcomed with ice, and from their mother's womb
the region's native snow hardens the soft limbs of infants.[18]
Almost no child is fed with mother's milk, but dragged from the breast
they drink instead horse's blood through a wound;[19] so ignoring milk
the whole race imbibes courage. Once they have grown a little,   40
they soon play at battles, with spears, these games being inspired
by the wound that nourished them. Accomplished hunters, now the boys
empty the wastelands of wild beasts; the youths, enriched by spoils,
respect the culture of the sword, and not to end old age
by the sword is a disgrace. They follow this pattern of life   45
as countrymen of Mars.[20] But you, surrounded by the sea,
breathe from both sides the mixed mildness of Europe and Asia;
for the Bistonian blasts of Aquilo are slowly calmed
by the nearby trumpet-blasts of the south wind borne from Calchedon.[21]
Meanwhile Susa trembles at you, and with a suppliant's homage   50
the Achaemenian[22] Persian bends his crescent tiara.[23]

17 In classical times the word *Quirites* was often used for 'Romans' (or 'citizens'), in
the plural, and occasionally by poets in the singular; in Late Antiquity this was seen as a
very rare and archaic usage. S. resurrects it here to link honorifically the Eastern Romans to
Roman citizens of former times.

18 This imagined picture of the upbringing of children in Thrace, which is near
Constantinople – but quite unlike it – and important for its manpower, has its roots in a
passage of Vergil's *Aeneid* where (9.603–13) the Italian Numanus Remulus, enemy of
Aeneas, makes a powerful speech extolling the toughness of early Italians: childrens' limbs
are hardened by immersion in rivers (603–4), and then by hunting and horseriding (605–6).

19 For this claim of drinking blood there is a parallel in Claudian *c.* 3.311–13, where the
Massagetes, a nomadic tribe, are said to wound horses and collect the blood to drink; cf. the
drama of Seneca, *Oedipus* 470, perhaps here embellished by S. Claudian's notion of drinking
from frozen sea-water is not borrowed here, but S. develops that commonplace in *c.* 7.42.

20 Mars, god of war, was thought to have originated in Thrace (Ausonius XXV. 3.8).

21 Chalcis or Calchis (read by the manuscripts) was the name of various Greek towns, but
here Chalcedon, across the Bosphorus from Constantinople, is certainly meant.

22 Achaemenes was the supposed founder of the Persian Achaemenid dynasty, with a
capital at Susa; the adjective equates as often to 'Persian'.

23 S. imagines an official of high rank and importance, wearing a 'crescent tiara' (with a
moon depicted on it, or perhaps shaped like a crescent moon) as part of his regalia.

The Indian, hair moistened with amomum's fragrant spice,[24]
for your profit disarms the throats of his land's wild animals
to to pay tribute in curving ivory; the elephant,
its glory gone, takes home a face stripped of the payment made   55
to the Bosphorus.[25] You extend your huge city within vast walls,[26]
and yet the populace makes them too cramped. With its buildings
the city takes to the water, and new land clogs the old waters:
transported here, the dust of Dicarchean sand is used,[27]
to be set fast by waters that it enters; the hardened mass   60
supports the new territory brought into the alien flood.
So organised, and looking at harbours on every side,
walled in by the sea, you are surrounded by the world's bounty,
most fortunate, having enjoyed a share in Rome's triumphs.
Now we complain no more; farewell, then, bisected empire.   65
In the balance both pans are equal; taking our weights upon you,
you have evened things out.[28]
                              A citizen of such a place,
you excel through your father Procopius,[29] whose ancient line
goes back to imperial ancestors: whose praise cannot fitly
be told by any eloquence, not even if the bard[30]   70

24 S. mentions Indians quite frequently (line 407 below, *c.* 5.42, 286, *c.* 7.74;) this is the
only passage that approaches a description. Vergil speaks of *amomum* in two pastoral poems
(3.89 and 4.25), which in his commentary Coleman calls both Cardamom and Cardomomum.

25 As in *c.* 5.42, S. concentrates on the elephant's tusks as tribute for the state; here he
draws a sympathetic picture of its distress. In *c.* 22.58–63 he shows curiosity about the strong
hides of elephants.

26 As it happened, it was an ancestor of Anthemius – his maternal grandfather (*PLRE*
2.94) – who was in charge of rebuilding the walls, completed in 413.

27 This is dust from the sand of Puteoli, an Italian harbour originally named Dicaearchia
after its founder Dicaearchus, which was both used for its own buildings and exported.

28 This point is made forcefully and more fully in lines 453–77 below, a catalogue of
Roman conquests and annexation. In this passage the tone is gentler, and tactfully vague.
The East has greatly benefited from Roman trade and in other ways; but having gained
Anthemius and so benefited, the West is not at a disadvantage.

29 Procopius (*PLRE* 2.920) was commander in the Persian War (422), and later patrician
and master of both forces (cf. line 90 and n. 38). (For these terms see general introduction,
section 10.) He was a descendant of the Procopius proclaimed emperor in 365, but held power
only briefly (*PLRE* 1.742–3).

30 Orpheus and his remarkable feats (*c.* 6 and *c.* 23.178–94), typically embroidered, are a
favourite theme of Kelly (2013), who argues that he is looking back to the poet Claudian.

should rise from Avernus – he whose song and tuneful fingers
moved rocks and made forests give ear and run towards his strings,
when the waters of Hebrus stood still, and with their current stemmed
the enchanted river's waves indeed were thirsty for his song.
To him, sometime in his youth, was entrusted the repair of peace   75
with Assyria.[31] The Parthians[32] were amazed that they could not
oppose the ripe judgement of one in his early years.[33] In fear
the satraps[34] placed below the king held back; so forcefully
did the envoy's genius impress them all. The lands of the Medes
trembled; Babylon, which had not closed its gates to the snake-born foe,   80
for once reckoned itself to be excessively exposed.[35]
But when a new deal for both sides had established a treaty
(the greater part dictated by Procopius),[36] they swore
by their gods fire and water, while he pledged that the agreement
would be valid, invoking his ancestral gods.[37] An old   85
Chaldean, over a victim's entrails, just like the pontiffs,

31 Assyria, formerly part of the Persian Empire, here stands for the whole of it. The context of this mission is the war with the Persian king Vahram V in 422 (Cameron and Garnsey [1998], 443). As well as negotiating the end of the war Procopius had a military role not mentioned by S. (Socrates [the historian] 7.20), which he might not have deemed relevant.

32 Elsewhere in this passage 'Persian' and 'Parthian' are used interchangeably, and with no distinction in meaning. In line 79 'Medes' is used to evoke a wide region.

33 The motif of precocious negotiating skill was used for Avitus (c. 7.207–14).

34 The satraps in the Persian empire were broadly equivalent to Roman provincial governors.

35 If the gates were indeed often left open there is no report that they were closed uniquely for Alexander. Alexander had a considerable struggle outside Babylon (Curtius book 4, *passim*), but the city was then surrendered to him (Curtius 5.1.17–24). His remarkable parentage is mentioned again in lines 121–2 below.

36 Magi have not been mentioned in the narrative; to understand the common Latin word *magis*, which would mean 'for the most part', would give good sense: he dictated the greater part of it, and the 'new deal' was essentially his.

37 S. will have known that, according to Claudian (c. 21.51–68), the young Stilicho (*PLRE* 1.854) went to the East to negotiate an 'Assyrian peace', dated to 383/4. There are considerable differences between their accounts, as one might expect: in Claudian the deities involved are Bel and Mithras; in S. the Persians swore by fire and water. Claudian specifies no Roman gods; S. speaks of ancestral gods,the traditional gods of Rome. Claudian speaks of a Chaldaean (a general term for 'soothsayer ' or 'diviner'), S. mentions the college of Roman priests known as pontiffs. In general, his description of the Persians' words and actions is more imaginative than Claudian's, though studiously vague. Claudian goes on to report the skill of Stilicho in killing lions and tigers (65–6).

droned secret words; the king himself, holding a jewelled bowl,
stooped and decanted cups onto the incense-burning altar.

On his return, a high-ranking double honour awaited:
patrician now and master of infantry and cavalry,[38]   90
he is put in charge of forts, where holding fast the Taurus Gates[39]
and moving on the roaming Ethiopians[40] by threat
of war, he had to see Orontes meek, with peaceful flow.[41]
His wife's father was Anthemius:[42] prefect, and also consul,
he ordered peoples with his judgments and the year with his name.[43]   95
Fortune, proffering purple, always follows those who wear it;[44]
the only change, in this case, is that he who was consul
becomes an emperor. But all the others I omit;
now come into my poem, you whose hair, creased by a helmet,
adopts the diadem; to whom a Caesar's purple garb,   100
without cuirass, is given, and the hand that must be filled
by a sceptre, disencumbered of the sword. Your cradle shone
with symbols of imperial power; the prescient countryside
gave promise of a golden age, with new, transformed, produce.
They say that at your birth rivers containing honey appeared   105
and were slowed down by their sweetened waters, and that oil flowed

38 '... the combination of supreme military rank together with the title of 'patrician' came
to mark the dominant figure in the West ...' (MacGeorge [2002], 5–6) The supreme military
rank was 'master of both infantry and cavalry' (also *c.* 7.377) or more briefly 'master of both
forces/services', as in line 206 below and other poems. See also the general introduction,
section 10.

39 The Taurus Gates (seen from the other direction they are 'the Gates of Cilicia')
guarded a pass vital to the protection of the various provinces in what the Romans knew as
Asia (roughly modern Turkey).

40 The nomadic Ethiopian forces were, it seems, less of a threat, but any trouble could
well destabilise Mesopotamia.

41 The Orontes was the main river of Syria, flowing south through Palestine and towards
Egypt in a valley that was notably fertile.

42 His career (mentioned here only in the words 'prefect and consul') began with the
consulship in 405, and the prefecture of the Orient (this lasted from 405 until 414); he was
patrician (see n. 38 above) by 406 (*PLRE* 2.93–5, Anthemius 1). According to Socrates the
historian (7.1.1), he was virtually ruler of the eastern empire.

43 He gave verdicts to litigants and his name to the year.

44 The purple (garment of emperors) is offered by Fortune; but she favours those who are
in the imperial house.

through startled oil-mills while the olives hung on the boughs, unpicked.
The plain brought forth its undulating crop without any seed,
and vine-branches were jealous of grapes grown without their aid.
Roses shone red in winter, and, contemptuous of the cold,   110
white lilies ridiculed the frosts with which they were surrounded.
When Lucina consummates such a birth, the customary
pattern of the elements gives way, newness of things creates
belief in an approaching reign. In this way nature affirms
that blessed gods have come to earth. Gentle flames played around   115
the tender locks of resolute Iulus;[45] Astyages,
fated to be deposed by Cyrus his grandson, shuddered
to see the grape-cluster that spread from the womb of his daughter;[46]
a wolf offered her udders to the fearless Quirinus;[47]
a laurel was blazing as Iulius first saw daylight;[48]   120
great Alexander and great Augustus are both reckoned
to have been conceived by serpent gods, and claimed Jupiter and
Phoebus as ancestors (dividing them): one of them sought
his father in Cinyphian Syrte,[49] the other gloried
to be thought, thanks to his mother's marks,[50] the offspring of Phoebus,   125
vaunting the Epidaurian signs of the Paeonian serpent.[51]
Many have been circled by eagles, and, by a sudden ring,

45 This is narrated in Vergil, *A.* 2.682–4; the description of Iulus here applies to the challenge of leaving Troy with his father, but other passages show him as resolute, as Aeneas certainly was.

46 Astyages's dream, and its explanation that his daughter's son would reign in his stead, is narrated by Herodotus 1.108–9. The prophecy is mentioned later in the Roman writers Tertullian *De Anima* 46 and Orosius 1.19.

47 The common story of the suckling of Romulus (Quirinus) and Remus is told in Livy 1.4.

48 This omen – a laurel burning in spite of its natural resistance to flame – may have been related in the lost beginning of the biography of Caesar by Suetonius.

49 Syrte: the oracle of Zeus (Ammon) in the desert is meant. Ammon was consulted by Alexander – and revealed him as son of Jupiter or Zeus, as various of his biographers allege: Curtius, 4.7.5–28, Arrian *Anabasis.* 3.3–4, Justin 3.11.11.

50 Suetonius (*Aug.* 94.4) relates that indelible marks of a serpent were left on Atia, mother of Augustus, as she slept in a shrine of Apollo, giving as his source the theological treatises of Mendes from the Nile delta.

51 He boasted that the signs were those of the holy serpent of Epidaurus, a major sanctuary for healing (cf. *c. 22.79*–80) and so of Paean, a god of healing identified with Apollo.

plumage has helpfully predicted crowns that were to come.[52]
But that this man, noble leaders, was summoned to the sceptre
could even then be known, when by chance in his father's home   130
a severed vine-branch brought forth shoots that were no longer its own.
That event presaged the springtime of his power; in the form of leaves
favouring omens flourished on that dry and withered branch.
But when he had completed the first years of infancy,
he would crawl round his father's armour; and though a tight plate   135
compressed his neck, he embraced it with both arms and made a space
where loosening the helmet he might place black and blue kisses.[53]
In boyhood for amusement he would feel with eager hand
arrows seized from the enemy, and, using captured bows,
he liked to pull strong bowstrings to their curving horns,[54] and to   140
propel the quivering javelin with tender arm, and also
transfer as he made a leap onto the back of a snorting horse
the steel chain mail that he wore, together with his heavy lance;
and to harry wild beasts he found and seek them out if hidden
by foliage, and to entrap them in entangling nets,   145
or else to pierce them with a throw of his spear. Often he enjoyed
his mates' loud praises, when the raging beast had taken a hit
and the weapon went into, and came out of, its fore-quarters.
Aeacides, spirited youth and huntsman, now conceal
your Pelethronian honours – though, when on your teacher's back   105
and thus unworried as you wandered through their lairs, in fact
a horse was guiding you.[55] Even Paean himself did not
aim arrows better than our chief when, standing over Python,

52 That is, plumage from a bird taking the shape of a crown. No case of this seems to be attested.

53 Playing with his father's armour, he struggled with the tight plate designed to protect the neck and made space so that he could loosen the helmet and plant kisses inside. The same word for 'black and blue' is found also in *c.* 7.242, referring to the marks or bruises on the face made in combat by real armour and a tight helmet; it is here applied to the boy's kisses, with the lips and probably much of his face being discoloured by his struggles and repeated endearments. The father is presumably not inside the armour, neither is the boy standing on his father's knees (Loyen [1960]).

54 He tightly strung the bow, attaching it to the (curved) ends.

55 Achilles should hide the accolades that he won in the glades of Thessaly – after all, the centaur who taught him was of great assistance.

distraught by an almost empty quiver, he embedded
within the serpent's numerous coils weapons without number.[56]   155

No less, among all this, did he attend to the old sages:[57]
how you, Thales, sprung from Miletus, condemned sureties;[58]
how you, Lindian Cleobulus sang, "moderation be our ideal";
how you, Periander of Ephyra, concentrate on the whole;
how you, Solon of Attica, think, wisely, of life's end;[59]   160
how you, Prienian Bias, hold the masses to be evil;
how you, Pittacus of Lesbos, urge us to observe the time;
how you, Chilon of Lacedaemon, wish all to know themselves.
Moreover, he studied various new sects and their dogmas:
what Anacharsis from the land of Scythia commended;[60]   165
whatever Sparta gained from Lycurgus the lawgiver;
whatever the crowd of Cynics questioned in Erechthean
schools, thereby imitating your companions, Epicurus;[61]
whatever the double Academy,[62] claiming nothing to be true,

56 He had only a few arrows left, and perhaps no other source of missiles, but there should
have been no difficulty in wounding the large serpent: has rhetorical playfulness ('numerous'
and 'without number') been overdone? The slaying of Python is mentioned as a theme of
poetry in *c*. 2.311 below.

57 This rendition (lines 157–63) of lines on the so-called 'Seven Sages' (these were
a group of ancient Greek philosophers whose maxims or mottoes were revered for their
guidance) closely resembles the versions in one of the epithalamia ('wedding poems') of
S. (*c*. 15.44–50); the differences of substance, mentioned below, are few. The date of the
epithalamium is not known, but it would be understandable if in his haste to write this
panegyric S. made use of something ready-made; written for a private occasion, it will
have been little known. The themes and manner of presentation may well be recollected
from his schooldays, and are more jejune even than the metrical playlet on the seven
wise men by Ausonius (Green [1991], XVI). The sages are mentioned, but without their
supposed advice, in *c*. 23.101–10.

58 Thales, in this version, condemned the giving of guarantees to appear in court.

59 Solon is not linked here with the common tag 'nothing in excess' as he was in *c*. 15.47.

60 Anacharsis was a largely legendary prince, who travelled widely in Greece and
elsewhere in the sixth century BC and came to exemplify the wise barbarian.

61 Cynic philosophers took doctrines or practices from other schools in Athens, as
(it is implied) Epicureans did too. These movements are disparaged less here than in
c. 15.124–5.

62 The word 'double' refers to the New and Old Academies, between which some,
like Cicero (*Academic Questions* 1.46), saw little difference on the point here mentioned;
Anderson (1936), quoting Semple (1930), 71–2, agrees.

proclaims; whatever Cleanthes of the bitten nails perceives;[63]   170
whatever Pythagoras, Democritus, Heraclitus
bewailed, ridiculed, kept silent on;[64] whatever Plato's mind,
located in the citadel,[65] teaches in threefold form;[66]
or whatever Aristotle, analysing kinds of speech,
teaches, weaving his nets of multiple syllogisms;   175
whatever Anaximenes, Euclid, Archytas, Zeno,
Arcesilas, Chrysippus, Anaxagoras have given,[67]
and the soul of Socrates as it lives on in his book *Phaedo*,
despising the vast fetters on his withered leg,[68] while death
itself trembled before the prisoner, and the pale hand   180
of the prison guard brought poison to the unperturbed master.
Moreover, whatever an earlier age applied itself
to present in Latin books,[69] he used to work his way through it all:
what battles and what seaborne dangers Mantua's bard described,
echoing the trumpet-tones of Smyrna;[70] and whatever help   185
in eloquence the consul from Arpinum contributes,[71]
having followed unceasingly the swordsmith's son, to whom,

63 In *Ep.* 9.9.14 (after a set of quick caricatures of philosphers) S. links Cleanthes's notorious gnawed fingers to his practice of counting (in fact Euclid's were longer). S. is more interested in his fingers than in his Stoic teaching.

64 The verbs are artistically deployed in reverse order. S. has more to say about Pythagoras in *c.* 15.51–78, where he mentions the philosopher's long silence before he presented his cosmology. In common parlance Democritus was considered the 'laughing' philosopher, Heraclitus the 'weeping' one (cf. Juvenal, the writer of satires, 10.28–30).

65 This point may derive from Cicero (*Tusculan Disputations* 1.20).

66 Cf. *c.* 15.100–1 for the threefold division of Plato's philosophy, into physics, logic, ethics.

67 This varied group includes two pre-Socratic philosophers (Anaximenes and Anaxagoras: cf. *c.*15.83–93), two Stoic philosophers (Chrysippus and Zeno), and two mathematicians (Euclid and Archytas). For Archesilaus see *c.* 15.94–6.

68 Plato described the painful fetter on Socrates' leg in his account of Socrates's imprisonment in *Phaedo* 60c.

69 It is not implied that 'Latin books' are presentations, let alone reproductions, of the Greek, though the strong influences on Vergil and Cicero – both denoted in what follows by their places of birth – are duly mentioned.

70 Smyrna in Asia Minor was the supposed birthplace of Homer, whom Vergil often echoes. The epic voice is often troped as a sounding trumpet (cf. *c.* 23.5).

71 Cicero, born in Arpinum, was consul in 63 BC.

spurning his father, a polished tongue meant more;[72] he also read
all the eternal books, Euganean pages, from Padua,[73]
the charming terseness of Sallust,[74] the weightiness of Varro,[75]   190
the genius of Plautus,[76] Quintilian's lightning,[77] the pomp
of Tacitus, name never to be spoken without praise.[78]

Now shaped by such studies, and born with such an ancestry,
imbued with these standards, by the lord to whom the world, from East
to West, was then giving sceptres,[79] to whom his only daughter,[80]   195
of marriageable age, now owed grandsons for the purple,
he was chosen as son-in-law, but not so that he should,
in idle luxury, content with her father's fortune,
seeking an easeful life, owe nothing to his own efforts.
But, with the rank of companion,[81] he traversed the Danube's banks   200
and the areas of its great frontier, exhorting, managing,
probing, arming. Just so Pius, under his father's sway,
governed his father's troops, so too Marcus, while Pius lived,

---

72 The excellence of Demosthenes (whose father made swords for a living) is described
allusively in c. 23.136–44.

73 Padua, in the territory of the Euganei, a tribe in the north-east of Italy, was the
birthplace of the historian Livy (as mentioned in c. 23.146).

74 Sallust wrote various highly regarded historical works in the first century BC.

75 Varro, a true polymath, wrote a wide range of scholarly works in the later first
century BC.

76 Plautus was a very successful writer of comedies in the second century BC.

77 Quintilian wrote books on oratory and education in the first century AD. The work or
works here noted are probably two series of *Declamations* attributed to him, declamations
being seen as fiery or cutting practice speeches. These are probably the basis of S.'s
description of Quintilian's 'pungency' in *Ep.* 5.10.3.

78 The name Tacitus means literally 'silent'; terseness being a commendable quality in a
scholar or speaker, to name him is a reminder of his quality.

79 The world was giving sceptres, or rather his imperial sceptre, to Marcian, as emperor
of the East 450–7, at this time (450), and also making possible powerful marriage alliances
with him.

80 This is Euphemia (Aelia Marcia) (*PLRE* 2.423–4, giving the date of the marriage as
ca. 453), named in line 482; and the 'royal wife' of 217.

81 He held the rank of 'companion' or military commander (see introduction), presumably
in Thrace. The date is probably 453 or 454, before his consulship (455) and after the death of
Attila in 453 (*PLRE* 2.96).

(both would be lawgivers) they then ruled legions without number.[82]
To Anthemius, when he returned, every honour was given,   205
and he shone out as master of both services,[83] and as
consul;[84] he gained the power, concurrent, of a patrician,
climbed fast, ran through the private distinctions,[85] and though a boy
rose to a curule chair, taking his gold seat like an elder:
a veteran youth.[86]

    By now your parent was a god;[87] but you   210
had no desire for supreme power. The diadems, after
a long rebuff, found an outstanding man,[88] whom, when in turn
chosen, you could not spurn; to you alone did Fortune grant

---

82 The point of this comparison with two famous second-century emperors, Antoninus
Pius and Marcus Aurelius ('being a lawgiver' means 'being emperor'; cf. *c.* 2.480–1 below),
seems to be to show the size of the forces ruled and responsibilities held by Anthemius at this
time, as well as the high probability that he would be next in succession (210–22). The father
of Pius was Hadrian, who adopted him a few months before his own death; there was thus
little time for the military arrangements implied here to come to fruition. Whether Marcus
helped Pius in the same way is not known. This idea of S. is a strange misunderstanding,
if not complete invention, an attempt to enhance the qualifications of Anthemius on the
military front.

83 Master of infantry and cavalry: see note 38 on line 90 above for this high rank and the
status of patrician, often as here awarded concurrently.

84 He was consul in 455, and gained the other titles at about the same time (*PLRE* 2.97).

85 'Private' indicates 'non-imperial' here. The impression is given of a meteoric rise.

86 Finding no evidence of gilded curule chairs for consuls (see introduction) or others,
Anderson referenced *Ep.* 8.8.3, where gold may be implied (as it sometimes is) by the word
bratteatas ('with thin veneer') that describes 'travelling-chairs'; but the curule chairs there
are of ivory. Perhaps S. exaggerates, as he certainly does in the description 'veteran youth'
(line 210). He is prone to imply that his honorands are younger than they really were (for
discussion of Majorian's age see introduction to *c.* 5). Loyen (1942), 89 stated perhaps
unnecessarily that Anthemius had to renounce the succession as too young.

87 Marcian, his father-in-law (the word 'parent' for this is a rare usage, but cf. *c.* 6.35
where Avitus is hailed as 'public father') died in 457, and was deified, as described in the
usual phraseology. Anderson thinks that literary tradition is more potent with him than
Christian feeling, which might have chosen another euphemism for 'die'.

88 Leo succeeded to the throne relatively quickly (*PLRE* 2.663–4 and 715): S. almost
describes him as worthy of Anthemius, and certainly acceptable to him. It is implied that
Anthemius might well have taken supreme power, but held back; but the opposition of
Aspar (nowhere mentioned by S.) is thought more probable by *PLRE* at 2.97. At some stage
Anthemius may have declined offers of power, contributing to the 'long rebuff' (for this
notion cf. *c.* 7.465), words that emphasise what an honour it was.

this honour: that although normal sequence cried out for you[89]
you were seen as emperor by selection, not inheritance.   215
You reign after your father-in-law, the Augustus, but the purple
came to you not by marriage; your royal wife was kudos
for your reign, not the cause; to hold the reins of power the state
did not seek out a son-in-law but a man of noble birth.[90]
I am deceived, unless the world with its twin poles proves this: 220
Zephyrus seeks you as its ruler, Eurus destines you
to be ruler; you fight in the North and are feared in the south.[91]

But – this precedes your colleague's making you his joint ruler –
I wish to touch upon the triumphs that the Illyrian coast[92]
had witnessed as it lamented its depredation by   225
the arms of Valamir,[93] through a Roman leader's fault, as it chanced.
Just as,[94] when once the slaying of Caepio had yielded up

89 This – the 'normal sequence' – is deliberately vague. Though his link with Marcian
made him the obvious candidate, that was not, S. argues, a deciding factor. Fortune is
brought in to emphasise the uniqueness of his situation.
90 The pun in this snappy line (between Latin words *gener* 'son-in-law' and *generosus*
'nobly born') cannot be reproduced in English.
91 From all quarters his election is acceptable. Major areas, as often, are denoted by
the winds that come from them: here the Zephyr from the West is Rome, the East wind
Constantinople, the North wind Germany and the Danube basin, the East wind Parthia. All
these areas knew him well.
92 The word 'triumphs' is probably ironic: they are triumphs for the enemy, not the
Romans, unless this description looks forward to the Roman victory (line 306) – which in
fact occurred far inland, not on the coast. The location is described only vaguely, and the
name of the enemy is not given; this seems to be the only source. Anderson sketches a broad
background to this and other 'raids' in his note (p. 26, n. 2), showing the effect of the end of
the Hunnic empire.
93 Valamir [Valamer], king of the Ostrogoths (*PLRE* 2.1135–6), who ravaged Illyricum
after the matter of their subsidy was not resolved (Jones [1973] 221 with note 6 and references
there: Jordanes, *Getica* 270–1, Priscus 37 Blockley). The date may be in the years 459–62
(*PLRE* 2.97).
94 Here S. in an ambitious historical simile makes an extended comparison of the situation
with a dangerous period in the late second century BC when Rome was challenged on two
fronts; it is designed to highlight the abilities of Anthemius under pressure and reassure
his listeners. He is tacitly compared with Marius, who at the battle at Arausio (Orange)
in 105 BC conquered the Cimbrian invaders after they, encouraged by the corrupt treaty
of Calpurnius Bestia, had defeated Caepio in Narbonese Gaul. Before that Marius (born

the might of Italy, with sudden ruin driving them,
when after the strangling of Jugurtha, the state in panic,
seeking a leader, chose the Arpinate huckster, avenger of   230
the corrupt treaties of Calpurnius, and set him against
the raging Cimbrians; then, when the province[95] saw your eagles,
it ceased at once to tremble at the enemy dragons.
Immediately subdued in war, and stripped of their plunder,
prostrate, they soon themselves became your spoil. But I ignore   235
these as mere plunderers; now I report acts of real war;
not a war devised by a petty gang, or a breakout from prison
by you, chained Spartacus, destined to be a gladiator,[96]
but an attack from a wandering horde from a region of Scythia,
full of cruelty, awful, greedy, vicious, even to   240
barbarians barbaric; a citizen, Hormidac,[97] was
leader. I now describe their lands, nature, and origins.[98]
Where the white Tanais driven from Hyperborean valleys
falls from Riphaean crags, there lies beneath the Greater Bear[99]

in Arpinum; the word 'huckster' is mildly derogatory) had overcome and humiliated the
African leader Jugurtha, king of Numidia, who was executed in Rome in 104 BC. There is
an even more compressed treatment of these events in c. 9.254–8.

95 This terminology, suggesting what had been the province *par excellence* to the
Romans, is more relevant to the warfare in southern Gaul (Provence) just described than
to the campaigning in Dacia. Roman 'eagles' are matched with enemy 'dragons' (though in
c. 5.402 the standards of both Roman and Vandal armies are called 'dragons').

96 The imprisoned gladiator Spartacus led a revolt in Italy in 73 BC and with a large army
defeated numerous Roman commanders before being overcome by Crassus and Pompey.
In Claudian's picture of him at c. 26.154–9, Spartacus is much more formidable; S. is less
dismissive in c. 9.252–3 than he is here.

97 Nothing else known of Hormidac (*PLRE* 2.571; Maenchen-Helfen [1973], 390 and
441). S. at least knows that he is not a slave or an outsider, but a 'citizen' or 'tribesman' (for
'citizen' applied to a barbarian cf. c. 7.375). The date is likely to be winter 466/7.

98 There are comparable descriptions of the Huns' physiognomy and way of life in the
historian Amm. 31.2.1–11 and (subsequent to S.) Jordanes *Getica* 24 and (on Attila) 35 (127),
as well as the briefer one in Claudian c. 1.323–31, which S. imitates only slightly, if at all
(*pace* Anderson, p. 29 n. 3, and Loyen *ad loc.*).

99 The Tanais is today's river Don, which flows south into the sea of Azov and the
Black Sea; the location of the Riphaean mountains, a trope for extreme cold, is set vaguely
in the furthest north; looking down is the (Greater) Bear, a northern constellation. A
bleak picture of the frozen north; but at the time in question the Huns lived mainly in the
Hungarian plain.

a race baleful in body and mind; the faces of infants   245
have their own hideousness. A bulbous body ascends into
a narrow head;[100] in two caverns beneath the forehead sight
is present but no eyes appear;[101] the light driven into
the arched recesses of the skull scarcely reaches the eyes,
which hide but are not closed; for in a vault of confined space   250
they have a wide range of vision, with the absence of more light
made up for by their pin-point perception, as if in wells.[102]
Next, so that nostrils cannot grow outwards between the cheekbones
a bandage placed around their tender noses constricts them
so as to leave room for helmets: thus, since they are born for battle,   255
motherly love disfigures them, because the cheek area
is stretched and made broader without the intrusion of the nose.[103]
The other male parts are handsome; their enormous chests stand firm,
shoulders are prominent, stomachs beneath the flanks compact.
The height of a foot-soldier is middling, but they seem tall   260
if you see them on horseback; hence they are often thought tall
when seated.[104] When the infant can scarcely stand without mother
a horse provides a back. You would think the limbs of animals
and human limbs were akin; so does the rider adhere to the horse
as if attached; any other race is carried on horseback,   265
this one lives there. Smooth, rounded bows and their arrows delight them;
horrendous are their hands, and sure; firm is their confidence
that their arrows bring-death. With shooting that is never wrong
their fury is taught to perform wrong actions. This race of a sudden

---

100 Amm. (31.2.2) compares them, with their compact limbs and thick necks, to the roughly hewn stumps of trees that are seen on parapets for bridges.

101 Jordanes (*Gothic matters* 24) describes their eyes as mere points; Semple (1930), 74, in his analysis of this complex passage, says the words 'must mean' the iris or pupil. See also Maenchen-Helfen (1973), 361–3.

102 S. ventures this comparison of their visual field with wells: they see as others might see looking into a deep well.

103 The flat nose follows from the description of the way the skulls of children were deformed, according to Maenchen-Helfen (1973), 364.

104 An interesting observation, whether by S. or not; it reads rather like a correction of someone's first impression of their height.

burst forth, and crossing with their wheels the stiffly frozen Danube   270
had come, scoring the water's dry surface with their wheelmarks.

Against this people, wandering over Dacia's countryside,[105]
you march at once; you attack them, you defeat them, you blockade them
and, when Serdica observed you and your camp all measured out,
you beset them with a siege.[106] The town was amazed at you spending   275
so much time placed on the rampart and that the soldiery
did not go into the fields on regular or furtive raids.
They often lacked Ceres, and always Lyaeus, but never
did they lack discipline; although the enemy was close,
they feared their leader more. So eventually it came about   280
that your ally (it so happened) but later on betrayer,
when battle started, drew away from the enemy – in vain.
For when he was already in flight, leaving the wings exposed,
you stood alone, an army in yourself; to you the troop
dispersed by the leader's flight, to you the cavalry rallied,   285
as you, fighting-on foot, sweated it out; beneath your standards
the soldiers did not feel themselves deserted in the conflict.
Come, white-haired generation of our fathers, now bring out
the tributes to old Tullus, that in his fine encouragement
he covered up the failing treaty with renegade Mettus![107]   290
There is no parallel, nor would bluffing an enemy

105 Dacia is, roughly, modern Rumania: see glossary.
106 Anthemius waited for the full might of his army to be visible from Serdica (near modern Sofia), but then lost no time. The population had by now presumably been overpowered by the Huns.
107 Tullus (Hostilius), the third king of Rome, punished his ally Mettus (or Mettius) for treachery in a battle against Fidenae and Veii in a signally cruel way: he was torn apart by horses. According to Livy (1.27–8) Mettus had deserted the Roman army but after its victory tried to cover this up and make amends. The 'encouragement' of Tullus (289) may relate to the speech he made to his troops early in the battle (Livy 1.27). Two powerful lines in Vergil's *Aeneid* (8.642–3) vividly present Mettus's treachery and punishment (here the epic poet describes a shield bearing various episodes in early Roman history). The address to the 'white-haired generation' and their imagined praises of Tullus (288–9) is sarcastic; they are straw men in his argument.

please you.[108] Then, the soldier conquered thinking he would be helped;[109]
this one conquered after learning that they had been deserted.
The leader fled, but you pursue;[110] he renews the fight, you win;
he shuts himself in, you storm through; he slips away, you catch him   295
and stipulate his death as the price of peace with the Sarmatians.[111]
You are obeyed; now the deserter duly meets his death,
and your victim has fallen by a foreign enemy's sword.[112]
Again, antiquity, take up, if you please, another debate.
The savage Hannibal, sought out to suffer punishment,[113]   300
although in his last hour he did not have the right to live
certainly had the power to die, and so, when the dark dungeon
and the iron hook awaited him, and the guard to break his neck,
he drank poison, a stauncher man than his Bebrycian host;
but he who abandoned you, killed in a death that was decreed,   305
perished by a judge's word rather than by a victor's mouth.[114]

Now come, Paean, whose hook-beaked gryphons skilful bridles curb
with their bonds of laurel, whenever through the leafy reins
you turn their feathered shoulders with ivy of twofold colour,
direct your lyre to this new theme: this is not the time to tell   310
the extinction of Python,[115] or to utter the twice seven

108 The cases are not comparable; and in any case 'bluffing', or concealing information, would not be Anthemius's way.
109 The old Roman army, still believing that Mettus and his Albans were on their side, were encouraged, and won the battle; the army of Anthemius won through though already aware of the desertion.
110 This and the following terse lines give a spirited account of the pursuit, in a style reminiscent of the emotional struggle of Avitus with the Hunnic enemy in Arvernum (c. 7.251–94, esp. 255–61).
111 The word Sarmatian, reserved by S. elsewhere for his lists of barbarians, is used here to denote the Huns.
112 The task was no doubt left to a barbarian, under orders.
113 Hannibal, defeated in the battle of Zama (202), was sought out, especially after the peace some ten years later between Rome and King Antiochus of Syria, who had sheltered him. His last host and protector was Prusias king of Bithynia, who was induced to hand him over.
114 The killing was coolly decreed by a Roman magistrate, and not in the heat of war.
115 A favourite theme of Phoebus, to judge from c. 22.74–5 (it is engraved on his lyre).

wounds of the Tantalids, whose deaths, preserved for you[116] in song,
and whose fatal catastrophes live everlastingly.
You too, Castalides, show briefly by what power divine
Anthemius came to us with a covenant between two realms;   315
make known how the imperial peace has sent him to wage wars.

By nature's law the Augustus Severus had joined the number
of deified emperors.[117] Soon, when Oenotria saw this
disaster from the lofty crags of the Apennine heights,
she made her way to the glittering home of greenish-blue Tiber   230
without a helmet to enclose her cheeks (and she had no
protecting corselet sewn with tightly fastened hooks).[118] Her head
was bare; instead of hair a vine-branch with clusters of grapes
ran round her forehead, squeezing together her many towns[119]
and over her smooth shoulders and her brightly shining arms   325
brooches adorned with precious stones held fast her hanging shawl.
Because of age she moved more slowly; and directed her
august limbs, as with a staff, to a branch of elm entwined with vines.[120]
Yet abundance followed her; wherever she drew near, she made
her path luxuriant as she walked; attending her progress   330

116 This is Phoebus (Paean above), responsible for their deaths, having avenged the boast
of Niobe that she had produced more children than his sister, the goddess Leto (numbers
vary: fourteen is also the number given by Ovid, *M.* 6.182–3). Niobe was daughter of
Tantalus.

117 The phrasing suggests that Severus died a natural death, and there may be some point
in the reference to nature's law being maintained; S. may, as suggested by *PLRE* 2.1004–5
(Severus 18), be implicitly denying the allegation that Ricimer poisoned him (Cassiodorus
Chronicle year 464). Loyen *ad loc.* implies that the comment by S. was influenced by the
presence of Ricimer.

118 Oenotria is an elderly and peaceable deity, living apparently in the Apennine mountains
of Italy, but clearly mobile when necessary, though not fleet of foot. The adjective Oenotrian
is relatively rare in Latin poetry, being used in Vergil's epic twice for the land and once for the
men who people her. In Claudian Oenotria has a small speaking part at *c.* 22.262–8, and at
c. 26.146 is distressed by the invasion of Pyrrhus; but the personification goes no further. Here
a corselet reinforced with hooks, almost like chain mail, would not fit her pacific purpose.

119 Rome's headware represents her towers; see line 392 and Roberts (2001); Oenotria has
such headware too, representing her towers (323–4), which somehow are folded away in the
vine branch around her forehead.

120 She moved her feet, as one might with a walking stick, towards the substantial branch
of elm, covered with vines as elms often were.

convivial Vintage sprinkled juice like dew in her footmarks.
At once she visited a cave in the river Tiber's flood.
There, sitting at leisure, the river ran;[121] in his green hair
there floated a forest, of the same colour, of rippling reeds;
the water falling from his chin was noisy, although his beard   335
with its bristles beneath helped greatly to muffle the din.
From his chest he belched out streams of water, which, falling in a rush,
flowed in torrents, cleaving furrows in his soaking belly.
The coming of the goddess shocked him, and his sagging hands
let fall his oar and urn.[122] He was preparing words of excuse,   340
but she spoke first: "Rome now has lost our ruler; in tears I come
to set her right, through you, if you agree. Let her seek out
the lands of Aurora, and putting aside all arrogance,
grant that alone and so deserve to be cherished yet more.[123]
Teach her what powers she must obtain and tell her in what world   345
she must seek leadership for her spent world. Whatever man,
born in my clime,[124] she has produced, Fortune has at once through him
shattered the wheels of his empire.[125] The Vandal enemy,
on one side, presses us, and with his massive fleet pursues
our ruin every year, and with Fate's order overturned   350
parched Byrsa inflicts on me the fury of the Caucasus.[126]

121 A joke by the poet; compare his description of the effect of Orpheus on trees and rivers at *c.* 6.4.

122 An urn is a river god's regular attribute in art, where it is an identifier, and appears sometimes in classical verse (Vergil, *A.* 7.792). The oar could assist going upstream, if needed.

123 'that alone': an end to her alleged arrogance.

124 That is, within the West.

125 Such people, within one generation, are the emperors Valentinian III, Petronius Maximus (references to them are made by S. at *c.* 5.306 and *c.* 7.356), Avitus, Majorian and perhaps the generals Aetius and Aspar – but not Ricimer; this question is addressed below (352–7).

126 The Vandal enemy was of course Geiseric (*PLRE* 2.496–9), a difficult enemy to counter or conquer, as the following lines indicate with some justice, though without underlining Rome's weaknesses. His fleet may not have been 'massive' (349), at least in terms of warships: on this question see MacGeorge (2002), esp. 308–10 in her Appendix 'Naval Power in the Fifth Century'. (The plea of Africa to have Majorian with his fleet, or any kind of fleet, in her harbours (*c.* 5.104–6) was quite impracticable). Geiseric's adaptability and energy are shown by his coming from near the frozen Caucasus to torrid Carthage (for Byrsa, *c.* 5.600, 7.455), thereby overturning Fate's order of things (a purely rhetorical point, this).

Moreover, unconquered Ricimer, to whom the nation' s fates
look for their safety, hardly with his own forces,[127] repels
the pirate who wanders over our lands, who shunning battle
pretends to be the victor, though a runaway.[128] Who can   355
endure an enemy who declines both peace and combat? For
he makes no treaties with Ricimer. Why does he hate him so?
Listen. He blethers on that he has no certain father,
although his mother was certainly a slave; to make himself
a king's son, he proclaims his mother's adultery.[129] Then he   360
is jealous that two realms call Ricimer to kingly power;[130]
Sueves on his father's side, Goths on his mother's. He also
remembers that Ricimer's grandfather Wallia crushed in
Tartesian lands the Vandal squadrons and allies in war,
the Alani, and that corpses covered Calpe in the far west.[131]   365
Why tell of past defeats, the losses of their forefathers?
He calls to mind the losses borne on Agrigentum's plain;[132]

127 The 'unconquered' Ricimer (this epithet often shades into eulogistic 'invincible':
cf. 517 below) had been a patrician and master of both forces for at least ten years (*PLRE*
2.942–5, at mid-943). His personal army (of federates) is mentioned also in line 380. See
MacGeorge (2002), 344–5 (an excellent itemised index).

128 The strategy of Geiseric involved seaborne raiding parties (including horses: cf.
c. 5.389–91) rather than piracy in the normal sense (Anderson calls him 'an incorrigible
pirate', p. 38 n. 2). The point behind 'wandering' is freedom from opposition rather than
wide territorial licence; even on 'our lands' he is evasive. The fact that no treaties have been
made (one might compare the regular treaties between Avitus and the Goths) is put down to
Geiseric's hatred of Ricimer, as S. tries to explain in the following lines.

129 Geiseric's father was Godigisel (Godigisel 1, *PLRE* 2.515–16 and 2.496–7), with
apparently good evidence (Procopius, BV 1.3.23). There is no uncertainty about his mother
– she was a slave – and so he presents himself as the illegitimate son of a king of the Vandals
(359–60).

130 This seems to mean that both Sueves and Goths were inviting him to be their king, or
could be expected to do so; this is unverifiable, but he is unlikely to have accepted if they
had. S. calls him grandson of the Gothic king Vallia in line 363, but in general knows little
of the Sueves.

131 Vandals (Silings) and Alans, as often, fought together. The date is 416–18, before the
Goths' move to Gaul (*PLRE* 2.1148): see Hydatius 60 [68], *Chron. Gall.* 511, no. 564. Various
regions of Spain (Calpe was one of the 'pillars of Hercules' by the straits of Gibraltar) were
involved.

132 Anderson's translation 'havoc' here is too strong, as indeed is Loyen's 'defeat'.
Neither corresponds to normal Latin usage: *dispendia* normally means 'losses' of some
kind, but not military reverses. There is no indication in the sources of a significant victory

He rages that his rival has distinctly proved himself
to be the grandchild of the man at the sight of whom, Vandal,
you constantly turned tail. Not more famous were you, Marcellus,[133]   370
on your return from Sicily's fields, through whom by land and sea
our arms beleaguered and beset the homes of Syracuse;
nor were you more illustrious,[134] whose fortune was to outdo
the triumph of Curius,[135] presenting throngs of elephants,
when the dark herd shrouded with their great bulk the white horses   375
and the triumphal show concealed the honorand.[136] The fact
that Noricum confines the Ostrogoth[137] shows that Ricimer
is feared, as does the fact that Gaul restricts the Rhine's armed might;
as for the Vandal plundering me, with his kinsman the Alan
gleaning what was left, he took revenge with his own private troops.[138]   380
But nonetheless he is only one man, who alone cannot
remove such dangers, though he can delay them; what we need
is an armed emperor, who like our forefathers would not

for Ricimer (cf. 353–4) or any other Roman. MacGeorge (2002), 187 lays out the scanty
detail of the context with the help of this passage; see also Loyen (1942), 93. See Priscus,
fragment 31 on the ravaging of Sicily by forces of Geiseric, and fragment 39 on Geiseric's
general tactics.

133 M. Claudius Marcellus (1) (OCD[4] 327) laid siege to Syracuse in 213 BC and captured
it in 212 BC.

134 L. Caecilius Metellus (OCD[4] 258) defeated the Carthaginians at Panormus in 250 BC,
with the capture of many elephants.

135 Manius Curius Dentatus, who had triumphed over Pyrrhus in 275 BC (OCD[4] 399), had
brought four elephants to Rome, the first ever seen there according to the historian Eutropius,
Breviarium 2.14.

136 A picturesque conjecture no doubt, part of S.'s fascination with elephants (cf. *c.* 2.54/5,
c. 11.103–4 and *c.* 22.59–63).

137 But for Ricimer (but note that victories by him are not indicated), S. claims, the
Ostrogoths would have broken through via Noricum, and Gaul would have failed to restrict
its potential invaders. On Ostrogoths in general, see Heather (1991), 332–3.

138 This plundering may have taken place in the Vandal capture of Rome in 455, or in
a later invasion of Italy, both of which could be said to have been avenged in a defeat by
Ricimer in 464 at Bergamum (*PLRE* 2.944), when Alans were defeated. A victory is also
mentioned in line 367 above, and there may have been other engagements. The panegyrist
has to give a good impression of sustained and successful activity. The metaphor of gleaning,
seen as a typical Alan strategy when fighting alongside the Vandals and others, may echo a
passage of Pacatus in *Pan. Lat.* 2. (12), 11.4, where, in an imagined protest to Theodosius if
he refused power, the Roman state mentions 'the pressures of the Goths, the seizures by the
Huns, and the purloining by the Alans'.

command wars but wage them, whom as he moves his standards onward
both earth and sea will dread, so that, control regained at last,   385
Rome's trumpets may assert command of Rome's inert navies."[139]

Hearing these words, Father Tiber agreed. To the city he goes
and straightway in person sees the goddess, and humbly adores her,
his horns touching her bosom and the breast that she offered.
Then he, as told, conveyed the prayers to her; agreeing, she   390
prepares for a journey. Grimly she bound her flowing hair;
her towers, enclosed in her helmet, were hidden;[140] laurel formed
a fillet. Rough with studs from enemy shields, a belt holds up
a sword protruding on her left-hand side. Her conquering arm
is placed inside the shield, the rounded form of which was filled   395
by the sons of Mars, the mother wolf, Tiber, Love, Mars, Ilia.[141]
A brooch holds with its biting teeth clothing liable to stray
from her breast.[142] Her menacing spear flashes, and an oak tree, bent
with trophies, sways and tires the goddess with its pleasant burden.
Her foot stands on a single, undivided sole; this strip   400
stops well before the toenails; from each big toe two laces
are drawn, in opposite directions, from the attached sockets[143]
so as to bind the sandal tight, and when the side-loops come
together, jointly weave-a curved network over the legs.
Attired in this manner, wafting through the unclouded air   405
she sought the rising of Hyperion, the dawning sun.

There is a place by the Ocean, close to the distant Indians,
neath the eastern sky, stretching towards the Nabatean wind:[144]

---

139 It is perhaps going too far to say that S. is referring to the Roman navy 'in the past tense' (MacGeorge [2002], 307), though the fleet was certainly unaccustomed to sail in anger.

140 The towers (see n. 118, on line 324) were hidden by her out of respect or veneration; she has been warned against arrogance (or the appearance of it).

141 Not unlike Claudian c. 1.96–9, though this is more concerned with metals; S. uses his quickfire style to be even briefer. He has a fuller picture on Rome's shield in c. 5.21–30. Ilia, who lived in the Tiber, is his wife, as in c. 5.28.

142 Cf. c. 5.18–20 for a similarly intricate picture of a brooch.

143 There is a comparably detailed description of footwear by S., perhaps excessive, given as advice to a friend about to travel, in Ep. 8.11.3 verses 7–17.

144 This is the south wind that blows from Nabatea (roughly speaking, northern Arabia); cf. Ovid, M. 1.61).

Here there is endless spring; the ground is not intruded on
by untimely cold or made pallid with frost; the fields, painted   410
with everlasting flowers, know not the chill of foreign lands,
the country is scented with roses; a sweet aroma bathes
the undivided fields; the plains bear viola, cytisus,
thyme, white privet, lilies, narcissi, casia, marigolds,
costum, malobathron, myrrhs, opobalsama and frankincense.[145]   415
It is from here that neighbouring Phoenix, when old age knocks,
seeks for the cinnamon that gives rebirth and life anew.
Here was Aurora's home, encrusted with shining red gold
exhibiting smooth stones of pearl on its roughened surface.
Diverse aspects bewitch the eye, and by fine artistry   420
whatever you focus on excels the rest; but all is dimmed
in the presence of its mistress, who with her blushing radiance
extinguishes the gems' assorted fires with those of her own.
Her well groomed hair presented saffron scents; the comb, as she
drew it downwards with bending arm, tidied her yellow temples.   425
Her eyes emitted rays; their colour was like that of fire,
yet in them was no heat, although when night is shaken off
the dews arising from it often ape perspiration.
Two bands encircled her bosom; and the slightness of her breasts
was mocked by the robe's hanging fold; the lowest part of her dress   430
extended its vermilion folds down to her roseate knees.
So did the queen sit on her throne: instead of a sceptre
her right hand clasped a lamp; alongside the goddess stands Night,
already turning round her feet to flee; behind the dais
the light, scarcely perceived as such, reveals a salient peak.   435
When from this place she saw Rome coming on her cloudless path,
she jumped up quickly, and taking the lead spoke kindly words:
"Wherefore, O head of the world, do you again visit my realm?
Or what do you command?" Remaining silent for a while,
then mixing harsh with gentle words Rome answered: "be not moved,   440
and do not be alarmed – I do not come so that Araxes[146]

---

145 English equivalents to the flowers mentioned are not in every case known; *casia* is
uncertain, as are *costum, malobathron, opobalsama*, which here are left in their Latin forms.
146 This refers to a famous line of Vergil (*A.* 8.728), a line that imagines this river's
indignant rejection of a bridge.

may flow, subdued by me, beneath a bridge imposed on it,
nor that, as once, Italian helmets drink Indian Ganges,
nor that beneath tiger-infested Niphates,[147] in fields
full of bowmen, a proud consul may lay waste Caspian   445
Artaxata;[148] I do not now seek the kingdoms of Porus,[149]
or that our battering ram should smash Hydaspean Erythrae.[150]
I am not rushing to attack Bactra, nor do the gates of
Semiramis mock our trumpets as they announce attack;[151]
I seek not Arsacid mansions, nor is a password given   450
to the army for a march on Ctesiphon.[152] This whole expanse
have we ceded to you. So do I not deserve protection
in my old age? You have long held, alone, all land between
Tigris and Euphrates, a domain bought by me with the blood
of Crassus (at Carrhae I paid the price);[153] not unavenged,   455
I did not lose the land so dearly bought. Or am I wrong?
No: you, Sapor, have proved it, slain by Ventidius.[154] Besides,
I gave up Pontus and the Armenias; with what struggles
they were sought, let Sulla tell you, or if a single voice is not
believed, ask Lucullus.[155] I now pass over the Cyclades;[156]   460
but Crete, gained by Metellus, is your slave;[157] Cilicia

147 Niphates is part of the Taurus range of modern Turkey, in Roman Armenia; the
bowmen are Parthian. S. mentions this region also in c. 23.94 and Ep. 9.13.5 verse 21.
   148 Artaxata was a royal capital in Armenia, often the target of Roman armies. No specific
consul is meant; anyone laying it waste might be seen as haughty.
   149 Unlike Alexander, Rome has no designs on the lands once ruled by Porus, the Indian
king (c. 24.72–4 and note).
   150 Erythrae: a town in India, imagined here to be on the river Hydaspes, now Jhelum. It is a
stronghold in c. 22.22, but elsewhere in S. functions as a geographical marker (c. 5.285, 11.105).
   151 Bactria lay roughly between the Oxus river and the Hindu Kush; the 'gates of
Semiramis' are those of Babylon, on the Euphrates.
   152 The Arsacids, descended from the first king of the Parthians, need not worry, nor the
town of Ctesiphon in Armenia (linked with Niphates in Ep. 9.13.5, verse 21).
   153 Carrhae: also mentioned in c. 9.22 and 251.
   154 The conqueror of Sapor (cf. c. 7.99) was P. Ventidius Bassus, the date 38 BC.
   155 The province of Pontus and the Armenias (Greater and Lesser) were gained by Sulla
in the first Mithridatic war, 89–85 BC; the struggle was continued by Lucullus in the third
Mithridatic war.
   156 The Cyclades, the archipelago in the south Aegean sea, frequently changed hands but
were finally included in province of Asia (line 466) in 133 BC.
   157 Crete was pacified by Quintus Caecilius Metellus in 69–67 BC.

I passed to you; Magnus routed them long ago.[158] I added
to Syria the Isaurians, now ruled by you: they were
made subject to our arms by Servilius.[159] I granted you
the ancient Aetolians and the Acheloan lands;[160] I made   465
over to you the bequest of Attalus – too trustingly;[161]
you keep Epirus: and you know to whom Pyrrhus owed it.[162]
I watch you extending your sway to Illyricum,[163] and to
the Macedonian lands[164] and yet you, Paulus, have descendants![165]
I gave you Egypt's corn; Agrippa had won it for me   470
long since in the Leucadian straits.[166] Judaea is held under
your jurisdiction, as if it had been yourself who sent
the famous Titus,with his father, there.[167] The trade of Cyprus

158 The province of Cilicia was created in about 80 BC; the pirates, who had made their
base there, were suppressed by Pompey the Great (Magnus) in 67 BC.
159 The Isaurians were defeated by Servilius Vatia Isauricus, who triumphed in 76–75 BC,
and Isauria was soon afterwards merged with Syria.
160 The Aetolians were defeated by Rome in 189 BC. By the Acheloan lands S. means the
basin of the long river Achelous in north-west Greece, subdued at the same time.
161 Attalus III, king of Pergamum, bequeathed his kingdom to Rome in 133 BC, when
it became the province of Asia. S. tersely implies unfavourable consequences, thinking no
doubt of political and economic challenges and conflicts in Rome itself. In the 80s Asia was
supported by Mithridates, and later took the losing side against Octavian.
162 The reference is to the story concerning Gaius Fabricius Luscinus, consul 282 BC and
278 BC; he turned down the offer of a renegade to murder Pyrrhus in one of the wars that he
waged on the Romans (Cicero, *On Duties* 3.22 [86]). See also *c.* 7.69 and *c.* 7.226–9.
163 The wording here is intriguing: the change seems to be deliberately depicted by the
poet as being in progress. The political situation of the province of Illyricum had been
disputed, as spelt out by MacGeorge (2002), 34–7, and the wording may be based on the
recent change in 437 that made Illyricum part of the eastern empire. If he knew of this,
perhaps S. was uncertain about the situation, or stood by a 'Western' and slightly anachro-
nistic view.
164 Macedonia was under Roman sway from 167 BC, and a province from 146 BC.
165 Paulus: Aemilius Paullus, victor over Antiochus at Pydna in 168 BC, thus ending
the third Macedonian war. S. adds the rhetorical point that the present situation is surely
unacceptable given that ancestors (who might contest this) still exist.
166 As a result of the battle of Actium (31 BC), won by Octavian's lieutenant Agrippa,
Rome gained control of Egypt and its resources.
167 Jerusalem in Judaea was captured by Titus (emperor 79–81) in 70 AD. His father
Vespasian had earlier suppressed a rebellion and pacified most of Judaea (note 'as if':
sarcasm is creeping in). In the poetic obituary that S. wrote for Abraham, a 'holy man', and
a refugee from Parthia, in *Ep.* 7.17 at lines 15–16 S. recalls that he had fled 'the walls [of
Jerusalem] once broken by Titus's archers'.

is brought to you: but being poor, I praise the fighting Catos.[168]
The Dorian land and the Achaean fields tremble at you,   475
and you stretch out your thriving realms over Corinth's two seas:[169]
Tell me, what Byzantine Mummius brought this to pass for you?[170]

But, if it pleases you to put aside old grievances,
grant me Anthemius. Let Leo be in these regions
emperor, and that for a long time; let the man whom I have sought   480
manage my laws;[171] may the star of her deified father rejoice
that his daughter Euphemia wears the ancestral purple.[172]
Add, furthermore, a private settlement to the public one:
let Augustus, as father-in-law, be blessed with Ricimer
as son-in-law.[173] The pair gleam with nobility: a royal   485
virgin is yours, I have a man who is royal.[174] If you
agree, you will permit some hope for Libya soon.[175] Look at
old marriages: no equal one presents itself to you.
Let Greece, unless ashamed, cite matches once made with danger:
let Pisa bring back her chariots and call forth Oenomaus,   490

168 In 58 BC the younger Cato was sent to annex the island of Cyprus. Rome here pretends
not to worry about the loss of Cyprus's considerable wealth, making a virtue of poverty and
recalling the Catos, renowned as both ascetic and warlike.

169 The eastern empire has also taken over most of Greece, including Sparta and the
Peloponnese (the 'Dorian' and 'Achaean' areas), and the isthmus of Corinth, important with
the Saronic and Corinthian gulfs for maritime trade.

170 This long disquisition ends with a highly sarcastic rhetorical question: Lucius
Mummius, consul 146 BC, who destroyed Corinth, 'organised the province of Macedonia
and dealt with the Greek cities' (OCD[4]), was in no sense 'Byzantine'; and the eastern empire
had no equivalent(s) to him. The Latin word for 'Byzantine' is not easily fitted into the metre,
and there may be no special point (such as scorn) in its use here.

171 In other words let him be emperor (on the implications of 'giving laws', see line 203
above).

172 The purple gained by Marcian and his ancestors is now worn by Euphemia (194–7), the
Augusta.

173 Euphemia and Ricimer had married in 467; as S. wrote in *Ep*. 1.5.10, the marriage
was taking place just as he arrived in Rome from Lyon. At the beginning of his next letter
(*Ep*. 1.9.1) he deplores the expense of it and the general jollification.

174 Cf. lines 360–2 for his potential to hold kingly power among barbarians. MacGeorge
(2002), 229–30 discusses whether he was ever actually denoted 'king'.

175 This marriage arrangement would make the defeat of Geiseric more likely. Libya
stands as usual for the provinces of Africa, and, of course, for Carthage.

who, undone by his daughter's deceit, was brought to ruin by
the substituted wax linch-pins and the loosening of the wheels;[176]
let the Colchian maiden, known to her husband by crime, not sex,
come forward;[177] from the barriers at the race's starting point
let Atalanta gaze up at the pallid suitors, and   495
collect the apples of handsome Hippomenes (not just
for the gold);[178] let Achelous, richly oiled from wrestling bouts
distinguish your wedding, Deianira; and when pressed hard
by panting Hercules, refresh his foe with spiteful spate —[179]
however much I might recall weddings of ancient times   500
he would stand out among the heroes, she the heroines.
This marriage, Ricimer, Courage as bridewoman, demands,
and thus the laurel of Mars brings you the myrtle of Dione.[180]
Come then, deliver one who does not dote on listless ease
or ruin himself with luxuries, but one now challenged by   505
the swelling sea, the bays of Abydus, the Sestian shore,
around which Hellespontine hurricanes reverberate.[181]

176 In Pisa the suitors for the daughter of Oenomaus would be challenged to a long-distance
chariot race and be killed if they came second. But his daughter Hippodamia, for the sake of
the suitor Pelops, persuaded Myrtilus, an expert charioteer, to replace the bronze linchpins
and so cause the hitherto undefeated Oenomaus to crash fatally.

177 Medea, who fell in love with Jason and, after killing her brother and escaping with
Jason (cf. *c.* 5.132), married him and had two children by him, whom she was later to kill.
She is mentioned by S. also in *c.* 5.133–6 and 9.67–75.

178 Atalanta challenged each of her suitors to a race: if they lost, they would die. Some
suitors were understandably pale at this arrangement, but Hippomanes was not, and he
gained her admiration. In the race he dropped some golden apples given him by Venus,
hoping she would stop to pick them up: she did, and he won.

179 Achelous, the river (and also experienced wrestler), who with his changes of shape
might distinguish any wedding, fought with Hercules for Deianeira. Hercules eventually
prevailed, finding the river waters, released spitefully by Achelous from his great beard, a
great help.

180 Courage itself is to accompany the wedding; female deities who accompanied and
assisted the bride had sometimes been described by the Latin word *pronuba*, used here.
The laurel of Mars gained by Ricimer has also brought him the myrtle sacred to Dione
(Venus).

181 This fleet in the Hellespont was probably in readiness to convey him to Italy to become
emperor, 'rather than evidence of a naval command' (*PLRE* 2.97); if so, S. obscures the
situation with his grandiose comparisons, first to the canal made by Xerxes (cf. *c.* 9.44–9),
and then to Lucullus, at the siege of Cyzicus on the Propontis (*c.* 22.164–6).

These entrances were not, I think, so well controlled even
by him who smashed through Athos and who with his Median rowers
sped through the wooded Alps with billowing sails;[182] nor do I think   510
that they were so surrounded by the ships of Lucullus
when the idle enemy laid siege to famous Cyzicus,
and in the stress of hunger chewed bodies of his kinsmen
and lived by the deaths of his own.[183] But why do I spin out my prayers?
Just hand him over!"

                              Then Tithonus' wife briefly replied: 515
"Come, take him, holy parent, though I have the greatest need
of a supreme, invincible leader – provided that
you show yourself more kind, and we manage the reins better,
working as one. Should it perhaps please you to recollect
old labours, and who fought for the fatherland of your Iulus,   520
(to mention just one thing) I sent Memnon from here, beforehand."[184]
So they finished; Concordia united the two sides,
with Rome having acquired at last the emperor of her choice.[185]
Now boast, antiquity, who always envied the outstanding,
that with like feeling and fervour you too made your choices: 525
bring back Camillus from exile against the power of Brennus,[186]

182 Xerxes sailed through the mountain using a canal dug by his engineers, as also described in *c.* 9.41–9. The Latin word 'Alp(s)' is occasionally used of any tall mountain or mountain range.

183 S. gives a longer description of this feat (evidently based on a picture he had seen) in *c.* 22.163–8. In the third Mithridatic war (74–73 BC), although he seems to have had a much smaller fleet, and Mithridates commanded the sea, Lucullus did get a message through to the besieged citizens (with good results), as recounted by Florus 1.40.16. See also Magie (1950), 323.

184 Aurora, here called, for variety, the wife of Tithonus, claims to have sent her son Memnon, a king of Ethiopia, who fought for Troy and so for Iulus and Rome; he is briefly and allusively mentioned in Homer, *Odyssey* 4.109–22, 12.522.

185 'at last': this may simply mean that negotiations are over, but it may hint at the weakness of Libius Severus, who reigned for four years (461–5). Compare the veiled criticism in lines 14–16 above.

186 For the exile of Cincinnatus cf. Livy 5.32.8–9 and 33.1. In *c.* 7.561–4 S. concentrates on the sequel of his return.

and, banishing Caeso, give Cincinnatus back his axes[187]
and call the weeping parent from the rake to the rostra,[188]
and in wretched tumult drive out leaders from whom, when beaten
you will seek help: if bursting through the Alps Carthage invades,[189]   530
fall back on men afflicted and condemned, so that to make
insatiate Metaurus redden with the slaughter of
Barca's son, let a once fined consul do it for you, one
who having made a shining sword beat Hasdrubal's thousands,
and let him present an unkempt head.[190] Not so our kindly choice: 535
though never convicted by us, he knows that he is loved.[191]

But now the winds that drive my sails onward are too powerful;[192]
enough, Muse, of my feeble verse and as I seek the harbour
let my song's anchor settle at last in a calm haven of rest.
But of the fleet and soldiery that you, prince, now control   540
and of the great deeds you achieve in a short time, I will tell
in proper form, if God should give fruition to my prayers,
in the second consulship of your son-in-law, or in your third.[193]
But now a festival calls us:[194] your presence is required

187 Livy relates the trial and exile of Caeso Quintius in 3.11–14; and then in 3.26–9 gives
the story of his father, Cincinnatus, made dictator while working on a farm (for this meme
cf. Pacatus in *Pan. Lat.* 2 (12) 9.5–7, and *c.* 5.300–4), and then saving Rome.
188 The word 'rostra' denotes the platform from which speakers addressed the people of
Rome.
189 Hannibal famously burst through the Alps in 218 BC; many others crossed them later.
190 The Roman victory of M. Livius Salinator on the Metaurus is narrated in Livy. 27.43–9
Having earlier been disgraced, he had adopted shabby clothing and long hair (Livy 27.34.5),
but did possess a sword, made by himself and used vigorously in the battle. The consul Caeso
was indeed fined (Livy 3.11), and his father, Cincinnatus, had to meet the cost.
191 Anthemius is a better choice, and a popular one (cf. lines 18–22), although he has not
undergone any such crises before being chosen.
192 Enthusiasm and inspiration are leading S. into dangerous waters, and he takes
advantage of the traditional picture of a poet's weakness, while holding out a promise of
more eulogy, to finish. Compare the confidence with which this trope is used at the beginning
of Avitus poem (*c.* 7.14–16), where he is not afraid of the seas ahead.
193 Ricimer's first consulship was in 459; Anthemius's first in 455 and his second in 468.
Ricimer is tactfully involved in the promised poem, but not so as to overshadow Anthemius.
194 The emperor's presence is required in the Forum of Trajan (cf. *c.* 7.116–18) for the
festival at which new consuls had the task of freeing slaves; this was performed with a blow

in the Ulpian forum[195] by those to whom you grant freedom,   545
whose cheeks experience with joy the ritual buffeting.
Proceed then, blessed father of your land, with good omen
set free old captives, then conquer and bind captives anew.[196]

to the cheek (line 546). Claudian has a similar passage in *c.* 8.611–18 – mixing it with praises
of Honorius in his new consulship – but does not use it, as S. effectively does here, to give
his poem a gentle diminuendo.

195 The Ulpian forum, or 'forum of Trajan' is described in OCD[4] 588. Cf. also *c.* 7.114–18.
196 The captives resulting from old victories must be freed, and new ones gained by war.

Poem 3
To my little book

INTRODUCTION

Referring closely to the poetic career of Vergil, these ten lines state that S.'s patron henceforth will be Petrus, who is a familiar character in his works (*c.* 5.564–73, *c.* 9.307–8 and *Ep.* 9.13 and 15, where there are snatches of praise from a later time). It is not known what this 'little book' – which interrupts the pattern of panegyrics preceded by a small poem in verse – consisted of (if not this simple poem alone), or its exact circumstances, but its point is clearly made: Petrus will approve and help to disseminate the future poems of S. That Sidonius sent Petrus poem 5 in its entirety, for him to forward to Majorian (*PLRE* 2.866, Petrus 10), seems unlikely. In fact this small poem is an important turning point for S., who boasts that, in Petrus, he has a star in his voyage to fame (line 6): this recalls language that he had used of Avitus in the panegyric, calling upon him as a star that will be a guide and protector over the sea of fame. That situation did not last; after the defeat, eclipse and death of Avitus in 456/7, S. has to plan carefully. Petrus will be his Maecenas in these new circumstances, as well as critic, being, as Martial might have put it, 'stern judge, nice man'.

To my little book

What makes the fields of corn rejoice, what season is to be
preferred for harvests and for herds, for vines and bees[1] –
these themes were once set out together with Maecenas' name;

---

1 The opening words of Vergil's *Georgics*, given almost verbatim in the first two lines, refer to the Vergilian topics of land preparation and care for herds, vines and bees. Vergil names Maecenas as a patron four times in the work, once in each of the four books (12, 241, 341, 42).

next, Vergil, you ventured to write 'arms and the man'.[2]
But my Maecenas in this present time will be Petrus: 5
for I travel the sea of fame beneath his star.[3]
If he approves my poems, he makes them known; if not, he hides them,
but does not censure me with rhinocerotian snort.[4]
Go forth then, book; believe me, he protects my modesty:
with him as critic, even to displease is a joy.[5]   10

2 'Arms and the man' were the opening words of Vergil's *Aeneid*, and often used as its title.

3 In lines 15–16 of the Avitus panegyric (*c.* 7) (which is earlier), the star that guides S. over the (metaphorical) sea is the emperor Avitus himself.

4 Turning up the nose was a recognised way of expressing scorn, social or literary; it is linked with the great upturned 'nose' or horn of a rhinoceros in Martial 1.3.5–6, where the epigrammatist caricatures critics who look down their noses and snort loudly with disdain; this passage is echoed here and in *c.* 9.340–3.

5 Petrus is a kind but not lenient critic.

Poem 4
Preface to the panegyric given for the Lord and Emperor Iulius Valerius Maiorianus, Caesar Augustus

INTRODUCTION

The preface makes clear that this poem, again clothed in reminscences of Vergil, but with allusions to Horace also, was written to recognise the mercy and kindness of Majorian. It may well have been designed as part of the encomium of Majorian in Lyon, together with *c.* 5; it strikes a suitably submissive tone. Compared with the prefaces of the other panegyrics, this one is more directly relevant; in comparison *c.* 1 and even *c.* 6 seem rather jejune. Whether or not S. himself fought in the battle of Placentia, there is an atmosphere of danger and remorse, but it is also clear that S. intends to use his poetic gifts however he can. The relationship with the emperor had moved on by the time S. wrote to him in *c.* 13. Metre: elegiac couplets

For Tityrus once beneath a spreading beech tree's canopy[1]
to be able to trill his sonorous songs on pastoral pipes,
Caesar avowed the wretch's right to life and landholding
and his anger did not persist against the humble suitor;[2]
but while she praised that bountiful ruler's return of land,   5

---

1 The opening line alludes very closely to the opening line of Vergil's first *Eclogue*, a dramatic dialogue in which the character Tityrus, a shepherd, speaks of his good fortune in being authorised to retain his land. By the time of S. this happy experience of Tityrus had long been seen as part of Vergil's own life, and the poem construed as a thanksgiving to Augustus. The opening motif of the shade of the 'spreading beech-tree' was emblematic of Pastoral poetry. Verbally speaking, the main novelty in this line is the word 'once', which immediately takes the reader back some 600 years to the time of Vergil.
2 Tityrus, the 'suitor' or petitioner, had pleaded successfully for the return of land confiscated by the triumvirs, who included Octavian, the future Augustus (here 'Caesar').

the rustic Muse gave him the heavens for the gift of fields.[3]
Nor was the repayment, using the gifts of Phoebus, less;
one man an owner made, but the other a god.[4]
For you too, Horace, who went with Brutus and Cassius,
the source of pardon was the source of poetry.[5]   10
Myself, likewise, in a different conflict recently fallen[6]
you bade, my conqueror, to be of an unconquered mind.
So, likewise, let the tongue of this poet preserved serve you:[7]
let compensation for my life be given in praise.
I will not criticise great Vergil now with mordant tooth,   15
nor, Sabine land, will I decry your citizen.[8]
This work is less than theirs in skill, but greater in its Caesar;[9]
let them boast eloquence; my boast will be my lord.

3 This line develops the joyful exclamation of Tityrus in the eclogue (line 6) that his
benefactor is a god. Later poems of Vergil come close in various places to deifying Octavian/
Augustus.

4 With his continued occupation of the land confirmed, Tityrus became effectively its
owner, a *dominus*; this Latin word contrasts with *deum* ('god').

5 On his own evidence Horace fought with Brutus and Cassius in their unsuccesful battle
against Augustus and Mark Antony at Philippi in 42 BC. S. does not distinguish between
Augustus, the giver of pardon, and Maecenas, the patron of poetry.

6 The word 'fallen' may refer to injuries of some kind in battle; it is not impossible that
he fought against Majorian at the battle of Placentia in 456, but there is no evidence, and
no hint of it elsewhere in his writings. Perhaps the encouraging advice of line 12 (but the
wordplay is surely due to S.) was given him at the same time as the meeting that he mentions
in *c.* 5.596–9.

7 With another play on words ('preserved'/'serve') Sidonius declares that he owes it to
Majorian to write encomiastic poetry about him, as he does in *c.* 5. In fact the panegyric to
Majorian, taken as a whole, is only in small part a personal thanksgiving: see introduction
to *c.* 5. Elsewhere (*c.* 13.32–4) S. promises encomiastic verse if Majorian grants his urgent
requests, as court poets typically do.

8 He will not in his poetry challenge Vergil or enviously claim to equal him, as the
common metaphor of biting implies, or attempt to go one better; nor will he find fault with
Horace by emulating him. Horace's birthplace was Venusia, on the border of Apulia, but his
farm in Sabine territory, supposedly a gift of the emperor, was more famous. These and other
details in the short ancient *Life* of Horace are discussed by Fraenkel (1957), 1–23.

9 A similar point is made by Ausonius in his speech of thanks to the emperor Gratian
(*Gratiarum Actio* 33), where he denies that he is comparing himself with Fronto, the eloquent
panegyrist of the emperor Antoninus, but asserts that his own emperor is superior.

Poem 5
Panegyric of Majorian

INTRODUCTION

This panegyric was delivered in Lyon, in late 458, soon after the arduous journey of Majorian, with his army and members of his staff, over the Alps. Majorian, who had been consul since January of that year, left Ravenna not before late November, presenting a particular challenge to many of his staff and new recruits and doubtless seeking to toughen them up. The description of the march by Sidonius in the last ninety lines is indeed a memorable attraction of the poem. In Lyon itself no formal or religious ceremony is mentioned; Majorian was already emperor, and no particular honour needed to be granted. The audience assembled in Lyon will have been in many ways unlike that of the Roman senate: we should imagine, as well as the emperor and his army, and his staff (some of them noted by name and complimented in the last twenty lines), citizens of Lyon, some friendly or at least inquisitive Burgundians from the neighbourhood and many Gallo-Romans from the Rhone valley, curious to see the emperor and hear the speech.

Majorian and his army were on their way to Spain, from where he proposed to cross to Africa and take on the Vandals; it may be that a visit to Lyon, if not part of his original plans (the way via Arles, by which he would return, is shorter), was sought by its citizens in their plight, which is forcefully and emotively presented at the end of the poem. (The causes of the dire situation are far from clear: scholars have suggested that roles were played by shadowy figures that Sidonus never mentions, warlords such as Marcellinus and Aegidius). Conceivably the imperial visit was in part devised by Petrus, the new patron of Sidonius (*c.* 3) – he was a major actor in the relief of Lyon sometime before Majorian arrived – with the more pacific purpose of publicly reconciling Sidonius and Majorian, providing open forgiveness for the former and offering a promising court poet for Majorian. It must be remembered that Majorian, with Ricimer, had overcome his father-in-law Avitus at the battle of Placentia in October 456

– little more than a year before – a fact to which Sidonius not suprisingly does not advert in this panegyric or anywhere else. It has been suggested that the speech was a *gratiarum actio* (speech of thanksgiving), but this official term describes usually the formal speech of a new office-holder to the emperor (Gillett [2012], 290).

The poem opens, not unlike the panegyric of Avitus, with a panorama, but it is not a panorama of the world seen from heaven but a panorama of the Roman empire, in which various lands bring their gifts to Rome. The atmosphere of happiness and prosperity is broken by the sudden arrival of Africa, whose ears of corn would signify plenty but are crushed on the ground in her deep distress: her fertile land has been taken over by the invader Geiseric. Through her bitter tears she denounces him as a frightened boar hiding in a thicket; like Rome in the panegyric of Avitus (but more fully) she recalls Roman traditions of last-ditch resistance (to Porsenna, Brennus, and Hannibal). For her rescue she wants Majorian, and proceeds to describe his origins and parentage.

Majorian was born in the province of Illyricum, presumably near Aquincum (close to modern Budapest), where a Majorian is attested in records as being the commander-in-chief of Theodosius, who was shortly to become emperor, in 379; the daughter of that Majorian married the wealthy man (the name is contested) who was father to the future emperor. It is not known, and not easy to guess or reconstruct from any available information, when the emperor Majorian was born. At various times in his adult life he is called a boy (*puer*), but in a way that arguably matches views attributable to the speaker, or a young man (*iuvenis*), but the importance of context and the tendency of panegyric (which is to praise what is thought a good quality) demand caution. For example, in his enforced retirement he is a 'veteran youth' or 'young man in retirement' (299), and later he sprints up the Alps 'like a youth' (524). Little is said about his early life: there are no omens at his birth or military toys as with Anthemius, no boyhood adventures or pursuits as with Avitus.

Much of the development of the future emperor is expressed, within the speech of Africa, in the fictive tirade of a Gothic noblewoman (her name is known to be Pelagia), who is resentful of the fact that her own prospects, whether in the Gothic world or Rome, are non-existent but strongly supports the hopes of her son Gaudentius in the Roman hierarchy, using her expertise in the occult. Within the speech of Africa, she takes over the role of narrator, describing his athletic abilities in fulsome comparisons with mythological exemplars in the Sidonian manner; she also records, more or less vividly, his military victories in Gaul (we might assume that her son was there too), his wealth, his popularity, his ambitions and his friendship with the likeminded Ricimer. Eventually she denounces Majorian as a rival to Aetius, her husband, and suggests that he be executed. Aetius immediately refuses, choosing to dismiss him from military service. Like Avitus, Majorian has a break in the country, and the topos of a politician ploughing fields in retirement is given new life.

The lament of Africa continues, ending with another bitter tirade against the Vandals (327–49). Personified Rome now grants her request for Majorian to be her avenger, and adds here (perhaps unexpectedly) a few vehement words on her own situation and the sufferings of Gaul over sixty years before. It is notable that S. announces (370–1) that he must tell of the afflictions of both Rome and Africa, so soon after the poet has made Rome sympathise with the sufferings of Gaul (354–7); this recalls the plaint of the Gauls in lines 532–43 of the Avitus panegyric and is, or might have become, a major thrust of the poet's thinking. Then (370) the poet himself takes over the narration of Majorian's victories (stressing the need for his own reportage). In the first of two campaigns he sent a subordinate officer to take on a band of Alamans who had crossed over the Alps; in the second Majorian in person repulsed a seaborne attack by the Vandals on Campania. Into this stirring narrative of military success Sidonius weaves an indication of Majorian's rise to power: at the time of the first engagement he possessed 'the authority of a commander-in-chief but the destiny of an emperor'; in the second, much more colourful and detailed, he actually was emperor, and emperor with the agreement and support of all orders of the state: the people, the senate, the soldiery and his (eastern) colleague Leo (384–8).

The march over the snowy Alps already mentioned, with soldiers slipping all over the place and suffering dreadfully from the cold, is a splendid *tour de force*, not without touches of sardonic humour. Once in Lyon, the poet makes a moving appeal to the emperor to assist Lyon after its sack and devastation by its unnamed Burgundians (usually deemed responsible for the tumult); he also makes a fulsome recognition of his power and a fervent hope that he may win victories in Africa and elsewhere that Sidonius could celebrate in poetry. But because of treachery the emperor and his great expedition had to turn back while still in Spain.

Synopsis

1–12 Initial accolade that situates Majorian, once a conqueror, now a ruler, in the traditions of Roman history and also alludes to his recent warfare.

13–53 Description of the goddess Rome, in warlike mode and seated on an opulent throne, from which she surveys the offerings of her varied territories.

53–88 Suddenly, in great dejection and anger, Africa enters, crushing the emblematic ears of corn on her head. She denounces the barbarian invasion of her territories and berates Rome for uncharacteristic lethargy and neglect, an attitude unworthy of Rome's ancient heroes.

89–103 The present enemy, the Vandal Geiseric, is feeble and fearful; there is no excuse for not resisting him, especially as there is a long foretold leader – whose life and accomplishments she will now narrate.

104–25 Explaining why she wants Majorian to save her and destroy her oppressor, Africa speaks first of his birthplace and his father, who had married the daughter of a famous leader who had fought alongside to the future emperor Theodosius.

126–39 Africa speaks of the wife of the general Aetius, who is jealous for her own son and exercises her knowledge of the occult.

140–97 Africa continues, speaking of Majorian's sporting ability and widespread popularity. (The long speech of Pelagia continues to line 274).

198–254 Turning to the military qualities of Majorian, Africa describes at some length a notable battle in Northern Gaul against invaders in which he stood out.

255–74 The wife of Aetius is portrayed as suggesting the execution of such a dangerous figure, a rival even to Aetius himself.

274–304 Aetius refuses, but Majorian is ordered to leave the army and turn to farming.

305–27 The death of Aetius is reported, and the subsequent killing of his murderer, the emperor Valentinian III. Still speaking through the mouth of Africa, Sidonius comments on the new situation as it affected the prospects of Majorian.

327–48 Africa observes that Geiseric, the Vandal leader, is now enfeebled – so too his followers – and totally dependent on tribes of North Africa.

349–69 Rome grants Africa's request for Majorian to be her avenger and adds that Majorian has already begun to put right the neglect of suffered by Gaul over many years.

370–440 Sidonius turns to the deeds of Majorian, describing two recent victories, one in the Alps and one in southern Italy.

441–83 Majorian plans to build a fleet and launch his invasion of Africa, and assembles a large and varied army.

483–510 The resistance of a Hun, Tuldila, is described, and Majorian's reaction justified.

510–52 Sidonius presents a vivid picture of the army's crossing of the frozen Alps, and the discipline exercised by Majorian.

553–86 Sidonius praises members of Majorian's staff who have accompanied the army, and beseeches the emperor to aid Lyon in its destitution.

586–603 Sidonius looks ahead to the eventual triumph of Majorian in Africa.

TRANSLATION

Recall to mind, O Roman state, your triumphs of the past:[1]
the imperial power is now possessed by a consul whom the purple
does not clothe more than a corselet does, whose brow a diadem[2]
by law, not luxury given, adorns, whose palm-embroidered robe,

---

1 S. begins by addressing the state, and asks his audience to consider unspecified triumphs of the past, setting the tone. Although the Latin word translated 'state' here is *respublica*, he does not mean the 'Republic' in particular, or the many triumphs of the Roman Republic, which is a period largely unsung and perhaps a set of mere names to many of the audience. At this time, the word is often used of the current situation. S. means no more than 'not recent', which also signals that to begin with Majorian's victories, related in detail later in the poem, will be passed over; as of course will the defeat of Avitus at Placentia two years before (Mathisen [1979a]). Otherwise the main function of these opening lines is to reassert the traditional values of a leader: military engagement and success, lack of ostentation and luxuriousness, hard work and modesty.

2 For the diadem see n. 5 on *c.* 2.

rewarding toil, follows his palm;[3] all power's honours are topped   5
by the *fasces*; the consulship exalts the emperor.[4]
Therefore "bravo!" resounds o'er sky and sea, country and city,
the cry of exulting Europe; victor once, now you are deemed
our ruler.[5] Once, I admit, the world had trembled, when you chose,
with too much modesty, not to have conquered for yourself,[6]   10
and, sad that you deserved imperial power, sternly declined
the government of what you had once thought to need defending.[7]

3 The wordplay on 'palm-embroidered robe' – the *toga palmata*, originally restricted to the celebration of formal triumphs, had come to be used interchangeably with the consular robe or *trabea* (see n. 3 on *c.* 2) – and the word 'palm', denoting victory, highlights the point that honours must be earned.

4 The *fasces* or 'consul's rods' are the bundle of rods and axes symbolising the consul's power of immediate punishment: cf. *c.* 2.1. The words that immediately follow (lines 5–6) are similar to those in *c.* 7.7–8, 'your *trabeae* exalt the diadem(s) already gained'.

5 The exclamation here translated 'bravo' is not usually associated with military (rather than literary) success; cf. *c.* 1.4 (the gods welcome their new chief) and line 108 of the verse in *Ep.* 9.13 (town and country greet the words of Petrus). The word 'deemed' (line 8) does not imply doubt about Majorian's status or his right to be emperor; he is now classed as ruler rather than victor, though both. Now, in late 458, he is accepted as one of the two emperors, and enjoys full legitimation and universal consent, clearly stated in lines 384–8.

6 The claim here attributed to Majorian that he did not wish his conquests to result in personal advantage – whether in terms of power or wealth – may be somewhat disingenuous. In the battle of Placentia Majorian played an important role, though subordinate to Ricimer, and might thus be seen as 'conquering for himself'; at least it opened the way to his assumption of power soon afterwards. If indeed there is an element of personal feeling here, it is covered up by S.'s 'admitting' that he concurs with a majority view, and by the presentation of Majorian as an emperor of exemplary modesty that quickly ensues. It is noteworthy that there is wording similar to that of line 10 in line 596 ('conquered for me': see note there); that passage could be seen as a way of making amends or at least clarification. Those two lines are almost symmetrically placed within the panegyric and arguably have intratextual significance.

7 Majorian is also praised for his reluctance to take supreme power, a reaction that was commonly ascribed to a prospective emperor or office-bearer: see *c.* 7.460–1, with notes, and *Pan. Lat.* 2.(12)11.1 (Pacatus's speech on Theodosius, which S. knew well), and Claudian *c.* 17.245–7. On such reluctance (*recusatio*) in general see Béranger (1948), 178–96, and Huttner (2004). What needed defending in Majorian's view was doubtless the state, the (Western) Empire, northern Gaul and central Italy, which are the sites of notable victories to be described later: but if the threats envisaged included Avitus and his Gauls or Gallo-Romans, S. would of course have strongly though silently disagreed. This issue is here well hidden by the hyperbolic general reference to Majorian's other victories; Avitus is never mentioned. (On the element of 'prudence' in this speech, see the many possible examples offered in Mathisen [1979a]).

Our warrior goddess, Rome, with breast laid bare, had taken her seat.[8]
Her head was crested with the city's towers,[9] and behind it,
slipping from out her ample helm, her hair streamed over her back.   15
Her reproof awaits all joy, by her modesty her awesomeness
Is increased, and although charm prevails it is opposed by virtue.[10]
Purple-coloured is her robe's fabric; this is pierced by a brooch,
biting with twisted tooth. Such covering as her breast disdains
a jewel fastens in the broad recess below her bosom.   20
Just here a gleaming shield,[11] of huge circumference, supports

8 In this personifying picture of Rome S. to some degree imitates Claudian's description
of Rome in *c.* 1.73–99, where after the victory over Eugenius she hastens to address the
emperor Theodosius in northern Italy. But S. gives a more nuanced picture of Rome, perhaps
seeking to outdo his predecessor, or at least offer a markedly different picture. In Claudian
Rome is speeding in a chariot, explicitly (84) like Minerva (and perhaps Homer's Athena); in
S. she is seated, indeed sedate, her hair less untidy, her clothing somewhat more disciplined
and showing less bare flesh. Both poets give Rome great severity of appearance, but in
S. there is a perspective beyond warfare, a perspective that reflects the dual emphasis on
military command and civilian life in lines 5–6 above.

9 In Late Antiquity Rome, and certain other towns, are sometimes depicted as having
towers on their heads or helmets, in a kind of 'mural crown' (Roberts [2001], at 539–40). The
towers may also be conceived as composed of the hair itself, as in two significant passages of
S.: in *c.* 2.324, where the many towers of Oenotria (Italy), as she travels, are somehow held
in by a vine-branch around her brow; and in *c.* 2.391–2, where Rome's towers need to be
confined by a helmet.

10 The picture of Rome's character begins with a statement (this has no counterpart in
the passage of Claudian) that joy is always liable to her censure, an ethical judgement that
broadly follows Stoic ethics. In the second of his short statements (on 'modesty': that is,
'propriety' or 'shame') S. also uses an ethical term of general application, whereas Claudian
presents a terrifying virgin warrior. S.'s third element expresses a philosophical tension
between virtue and pleasure (or 'charm'), recalling the Socratic 'choice of Hercules' between
pleasure and virtue and, again, Stoic philosophy. This last point is concisely presented in
language drawn not from Claudian – his point ('virtue is mixed with grace': line 91) is less
subtle – but based on a passage of the epic poet Statius (*Achilleid* 1.335–6): 'grace remains,
though virtue resists'.

11 From her clothing and body the gaze turns to the shield, which supports her left side
(she is left-facing, and to be imagined as in full profile or perhaps three-quarter profile). The
shield is described in detail; this is an example of the literary genre of *ekphrasis* prominent
in epic, notable among them the shield described in Homer's *Iliad* (18.478–608) and, with
themes illustrating salient points of Roman history, the one in Vergil, *A.* 8.625–728. The
remoulding of the Vergilian material, apparent in various ways, contributes to a sense
of continuing traditions, both literary and ideological, that link Rome with her small but
celebrated beginnings. The abovementioned passage of Claudian also includes in lines 94–9

Her left side; on this you could see,[12] cast in robust metal,
The cave of Rhea,[13] and the mother wolf, with jaws agape,
fearsome even when fondling them, though fretting, even in
the likeness, that she might devour the sons of Mars.[14] The next   25
part shows the Tiber; he, stretched out beneath the porous tufa
was breathing out moist sleepiness through his grey-greenish throat;[15]
A cloak covers his chest, woven by his wife Ilia,[16]
who close to him in his watery bed desires to still the noise
of the tumbling waters and maintain her billowing husband's sleep.[17]   30
These scenes glint on her shield; her spear with ivory shaft rises,[18]
drunken with human gore. Close by, Bellona builds a trophy
and bends an oak tree down with the heavy weight of captive spoils.[19]

a description of Rome's shield that lists the themes and the various metals used, but has not influenced S.

12 The reader is often addressed as viewer in the genre of *ekphrasis*.

13 The cave of Rhea (she was also known as Rhea Silvia, and as Ilia), like Vergil's 'cave of Mars' (*A.* 8.630), sets the scene, alluding to the place where Mars came to her. The story is told in Livy 1.4.

14 Developing Vergil's empathetic picture of the wolf gently licking the babies – who as good Romans, and sons of Mars (25), had no fear (*A.* 8.632–4) – S. focuses on her open jaws, formidable though benign.

15 On another part of the shield the personified river Tiber, in a cave of tufa that shows Vergilian influence of a different kind (*Georg.* 2.214), breathes out 'moist sleep' and perhaps snores, in an expression modelled on Vergil's description (*A.* 9.326) of a man 'breathing out sleep', a phrase the Vergilian commentator Servius (of the late fourth and early fifth centuries) explained as snoring. His throat, appropriately for a river-god, has the colour often ascribed to watercourses or the sea; what emerges from it is at once human drooling and river water.

16 The garment woven by Ilia (on underwater looms) is almost the only feature taken from Claudian's description of Tiber in 1.209–25, at 224–5.

17 In bed with him, or close at hand, Ilia tries to ensure that he is not awoken by his own noise. Their bed is watery (but no pun with the sense 'river-bed' is possible in Latin; otherwise S. might well have made one), and the description of the sound represents both the snoring and the flowing river.

18 Contrasting with the sparkling shield in colour, shape and material is the spear, held presumably in her right hand and so partly visible above the shield.

19 The goddess Bellona (literally, 'goddess of war') assists her brother Mars in Vergil *A.* 8.703, and is introduced by Claudian in various roles, including the erecting of trophies, in *c.* 22.371–2 and 26.34. Spoils taken from the enemy are often portrayed in epic as hung on oak trees.

The throne towers up,[20] composed of rocks hewn out and lowered down
from the red mountain of the Ethiopians,[21] where in 35
the ever near sun the native purple has breathed on scorched rocks.
Close to it is Synnadan marble, added is Numidian,[22]
mimicking ancient ivory;[23] then, from Laconian stone,
interwoven with them there glints a grass-green seam of marble.[24]
So when she had taken her central place, enthroned, each land 40
hurried to her at once.[25] Then every province offered up
its produce:[26] the Indian, ivory; the Chaldean, spices;

20 Rome is imagined as seated high on a throne consisting of red granite and various
precious stones, which decorate the steps up to the throne and the throne itself, no doubt
to some extent modelled on that of a Roman emperor. In his luxuriant description S. draws
upon descriptions of coloured marble in the poet Statius (*Silvae* 1.2.148–51, 1.5.36–41 and
2.2.85–93), rather than a technical treatise; although Pliny in book 36 of his *Natural History*
has scattered references to these stones (Ethiopian (63), Phrygian (143), Numidian (49)
and Spartan stone (55)) there is no sign that S. quarried his descriptions. For illustrations
and relevant information, see Gnoli (1988). Exactly how the stones – respectively purple,
spotted, yellow and green – are placed and combined is left to the imagination, except in
lines 38–9. For similar descriptions by S., see *c.* 11.17–19, *c.* 22.136–41; in *Ep.* 2.2.7 he lists
kinds of marble not present in his (humble) villa Avitacum.
21 Ethiopian stone is a rose-coloured granite from Syene [Aswan], at the southern
extremity of Egypt. S.'s point here is that the extreme heat bakes in the natural colouring of
the granite; in *Ep.* 2.2.7 the source of the colour is just a 'natural tinge'.
22 Synnadan, or 'Phrygian', marble is from north-west Turkey. It is, as may be seen from
Statius *Silvae* 1.5.37–8 and 2.2.87–9, 'purple' and 'spotted'; so in S. *c.* 11.19 it is 'spotted' and
in *c.* 22.137–8 a purple quarry is mentioned.
23 Numidian (also described as 'Punic' or 'Libyan') stone was yellow (Statius, *Silvae*
1.5.36 and 2.2.92); in *c.* 11.19 and 22.138 S. describes it as 'like ivory'.
24 Interwoven between the purple and the yellow are bands of green Spartan stone
(mentioned by Statius in *Silvae* 1.2.148–9, 1.5.40, 2.2.90–1).
25 The assembly over which Rome so conspicuously presides is one in which various
regions of the Empire (S. calls them 'provinces' [41], but they are not provinces in any official
sense), and some outside it, are imagined as offering gifts of their produce. The picture
represents Rome's political and economic dominance and success, but the meeting itself
bears no close relationship to any regular feature of Roman procedure, except perhaps
the reception of embassies from individual communities. Is this picture of plenty in fact
modelled on the entrepôt of Arles (see Leo, *Ep.* 65.3 'of many profitable things') cited by
Matthews (1975), p. 334, n. 5 (circa 450)?
26 The long list of peoples (or places) and the gift of each one are presented in a mode of
'listing' typical of S. The offerings mentioned derive to some extent from passages in Vergil
(*Georg.* 1.56–9) illustrating the varied productivity of the known world, and, much more
briefly, from Claudian (*c.* 7.211), where offerings are envisaged from remote peoples to be

the Assyrian, jewels; the Chinese, silks, the Sabaean, incense;
Attica, honey; the Phoenician, palms; Lacedaemon, olives;
the Arcadian, horses; Epirus, mares; the men of Gaul, cattle;   45
the Chalybian, armour; the Libyan, corn; the Campanian, wine;
the Lydian, gold; the Arab, amber; the isle Panchaia, myrrh;
Pontus, castor-oil; Tyre, purple; Corinth, bronze ornaments,
Sardinia, silver; Spain contributes ships,[27] and also brings
thunderstone; the lightning hurled from on high colours the rocks   50
and the heated flint is fertilised by the impregnating
divine anger; whenever there the vault of heaven is stirred,
the more valued earth there becomes.[28]

Suddenly Africa,
weeping, her dark cheeks rent, fell prostrate and with downturned brow
crushed the corn-ears, now sadly so prolific, on her head,[29]   55

subjugated. S.'s list includes five producers and their products from Vergil (India, Sabaeans, Chalybians, Pontus, Epirus), and all three of Claudian's (India, Panchaia and China). His assignment of other products is somewhat schematic: Gaul, for example, is praised for cattle, not its corn as in *c*. 7.139–48; Sardinia was indeed known for its silver, but was probably not the major producer.

27 Spain's first gift is of a different kind; she was not famed for ships, and this detail may reflect the fact that ships would be needed very soon by Majorian, at least to transfer his army to Africa, and were being assembled there. S. may have thought that timber was even more readily available in Spain than it was in Italy (for which cf. lines 441–4 below).

28 Spain's second gift, thunderstone, a kind of stone created by lightning when it touches earth, came in two kinds, according to the seventh-century encyclopaedist Isidore of Seville (*Etymologiae* 16.13, 5): one kind, that looked like crystal, came from Germany, the other, a reddish stone that resembled an alloy of gold and bronze, was produced on the shores of modern Portugal and western Spain. According to Isidore this second kind had the power to ward off lightning, and the 'quality of fire' (as well as the appearance of it); these might have been of practical use in battle, and were also perhaps thought to have some talismanic effect, or to mimic divine support.

29 The sudden entry of Africa, very visibly dismayed, is a complete contrast. She was a prolific producer of grain, and so essential to Rome, but her abundance, emblematised by the corn-ears on her head (as also on coins of Africa), was now, since her capture by the Vandal Geiseric, a matter of regret. A similar situation had occurred in 397–8, when Africa was controlled by the rebel Gildo, as vigorously addressed in Claudian's poem (*c*. 15) on the crisis. The description of her appearance, in thrall to Gildo, in Claudian (lines 134–9) is broadly similar to that of S., and later, in line 153, Africa lamented that she has been 'fertile for Gildo', just as S.'s Africa regrets being sadly prolific (55). But in S. her arrival has a

and thus began to speak: "A third part of the world,[30] I come
unfortunate through one man's good fortune. Once born to a slave,[31]
this plunderer, with his masters killed, has now for a long time
held his barbarian sceptre in my land and, driving far
my nobles, hates whatever he, raving upstart, is not.[32]   60
Alas for Latium's torpid energy! He laughs that your walls
gave way to his treachery.[33] Do you not shake your spear at him?
Captured yourself once, do you not feel pain? Indeed, your fortunes
are thought to rise with troubles, and be greater after a fall;[34]
but it is better now that the fear has gone: conquest awaits you   65
if you fight back as usual when conquered. Porsenna
when thrusting proud Tarquin on you, filled the Janiculum
with Tuscan soldiers, but when he prepared to burst your gates
by siege, he faced your total might in the shape of a single shield,

stronger effect, due to the way that she violently interrupts a scene of happy prosperity rather
than seconding the complaint of an equally downcast Rome (Claudian *c.* 15.17–27) to Jupiter
in Olympus.

30 In describing Africa as the 'third part of the world' (so too Claudian at *c.* 15.161–2),
S. refers to the classification by some writers, notably Pliny (*NH* 3.1.3), of Africa as a third
continent, besides Europe and Asia. The matter was controversial, as noted by Lucan (9.411)
and by Paulinus of Nola in a rendering of Suetonius's book 'On Kings' (Ausonius, *Ep.* 17
[p. 216 Green]). The geographer Pomponius Mela (1.1) distinguished four main regions of the
known world.

31 This passage is the only evidence, with *c.* 2.358–9, that Geiseric, the Vandal king, had
been born to a slave. Procopius (*Wars*, 3.3.23 [BV. 1.3.23]) describes him as an illegitimate
son of the Vandal prince Godigisel (*PLRE* 2.496–9). The word 'masters' in line 58 might
refer to slave-masters, but could equally well imply superiors in general.

32 Geiseric the outsider hates everything and everybody that is unlike himself. It may
be that this condemnation includes the religious antipathy ascribed to him; according to
Prosper s.a. 439, he was particularly hostile to the nobility and the religious in Africa.

33 No other source mentions treachery. It is possible that S. was aware of the rumour
that he had been invited into Rome by Eudoxia, widow of the murdered Valentinian III
(Hydatius 160 [167], John Ant. fr. 201.6: see *PLRE* 2.411), and construed this as a treacherous
agreement; but it is quite plausible that with his low impression of Geiseric (cf. *c.* 2.17) S.
made the assumption himself. 'Latium' in S. stands variously for Rome, her environs or the
Roman state, as does the adjective *Latius*, as in *c.* 7.513.

34 The stirring sentiment of this line, also exploited by S. in *c.* 7.6–8, recalls the rousing
words of the early fifth-century poet Rutilius Namatianus ('On his return', lines 115–40).
The *locus classicus* for the theme is Horace, *Odes* 4.4.65–8, lines praising Rome's resilience
put into the mouth of Hannibal, their supreme enemy.

the shield of Cocles.[35] Many thousands pressed on this one man,   70
their access hanging in the balance; when the bridge was broken
he fell, but was not felled. In the end this king, warned by the death
of his scribe, realised that warfare was not only launched against him
when wars were under way; before long, seeking peace, he returned[36]
to his kingdom, defeated not so much by the hand's blunder   75
as by its blaze. For Scaevola, standing with icy heart,
passed judgement on his errant right hand in the fire close by,
more fortunate from his mistaken hand; as it happened,
the attendant paled at the man's resolve, and the captive's torments
frightened away his tormentor. You trembled, too, at Brennus,[37]   80
although later supreme. All that was yours, all that was then
called 'Rome', was only the Tarpeian hill; a single man
repulsed a whole array, when the gabbling goose announced the presence
of the Senones, and without soldiers your Fate kept watch.[38]
Me too – grant me forgiveness that we once waged war on you –   85
you overcame after Trebia and Cannae,[39] and the roofs of Rome

35 The story of the heroism of Horatius Cocles in the face of Porsenna's besieging army
is told in Livy 2.9–10. Ordering the Romans to destroy the bridge behind him, he fought
until it was broken; then he fell along with the bridge, but, as S. puts it in line 72 with typical
wordplay, did not 'fall' in the sense of meeting his death; he was able to swim away in full
armour.

36 The story of Mucius Scaevola's bravery is told in Livy 2.12, and its sequel in Livy
2.13 and 14. The detail in lines 72–4 may derive directly or indirectly from Livy's story of
Mucius' warning to the enemy king that he need not fear 'pitched battles and the clash of
arms' (tr. Luce) but should fear individual young assassins like himself (2.12.11). There were
other ways of waging war.

37 For Brennus, the leader of a Gallic confederacy (of which the Senones were part), see
Livy 5.34, and for the fear he could inspire, Livy 5.38; for the eventual Roman victory, Livy
5.49. Camillus is mentioned in all three panegyrics (c. 2.526, c. 5.557, c. 7.563) as an example
of valiant resistance.

38 The story of how the geese saved Rome – then a small community on the Tarpeian hill,
centring on the Capitol – when the Gauls, led by Brennus, attacked Rome, is related in Livy
5.47, and poetically in Vergil A. 8.652–62. S. ignores the role of the soldier Mucius Manlius,
who in both their accounts was awoken and then organised fightback, in order to emphasise
the role of Rome's Fate, here semi-personified.

39 For the Carthaginian defeat of the Romans at the Trebia in 218 BC see Livy 21.52–6;
and for their victory at Cannae (216 BC) Livy 22.36–49.

were seen by Hannibal before my Scipio saw ours.[40]
What have I done? I am driven by Fate to stir up wars against you,
whether I wish or do not wish. It's a trembling foe that scares you,
kept safe by the protecting sea, just as a bristly boar[41]   90
lies close to thick wasteland and there, concealed, sharpens the weapons
of his black snout, laden with white teeth; round it yelps a huge
pack of dogs, ready if the beast should choose to run at them on the plain;
within the screen of thorn-bushes it swaggers and swells with pride,
in energy weak but in position strong, until 'get 'im!'   95
shouts the nearby hunter from the hill; the master's well-known voice
renews their flagging savagery, and then unheeding fury
disdains to feel the hurt of wounds. Why do you put off battle?[42]
Why do you cringe before the sea, you for whose triumphs often
even heaven is used to fight? Consider this, moreover: now   100
you have an outstanding emperor, who prescient ages avow
is coming for Libya's overthrow, and who, a third victor,
will receive my name.[43] The Fates owe this to you, Majorian,
for all your toil. Why it is he that I desire to take

---

40 According to Livy 26.9–11 Hannibal was very close to Rome in 211 BC, and indeed at
one time was at the Colline gate (cf. *c.* 7.129–34). Hannibal's closeness to Rome at this point
in time was often regarded as her gravest crisis (Lenski [1997], 165–8). Scipio is 'my Scipio'
to stress again Africa's present loyalty.

41 The position as Africa sees it (89–98) is presented in a simile (a discursive comparison
to enhance elements of narrative, especially in epic) and, as often, there are multiple points of
similarity between the simile and what it illustrates. The picture here highlights the swagger
of the boar, its cowardice (though it remains formidable), the hunter that lies in wait and the
struggle. Vergil, in one of the longest of his similes, portrays a boar long defended by forests
and marshes (*A.* 10.707–13), but its application is very different. Elsewhere S. condemns
Geiseric as one who leaves fighting to others (327–41), and his picture here applies to the
Vandals as a whole.

42 The angry questions are addressed to Rome, like the lament in line 61.

43 In this sentence S. exactly repeats three words used by Vergil when speaking of the
fated arrival in Carthage of the powerful people of Rome: 'coming for Libya's overthrow'
(*A.* 1.22). Majorian, it is implied, follows in the footsteps of the victorious Roman armies.
When he has defeated the Vandals he will be the third hero to be awarded the name
Africanus, following the abovementioned Scipio, who defeated the Carthaginians at Zama
in 202 BC, and the Scipio (Cornelius Scipio Aemilianus Africanus) who overthrew the
city in 146 BC.

to his fleet and enter my harbours and come into my city,[44]   105
I will carefully explain in a few words, if you command.

It is said that in Pannonia, ruled by Mars' city, Aquincum[45]
the man who governed Illyricum, and the Danube regions,[46]
was grandfather to our emperor, for when at Sirmium[47]
Theodosius took the name Augustus, he had as master   110
of both services, as he left to visit the eastern parts[48]
a Majorian. Reported in Latium's formal records[49]
are this man's feats when our trumpets bore down on Scythian farmers
and the army trampled on the Hypanis, and ice-bound Peuce

44 Or perhaps 'a fleet' (not 'his fleet'), if the points made by MacGeorge (2002), 306–11 ('Naval Power in the Fifth Century') are taken into account.

45 The formula 'it is said' does not so much imply uncertainty about the senior Majorian's appointment as provide poetic colouring for the new episode. S. doubtless had a good source for what follows, perhaps Majorian himself. Aquincum, close to the site of modern Budapest, was, or had been, a major fortress and centre, with its own arms factory, governing the province of Lower Pannonia, and sometimes also that of Upper Pannonia (Mócsy [1974], 94, 111, 237). The description fits the time of Theodosius I, but not the time when S. wrote; by then Pannonia had been overrun by Huns and others (Mócsy [1974], 297–332, 339–52), as he may have known. Cf. c. 7.589–90.

46 This strategically vital area stretched from the Adriatic coast to the lands bordering the middle Danube and included the large territory of Illyricum; it was under the military control of a 'master of infantry and cavalry' (see c. 2.90 and note).

47 The Roman city of Sirmium, now Sremska Mitrovica in northern Serbia, on the Danube 55km west of Belgrade, was one of the main imperial residences in Late Antiquity. Whether Majorian senior became master of both services at the time of Theodosius's elevation to emperor (19 January 379 [PLRE 1.904–5]), or had held the post already, is not clear; perhaps Theodosius had held it until then, and was followed directly by Majorian. Majorian's genealogy, obscure and known only from here, is enhanced by this link with the famous and highly respected Theodosius I.

48 This visit, not otherwise attested, was probably a quick tour of inspection; Theodosius was soon concerned with problems elsewhere, and is known to have been seriously ill soon afterwards (the exact time is uncertain (Piganiol [1972], 233 n. 6). The point of this observation may be to suggest that Majorian's later strategy originated with Theodosius, and that he enjoyed the emperor's confidence.

49 There is no other evidence of these victories, and perhaps never was; the poet's reference to the Fasti or official records of Rome is designed to give the impression that they were well known or had at least deserved formal announcement. Elsewhere S. appeals more plausibly to the Fasti for the achievements of emperors, Anthemius' two consulships (c. 2.4 n.) and the honours of Consentius' s grandfather (c. 23.177). The achievements of Majorian that S. hopes to celebrate in the future (c. 13.33) would also be recorded there.

was sneered at by camp-followers, who in mind welcomed its frosts.[50]   115
To the emperor's father he was father-in-law,[51] who, a man of note,
was always happy with a single public office, so that
he might in perilous times closely care for his single friend.[52]
More than once, by offering a consulship, did the court attempt
to snatch him from his friend Aetius, but he stood fast,   120
a greater man than those who were so honoured; his loyalty,
not gained by such a prize, began to be more prized. He was
what the quaestor was once to consuls:[53] he managed public funds
with the powers of his own office; such restraint did he observe
that rumour averred that even then he was saving for his son.[54]   125

50 Hypanis is now the southern river Bug, which flows into the Black Sea west of Crimea;
it is mentioned by Claudian in c. 28.337 to show the dimensions of the earlier emperor
Trajan's authority. Peuce denotes an island near the mouths of the Danube (but also one of
the Danube's mouths); according to Claudian c. 28.105 Alaric grew up there, and in c. 8.630
he describes it as clogged with corpses of Gruthungi.
51 This person, Majorian's father, cannot be certainly identified; he is Anonymus 114 in
PLRE 2.1235–6. Domninus (PLRE 2.373), with whom he has been identified, was father of
a Maximianus, according to the text of Priscus (fr. 30 Blockley), not a Maiorianus; but if the
name Maximianus is a scribal error, caused by the similar word Maximus that immediately
precedes, as suggested by Blockley (1983), ii, 393, n. 134, the identification could stand.
The details would match the financial concerns of Domninus. The person mentioned was
probably *numerarius* (financial official) in the office of master of both services. Such men
were, in the words of Jones (1973), 599, 'men of some consequence', as the careers of two
fourth-century holders attest (Amm. 15.5.36 [Remigius] and 26.1.6 [Leo]).
52 This friend was Aetius, an outstanding general, thrice consul and later 'the most
powerful person in the western empire' (PLRE 2.28), indeed effectively the 'ruler of the
western empire from 432 to 454' (OCD⁴). The position of *numerarius* to such a person was
a very powerful one, and it is hardly surprising that Majorian's father declined to relinquish
it, notwithstanding the strict time-limits laid down. (For the evidence of limits, see RE
17.2, 1304–5.) He had much to gain from sticking to such a successful general, who could
shield him from the pressures of the imperial court, and he was perhaps not the disinterested
paragon of friendship and loyalty that S. depicts.
53 The comparison with the quaestors of the Roman Republic is misleading, since the
consuls and their quaestors were answerable to the Roman state, whereas Aetius was in
practice beyond it, and had effective power for longer than any consul. He may (Anderson
says 'must') have controlled the war-chest of Aetius.
54 This rumour is not otherwise attested, and it is not clear what exactly it conveyed,
or what S. is making of it, but it is likely that he is countering a hostile report. What to
him was 'restraint' (line 124) might have appeared differently to others, perhaps as secret
embezzlement; to rebut this idea, S. stresses that the man was acting in accordance with
his legal authority, and he may indeed be seeking to defend it retrospectively by noting that

But, as it chanced, the general's wife,[55] jealous already, had seen
that the boy's repute was growing, and, bubbling with indignation,
she had boiled up corrosive poison in her barbarous heart.
Straightway she scans the heavens, and, pondering various numbers,
explores the whole subject of astrology, consults the shades,   130
searches for thunderbolts, inspects entrails,[56] delighted that
in all these ways she had seized God's secret. Thus the grim Colchian[57]
stood on the stern of the Pelasgians' boat with fearful husband,
before she scattered Absyrtus for his father to find, and made
this evil worse than fratricide by using in the struggle   135
her brother's corpse and weaponising him; or when she tamed
the fiery bulls, herself more fiery, and a chilling flame
guarded the trembling hero, who with the ointment's screening drug
even felt cold (they say) among the cattle's flaming breaths.[58]
So after long repining, when she heard that imperial power   140
and lengthy rule was preordained for him, with her arms slashed
she went into the room in which her husband's bed was, and
madly burst out: "You lie here unconcerned, forgetting kinsfolk,
you laggard; and as emperor (so the ages pray) the world
will have Majorian: the stars proclaim this with their signs,   145
and men do in their prayers. But why do I seek this man's stars,
for whom men's love has made a separate Fate? Than that nothing
is stronger. The boy is never greedy, but lives frugally;
already, though still poor, he spreads his wealth, he floats great plans,
and sticks to them; all that he purposes is on a grand scale.   150
He presses ahead with his hopes. If I may speak, perhaps, of sport,

the beneficiary, the official's own son, was now emperor, thus putting the matter effectively
beyond dispute. The son certainly had money to spread around (line 149: there S. explains
it as due to frugal habits).

55 Her name was Pelagia (*PLRE* 2.856–7).

56 For indications of future events she views the stars (astrology), examines dead bodies
(necromancy), scrutinises animal entrails (haruspicy, extispicy) and studies thunderbolts
and places struck by them (fulgurature).

57 This is Medea (cf. *c.* 2.493), who came to the aid of Jason and the Argonauts when
they arrived in her homeland, Colchis on the Black Sea, in search of the Golden Fleece. She
married Jason and, as they later tried to escape, sought to delay the pursuers by scattering
the pieces of the body of her murdered brother Absyrtus from the ship.

58 At an earlier stage, Medea's father Aeetes required Jason to subdue two fire-breathing
bulls; he was helped by Medea, already in love with him, who gave him this ointment.

whatever you are thought to have achieved with the bow is eclipsed
by a single day of his: at three arrows snake, deer and boar
trembled and died. Not so exact in shooting at the foe
was the father who, with his son enveloped by a snake's body,   155
feared even more as he sought to help, until with the same arrows
he brought both life and death, and, as he kept a steady hand
in spite of a quivering heart, his fear (though hope was closer) issued
in perfect skill, as he produced amidst the limbs of two
but a single death.[59] Suppose he opted for a boxing bout,   160
Eryx of Sicily is outshone;[60] and Sparta did not flourish
with such skill when, felled on Bebrycian sand, Amycus looked up
to see his foe, conditioned by Therapne's wrestling-school.[61]
And what power is there in his feet! In vain did Opheltes's son
gain victory for himself in Sicily's games;[62] not in this way   165
did the swift Arcadian drive his haughty feet through dry Nemea,[63]
he whose mother, as she flew over the dusty Aetolian track,
Hippomenes feared (although placed far ahead, contemptuously,
on the racecourse's turf), when from her starting-place sprang out
the swift young heroine before the excited spectators,   170
never to touch the ground with a whole foot; when he, now pale

---

59 The father and son are respectively Alcon and Phalerus, mentioned by Manilius
Astronomica 5.304–10 (without their names), by the epic poet Valerius Flaccus at *Argonautica*
1.398–401 (with only Phalerus named) and very briefly in Servius's commentary on Vergil,
Ecl. 5.11.

60 Eryx the boxer is mentioned at Vergil, *A.* 5.392 and 402–4 (the Funeral Games).

61 Amycus, the king of the Bebrycians, challenged visitors to his land to a boxing match,
only to find Pollux, who arrived with the Argonauts, too much for him (Valerius Flaccus
4.222–314). The Latin phrases for 'Bebrycian sand' and 'Therapne's wrestling-school' are
derived from Statius (*Silvae* 4.5.28 and 4.2.48).

62 Euryalus was adjudged the winner of the footrace in Vergil, *A.* 5.286–338; his father is
named in Vergil, *A.* 9.201.

63 This is Parthenopaeus, the son of Atalanta from Aetolia in west central Greece, whose
victory in the Nemean Games is narrated in Statius, *Thebaid* 6.550–645; from this S. derives
the detail of the feet that hardly touch the ground (6.638–40; neatly phrased at line 171) and
the depiction of the pursuer's breath and shadow (6.604–5), saved for the climax of this
twofold comparison at 173–4. Suitors of Atalanta were challenged to race with her and put
to death if they came second; but one suitor, Hippomenes, was successful, thanks to the
trick here described in line 176. Like Vergil (but not Statius), S. uses words for 'racecourse',
'starting-gate', 'turning point' that suggest the chariot races of classical Rome (Vergil,
A. 5.145, 5.171, 5.289).

looked back and saw the expanse of plain between them was decreasing,
and knew the rest of the race was long; when, harried by her breath
he now was running in his rival's shadow, in deep distress,
till at the turning point, so close to being left behind,   175
he upset her speeding footsteps by three times dropping an apple.
Someone who sees this man on horseback scorns the child of Leda[64]
and your young man, Stheneboea, on whom antiquity bestows
the back of a winged horse to ride and who, as it reports,
vanquished the Lycian Chimaera, when a single wound   180
ended three lives.[65] Had the Fates made you live then, valiant Majorian,
you would have disallowed Castor his expert horsemanship,
Pollux his boxing skills, Alcon his skill in archery,
and even ridiculed Bellerophon's sensational spoils.[66]
Taking a shield, he surpasses the son of Telamon,   185
who battling among the Greek ships, faced with the fires of Hector,
repulsed them even from the fleet of treacherous Ulysses.[67]
If you ask with what power he hurls a spear, then Metabus,
when fearing for the bundle which enclosed tiny Camilla
propelled his spear less forcefully;[68] and not with such momentum   190
did Achilles' hissing ash-tree lance emerge from Troilus's body,[69]

64 Castor, son of Leda and brother of Pollux, was famous as a horseman.

65 Bellerophon, who was loved by Stheneboea, is meant; with the help of the winged horse Pegasus he slew the tripartite Chimaera (part lion, part goat, part snake). In a different context, Claudian speaks in his *Gigantomachy* of three souls being extinguished with one shot from Mars (*Shorter Poems* 53.82).

66 Castor was the brother of Pollux (cf. 287, and above n. 64). The spoils of Bellerophon came from his involvement with Iobates, king of the Lycians, who, unable himself to overcome Bellerophon, gave him half his kingdom and also his daughter. The golden bridle given him by Athena to use on Pegasus is seen here as part of the exceptional spoils.

67 In Homer's *Iliad*, after much fighting round the Greek ships moored at Troy, Hector sets fire to them (16.112–24). The treacherous nature of Ulysses is a common Roman motif; the point that Ajax, son of Telamon, protected even his rival's ships derives from the debate between them in the narrative of Ovid, *M.* 13.1–398, especially lines 5–8, 91–4, as do the Latin words used for 'the son of Telamon' in line (13.22).

68 Metabus had carried his daughter Camilla away from the enemy, but faced with a river in spate was forced to throw her across in a bundle attached to his spear (Vergil, *A.* 11.539–66).

69 Achilles' killing of Troilus is alluded to by Vergil at *A.* 1.474–5, but in a quite different version. S.'s picture probably derives in part from Statius, *Silvae* 2.6.32–3: as Troilus fled around the walls of Troy he was killed by Achilles' lance. S. enriches this

nor did the Attic son of Aegeus with Marathonian oak
so smash Creon for hindering the heroes' burial.[70]
Nor did the goddess who avenged the abused priestess of Phoebus
throw such a thunderbolt against the Greeks, when Greece endured   195
a night like Troy's, and a fire like Troy's, and when the son of Oileus,
impaled upon Caphaereus' rocks, belched flame over the waters.[71]

But these are minor things. More to the point, when you wage war
he is there as learner, not a soldier; in pretence a pupil,
he's really watching as your rival. Your conquests he hates   200
and loves those whom you conquer. When compared with him, the great
Alexander, racked by his father's glory, was a sleep-walker.[72]
What am I to do, in my sad plight? What kingdoms for my son
will I obtain, debarred from Gothic rule, if Rome ignores me
and, more than that, my little son Gaudentius is trampled   205
by this youth's Fates?[73] Gaul lionizes him already, as does
the whole of Europe too. He washes in the ice-bound waters
of the rivers Rhine, Arar, Rhone, Meuse, Marne, Seine, and Lez, and those
of Lot, of Allier, Aude, and Waal; the Loire, hacked out by his axe,

episode by combining Homer's description of Achilles' great (ashen) spear, using a word
from the Latin rendering of *Iliad* 16.143 by Ausonius (*Ep.* 23.28 Green) with the epithet
'hissing' from Vergil, *A.* 12.267. Weapons not infrequently pass right through bodies in
classical epic.

70 At the climax of his epic poem *Thebaid* Statius (12.730–81) relates how Aegeus'
son Theseus finally killed Creon, who had forbidden burial for the brothers Eteocles and
Polynices. The words for 'Marathonian oak' derive from line 730 of that passage; the name
Aegides ('son of Aegeus') occurs at 12.546 and 769.

71 Pallas Athena, with Jove's thunderbolt, avenged Cassandra's violation by Ajax son of
Oileus.The wreck is alluded to by Vergil at *A.* 1.39–45; the promontory Caphaereus, to which
the ships were lured, is named in *A.* 11.259–60. Cf. *c.* 15.1–3.

72 This element in Alexander's motivation is expounded in Plutarch, *Alexander*, 5.

73 She regrets that she, as a woman, is unable to hold office among the Goths, and that
her son Gaudentius (*PLRE* 2.494), whether because of her research into Fate, or because of
his being younger than Majorian, or because of possible mooted betrothals, is the less likely
candidate. Prosper (454) mentions a possible betrothal of Majorian and Placidia, a daughter
of Valentinian III; there may have been other such plans. As for their ages, Gaudentius was
born in 439 or 440 (Clover [1971]) but Majorian, though the indications are vague, was the
older (on his age, see the introduction to this poem). The general situation is discussed by
Oost (1964). In 455 (after the death of Aetius) Gaudentius was seized by Geiseric and taken
to Africa as a possible negotiating tool.

he drinks in chunks.[74] When he went to defend the Turoni,[75]   210
who were in fear of war, you were absent; soon after that
you fought together at the place where Frankish Chloio entered
the open lands of the Atrebates.[76] Here converging roads
met in a tight defile, where under the arch of a bridge the village
Helena, and a river, were crossed in one long viaduct   215
by a narrow road with beams supporting it.[77] There you were posted;
Majorian, on horseback, fought under the bridge itself.[78]
As it happened, on a hill close to the river bank rang out
the noise of a barbarian marriage-song; with Scythian dancers[79]
a young bride was wedding a bridegroom fair-haired like herself.   220
These people, it is said, he overpowered; his helmet rang

74 This virtuoso list of Gallic rivers, designed to show how well known Majorian had
become in Gaul and how well travelled he was, is a carefully constructed mosaic of names
(for the details and general structure, see Extended note (i)). It should not be inferred that
Majorian had at some time lived near each of these rivers, or, conversely, that he had never
been close to rivers that are omitted. Loyen ([1942], 64 n. 2) suggests that the names Lez and
Lot are set in places of honour, being locations where he was born or spent early years; in fact
they are not exactly central in the list, and are not close to each other.

75 Nothing else is known about this defensive operation around Tours, but it is possible
that Majorian had been fighting under Litorius during the Aremorican invasion of 437,
mentioned in c. 7.246–8, or perhaps a later war in c. 446–8 (446 in Anderson, 448 according
to Loyen [1942], 66; the evidence is thin).

76 For Chloio/Chlogio king of the Salian Franks (there are various forms of the name), see
PLRE 2.290–1.

77 The location of this battle has yet to be identified, although S. describes the site with
care: the vicus stands where two roads join in a narrow defile (perhaps this is a crossroads,
or a junction of roads leading into Gaul [Semple (1930), 82–3]), and lies by a sizeable river
(or gorge; or marsh?) that required a viaduct with long beams. No signs of joining roads,
and no watercourses in the area that would need such bridging, have been put forward, and
could have totally disappeared. The name ('village [of] Helen'), not implausible in itself,
has yielded some toponomastic suggestions of uneven quality, notably Hélesmes in the
Départment du Nord. Loyen opted for a site 'near Arras' (capital of the Atrebates, who are
mentioned in line 213), a large area; more precisely, Anderson (p. 80) mentions the older
suggestions Vieil-Hesdin and Lens. I have not seen Franzoi (2016).

78 This detail, probably provided by Majorian, invites the inference that he was more
exposed than Aetius, or at least more active. He may have been the magister equitum ('master
of cavalry') of Aetius, as suggested by Semple (1930), 83.

79 Scythian: this epithet, and the noun Scythia, has various denotations in S. (general
introduction, section 9). Here it indicates the exotic nature of the entertainers, who, like their
leader, were presumably in fact Frankish.

with blows; his corselet with its covering of metal scales
kept off the enemy's thrusting spears until they turned their backs
and took to flight.[80] Resplendent on the wagons you could see
the scattered trappings of their celebration, the dishes   225
and the captured foods thrown randomly about, and fragrant garlands
atop heads that bore on their sweet-smelling locks wine-bowls with wreaths.
Then the rage of Mars grew more ferocious, and the wedding torches
were smashed by Bellona, yet more inflamed; the victors seized
the chariots and the bride herself. Not to such an extent   230
were Pholoe's monsters and the Pelethronian Lapiths mired
by Euhan, son of Semele, when sacred symbols roused
the Haemonian mothers, and kindled Venus and Mars together;[81]
to start the battle they use bloodied foods, then whirl around
the wine, treating their cups as weapons; with growing bedlam   235
the spilling Centaurs' blood stains and pollutes Emathian Othrys.
Nor should the cloud-born brothers'quarrelling be given more praise;[82]
this young man too subdues monsters, on whose red-coloured heads
the hair is pulled over the forehead, and whose bare necks shine
having lost their covering of hair; while their pellucid eyes   240
are white, with grey pupils; on both sides their faces are shaven;
they have no beards, but thin moustaches, furrowed by the comb.
Strongly sewn patchwork garments bind the elongated limbs
of the men; with covering drawn up high their knees are unconcealed,
and a broad waistband keeps in place their underweight bellies.   245

80 Though they attacked the Romans as violently as they were attacked, the Franks
were a feeble and seemingly unprepared enemy. The importance of this Roman victory was
greatly overestimated by Stein (1959), I, 332 and 493, and (to use S.'s word from line 8) is not
deserving of many 'bravos'; but it is a vivid tableau, and S. focuses on what is colourful and
unusual, albeit with little light on what might be specifically barbarian. Torches, dancing,
eating and drinking are prominent in all societies.

81 The mêlée, on which S. focuses with gusto, was greater, says S., than the brawl
which embroiled the Centaurs (the 'monsters of Pholoe') and their enemies the Lapiths, a
'Thessalian clan' of some kind, (OCD⁴ 297 s.v. Centaurs), in a battle imagined by Ovid
at M. 12.210–535; there are traces of this here in lines 234–5. The outbreak of fighting is
explained in other writers not, as here, by the frenzy of the 'mothers', inspired by Bacchus,
but by the Centaurs' lust and drunkenness (for example, Eurytus in Ovid, M. 12.219–21).

82 Majorian's exploits deserve no less praise or admiration than the quarrels of the
cloud-born Centaurs. The epithet is from Vergil, A. 7.674, whose epithet is also used by
Claudian in c. 3.329.

To throw their axes swiftly through the vast expanse of air,
and know in advance the exact spot they will strike, and twirl their shields
is a joy, and to precede with leaps and bounds the spears they have thrown,
and reach the enemy first.[83] In the years of their boyhood they have
an adult's love of warfare. If by chance they are overcome,   250
whether by weight of numbers or the lie of the land, it is death,
not fear, that crushes them; they stand unshaken, and live on
through their spirit, almost after their final breath. Such men
this youth has routed; you have seen this, and praised him. Who can
endure this? He does all that you do, but many things without you.   255
All men fight for the emperor: but he now fights, I fear,
for himself. If he wins power, then all your conquests are for him.
The Fates here leave no middle course; if you disdain to be
his killer, then you will be his slave. If the Chaldean observes
the stars aright, if the Colchian knows her herbs, and the Etruscan   260
his thunderbolts, if the Thessalian really evokes the dead,
if the Lycian oracle shows wisdom, if by their flight the birds
truly reveal our destinies, if Hammon of the Syrtes
with his learned bleatings sighs out something sacred, if indeed
you, Phoebus, you, Themis, and you, Dodona, sing the truth,[84]   265
after our times this Julius will be Augustus.[85] What is more,
joined with the youth in love is one equipped with the spirit
of his royal grandfather.[86] Where can you turn? The heights of the world
are the goal to which both of them guide their minds, and he his fate.

83 The detail of twirling their shields derives from the epic poet Valerius Flaccus 6.551.
The following item, the pursuit of their thrown spears, may have been suggested by Statius:
Achilles was so trained (*Achilleid* 2.112–13).

84 Pelagia mentions a wider selection of methods of foretelling the future than are
mentioned earlier (129–31): they are, respectively, astrology; herbal remedies, necromancy,
lots, augury, oracles and prophecy.

85 Iulius (Julius) was one of the names of Majorian, as shown in the inscription containing
his names (Dessau *ILS* 810) and some manuscripts. 'To be Augustus' means 'to be emperor';
to 'be Julius Augustus' would mean nothing.

86 This friend of Majorian is Ricimer (*PLRE* 2.942–5); his maternal grandfather was the
Visigoth Wallia (*PLRE* 2.1147–8). By 457 he had become 'companion of soldiers', and then
became 'master of soldiers' and patrician (for these terms, see general introduction, section
10). He rebelled against Avitus and executed him; after helping Majorian to become emperor
(John Malalas 375) he deposed him, and executed him four years later. See also *c.* 2.352–70
and 484–6.

Arise, attack them unawares, at once. Order them both   270
to die, and you will be unable to kill either one;
but plan false flatteries for one, and let Majorian
be sought with the sword. But why do I speak useless words? In vain
do we fend off such things; he will live, and therefore reign." Provoked,
Aetius briefly replied: "Restrain your raving mind's   275
wicked desires. Will I be able to ordain the death
of a blameless person, not to say one of us? Does anyone pray
that it be made a crime for the innocent to be well-born?
Who could charge Fate to pay a penalty? I will attack
you with a sword, Majorian, if the sun shines bright by night   280
and the moon by day, or if the two Parrhasians renew
their ploughs in the Ocean,[87] or if Tanais can see Atlas,
Bagrada the Caucasus,[88] if a boat made of Hercynian wood
sails on Nabataean Hydaspes rather than the river Rhine,[89]
if the Spaniard drinks from the Ganges, and if from warm Erythrae   285
the Indian water-carrier comes to Tartesian Ebro;[90]
if Castor drenched himself in the blood of Pollux, if a mad
blow from Pirithous killed Theseus, or one from Orestes
slew Pylades when the pious matricide was carrying off
the sacred image from the Taurians.[91] But lest perhaps   290

87 This series of 'adynata' (rhetorical expressions of impossibility) is based here on the
cycle of day and night, on astronomical fact, on geographical data and on myth. The 'two
Parrhasians' were the country nymph Callisto and her son Arcas, who were made by Jupiter
respectively the constellations Great and Little Bear (Ovid, *M.* 2.401–530).

88 The Tanais (now Don) was a river in southern Russia, emptying into the Black Sea
(cf. *c.* 2.243, *c.* 7.75); the Bagrada (now Majerda) was a river in Africa, entering the sea near
Carthage.

89 The Hercynian forest was in Germany, quite close to the Rhine (*c.* 7.326; cf. 531),
the Hydaspes a river of India, probably the modern Jhelum in the Punjab. The adjective
'Nabatean' in Latin poetry (also in 2.408) refers to a large area around and beyond the
Arabian Gulf.

90 The distant Spaniard could not use the Ganges for drinking water, nor could an Indian
water-carrier draw from the Spanish river Ebro, which rises in the Pyrenees. Erythrae,
vaguely placed somewhere in India, is described in *c.* 2.447 as on the Hydaspes.

91 These expressions of impossibility are based on famous friendships between
mythical heroes, as in Claudian, *c.* 3.107–8, following Ausonius *Ep.* 23 Green, 19–22. For
one of these pairs to kill the other was quite unthinkable: Castor and Pollux were devoted
brothers; Theseus and Pirithous were linked in lifelong friendship, as were Orestes, the son
of Agamemnon and Clytemnestra, and Pylades. Even if mad (the temporary madness of

I seem to have scorned your sorrow, let him live, but for a while
be freed of his duties. Alas! Had you not thought such thoughts,
he might have owed good fortune to us both!"[92] So did he speak,
and bade the youth exchange his usual work for labour on his
ancestral fields; Fate's wheel was moving round, so that he could learn   295
what tasks await the landowner, and then what character
the civil law instils, and so that he should bring not just
a soldier's skills to imperial rule.[93] He had at once hung up
his arms, now a young veteran, and his plough was now enriching
the poverty of a barren soil. Just so did you, Rome, once   300
with the help of a bending consul,[94] plough your fields, if for a while
under peace's protection you had set aside war's trumpets;
his strong left hand, that had borne the eagles, plied the plough-handle,
while close to a humble fire the victor-ploughman's robe drank smoke.[95]

Meanwhile, cut down by the emperor's sword, Aetius had reached   305
his mournful destiny;[96] so as more safely to combine
Aetius' huge army with the Palatine detachments,[97]

Orestes in myth is not relevant) they would not have killed their respective friends; the focus
is on firm devotion. The exploit of Orestes here referred to is his seizure, with Pylades' help,
of a statue of Artemis (Diana) from the tribe of the Taurians (in the Crimea).

92 In this comment, almost an aside, or a word to himself (and the hearer/reader), Aetius
is made to regret the lost opportunity of having an emperor under his (or their) control.

93 Majorian's forced withdrawal was not pointless in the overall scheme of things. S.
shows the value of this hiatus in Majorian's career. Similarly, Avitus is shown in c. 7.312–15
to be not just a soldier but equipped to be a champion of the laws and, later, as emperor, a
maker of them.

94 Cf. c. 7.378–81, where the news of an appointment finds Avitus working his land, and
he is explicitly compared to the well-known hero Cincinnatus, who is also meant here. It
seems that the word for 'bending' is a pun designed to recollect the word for 'curl' or 'ringlet'
(cincinnus), from which the name derived.

95 In this picture based on the meme of the traditional consul–farmer (cf. Pacatus in Pan.
Lat. 2. (12), 9.5–6) the left hand that carried the standards now guides the plough and the
right hand, presumably, the horses. The consular robe ('palm-embroidered', as in line 5), which
might be needed by one recalled to office, hangs from the rafters, inevitably affected by the
smoke from the fire in the small dwelling. The expression derives from Horace (Odes 3.8.11).

96 This pivotal event is also briefly noted in c. 7.357–9, with some differences: the word
'mournful' shows sympathy for Aetius; the emperor Valentinian III is not described as 'mad'
(to have murdered him).

97 Valentinian sought to combine the armies of Aetius with his own imperial or 'palatine'
armies (these were 'the inner core of the field army... at the disposal of the emperor' [Jones

the emperor calls Majorian, with prayers. But vengeance for
his bloodshed did not wait (he had gathered hordes of people
but not their hearts); he paid with the sword for his sword's violence   310
and his fall, coming on top of your own ruin, Rome, was heavier.[98]
Even then the present emperor's régime was being woven
on golden distaffs by good Fates; but the public losses
fell short of making him Envy's target.[99] All the emperors
chosen to bear the name Augustus occupied a throne   315
left by Caesars,[100] but when you, Rome, were reeling from your capture

(1973), 1.125–6]), and to achieve this – no easy task – appealed to Majorian, with, no doubt,
the prospect of an appointment. Majorian may at this time have become *comes domesticorum*
(commander of the corps of officer cadets), as suggested by *PLRE* 2.702; this is the rank
which he held soon afterwards, at the battle of Placentia.

98 Valentinian was not popular with the people, in spite of attempts to gain popularity
by assembling them and palliating discontent. According to Gregory of Tours he was
haranguing the people when attacked (*History of the Franks* 2.8). Our many sources
(*PLRE* 2.1139) are unanimous that there was a prearranged plot fomented by or agreed
with Petronius Maximus, and that the murder was committed by Occila and Thraustila,
bodyguards of Aetius, or by Occila alone, in the Campus Martius. Whatever he might
have thought of Valentinian's previous qualities (there is an overview of Valentinian III by
Humphries [2012]), S. comments that his death was well deserved, and the more disastrous
because Rome was in a state of ruin.

99 Similar words (on the weaving of the favourable Fates) were used at the jubilant
ending to the panegyric of Avitus (*c*. 7.600–2); this one, though certainly optimistic as far as
Majorian was concerned, is rather more restrained. If Majorian was favoured for elevation
then by Eudoxia, Valentinian's widow (Priscus [30] Blockley), this would justify high
optimism, but might come at a price, for good fortune was thought to be attacked by the spirit
of envy (*invidia*). However, (S. argues, none too clearly) in fact Majorian was not blamed
for the disasters which then befell Rome. The phrase 'public losses' (313) is ambiguous,
and S. has chosen a verb (literally 'fled' 'avoided') that does not point an accusing finger
at anyone. The Latin is strained, as shown by the literally correct translation of Shackleton
Bailey (1976), 244 'public calamities avoided jealousy of the hero', but the purpose is clear:
Majorian's position was at this juncture unaffected.

100 The following discussion of emperors from the first and early second centuries AD
(S. regularly ignores the intervening epochs, as in *c*. 7.104–13, and in the fifth century they
would not be applicable to this case) is not straightforward, but two main points emerge,
to Majorian's credit. Firstly, Majorian was in some sense a self-made emperor; he had
everything to do, even if that was not exactly 'creating the Empire anew' (Shackleton Bailey
[1976], 244). The throne was not in any sense 'left' for him by a previous emperor (here
'Caesars' means 'emperors'), either by hereditary succession or specific preparation. The
second point, elaborated at some length, is that Majorian was one of few emperors who had
actually earned the title of emperor, the others being Trajan and Vespasian (317–19 and 327).
The standard form is illustrated in lines 318–19: Nerva's adopted son Trajan, when 'called

this man created what he holds. So Nerva called on Trajan
when his son was already victor; to be Germanicus
in title, he had earned by his deeds. Things follow a pattern:
whoever starts like this seeks out such fame. In earlier times   320
after Tiberius' Capri,[101] and Gaius' shameful claims,[102]
then the censorship of Claudius,[103] and Nero's lyre and weddings,[104]
after the vanity of the monstrous mirror, in which Otho
gawped – this was ugly though he was handsome[105] – and the five millions
condemned to the abyss of Vitellius' shameless belly,[106]   325
an emperor was chosen who had earned these titles and
shown like patience of toil – Vespasian.[107] But in case, perhaps,

on' to be emperor, had already earned the title Germanicus by his military prowess, and the title was thus very apt. In the survey of the other, supposedly less deserving, emperors – who all palpably fell short, at least according to his simple, almost caricaturing, summaries – S. recycles, with some important differences, material he had used for another purpose in c. 7.104–11, as will be shown in the individual comments below. In general, the evidence to which S. appeals is flimsy in the extreme, and the 'pattern' or 'fixed order' that 'things' follow (in line 320) is far from obvious. For more careful treatments of these emperors, see Kneissel (1969), 27–69, referenced by Tan (2014), 83 n. 13.

101 The extravagances that reportedly followed Tiberius' retirement to Capri are prominent in Suetonius, *Tiberius* 39–44; their gravity is noted in Tacitus, *Ann.* 4.67, and they are enough to damn him here. As in c. 7.104, no mention made of his military success before he became emperor, or that he then as a matter of policy undertook no military campaigns (Suetonius, *Tiberius*, 37).

102 This differs from the point made in c. 7.105 concerning his boots; here they are not appropriate. For the claims made by Gaius, see Suetonius *Caligula* 22, where he begins a section on Caligulan monstrosities.

103 As in c. 7.105, S. picks out the censorship of Claudius, who became unpopular when he revived this office (Suetonius, *Claudius* 16).

104 In c. 7.106 Nero's lack of manliness until his death was the point; here S. focuses on his lyre-playing (Suetonius, *Nero* 20 and esp. 21) and his weddings (7 and 35; in Tacitus they may be traced in *Annals* 12.58, 14.59 and 63–4 [the death of Octavia]).

105 Otho's use of a vanity mirror 'made Rome ugly' in poem c. 7.107–8, but here is seen as destroying his claims to be handsome. Both points derive from Juvenal, *Satires* 2.99–101.

106 Vitellius' greed (Suetonius, *Vitellius* 7, and especially 13) is treated rather more vigorously than in the earlier passage (c. 7.108–10). Suetonius' sum of 400,000 sesterces (he offers this as typical) becomes 500,000 sesterces in S., constrained by metre. The sums are huge.

107 'Patience of toil' (327) is a new criterion. The argument has slipped: the plural 'these titles' (326) is unexplained, and the nature of the 'pattern' (119–20) remains unclear. Vespasian was never *Germanicus*, but had already won the titles of *Iudaicus* (Kneissel [1969] 42–3), and this seems to suffice.

you think me trapped by the plunderer's power, a vicious life has drained
from him the vigour of his race; his Scythian savagery[108]
is guided not by strength of will but weak desires; by gaining   330
vast plunder he has lost by self-indulgence all the strength
with which when poor he flourished. Now, for his own ends, he arms
my flesh and blood against me; I, captive for all these years[109]
am torn between his writ and my virtue; fertile in woes
I bear men for my suffering. With his own arms he does   335
naught; it is Gaetulians, Nomads, Garamantes, Autololi
Arzuges, Marmaridae, Psylli, Nasamones[110] that make him feared,
the sluggard, and, with gold aplenty, of steel he knows nothing.
His colour is pale, with drunkenness destroying him he is gripped
by enfeebling corpulence, and overwhelmed by constant stuffing   340
his stomach cannot liberate the acid flatulence.
His men's lives are the same; not as much was Hannibal Barca
destroyed in sumptuous Capua, when bodies strong in war
amid enchantments were weakened by luxury-loving Baiae,
and, where Mount Gaurus dips itself into the Lucrine lake,[111]   345
now swimming, the Massylian exerted his dark arms.
And so, I pray, albeit after all these centuries,
give me this master to be my avenger, so that no more
will Carthage fight with Italy".[112] So speaking, in agony,
she groaned aloud, and reinforced her pleas with floods of tears.   350

108 The 'plunderer' (in *c.* 2.17 and 354 he was a 'pirate') is Geiseric, who is never named
in these poems; cf. 2.17 n. Men from the wide area denoted by Scythia are expected to be
savage; Geiseric's bithplace is unknown.
109 Almost thirty years; Geiseric invaded Africa in 429.
110 This cluster of eight races, ranging from today's Morocco almost to the Nile Delta,
uses the evidence of African tribes in Lucan's *Civil War* (4.677–84), which mentions them
all (Psylli feature in book 9). Three names in Lucan's list – Afer, Mauri and Mazax – are not
used: for S. the first two are generic rather than tribal. The names were perhaps all in current
use, but of little value as real information on the armies of Geiseric.
111 The enfeeblement of Hannibal Barca and his men in Capua, and their abuse of its
pleasures, are related in Livy 23.18.10–16 and alluded to in 23.45, 1–3. Baiae became a
famous resort after Hannibal's time, and gained the reputation for luxurious living that Livy
doubtless had in mind. In his account Florus adds the sunshine of Campania and the hot
springs of Baiae (1.22.21–2). Mount Gaurus and the Lucrine lake (cf. *c.* 18.7) were nearby.
112 S. uses three exact words from the weighty prologue of Vergil, *A.* 1.13 ('Carthage,
opposite Italy'), changing the meaning to 'against Italy'.

Rome made the following reply: "Cut short your long complaints,
my loyal friend; in heaven's name your saviour will indeed
be Majorian. But let me call to mind a few matters,
concisely. Ever since Theodosius returned a share
of power to his patron's banished brother – this man's neck was   355
broken by a hand that would later turn on itself[113] – my Gaul,
ignored till now by the world's masters, unknown, has been a slave.[114]
Since then much has been lost, for with the emperor (whoever
it was), strictly confined,[115] in diverse parts of the wretched world
devastation was the rule.[116] What sort of life could give pleasure,   360
when the ruler needed governing? Despised for many years,
the nobles were of no esteem; for the strong the recompense
from the state was ill-will.[117] Now our emperor is setting all

113 Rome neatly, almost casually, adds a severe complaint about the government of 'my
Gaul', in a narrative which goes back some seventy years. In 388 Theodosius, appointed
emperor in 379 by Gratian, who is accordingly described here as his 'patron', restored
Gratian's brother Valentinian II to the throne after he had fled as a result of the invasion
of Italy in 387 by the usurper Maximus. The circumstances of Valentinian's death in 392
are uncertain; he may well, as stated here, have been killed by Arbogast (so Harries [1994],
90 and n. 33; according to *PLRE* 1.935 it was 'probably by suicide'). For Arbogast, who
committed suicide in 394, see *PLRE* 1.95–7; for Gratian see *PLRE* 1.401–2; for Valentinian II
see *PLRE* 1.934–5.

114 Compared with the tirade of Theoderic in *c.* 7.537–43 – stressing weak emperors, weak
laws and the problems of living with them – this complaint, expressed by Rome herself to the
Lyon audience, focuses on the condition and feelings of the Gallo-Romans: they had been
ignored by the empire's leaders, treated as outsiders and so unaware of wider policies and
opportunities, and slaves, bound to pay taxes, which were politely accepted however severe,
and to fight as required.

115 Honorius, from 402, and subsequently Valentinian III, lived for some time in the
relative but remote security of Ravenna; being young at the time of their accessions (cf.
c. 7.532–43) they needed 'governing' (line 361). See McEvoy (2013), 135–50 and 220–34.

116 Devastation (360) both mental and physical; for the latter, see the study of various
poets of Gaul by Roberts (1992), 97–106.

117 Nobles are certainly inconspicuous in our records of Gaul (Stroheker [1948]):
though Harries (1994), 27, stressing the inadequate evidence, thereby makes an important
caveat. Harries also notes (246–9) the lack of an agreed policy or shared interests among
the nobility. Cf. also Matthews (1975), 329–51. In the word for 'the strong' (a singular in
the Latin) an allusion has been seen in particular to Avitus, but the 'collective' singular
is a common usage, and as has been plentifully shown there is an element of 'prudence'
and avoidance of controversy on the part of S. in this panegyric (Mathisen [1979a],
165–71).

to rights, and adding new forces from his various peoples[118]
he is advancing, via other wars, to yours. The march   365
is the main issue, not the fight.[119] But why waste time with words?
He comes; he conquers". With this speech the council came to an end
and with the metal bending to the words of the goddess
in harmony the three sisters drew out new threads of gold.[120]

To express these sufferings of Rome and Libya that I have sung   370
men's prayers have taught me; now it is time to move to deeds, of which
I must speak even if within me Apollo should fall mute.[121]
Mars, not the Muses, will inspire me now. The fierce Alaman
had climbed the Alps; led over the Rhaetian ridge through long, still wastes,[122]
he had left the mountains, after ravaging the Roman side,   375
and all over the plains once given the name of Canius[123]

118 Perhaps a victory over the Vandals would indeed enable these things to be attended
to, but this reads as if the problems are being brushed away in a spirit of gung-ho; Rome
naturally concentrates on the military preparations for that war and other wars which
would enhance security and add to manpower, notably that provided by the Burgundians
(Anderson, on line 364).

119 In case Majorian should be thought slow, Rome adds that his gathering of allies is the
vital thing; eventual victory (it is implied) is assured. He intended to march (and did) through
Gaul and Spain, reaching Carthage in 460. On the unfortunate outcome, see Hydatius 195
[200].

120 As at the end of the panegyric of Avitus (lines 600–2), the Fates (NB here 'sisters') at
once see to Rome's wishes. Repeating this commonplace in a new context would not cause
embarrassment or risk envy. A panegyrist must be upbeat. The notion of metal obeying
Rome's might reinforces the impression of her military power, as would the power of the
three Fates, who support her.

121 Enough has been said, the poet declares, of the afflictions of Rome and Africa (370).
The underlying conceit that follows is that even if he (the poet) received no inspiration from
Apollo or the Muses, as a poet might expect, he would be bound to recount the following
feats of Majorian; the divine inspiration would then be Mars, god of war.

122 The existence of this route is known from Amm. 15.4.1, where the emperor
Constantius II proceeds from Milan into Rhaetia (equivalent to Tyrol, parts of Switzerland
and of Bavaria) against an Alemannic tribe, and from Gregory of Tours, *History of the
Franks* 10.3, where one of the dukes of King Childebert (Duke Olo) makes for Milan via
Bilitio (modern Bellinzona). This and nearby passes are discussed in *RE* 1.1608.

123 The name (Latin, *Campi Canini*) is given by Amm. and Gregory in the passages cited
above. Nothing is known about Canus or Canius, if indeed he existed: always ready to make
a periphrasis, S. may have assumed that they had been called after a person of that name.

he had sent out nine hundred of the enemy to plunder.[124]
Now master of both services you direct Burco there,[125]
accompanied by a tiny task force, though that is enough
when the order to engage is yours; the victory for our side   380
is sure when you command combat. Fortune wins triumphs not
through numbers, but devotion; I want not armies in battle,
if you send just a few to fight.[126] The success is down to you;
you fought empowered with the rank of master of services
but with an emperor's predetermined fate. More recently,[127]   385
the enemy roved at leisure on the open sea, after
each order of the state had duly given you supreme rule –
plebs, senate, soldiers, and your colleague too.[128] With southerly winds,
they invade the land of Campania, and with Moorish soldiers
attack the unsuspecting farmers; sitting on the thwarts   390
the bloated Vandal waited for the spoil, which he had ordered
to be dragged there – spoil captured by captives.[129] But suddenly

124 Literally 'nine times one hundred'. It is notable that S. does not adopt the simpler
expedient of rounding up to 1,000 (that would be an excusable exaggeration, smaller than
many): he may have had exact information, or wished to give such an impression of doing so.

125 This engagement took place after 28 February 457 (*PLRE* 2.703), the date when
Majorian received this appointment as master of both services and probably in early spring
of that year. Burco may have had the rank of military commander, as suggested in *PLRE*
2.242–3.

126 The patriotic poet speaks as Rome herself might ('I want … '). In this second battle the
destiny of the future emperor, which Majorian was to become a few months later (see below)
is presented as another vital factor.

127 A new episode in a different part of Italy. Having roved apparently at leisure (cf.
c. 2.354), the Vandals attempt to land infantry and cavalry in Campania (west central Italy).
See notes on the text used.

128 With this insertion (387–8) S. makes it very clear not only that this episode took place
after Majorian was made emperor (this happened on 28 December in 457; with primary
refs in *PLRE* 2.703) but also, and very significantly, that his claim had received universal
consent from constitutional bodies (cf. *c.* 2.18–20).This claim to high legitimacy goes back
to Augustus (*Res Gestae* 34.1: see MacCormack [1981], 243); most importantly, it includes
a reference to the assent of the Eastern emperor, his future colleague, which was essential.
Leo, the Eastern emperor concerned, had become emperor some time after February 457
(*PLRE* 2.664).

129 The 'captives' are the Moors, who, it is implied, are being exploited in this case;
stylistic embroidery by S., perhaps, to blacken the Vandals. The two peoples are regularly
mentioned together, as equals, by Victor of Vita in his account of the sack of Rome; see also
Courtois (1955), 232 nn. 7 and 8, and 340–1 on this invasion.

your troops had thrust themselves between the two enemy sections
on the plains that separate the sea and the nearby hill and make
a harbour with the river's backward bend.[130] At first the horde   395
in panic head for the mountains, where, cut off from their ships,
they became spoil for those despoiled. The excited pirates then
muster at full strength for the battle, some from the hollow boats
disembark their well-trained horses, others put on iron mail
of the same colour as themselves, others prepare curved bows   400
and arrows that bear poison smeared on the iron tips, so that
a single shot may inflict a double wound. The woven dragons
in each array already dart this way and that;[131] their throats
swell in the Zephyr winds that jostle them; with gaping mouth
the embroidered image imitates mad hunger, and the wind   405
creates a fury in the cloth whenever its twisting back
is pumped up by the winds and its stomach cannot hold the air.
But then with terrifying din, the blaring trumpet brayed;
a roar answers the clarions and courage suddenly flares,
briefly, even in faint hearts. From everywhere cascades cold steel,   410
but from one side it enters enemy throats; a hurled missile
crushes one man, then hardly stopping speeds to a second kill;
a lance's blow spins one man round; pierced by a javelin,
one man falls from his horse, and then, pierced by a dart, one more.[132]
One falls to a missile from some distant hand; some with smashed knees 415

130 The river is probably the Volturnus, the principal river of Campania, and the plain the
plain of Sinuessa. S. may have thought that the place-name is derived from the word *sinus*
('bend'), as it well might be.

131 'Dragons' were the standards of the Late Antique army (cf. *c.* 2.333), mentioned by
Amm. and Claudian among others, who sometimes note, as S. does here, the impression
they give of strong emotion when fluttering in the breeze: in Amm. 16.10.7 they hiss with
anger, in Claudian they are made gentle (*c.* 5.365) or angry (*c.* 7.138–41) by the wind. Clearly
both Roman and Vandal flags are meant. The picture in line 407 rather suggests abdominal
flatulence, echoing the gorged Vandal of line 341.

132 S. uses an imaginative diversity of words for the weapons, notably some abstruse ones
from Vergil's *Aeneid*, which are difficult to translate closely if at all. The 'hurled missile'
is the *falarica* described in *A.* 9.705. The word 'javelin' (OLD) renders *aclys*, an exotic and
evidently unfamiliar weapon from *A.* 7.730, described by the commentator Servius as a
'spiked club thrown with a cord or strap' (for retention purposes). The 'dart' is the *veru*
(*A.* 7.665); this word more commonly means 'spit'(as used for cooking).

live on to make death seem grudging.[133] Someone then chops off half
a brain, along with half a helmet, and with powerful arm
scatters the wretch's miserable skull with two-edged sword.
When once the Vandal, with his troops driven back, had turned to flight,
battle gives way to slaughter: with no discrimination   420
they are spreadeagled on the plains. All kinds of valiant things
were done by cowards.[134] Pale and panicking a fleeing horseman
enters the sea, goes past the ships, but shamefully swims back
from the open sea to his own skiff.[135] So was it in the third
battle with Pyrrhus long ago: after, with thousands killed,   425
Dentatus was defeating him, Pyrrhus could scarcely drag
the shreds of his navy to Epirus – he, who had dispersed
Chaones and Molossi, and bands from Thrace and Macedonia
over your shores,[136] whose power had panicked pale Oenotria
and even dissolute Tarentum, which had sought his help.[137]   430

---

133 Death, which in war presents itself so freely, is sometimes niggardly, begrudging
release to the horrifically wounded.

134 The language here in some ways recalls Vergil *A.* 2.364–5, a scene from the sack of
Troy, but is adroitly adapted to this context: the 'spreadeagled' enemy of line 421 are dead,
not sleeping, and the word in Vergil that describes the 'defenceless' or 'motionless' bodies
is here actually applied to 'cowards', in a clear contrast with others who were brave. These
adaptations are interpreted very differently by Brolli (2013), 95–9.

135 The picture is unclear: it is not obvious what if anything here is brave, but the idea
must be that potentially brave (in Loyen's word, 'vigorous') actions are committed under
stress. The shame felt at returning to one's boat (whether a converted transport as suggested
by MacGeorge (2002), 309, or the small boat or 'skiff' (*cumba*)) shows the pointlessness
of racing into the sea and perhaps losing one's horse. It is not clear if the cavalry left their
horses behind, or whether the picture is of a single horseman or a greater number, or even
an unhorsed warrior. No Roman ships are mentioned or implied in this episode, which is
probably typical of Vandal raiding.

136 For a description of this battle between Pyrrhus and Curius Dentatus Manius at
Beneventum (275 BC) see Plutarch, *Pyrrhus* 25. The points of the comparison are, first, the
powerlessness of the fleets and, secondly, the unhappy retreat of an invader from overseas
who had brought many peoples with him (cf. 336–7). The detail of these peoples may owe
something, directly or indirectly, to the rhetorical passage in Florus 1.13 (1.8) that mentions
Molossi, Thracians and Macedonians, and then Italian peoples. The Chaones were, like the
Molossi, inhabitants of Epirus (in north-west Greece).

137 Oenotria (cf. *c.* 2.318, with note) originally referred to southern Italy, as it does here,
but refers to Italy as a whole in Vergil *A.* 7.85 and Claudian *c.* 22.262. Here, as in Claudian
c. 26.145–6 (where Oenotria is also stated to have suffered from Pyrrhus), it is more likely to

With the enemy expelled, the plain, now rising high with dead,
could be surveyed at leisure. There, down in the confused mass,
you could detect each army's character; none of your men
did not have frontal wounds, while not a single one of theirs
was not pierced in the back.[138] This was proclaimed aloud by the wounds   435
of the pirates' leader (as he then happened to be), to whom
the sister of the greedy king is said to have been married;[139]
though coated in black dust and smashed with pikes he carried still
the shameful signs of ignominious flight. So did your troops
with all their spoil control the plain, enjoying the fruits of Mars.   440

Meanwhile, as you construct a fleet on both Italian coasts,
for the lower and the upper seas,[140] every forest falls down
seaward for you, and on both sides cut back incessantly
you, Apennine massif, so rich in trees for shipbuilding,
send to the sea as many forests as you send rivers.   445
Though wearied by successive payments of tribute, Gaul wishes
to gain favour through this levy, and does not feel its weight,
which she accepts as a benefit.[141] Not with so many ships
did the elder son of Atreus mantle the Carpathian sea
when the Doric foe, to seize Sigeum's wealth, besieged Rhoeteian   450
Pergamum;[142] nor was Xerxes lord of such a fleet when he,
to join Sestos and Abydos, levelled the billowing waves
and brought the breakers beneath a bridge, when with hybristic steps

refer to southern Italy. Tarentum is described with the same pejorative epithet that the satirist
Juvenal applied to Corinth, in a passage that S. seems to echo (8.113).

138 Frontal wounds signal the courage of the victors, wounds on the back the cowardice of
the defeated, a common theme in descriptions of battle.

139 It is possible that this man is Sersao, the relative of Geiseric mentioned by Victor of
Vita 1.35 (Courtois [1955], 394, n. 11; *PLRE* 1.996–7).

140 The words denoting the Tuscan and the Adriatic seas ('the lower and the upper sea')
are derived from Lucan 2.400 (just before a passage (416–27) on the rivers of Italy – and one
which could have inspired S.'s list of French rivers (lines 208–9).

141 S. here presents Gaul as nobly suffering in silence.

142 The elder son of Atreus was Agamemnon, leader of the expedition from southern
Greece (so 'Doric') against Troy. This whole description is richly poeticised: the epithet
'Carpathian' (Carpathos is an island between Crete and Rhodes) is unusual for the Aegean
sea; there are various poetic words – 'Sigean', 'Rhoeteian' and Pergamum – that all refer to
Troy.

he slighted and profaned the waters, and his thronging troops
outrageously cavorted over the Hellespontine depths.[143]   455
Not so much did the Mareotic fleet in Leucas' port
conceal the seas round Actium, when to her husband's war[144]
the crew, part of a dowry, came from Pharian Canopus
and fierce Cleopatra, accoutred with traditional sistra,[145]
and, having loaded her gold-coloured boats with dark-skinned soldiers,   460
weighed down the extensive waters with her Ptolemaic treasure.[146]
You, Rome, fight not with finery like this, but as of yore
with something richer – steel. Justly less treasured is the gold
of a wealthy sluggard. But do not despise such enemies:
though no embellishment in battle, they do embellish triumphs.   465
Nor will it be a regret to have evoked the Lagean line
to exemplify your enemy, because for these kingdoms
I see a similar fortune, since on one side there is equal
extravagance, and on the other no less great a Caesar.[147]
Immediately you undertake something that in our time   470
no emperor could achieve: the rugged troops of seven-mouthed Danube
you sweep away to fight.[148] For all the folk that the inert sky[149]

143 The Persian king Xerxes, invading Greece in 481 BC, linked Sestos and Abydus with
a bridge of boats, over which he and his army marched across the Hellespont, as related by
Herodotus (7.33–43). For other feats of Xerxes, cf. *c.* 2.509–10 and *c.* 9.41–9.

144 The battle of Actium (31 BC) between Octavian and Mark Antony, husband of
Cleopatra, was often represented, as in Vergil *A.* 8.671–713, as a clash between Romans and
Egyptians. Here the wealth of poetic adjectives meaning 'Egyptian' (456, 458, 461, 466)
contrasts with the simplicity with which Rome is described (462–4). Leucas (456) was a
town close to the promontory of Actium.

145 Cleopatra also wields rattles (*sistra*) – these were employed in the worship of the
goddess Isis – in the Vergilian description of Actium (*A.* 8.696).

146 The treasure of Cleopatra is a significant feature of various narratives of the battle,
including Vergil, *A.* 8.685, Plutarch, *Antony* 67, and Dio 15.50.

147 The luxury-loving Vandals are compared with the Egyptians, here called 'Lagean'
after Lagus, the supposed founder of the Egyptian dynasty and father of the first Ptolemy;
Majorian is compared to Octavian, the future emperor Augustus, here as often called Caesar.

148 It may be correct that no recent emperor had tried to utilise so many such forces,
whose description here as 'rugged' corresponds to the icy climate; Theodosius I perhaps
came closest, with his recruitment of Goths in an earlier crisis, for which see Pacatus, *Pan.
Lat.* 2. (12). 32.3–4, with Nixon and Saylor Rodgers (1994), nn. 67 and 117, and Heather
(1991), 160–1. Majorian is again inspired by Theodosius (cf. lines 109–12 above).

149 The word 'inert' refers to the stillness of deep winter.

gives birth to in Sithonian climes beneath the Parrhasian Bear,
all these quake at your standards: Suebian, Bastarnian,
Pannonian, Neurian, Hun, Getan, Dacian, Alan, Alites   475
Bellonotian, Rugian, Burgundian, and Visigoth,
Bisaltian, Ostrogoth, Procrustian, Moschan, Sarmatian,[150]
all these came to your eagles, and for you campaigns the entire
Caucasus range, and the drinker of Scythian Tanais.[151]
What could the man's fortune achieve? until now Rome has feared   480
all those armed groups which she enrolled to threaten others; now,
with you as emperor, freedom from fear seems trivial
without subservience from a tribe she feared when another reigned.[152]
You were now on the move, surrounded by manifold standards
of thronging thousands; just one race refused obedience,   485
fiercer than normal, having just pulled back from the Danube
its untamed army, its leaders lost through wars. In this proud race
a wicked battle-lust was being stoked by Tuldila.[153]

150 A combination of well-known and obscure names designed to indicate the vast area of
central Europe (in today's terms) from which barbarians came to serve Majorian. It is of course
quite unlikely that an official record was taken or that such details were reliably researched
later, but they should not be dismissed as partly 'fantasy' (Loyen), as in some cases 'obsolete'
(Maenchen-Helfen (1973), 161 and n. 810), or as enforced by metrical needs. Several of the
names, according to Maenchen-Helfen, are from book six of Valerius Flaccus, a poet used
elsewhere by S., where the Argonauts meet a variety of local tribes. Many of the names are
familiar, especially from Claudian; some are in Amm. and in geographical writers. The tribe
or race here called Alites has not been identified or explained; the word Procrustian is quite
implausible, and may be a corruption of Pirustae (an Illyrian people known to Caesar and Livy).
For Bellonoti, see the endnote to c. 7.321–5, a passage which raises similar problems.
151 The Caucasus mountain range campaigns (its inhabitants becoming soldiers) for the
emperor, while the river Tanais (now the Don, in southern Russia, so 'Scythian') supplies
water to countless drinkers. There is little similarity between the description of the drinker
here and that in Claudian c. 3.312 as Maenchen-Helfen suggests; his evocation of Horace is
more plausible, but the expression ('drinker of such and such a river') is a common topos.
152 The point of this claim is that although it had been regular Roman policy to enrol in her
armies foreign peoples whom she herself found formidable, now she not only does not fear
such tribes, as under previous emperors, but lords it over them. As will shortly be seen (lines
505–10), Majorian is a hard taskmaster, and by implication a tougher and more successful
one than Julius Caesar (lines 505–9); here, perhaps, superiority to Theodosius I also is
implied (cf. note 148).
153 Tuldila was probably a Hun (PLRE 2.1131, inferring this from the fact that they were
now leaderless). For the name see Maenchen-Helfen (1973), 405, 422, 441 for comparisons
with other names, and in general 161–2.

At this point, having only just laid down your arms, you take
them again, just as the Bistonides when (it may be) they fill   490
with Ogygian dancers the frosty lands of the Cicones,
by the fields of Strymon, or on Rhodope, or where in cloud
midst Hyperborean crags Hebrus rolls down from Ismarus,[154]
the wandering crowd gives way to sleep, the exhausted revellers
weary and rest; the flute does not respond to the double breath;   495
but now ...[155] with scarcely any rest, whirling the thyrsus round
a god-filled Bassarid, shaggy in an Erythraean fawn's
kenspeckle coat, excites the Odrysian devotees to sound
the languid timbrel.[156] You postpone their punishment, and thus
become responsible for more bloodshed. Part of your army,   500
with more concern for you, no longer tolerated this
but, on your behalf, scorned your restraint; victims of the new war,
each mutineer fell dead. And you distribute spoils to those
who had displayed a loyal mind; those who out of terror
helped with this harsh lesson are cheered by their reward. Caesar,   505
seeking Pharsalia's plains, quelled sudden mutinies with the sword,
but having thus cut off his own limbs, driven by his great cause,
he grieved for those that he killed;[157] but this revolt helped your campaign;
if the barbarian does not heed whatever you command,
he dies, to make the soldiers fear.   510

Already, in winter-time,
through Alps white as marble and crags that rear to join the sky

---

154 Among the names that recall Thrace and its landscape is an epithet 'Ogygian' (491),
which refers to Thebes, in Boeotia, where Bacchic cult is said to have originated and been
developed.

155 The ellipse in line 496 replaces two words of the Latin original that yield no sense at
all (literally, 'they tie with a bridge'!); the text is corrupt. See note on the text used.

156 The thyrsus is a kind of wand, decorated with a fir cone, a tuft of ivy, or perhaps vine
leaves. It is one of a number of words that enhance the richness of this outstanding bipartite
simile set in lesser-known Greek lands; the word for 'god-filled' is another, and so too the
word for 'fawn skin'. The originally Greek name Bassaris, of uncertain meaning, denotes
'Bacchante'; 'Erythrean' indicates the warm countries around the Arabian sea (cf. c. 5.285
and the references there).

157 Caesar's management of the mutiny at Placentia in 49 BC is described by Lucan at
5.237–373 and in other sources (Suetonius, *Caesar* 69; Dio 41.26–36; Appian 2.47). None
of these claims that he felt grief in the aftermath; the detail may have been invented by S. to
emphasise Majorian's mental toughness.

and rocks like glass, and louring cliffs that threaten freezing rain,[158]
you lead the way on foot, and you prevent your slithering feet
from falling with a lance that you pushed out in front of you.
When halfway up the mountainside, most soldiers had begun   515
to feel their vitals stiffening with frost, as on the slope,
restricted to the narrow paths, they could not even crawl
but slid back on the frozen ground. By chance, one of that column,
a man whose vehicle's wheels had crossed the Danube white with ice,[159]
cried out, "rather would I suffer the sword and the usual chill   520
that comes with a quiet death, but now with paralysing cramp
languor binds fast my limbs; scorched with a sort of fiery cold,
my body perishes. Without respite we follow this youth
as he pursues his enterprise; all those who are the strongest,
whether king or people, now bed down, sheltered in camp or   525
in a sun-warmed tent, while we subvert the order of the year.
What he commands will be the law for all; never is he
deflected from an enterprise; if he fears time's wrath, even
through losses, he sees it as loss of face.[160] To what race should
I assign this man, whom I, a Scyth, cannot bear? What tiger's milk   530
did he imbibe as an infant neath Hyrcanian cliffs?[161] What land
bred him – some land more gruesome than my own country? See there,
at the top, how he marshals his frozen troops, and laughs at the cold,
being himself in mind uniquely ablaze. When I followed
the trumpets of a northern king, I heard that the emperor's troops   535
and Caesar's guard languished, effete, in constant luxury;
it is no good to me that earlier masters are no more

158 The focus switches to the Alps. The exact itinerary is not in any way indicated; the date is some time after 6 November, when Majorian is known to have been in Ravenna. The paradox 'dry rain' indicates falls of ice or snow from cliffs or cornices, or even avalanches.

159 This soldier had previously fought beyond the Danube, perhaps in a campaign involving a chariot; but the wheels of a wagon are more probably meant.

160 A difficult passage, partly because of the wordplay. The passing of time may bring losses, but, far from taking this as a warning or a deterrent, he considers such fear on his part to be a loss of face or an insult to his ego. The words 'time's wrath' personalise the struggle, as if time (the notion here includes 'insufficient time' or 'unfavourable time', or simply 'what happens') was a rival that should adapt to him, not the reverse.

161 The influence of Vergil, *A*. 4.366–7, where Dido denounces the departing Aeneas ('I believe harsh Caucasus begat you … and Hyrcanian tigers suckled you': tr. Day Lewis) is apparent; as often, S. thoughtfully adapts.

if here too is a mighty king".[162] As he prepared to speak
more strongly, you incited him, from a crag, with biting words:
"Whoever you are, who dread the glassy ascent in front of you,   540
just break the surface of the hanging water, carve the stream
and use it as a step.[163] No more of these shameful complaints!
The idle feel the cold. Did nature endow me with the limbs
of two-bodied Hylaeus?[164] Surely no Pegasus with wings
assisted me in this march, nor did Calais and Zetus   545
give me their wings to fly with[165]– can't you see me now trampling
the snowy summit of this ridge? Are you broken by the cold,
and by the Alps? Let me now devise redress for all these frosts –
ah yes, a summer by the Syrtes!".[166] Thus do you revive
the army with harangues, and lift them by example; you   550
are the first to undertake the exertions you command; the rest
then gladly obey the leader who submits to his own demands.[167]
And what a staff is yours, and what a master of services
was he who drove your army after you,[168] though by no means
one that was unwilling. He alone deserved to take the palm   555
of Sulla in arms, Fabius in talent, Metellus in piety

162 He had probably served Attila ('the northern king'), and naturally refers to Majorian
also as 'king', a term unusual for a Roman ruler (though related words like 'kingdom' and
'rule' are not).

163 The soldier is advised to cut steps in the ice and make a ladder, as mountaineers must
often do. The paradoxical words 'hanging water' and 'stream' that refer to the icy slope have
a point beyond elegant variation; it is as if he dismissed the obstacles as only water.

164 Hylaeus the centaur, one of two such beings mentioned in Vergil *A.* 8.293–4, would
have found it easier with its four legs (and indeed with its experience of high mountains in
Thessaly [cf. lines 492–3]). Pegasus, the winged horse, would simply have deposited the
emperor on the appropriate summit.

165 Calais and Zetus were the winged sons of Boreas, the north wind. The form Zetus, as
again in *c.* 24.48, is used rather than the commoner form Zetes.

166 The desert of that name, not the sandbanks. This heart-warming piece of good cheer,
albeit sarcastic, suggests that Africa will be reached before long.

167 The Latin word translated 'demands' is literally 'laws', but although Majorian (like
any emperor) was indeed a lawgiver, to introduce this notion here would be pointless. He is
a leader who follows his own precepts.

168 Here S. introduces the emperor's 'companions' (the Latin word *comes* was part of
various titles of higher magistrates), beginning with his 'master of services', who is nameless,
but identified by most scholars as Nepotianus (*PLRE* 2.778). See further in Extended note (ii).

Appius in speaking, Camillus in skill, Fulvius in verve.[169]
If you enquire how great a man it is who holds the honour
of being prefect where Gaul spreads her wide bounds,[170] hardly equal
in conduct was the man to whom Trajan, before the senate,   560
entrusted his drawn sword for use even against himself.[171]
Under your judge the one who now dictates laws to the Goths,
the skin-clad enemy, looks up to the our harsh-voiced court usher.[172]
Why speak here of the one who governs the Sacred Bureau
who, as he manages the reins of a civil sector,   565
also sustains a soldier's cares, with whom as mediator
a savage race is reconciled to your conditions? Why,
with your weak powers, rash Clio, do you try to praise Petrus?[173]
From this man's mouth Caesar sees fit to address the world, although

169 The (older) worthies with whom he is favourably compared are each characterised in a
single word, in the Sidonian manner. See Extended note (iii).

170 This refers to Magnus (no other names of his are known: (*PLRE* 2.700–1)), now
praetorian prefect of the Gauls and so their most high-ranking judge (562–3). Magnus is
praised by S. in *c*. 15.154–7 (where his prefecture is again mentioned), and extolled for many
virtues in *c*. 23.455–63 – and for his library in 24.90. He was consul in 460. At a banquet
attended by Majorian, Sidonius and others (*Ep*. 1.11.10) his conversation was about literary
subjects, and in the preface to *c*. 14 he is cited as an expert in philosophical terminology.

171 This action of the emperor Trajan is referred to in Pliny, *Panegyricus* 67.8, and
described by Dio 68.16.1 and Aurelius Victor, *De Caesaribus* 13.9, who names the person as
the praetorian prefect Suburanus.

172 The skin-clad enemy (for the epithet, cf. *c*. 7.219 and 349) is Theoderic II, king of the
Goths, lawgiver to his people but portrayed here as submissive to a minor court official (cf.
c. 7.467), who is in turn under the judicial authority of a judge subject to Magnus (line 562).
The contrast between the friendly negotiation between him and Avitus in *c*. 7.460–86 and his
support of Avitus in *c*. 7.496–9 is marked: he was now an adversary. Later, but at an uncertain
date, S. gives a very detailed and respectful description of the king's lifestyle in *Ep*. 1.2.

173 With ten lines (including a parenthesis on another man in lines 570–1: see below,
n. 179), Petrus (*PLRE* 2.866) has the longest of these tributes (lines 564–73), and S. pretends
to be unequal to the task, rebuking Clio, his Muse, for even trying. Clio was traditionally
Muse of history; that might have some point here, given his recent achievements. Petrus (cf.
c. 3) was an orator of some repute; his eloquence is praised in *c*. 9.307–8, and see also *Ep*. 9.13
(lines 83–7), *Ep*. 9.15 (lines 39–42). Petrus was head of the 'Sacred Bureau' (565) 'secretary
of state for imperial correspondence' (Jones [1966], 381) or, literally, 'master of letters'. The
'soldier's cares' that he sustains are the heavy responsibilities incurred in the operations
briefly described. He had evidently taken on (as S. reminds the 'most mild of emperors, 571)
the task of confronting the 'savage race' (567) within Lyon; who exactly these occupiers
were is not clear (though they are often not improbably identified as Burgundians), nor is it

he also enjoys the asset of his quaestor's eloquence;[174]   570
indeed this selfsame man lately, O most mild of emperors,
having taken hostages, removed from this our city's walls
the sword that had been thrust into our miserable guts.
And since you, who are our sole hope in this exhausted state,
have come, we beg you hasten to relieve our present ruin   575
and as you pass, victorious, look upon your own Lyon.[175]
Exhausted, she implores of you rest after such great hardships.
Having given us peace, give us new heart. The steer with toil-worn neck
unlocks the solid soil far better when the plough is removed.[176]
Our land has been emptied of oxen, of fruit, of farmers,   580
of citizens. When standing fast, its true state lay hidden,
but when captured, (alas) how dire it was! O emperor,
when joy has come, remembering woe delights. Rapine and fire
have sapped our strength; but as you come you bring with you total
renewal, and since we have been the cause of your triumph   585
catastrophe itself pleases. When you, victor, begin
to mount your chariot,[177] and your hair is bound by laurel crowns
– mural, rampart, and civic crowns – in the traditional style[178]

clear what exactly lies behind the metaphorics of 'sword' and 'guts' or the blunter 'rapine and fire' in line 583. A fuller, but not unproblematic, narrative is that of Loyen (1960), xiv, with n. 2, who argues, following a remark of Stein, accepted by others, that the city was occupied by Aegidius (*PLRE* 2.11–13) with his Frankish auxiliaries, who on their leader's departure drove out the Burgundians and left the city in ruins.

174 The quaestor introduced here, who shares the task of being the emperor's mouthpiece, is Domnulus (*PLRE* 2.374), described by S. in his prose introduction to *c.* 14 (some time later) as 'a man of quaestorian rank'. He was also a poet (*Ep.* 9.13.4; 9.15.1), a philosopher (*c.* 14 pref. 2) and a 'churchman' (Anderson [*Ep.* 4.25]). Mathisen (1979b) conjecturally reconstructs his political career in *Francia* 7, 613–14.

175 No particular connection of Majorian with Lyon is attested, by birth or otherwise; S. was born in Lyon, but never elsewhere links Majorian with the area. His words 'your own Lyon' is a statement of devotion, to show that he is a welcome victor as he passes through.

176 The exhausted steer ploughs better after a rest.

177 For the victor to mount the chariot (as promised [in vain] to Avitus, *c.* 7.10) was a pivotal moment in the Roman triumph. For thorough discussions of the Roman triumph in general, and details mentioned in the ensuing lines, see W. Ehlers, 'Triumphus', *RE* 2. VII A. 1.493–511, updated in many ways by Beard (2007).

178 Six kinds of military crown, including the ones here named, are listed by Aulus Gellius, the second-century AD miscellanist, in his *Attic Nights*, 5.6.1: civic, mural, camp-related, naval, triumphal, obsidional (that is, related to sieges). The three kinds mentioned by S. here

and the golden Capitol gazes upon the chains of kings,
when you embellish Rome with spoils, when with expensive wax   590
you represent the captive huts of Cinyphian Bocchus,[179]
then I myself through thronging peoples and screaming applause,
will walk before you and, as now, sing with my feeble voice
that you have conquered both Alpine massifs, and the Syrtes,
the great sea and the smaller seas, and Libya's armed bands too,   595
but first, that you conquered for me.[180] Now that you turn your eyes
and look upon us wretches with a placid countenance,
we may exult. I do recall that, when you wished to pardon,
this was the appearance of your face.[181] Mild charm gives signs of itself.
Answer my prayer; so may Byrsa recover through your triumphs;   600
so may the Parthian flee without pretence, and the Moor turn white
with terror; so may Susa quake and, with quivers laid down,
may Bactrians stripped of weapons surround your judgement-seat.[182]

are also found in Livy 10.46.3, in his account of the sumptuous triumph of Lucius Papirius
Censor in 293 BC.

179 The Capitol was the traditional destination of the triumphal procession, and saw
members of the defeated armies in chains, and floats carrying the victor's spoils and pictures
to illustrate their defeat (Beard [2007], see index s.v. Triumph: 'Placards', and 'Models and
Paintings'). Bocchus, the name of two kings of Mauretania centuries earlier, is here a typical
name for an African king, with Geiseric the real target.

180 The Pyrenees were often known as 'Alps'; the 'great sea' is the Mediterranean, and
the 'smaller seas' various bays or straits; the Syrtes (cf. line 549 above) denotes the desert.
S. will be proud as he walks in front of the chariot praising the emperor's successes; but
first and foremost he will rejoice that Majorian conquered for him, the humble poet. Two
short Latin words in 596, here 'conquered for me', recall the phrase in line 10 'conquered
for yourself' – this line and the present one are arranged almost symmetrically in the poem
– where it was suggested that the earlier words might have been thought disingenuous, even
sarcastic, in which case S. could be seen as now putting that right in this imagined acknowledgement of Majorian's achievement and his own personal gratitude.

181 S. claims to see the same expression in Majorian's face as when the emperor was
once giving pardon, perhaps to S. himself (see on c. 4); this can now encourage the city's
inhabitants.

182 May the emperor, if he succours Lyon, enjoy the revival of Carthage (Byrsa, as in
Vergil, A. 1.367, and c. 2.351), further confusion of the Moors and success in remote places:
in Parthia, famous for the pretended flight of its cavalry (cf. c. 2.455), in Susa, the capital
of Persia, and in Bactria, where the picture is one of disarmed natives waiting around the
tribunal to receive justice. The last two places recall the list in Claudian c. 7.201–3, addressed
to Honorius, but are developed in original ways.

Extended notes

(i) The rivers of Gaul (207–10)
The rivers are not chosen for their documentary value, but to give a general impression of Majorian's travels and adaptability. The first three, Rhine, Saône and Rhone, all of them large, roughly indicate Gaul's eastern frontier; then follow three substantial rivers of north-eastern France, the Meuse, Marne and Seine. Then there are some smaller rivers from the south: the Lot (presumably Oltis, as Loyen states; this is more likely than the Orb [Latin *Orbis*, mentioned by Mela, 2. 5, which passed through Béziers]); the Lez, a small river near modern Montpellier; the Allier (*Elaver*), known to S. perhaps through Caesar's account of the battle of Gergovia; and the Aude (*Atax*) in the far south-west. This last river and the one that follows it, the Waal (*Vacalis*), show the extent of Gaul; they could not be further apart. Gaul's longest river, the Loire, concludes the list, with an important change: it is used not merely for washing but for drinking, according to the well-known conceit used by classical and later poets.

(ii) The emperor's Master of Services (553–55)
Majorian's 'master of services' is nameless, but identified by most scholars as Nepotianus (*PLRE* 2.778). This man was one of three 'masters of services' holding the office at the time; two of them were designated *praesentalis* – that is, 'at the imperial court' – and were closely linked to the emperor's presence. One of these, Ricimer, had responsibility for Italy and is unlikely here; so the other *praesentalis*, Nepotianus, is probably meant. Less likely is Aegidius, companion and master of both services in Gaul at this time; a man less likely to be praised by S., even anonymously; he is never mentioned by S., a fact which to Harries (1994), 247 'cannot be fortuitous'. Mathisen (1979b), 607–10 opts for Nepotianus. Relevant office-holders are tabulated, and individuals briefly discussed, by Demandt in *RE* Suppl. 12.553–790, at 683 and 790.

(iii) The Roman Exemplars (556–7)
Sulla fought in many of Rome's wars in the late second and early first centuries BC. Fabius is the general especially famous for the delaying tactics that helped to wear down Hannibal in Italy (Livy 22–8 *passim*, with a summary in 30.26.9); the Latin word *genius*, which seldom equates to English 'genius' (but cf. 2.79), could do so here. The Metellus referred to gained the name of Pius for the filial duty showed in his efforts to restore his father from exile in 100–99 BC. Appius is Appius Claudius Caecus, censor in 312 BC, praised for his oratory by several classical writers. Quintus Fulvius Flaccus was consul and dictator as well as a leading general, one of whose achievements was the capture of Capua in 211 BC. M. Furius Camillus (2.526 and elsewhere) was a famous general of the (early) fourth century; the tribute may include his political as well as his military skills.

Poem 6
Preface to the Panegyric of the Emperor Avitus

INTRODUCTION

The theme of this preface is the common one of the Gigantomachia –
the battle of the gods of Olympus against the giants, often treated as an
allegory, as here. This presentation concentrates on the peerless figure
of Athena, whose miraculous birth from the head of Jupiter comes in the
nick of time and repels the attacks of the monsters. Athena foreshadows
Avitus, who has come to the rescue of Rome; he too is a combination of
great strength with outstanding wisdom. The tale is told by the minstrel
Orpheus, a favourite figure of Sidonius, who in various places in his poems
describes the countryside of northern Thessaly with which Orpheus was
especially associated. At the end of his song S. makes a comparison between
Orpheus's praises of his mother and his own encomium of his father-in-law,
Avitus. In this neat, colourful and amusing short poem, which is subtly
relevant to the wider goals of his panegyric, S. presents himself as well
versed in the classical tradition. Metre – elegiac couplets.

TRANSLATION

As with much song the joyful birth of weapon-clashing Pallas[1]
was praised by the Ismarian seer with Thracian lyre,[2]
as throughout Mopsopian Marathon[3] rivers stood still, amazed,

---

1 The phrase 'weapon-clashing Pallas', which actually forms the first two words of
the preface, was used by Vergil (*A.* 3.544) and certain epic poets after him, and provides a
spirited and serious beginning to the poems on Avitus, who is in some ways foreshadowed
by the goddess (see also on line *c.* 7.436, where Toulouse is 'city of Pallas').

2 This is Orpheus, often associated with Ismarus, a mountain range in southern Thrace.

3 The epithet 'Mopsopian' combines with the name Marathon, which here (and in
c. 15.35) denotes Attica, to make a sonorous phrase, while the recollection of Marathon,

while all the countryside ran after him, spellbound,[4]
as a sweet sounding hum was made by his plectrum on the strings, 5
they say that the goddess approved with praise these praises:
"O goddess, born during the crisis of the Giants' war,
emerging armoured from your father's parted head,
whom neither did Latona bear within the caves of Delos[5]
– she who would fix this wandering island for her children – 10
nor did the mother who, pregnant with Hercules, prolonged
his birth over a triple night in Cadmus' lands,[6]
nor did the woman whose tower was flooded with metallic rain
as the son begotten of gold seed filled out her womb.[7]
No: but when Phlegra's fields were looking to a panicking Jove,[8] 15
his head was split and shot you forth from out his brain,
and when it was brute force alone that spurred the gods to battle
and, without you, their powers were in gross disarray,
when once your father's head had given you birth, divine Wisdom,
then at once the gods really prevailed, when they had you.[9] 20
Through you, the structure built up by the giants' frightful hands,
almost stretching to the fiery firmament, crashed down.
Pindus, Othrys, and Pholoe fell from the Giants' hands,

best known for the famous Greek victory over the Persians in 490 BC, supports the poem's emphasis on brave warfare and strategic wisdom.

4 A paradoxical antithesis expresses the central picture of the Orpheus myth: the rivers 'stand', transfixed, but the countryside in general (literally) 'runs' (cf. *c.* 2.334). For other descriptions of such countryside, without the humour evident here, see *c.* 5.490–8, *c.* 23.181–95.

5 After Latona (Leto), though persecuted by Hera, was enabled to give birth to Apollo and Diana on the island of Delos, it received its firmly fixed position in the Aegean sea as a reward for its brave hospitality.

6 Hercules, son of Jupiter, was born to Alcmena in a night thrice as long as a normal night, in Thebes, a city associated with Cadmus.

7 Perseus was born to Danae, confined in a tower to keep suitors away, but visited by Jupiter in showers of gold.

8 Phlegra is the site of the war with the giants (cf. *c.* 9.88). The motif of panicking Jove (aka Jupiter), used also in *c.* 7.133–4, is derived from the poet Horace's politicising treatment of the theme in *c.* 3.4.49–52, and perhaps inspired by Claudian (see below).

9 The futility of brute force is a point made in implicit praise of the emperor Augustus in Horace, *Odes* 3.4.65, following four stanzas describing the gods' battle with the giants; they meet their match in Athena, who was often identified by philosophers with wisdom and rationality.

and massive Ossa now slipped from the grip of Rhoetus.[10]
Aegaeon, Briareus, Ephialtes and Mimas,[11] once wont   25
to brush the northern Plough with their heels, were all laid low.[12]
Your father felled Enceladus, your brother, Typhoeus;[13]
one undergirds the Euboean's rock, one Sicily's."[14]
Orpheus then switched and made his one and only theme his mother,
and taught his strings to celebrate Calliope.[15]   30
The Muses rose to cheer their sister's praise; his filial love
delighted the goddess even more than his music.

10 The mountains Pelion and Ossa are mentioned in many versions of the Gigantomachy;
S. has added other mountains of Thessaly from various poetic contexts. He does not state
explicitly, as many ancient versions do, that Ossa was piled on Pelion, or the reverse, or that
either was placed on Olympus, but the notion of mountains being picked up and falling from
the giants' hands in these lines provides a truly gigantic scenario. In his longer and more
vigorous description of the battle (in an epithalamium) the island of Lemnos is explicitly
weaponised (*c.* 15.25–6), as almost happens in Claudian, *Shorter Poems*, 53, lines 85–7.

11 The names of Rhoetus and Mimas were used by Horace in *Odes* 3.4.53–6; the names
Aegaeon and Briareus, normally considered to denote the same giant, are in Vergil (*A.* 6.287
and 10.565) and other poets. Mimas also figures in Claudian's short poem *Gigantomachy*
(*Shorter Poems* 53), at 85–8; and the name Ephialtes could be derived from Claudian's
treatment of the theme in *c.* 26.61–76 (at line 75), where the notion that Jupiter trembled (line
15 above, and later *c.* 7.133–4) is present. Other giants are included in the abovementioned
portrayal in *c.* 15.17–35, where S. gives an even more muscular rendering.

12 The giants were often depicted with snaky feet (cf. *c.* 9.79–81; hence the poet's conceit
that they 'brush' rather than trample or kick the constellation. (Perhaps this notion is
modelled on Vergil's description of the fires of Etna 'licking the stars' [*A.* 3.574; the volcano
is mentioned in line 28 below]). In another Sidonian description of giants (*c.* 9.76–93) they
have feet that end in mouths, in lines 79–81.

13 Enceladus was killed by Jupiter's thunderbolt according to Vergil (*A.* 3.578); this is
alluded to in Statius, *Thebaid* 11.8 and Claudian, *De Raptu Proserpinae* 1.154–5. Vulcan, the
brother of Athena, has a general role in the abovementioned Horatian ode (lines 58–9); he is
not just opposing Typhoeus, as here.

14 The defeated giants were, according to most traditions, and in Vergil, buried beneath
volcanoes: Enceladus beneath Etna in Sicily (Vergil, *A.* 3.578–80), and Typhoeus beneath
the rocky island of Ischia, at Jupiter's command (Vergil, *A.* 9.716). Known to the ancients
as Inarime, this island is supposed to have been founded from the Greek island of Euboea,
whence the epithet here. S.'s couplet is similar to that of Claudian's in *c.* 27.17–18 ('Enceladus
and conquered Typhoeus were my song: one sank under Inarime, one massive Etna subdues')
in interesting ways: the names of the two giants frame the first line, as here, and the next line
does not, in Latin or the English, state unambiguously which giant was where – perhaps a
deliberate riddle.

15 Calliope, leader of the Muses, and a Muse herself, was mother of Orpheus.

But if to sing a mother's praises wins acclaim, and if
to equal the ancient music is beyond my powers,
then my poem's hero is Avitus, father of his people:[16]   35
my theme is greater, even if my Muse is less.

16 More important than the pallid contrast of mother and father (line 33) is S.'s (modest)
contrast with Horace, and his declaring the superiority of his theme, Avitus: cf. *c.* 4.18.

Poem 7
Panegyric of the Emperor Avitus

INTRODUCTION

Avitus and his Gallo-Roman supporters arrived in Rome in the second half of the year 455, and he was duly appointed consul for the following year. Sidonius, his son-in-law, aged perhaps twenty-five, was no doubt heavily involved in preparations of various kinds, and was tasked in particular with the delivery, on 1 January, of the panegyric of the new emperor and consul; a suitable choice of a learned young man and stylish writer, already with ambitions (one might guess) to be involved in politics, and already perhaps foreseeing a career as some kind of court poet like Claudian, whose panegyrics he knew well.

The task he took on, to commend Avitus to the senate, was certainly not straightforward, and there were many difficulties. In this and a later poem he introduced bitter complaints by Gallo-Romans that they been sidelined and left out of government; the underlying conservatism of many decades would be working against him. There was known opposition in Rome, both from individuals such as Majorian and Ricimer and from vested interests within the senate. The involvement of Avitus with the Goths, based in Toulouse but with wide territorial ambitions, would have been no secret to his peers. The ancestry of Avitus was perhaps less impressive than Sidonius made out (and may have been overestimated by modern scholars: (cf. *PLRE* 2.196: it was 'very distinguished', following his exaggerations). He, Sidonius, whatever his talents, was inexperienced, though no fool and no callow youth. The greatest challenge in the long term was the military situation, the need to defeat the Vandals – this would indeed be paramount and inescapable throughout his lifetime – which was fluid and threatening. The previous year in Rome had been turbulent in the extreme. The emperor Valentinian III had been murdered by Petronius Maximus, who thus put an end to the Theodosian dynasty, which if nothing else had been stable, and who after the shortest of reigns was himself killed when the Vandals invaded. The strong points of Avitus, according to Sidonius in this the most biographically orientated of his three panegyrics, were that he had a good legal brain, or at least was good and effective at drafting treaties, that he was a first-class general, and that, in broad terms – this is a leitmotif of the panegyric – he had shown himself to be very resourceful in a crisis.

Most of the panegyric's 602 lines (123–598) present a speech of Jupiter in essentially narrative mode (but regularly including speeches by others) delivered to a council of the gods that he has just convoked. Its atmosphere of calm and dignity is rudely broken by the entry of Rome (such divine journeys happen in panegyric, just as they do in epic), bedraggled and crestfallen. Rome gives a pitiful and despairing speech lamenting her long decline and her present parlous condition (51–118). Jupiter gives reassurance: he too knows the power of Fate and the inevitability of its fluctuations; in the present sad case he has a solution (123–38).

Following the conventions of panegyric, he begins with the birthplace of Avitus, Arvernum, a most fertile area of central Gaul and also a source of great fighters. Julius Caesar's well-known problems in besieging nearby Gergovia are mentioned to reinforce that picture: Jupiter explains that he was preparing the race for its present opportunity. Avitus has a long lineage, and claims to nobility: strangely, he has by his elevated rank made his ancestors famous, but we are not told more. His father (never actually named), aware of Avitus's destiny, diligently guided his boyhood, and some interesting (but minor, as Sidonius admits, in line 187) pursuits – hunting with dogs, and with birds of prey – are recorded. His mind was developed by studying poetry, and also Cicero, and he read books on warfare and military tactics.

Thanks to his legal studies he was chosen to negotiate for his fatherland on a substantial issue, and won the admiration of Constantius, who soon afterwards was briefly emperor, and obtained from him relief for his region from a heavy tax (207–14). He also impressed the Gothic king Theoderic; this was when Avitus visited a kinsman who had been given to the king as a hostage. No doubt (though this is implied rather than stated) he also impressed the outstanding general Aetius, whom he later accompanied in numerous battles, in some cases leading Roman armies against races that destabilised parts of south-eastern Gaul (now largely Austria). Notable weight and literary colour is later given (242–94) to what might have been passed over as a minor incident; it involved a Hunnic soldier, serving under Litorius, another Roman general, who attacked and killed a friend and fellow citizen of Avitus in a sudden clash. By his dramatic narrative in full epic style S. makes it vivid, indeed Homeric; it is one of the poet's memorable *tableaux*, a kind of centrepiece, and leaves in the mind a vivid picture of Avitus's strength of devotion as well as his prowess in fighting. But he is also the maker of treaties, and within a few years a prefect (296), and by creatively renewing a treaty (nothing is known of the details) he checked the expansive ambitions of Theoderic and his Goths when leading Roman generals were powerless. A greater enemy (and a strong enemy of the Goths) was the Huns: in the ensuing crucial defence of Gaul in 451 against an enormous host of Huns and many other races Avitus's role is presented as pivotal, and more significant than the vacillations of the once great Aetius.

Synopsis

1–16 Invoking the sun-god, and Janus, the poet addresses the senate and praises the new emperor.

17–44 Jupiter, father of the gods, summons all the gods to an assembly.

45–58 Rome enters, a piteous sight (45–9), and bursts into a lament deploring her decline and lack of safety after her promising beginnings all those years ago.

59–100 Rome reviews the challenges of her subsequent history, successfully overcome thanks to a host of heroes.

100–18 She regrets the way in which she, Rome, has been somehow merged with the successive emperors, whom she quickly enumerates; reaching Trajan, she wonders if an equal of the great Trajan might be forthcoming, from Gaul, perhaps?

119–38 With sympathy from the assembled deities, Jupiter begins his reply – which fills all but the poem's last four lines – with consolation and encouragement: it happens to him too, and Rome has always come through her ordeals.

139–63 Jupiter describes the region of Arvernum, fertile in crops and in warriors, birthplace of Avitus.

164–206 The birth of Avitus, and his early days.

207–29 His early experience of negotiation, and his acquaintance with the Gothic king.

230–40 Avitus engages in warfare on the borders of eastern Gaul, serving under Aetius.

241–94 Soon after this, after a sudden attack on Arvernum by marauding Huns, Avitus pursues and kills a Hun in single combat, so avenging a murdered servant.

295–315 As praetorian prefect, Avitus frustrates Gothic expansionism
   with a renewed treaty.
315–56 Faced by a massive invasion of barbarians, the general Aetius
   pleads with Avitus.
357–91 There is a crisis at Rome, with the execution of Aetius by the
   emperor Valentinian III; he is succeeded by Petronius, who
   appoints Avitus as his commander-in-chief.
392–430 Avitus goes to Gaul and negotiates with Gallic leaders.
431–40 An alliance is made between the Gothic kings and Avitus in
   Toulouse.
441–58 Rome is captured by the Vandals; immediately reacting, the Goths
   call a council of their elders.
458–86 Avitus addresses this council, and his offers of peace and a treaty
   are well received.
486–520 The reply of king Theoderic; the treaty is then confirmed.
521–30 Avitus has reservations about taking power, but a large crowd
   creates a platform for him.
530–71 A senior figure from among the Gallo-Romans makes a speech
   supporting Avitus.
572–97 Avitus is made emperor; Jupiter looks forward with great
   expectations.
598–602 There is loud applause in the council of the gods; a Golden Age
   is woven by the Fates.

TRANSLATION

Phoebus, who are to see, at last, in the world that you traverse
someone that you can bear as equal, give your light to the heavens;
for the earth, this man gives light enough. Nor let the zodiac,
which Marmaric Atlas grazes with his head, flaunt any more
its stars, this man has his own.[1] Just as the stars sparkle anew   5

---

1 Phoebus (the sun), the heavens and the stars of the zodiac form a strong opening
prayer and a striking backdrop to Avitus, whose light is all-encompassing on earth. Atlas
is the god who gave his name to the mountain range in north-west Africa (the epithet
'Marmaric' is used in general for 'African', and not, as originally, for a specific part
of Africa) and in myth was considered the upholder of the sky, including its stars. The
words about Avitus's stars (that is, his fates) are few and cryptic; interest in an emperor's
horoscope was a sensitive subject.

after their setting, so does Rome shine in adversity, Rome
whose way has ever been to grow by afflictions. Now she rises
with the emperor consul. Surely, O senators, you rejoice to see
the rods combined, and to have voted a curule chair to join
the sceptre; but, believe me, you will give much more: chariots.[2]   10
Now, double-headed Janus, join the hair of both your foreheads,
and be girt with twofold laurel.[3] Glorious was the emperor's year;
now too is this, the consul's year, glorious. Your *trabeae*
exalt the diadems already gained.[4] No need to fear,
my Muse, because Auster has caught our sails;[5] we have begun   15
to cruise on fame's ocean. Behold the star to keep us safe!

As it chanced, the Father of the gods looked out from the heaven at the earth,
and lo, all that he saw was flourishing; to behold the world
was to restore it; just his nod alone makes all things thrive.
And now, to muster the gods, the winged god of Tegea flies,   20
now using his winged feet, now his winged brow.[6] Scarcely has he
landed on earth, passing the whole length of his grandfather:[7]

2 The 'rods' of authority (*fasces*: see on *c.* 2, line 1), those wielded by both consul and
emperor, are now combined in one person. A 'curule' chair (line 9) is a chair of state used by
certain high-ranking magistrates. The mention of chariots here implies an eventual triumph
for Avitus when the Vandals have been defeated (cf. lines 587–91 below). Triumphs of the
traditional kind were by now very rare, but the imagery remains potent.

3 Janus, the god of the new year as well as the old (hence his portrayal in art with two
faces), must now be suitably decorated; cf. *c.* 2.8–9. In the present case laurel, suggesting
victories, is apt. The language is suitably traditional, with one epithet of Janus from Vergil,
A. 7.180 ('with twofold foreheads'), the other ('double-headed') from Ovid, in a didactic
poem (*Fasti*, 1.95).

4 For the *trabeae*, see *c.* 2 n. 3; for diadems – here in the plural, for effect – see *c.* 2 n. 5.
Lines 13–14 here make the paradox that a consulship enhanced the position of an emperor,
as in *c.* 5.6.

5 The trope of the small boat, signifying poetic inability, was often used by Latin poets
when declining an invitation to write panegyric, but not here. S. has begun, and is confident.
The name Auster often denotes the south wind, feared by sailors; Loyen (1960) sees in it a
reference to the Vandal enemy, likely to sail with it from Carthage.

6 Mercury was born in Arcadia, in southern Greece, of which Tegea was a leading city.
He is regularly depicted with wings on his forehead and feet.

7 The expression echoes Vergil's description of Mercury's descent to earth in Vergil,
A. 4.258 ('on his way from Atlas, his mother's sire' [tr. Day Lewis]), but S. goes for
humorous parody, as if a reclining grandfather of unusual length is part of the long way
down from the sky.

at once sea, land and air send their own gods. Brother of Jove,
you are the first to come, you who are wont to cleave the sea
in sea-green chariot and spread calm over the marvelling main.   25
Phorcus accompanies the dripping Nymphs, and you come too,
O grey-green Glaucus; you too, Proteus, surest of prophets
were there, for sure.[8] Behind them come others in a long line:[9]
vine-clad Bacchus, ferocious Mars, shaggy Tirynthian,
naked Venus, fertile Ceres, quiver-bearing Diana,   30
relentless Juno, prudent Pallas, turreted Cybele,
Saturn the exile, wandering Cynthia, youthful Phoebus,
panic-inspiring Pan, the uncouth Fauns, the saucy Satyrs.
In the assembly, too, were those who dwell in heaven by merit:
Castor, for horsemanship, Pollux for boxing, Perseus for   35
his scimitar, Vulcan for his thunderbolt, Tiphys the helmsman,
Quirinus for his race.[10] What man could sing heaven's court, whose pavement
the shining stars themselves provide? Now, all serene, the father
assumes his place on the golden throne, and then the leading gods

8 Neptune, brother of Jove, is accompanied by the sea-god Phorcus and his retinue
of nymphs (Vergil, *A.* 5.240, 824), by another sea-god, Glaucus, who is grey-green as his
name suggests, and by Proteus; according to Vergil (*Georg.* 4.387–400) Proteus knows past,
present and future, but is hard to catch (note the words 'for sure') because of his disguises
and changes of form. This triad accompanies the sea-god Nereus in Claudian's *De Raptu
Proserpinae*, 3.11–13, where the narrator's assurance that Proteus would in the divine
assembly 'remain in his true shape' might have led S. to make the point in his own way.

9 Each god in this list is described by a single adjective, in a favourite Sidonian mode of
condensing the presentation of several items. 'The Tirynthian' is Hercules, born in Tiryns,
shaggy because of the lion skin he wore; Juno is relentless, as she is depicted throughout
Vergil's *Aeneid*; Cybele (also known as *Magna Mater* ['the Great Mother']) wears the
turreted crown that she has in Vergil (*A.* 6.785), in later poets, and in many artefacts; Saturn
is described as an exile from Olympus; he was ousted by Jupiter (Vergil, *A.* 8.319–20);
Cynthia is the moon. The quality chosen for Pan is (for the wordplay) that he can create
panic. Like Pan, the Fauns and Satyrs are deities of the countryside.

10 In lines 34–7 we have what is in some ways a surprising collection. Vulcan was
fully divine, as son of Jupiter and Juno. Castor and Pollux enjoyed divinity for six months
in each year, on the timeshare principle (Vergil, *A.* 6.120–1). Perseus, associated with the
sword or scimitar with which he rescued Andromeda, became a star, and so was immortal,
but not a god; neither was Tiphys, the pilot of Argo, the first ever ship, considered a god.
Romulus, founder of Rome (also known as Quirinus, as here), and so very appropriate to the
poem, had been seen ascending to heaven and was honoured as divine. Hercules, already
mentioned in line 29, who was made a god for his labours, could well have been presented
here rather than above.

sat down (it was permitted for the rivers, too, at least   40
the older ones) to sit:[11] for you, mightily flowing Po,[12]
and you, the swelling Rhine, chopped up by blond Sygambrians
for drinking, and you, Danube, ridden through by wandering bands
of Scyths, and you, Nile, better known for having a hidden source.

Then, from a faraway, elevated region of the sky   45
came Rome, dragging her sluggish feet, with face downturned, neck bowed;
from her head her hair hangs limply down, covered with dust but no
helmet; her shield dashes against her feebly moving legs;
the spear she carries is a mere dead weight, not a dread threat.[13]
And having cast herself at the feet of the kindly Thunderer   50
she spoke: "I call to witness you, divine father, and the
godhead which I, Rome, used to be: quite crushed by my huge fate,
I envy those who are abased; the weight of a vast roof
a small house cannot bear. Lightning does not molest the valleys.
What did the Etruscan seer, I ask, with his twice six vultures,   55
predict for me?[14] O why, when building walls for my young race,
was I already exalted by the omens, at the time

11 The joke about the seating arrangements derives (though it may be older) from Claudian's description of the assembly of the gods in *De Raptu Proserpinae* 3.14–16, where older rivers sit and younger ones stand, 'in the plebeian manner'.

12 The Italian Po is described in Vergil, *G.* 1.482 as 'king of rivers'; according to Vergil, *G.* 4.372–3, there is no more violent river. The Rhine is described here as both 'swelling' and frozen (it could be either); the Sygambrians, living on the east bank of the Rhine, are said to need to break the ice to drink. Vergil draws a chilling picture of the frozen Danube at *G.* 3.360–2; it could be crossed in carts, as mentioned in *c.* 5.519. The source of the Nile was famously unknown.

13 Claudian drew a sad picture of weak and bedraggled Rome at *c.* 15.17–25, worried that her end had come, which focuses on her shield, her unruly hair and her rusty spear before her long speech denouncing the usurper Gildo to Jupiter (lines 28–127). By contrast, S. concentrates on her lethargy as she presents herself to the assembly (46–9).

14 This prophecy, based on the twelve birds that appeared to Romulus (see next note), forecast for Rome a lifespan of 1,200 years from its foundation date, reckoned to be 753 BC. It was known to Varro, the antiquarian of the first century BC, and is alluded to by Claudian, *c.* 25.265–6. The statement of Gibbon (1776–88, chapter 35) that it 'inspired the people with gloomy apprehensions' may be exaggerated; on the available evidence, it was not a major part of fifth-century anxieties. The fact that the exact 1,200 years (twelve ages) had passed some time ago would not remove all worry; as Loyen (1960), 182 points out, the length of *saecula* ('ages') could vary. See also lines 357–8 below.

when you, poor Romulus, on the peak of an Etruscan hill
dug my foundations?[15] I felt much more confident in my sword
when in a perfect storm Rutulians and Veientines,   60
Auruncans, Aequians, Hernicians, Volscians together
were pressing.[16] Even to you I seemed quite strong when the woman rent
her abused body with the knife and you, her stolen modesty,
returned to the chaste wound,[17] when Tarquin and the Etruscans hemmed
me inside my wall. Oh, the flames of Mucius, and Cocles' leap![18]   65
Oh, the grief! Now where is he who brought under my rule the Samnite,[19]
Gurges, and he who slew the fleeing Volscians, Marcius,[20]
and he, dictator and exile, who scattered the Senones?[21]

15 These omens were seen, as walls were being built and foundations dug, when Remus
and Romulus were disputing where exactly the city should be and what it should be called
(Livy 1.6–7 and Plutarch, *Romulus* 9.4–5). S.'s account emphasises the Etruscan background
(55, 58; cf. 64), perhaps hinting at an atavistic suspicion of Etruscans by the distraught
speaker.

16 In the words 'perfect storm' (more literally 'a combined whirlwind') the speaker
exaggerates. These attacks (but Rome herself was sometimes the aggressor) were to a
large extent not joint ventures against her or continuous wars, and S. compresses several
centuries of history. Hostility between Rome and the Veientines lasted for most of the fifth
century, until the capture of Veii in 396. The Volsci, often accompanied by the Aequi,
were regular enemies of Rome in the fifth century; the Hernicians then were staunch allies
of Rome, but gave trouble in the fourth century (Livy 6.2–10, 7.6.7–12). The Rutulians
and Auruncans have a low profile in the history of the early Republic and probably owe
their inclusion here to Vergil's *Aeneid*, where they are mentioned together, as opponents
of Aeneas, in 7.795 and 11.318.

17 The legend of Lucretia ('the woman') in Livy 1.57–9, was famous and much debated.
S. declares, unlike Augustine (*City of God*, 1.19) when advising Christian women, that
Lucretia's modesty, which had been stolen or ravaged by Tarquin, was restored by her suicide.
The poet's direct address to 'modesty' (or 'shame') may have been inspired by a similar
apostrophe given to Dido in Vergil, *A.* 4.27, although such apostrophe (see introduction) is a
common feature of his style.

18 When threatened by Rome's enemy Porsenna, Mucius Scaevola held out his hand to be
burned, showing his contempt of pain (Livy 2.12–13). Horatius Cocles destroyed the bridge
that would have allowed the besieging enemy within the walls and, leaping into the water,
swam, fully armed and under fire, to safety (Livy 2.10). Claudian at *c.* 8.406 and 18.445
refers to them both, highlighting the flame and the bridge, emblems of their heroism.

19 Quintus Fabius Maximus Gurges defeated the Samnites at Sentinum in 295 BC (Livy
10.30).

20 This refers to the role of Marcius Coriolanus in the capture of Corioli in 493 BC, after
the repulse of a relieving force (Livy 2.33.5–9).

21 The repulse of the Gauls, including the Senones, who may have been the leaders of the

Would that the life of Fabricius was mine, and the death of the
Decii, to conquer like the one or, like the other, be conquered![22]   70
Give me back my early days! Alas, where now are those parades
with rich triumphs but poor consuls? My spear then terrified
the Libyan world; I placed the yoke three times on treacherous Carthage.[23]
The Indians' Ganges, Phasis of Colchis, Armenia's
Araxes, Ger of the Ethiopians, the Goths' Tanais,   75
trembled before my Tiber.[24] Crushed with your Teuton ally
You, Cimbrian, submitted to me once; hands formerly
weighed down with swords I ordered to bear nothing but their chains.[25]
Alas, to think how great I was when by my orders Sulla,
Asiaticus, Curius, Paulus, and Pompey made demands on   80
Tigranes, Antiochus, Pyrrhus, Perseus, Mithridates
for peace and kingdoms, banishment, tribute, prison, and poison.[26]

Gallic invasion in 390 BC, was credited to Marcus Furius Camillus, dictator in that and other
years but subsequently exiled. Books 5 and 6 of Livy relate the stories of his achievements
and career. He is an important figure for S., present in each of the three panegyrics (c. 2.526,
c. 5.557 and line 563 below).

22 Caius Fabricius Luscinus (consul in 282 and 278 BC) was famous for his poverty and
austerity, as well as conquest; Publius Decius Mus (consul, died 340 BC) and his son (died
295 BC) for their 'devotion' (sacrifice) of themselves, along with their enemies, to the gods
of the Underworld.

23 There were three wars against Carthage ('Punic' Wars): in 264–241, 218–201 and
149–146 BC. To the Romans 'Punic perfidy' was notorious (cf. line 445 below), and a main
theme of propaganda.

24 Distant rivers are used, as they were by poets of Augustan Rome, to mark out a
vast area within which Rome's power received or deserved respect. Each of the river
names here is used quite commonly by Claudian, except for Ger (which he calls 'the best
known river of the Ethiopians'), which occurs only at c. 21.252. This may have suggested
to S. the idea of adding the name of an appropriate people in each case, for ornament, of
course, rather than information. The Tiber stands for Rome, as if sharing her power, and
so earning reverence.

25 The invading Cimbrians and Teutones were defeated by C. Marius in 102 and 101 BC
(cf. c. 2.230–1), victories mentioned again in c. 2.229–31, c. 9.256–8 and c. 23.18–19 and
472. The word 'chains' suggests his celebratory triumph. S. shows a degree of pride in these
successes in southern Gaul.

26 This sentence consists of three elaborately constructed lines, of which the first gives a
list of victors, the second a list, in the same order, of their five opponents, and the third a very
brusque list of the five kinds of loss that each enemy was made to suffer; a good case of the
poet's stylistic finesse. The arrangement is formally impressive, but not historically exact;
see Extended note (i).

I pass over the Sarmatians, the Moschians, and the Getae,
accustomed to drink bloodstained milk and spice their drinks from their veins,
and Parthians who the more they flee, the more they should be shunned.[27] 85
Nor is it enough to mention land wars; with gleaming weapons
I have with you as guide entered so many seas, and distant
races beneath the setting sun.[28] Caesar, victorious,
carried his standards all the way to Caledonian Britain
and even though he overcame the Scot, the Pict, the Saxon,   90
sought out new enemies, though Nature barred further searches[29]
for men that he might attack. Leucas beheld you, fierce Augustus,
crush Egypt, when the fleet's soldiers convulsed the seas round Actium
and drunken Antony, his troops in headlong flight, thrust out
the impure daughter of the Ptolemies from her ancestral realm.[30]   95
And though I earlier complained of the world's narrow extent
I am now not a frontier to myself.[31] Highest of the gods,
I seemed to you more powerful than was right, because Parthian
Sapor gave back my standards willingly, and, with tiara

27 The Moschians were a little known tribe (at least to Pliny *NH* 6.13), linked with the
better-attested roving Sarmatians of Lucan 3.270 (linked also in *c*. 5.477). Here a simple
name is enough for his purpose, especially as they are 'passed over' (with the rhetorical
figure of *praeteritio*). The Getae here (a Thracian tribe) are not the same as the contemporary
Goths, whom S. also calls Getae. Not all of these tribes drank blood or spiced milk with it;
perhaps none did. The Parthians (or Persians) were famous for their tactic of feigning flight
and then rounding on the enemy with deadly volleys of arrows, as at the battle of Carrhae in
53 BC (see on line 100 below) and *c*. 2.454–5.

28 Summing up the picture of Roman expansion, S. makes a very apt and almost verbatim
quotation of a line and a half in Vergil, *A*. 6.59–60, where Aeneas describes his far-ranging
travels undertaken at the command of Phoebus Apollo; Rome over the centuries has done
likewise.

29 Caesar's activity in Britain marks a north-western boundary to this broad picture of
the empire. His activity in Britain is elided, but at least S. knows of the 'conspiracy' of Picts
and Scots and others in the 360s that Amm. describes in 27.8.1–8 (cf. also 26.4.5).

30 The battle of Actium, near the island of Leucas in north-west Greece, at which Octavian,
the future Augustus, defeated and put to flight Mark Antony and Cleopatra, daughter of
Ptolemy XII, king of Egypt, took place in 31 BC (*c*. 2.471 and, more pictorially, *c*. 5.456–61).

31 In this pithy sentence Rome refers to the invasions of Rome by Alaric in 410 and
Geiseric in 455 (see lines 505–6 and 441–9 below, respectively). From being short of lands to
conquer (lines 87–92), Rome has seen her walls breached by others.

set aside, mourned, as he atoned for them, the deaths of Crassus's men.[32] 100
And then, with the removal of the authority (alas!)
of people and senate I suffered what I feared: I am
synonymous with the emperor, entirely his property;
a queen once, now I am, through many a Caesar, a realm in shreds.[33]
Tiberius's Capri, Caius's bootlets, led to   105
the censorship of Claudius, and Nero, a man only
in dying;[34] Galba, made respectable by dour Piso,
you, Otho, slew, you who aspired to look good in your mirror
but disgraced me. Vitellius's vile greed brought me a paunch,
which though it reigned for but a short time, expired far too late.[35]   110
Next, quite worn out, Vespasian, famous in warfare, held me;
then Titus, then his brother; next was the quiet Nerva,
made greater by the Caesar he adopted, who began

32 The Roman standards lost when the Parthians defeated Crassus at Carrhae in 53 BC
were restored to Rome in 20 BC by King Phraates IV. This terse account of the relationships
makes no distinction between Parthians and Sasanids, and uses the generic kingly name
Sapor to suggest the once fearsome Sasanid adversaries Shapur I and II. See also *c.* 2.457.

33 Loyen (1960), 182 notes briskly and briefly that the capital had been Ravenna, not
Rome, since 402; but in her distressed exaggeration Rome surely suggests much greater
damage than the transfer of the imperial court could have caused. (On the actual impact
of that, see Gillett (2001) and Humphries (2012), and my note on *c.* 23.305.) However, the
concentration of power in the various imperial capitals in the fourth century, as practised by
individual Caesars, such as Constantinople (Constantine) and Trier (Valentinian 1), though
important in military terms, might be seen as contributing to the general decay alleged
here. Lines 101–2, after an unexpected harking back to the rule of 'senate and people' (a
traditional phrase not paralleled elsewhere in S.) introduce quickfire comment on the growth
of the principate in the first centuries BC and AD, and help to explain the poet's momentary
republicanism.

34 Tiberius's retirement to Capri is prominent in Suetonius, *Tiberius* 39–44; the origin
of Gaius's name Caligula in the small military boots he wore as an infant is explained in
Suetonius, *Gaius* 9, and also Tacitus, *Annals* 1.41. In the parallel and very similar (slightly
later) passage that describes these emperors at *c.* 5.320–7 S. describes the name Caligula as
shameful or degrading, and there too he picks out the censorship of Claudius, who became
unpopular when he revived this office (Suetonius, *Claudius* 16). Nero showed some dignity
in his death (Suetonius, *Nero* 49), after a self-indulgent life.

35 For Galba's adoption of Piso see Suetonius, *Galba* 17, and for Piso's severe and
inscrutable character Tacitus, *Histories* 1.14. Otho's vanity mirror, a theme highlighted
again by S. in *c.* 5.323–4, is mentioned by Juvenal in *Satires* 2.99–101 (this is no doubt his
source), and the gluttony of Vitellius by Suetonius, *Vitellius* 13.

to make me again myself.[36] Then came Trajan, by whose labours
the colony Agrippina became feared by the Sygambrians.[37]   115
He was brave, devout, upright, eager. A captive now, I pray
for such a man – can anyone equal him?[38] – unless perhaps
you, Gaul, could once more send a conqueror." Tears choked her voice,
and grief delivered any other pleas that she had. As one,
heaven's leaders rose in sympathy: Mars, Venus, Romulus   120
and all the gods that helped you, Rome; even Saturnia
is moved to kindness and abjures her ancient grievances.[39]

Jupiter answered in these words: "Fate, by whom everything –
myself included – is governed, could not be broken. Great
things always suffer, and your power, by my own gift raised high,   125
made Fortune envious of herself. But be of great courage,
enfeebled as you are. If raging Porsenna took fright
even more after the bridge was cut, if your surrounded walls
saw Brennus soon take flight,[40] and if we drove fierce Hannibal back

36 As in *c*. 5.327, little is said here about Vespasian and his military victories, and there is
even less about Titus and his brother Domitian. In the last case, it is a matter of his general
ignominy; he is not mentioned, for example, by Pliny in his panegyric of Trajan included in
the collection recently made by Pacatus (*Panegyrici Latini*). The speaker hurries on to the
highly regarded Trajan, adopted by the short-lived emperor Nerva.

37 The colony of Agrippina (where the city of Cologne now is) was the centre of the
province governed by Trajan when he was made emperor there, in 98 AD. Trajan is honoured
by the implicit contrast between the alleged fearsomeness of the Sygambrians then and their
relative quiescence in the fourth and fifth centuries.

38 Trajan was considered the ideal emperor by writers in Late Antiquity: according
to *Anonymus Valesianus* (also known as 'Excerpts of Valesius') II, 12.60 the Ostrogoth
Theoderic (*PLRE* 2.1077–84) was called Trajan by the Romans of the time, and even
saw Trajan's times as exemplary. Trajan was born in Spain, part of the prefecture of the
Gauls; hence the implication that Gaul could again 'send' him to Rome to be emperor. His
fame at this time is reflected in the Forum of Trajan in Rome, a highly important space
in the urban landscape (with many statues, including one of S. himself: see *c*. 8.7–8 and
Ep. 9.16.3, verses 25–6). It was, according to Amm. 16.10.15, 'a construction unique under
the heavens'.

39 The hatred of Juno (Saturnia) for Rome is for Vergil (*A*. 1.8–33) the fundamental
reason for his hero's sufferings throughout the poem. In Claudian *c*. 15.130, after Rome's not
dissimilar plaint about Gildo, when the other gods break into tears, Juno simply 'does not
have dry eyes'.

40 For Porsenna's attack on Rome and subsequent siege, see note on lines 64–5, and
c. 5.66–80, and for the invasion by Brennus, leader of the Gauls, *c*. 5.80–4 and lines 561–2

with a tempest that combined uproar from heaven and earth (when his camp 130
already stood close by your walls, a thunderbolt shot forth
in front of the Colline tower, and Nature feared that there, once more,
as at Phlegra, Jupiter was fighting in panic)[41] – then lift
your drooping, sleepy eyes, and let the clouds of doom and gloom
be wiped away and banished from your minds. For you, to be sure,   135
to be conquered is a miracle; when you begin to conquer,
it will not be.[42] To make it clear how you can arise at last
from your fatigue, I will explain in a few short words; listen.

A land is mine, which proudly claims to be of Latin blood,[43]
a land renowned for men, a land to which Nature, lavish   140
creator, never formed an equal. From the city extend
fields rich and fertile, which when barely touched by the early plough
thirst for the awaited seeds, and, giving oxen an easy time,
present a pitch-black soil endowed with some secret richness.
To this land, baked by torrid southerly winds, the soils of the Nile   145
and of Libya, give pride of place;[44] the fields of Gargara,
always compared to them, have been condemned as arid by
Mygdonian scythes; Apulia's and Calabria's farmers yield.
The world's sole hope, Arvernian, who live here, in armed combat
on foot you yield to none, on horseback beat anyone. Let Caesar   150
– whose Fortune here was very fearful – be my witness: when
driven from Gergovia's hill his soldiers scarcely stopped running,

below. S. redeploys references to these two made in Claudian *c.* 15.123–6, where they mark
the depths of Rome's despair.
    41 When Rome came close to capture by Hannibal in 211 BC, a great storm drove
Hannibal from the walls (Livy 26.11); interpreted as a thunderbolt, this recalls Jupiter's panic
when fighting the Giants (*c.* 6.15; Claudian *c.* 26.64); in the present case Jupiter admits that
he fears Hannibal on Rome's behalf. This event was seen by the Romans as the gravest
danger in their history; in the opinion of the philosopher Themistius in the fourth century
only Hannibal approached the Goths in terms of the terror he caused (Lenski [1997], 162).
    42 A strong assurance from Jupiter to inspire the Romans, which is placed so as to
highlight Avitus, the new saviour.
    43 The place is Arvernum, modern Clermont, and the people the Arvernians (addressed
in line 149), who, in the words of the poet Lucan (1.427–8) were proud to claim brotherhood
with Rome on the grounds that they too had Trojan blood. The claim is alluded to in *Ep.* 7.7.2.
    44 Gargara, which is in the Troad, in north-west Turkey, is mentioned for its fertility by
Vergil, *G.* 1.103, and by Pacatus in his panegyric of Theodosius I (*Pan. Lat.* 2(12).4.4). Apulia
and Calabria are in the south of Italy.

even in their camp.[45] This enemy I willed to be so strong,
but only while preparing to give you, Rome, Avitus,
whose line, having embraced the highest families, shines bright,   155
whose consulships run back to distant ancestors, whose race
glows with patrician worth as you, Philagrius,[46] attest.
But what a small part of his praises is the praise of forbears,
who owe their consulships and prefectures to their descendant!
There may be others of whom their most recent issue boast,   160
and others who can count their families by old titles,
but only you, Avitus, elevate your ancestors.[47]

Now I will tell this great man's feats and sketch his early life.
When in childbirth his noble mother had freed her chaste womb's weight,
I quickly gave clear signs of the future emperor, and filled   165
the anxious father's whole residence with auspicious omens.
Although he was uneasy with his son's great destiny,
yet realising already that the boy would be emperor,
he saw that in so great a child he had been entrusted
with an obligation to the world; and so that you, Rome, should   170
incur no loss, he zealously assisted Fortune. First,

45 The battle of Gergovia (52 BC) is described by Julius Caesar, *De bello Gallico*, 7.34–52. In speaking of the 'Fortune' of Caesar S. makes a skilful reference to the moment in the battle of Pharsalia when, in the words of the epic poet Lucan, Caesar's fortune seemed to be in trouble, indeed at a standstill (*Civil War* 7.547).

46 Philagrius, presented as outstanding among Avitus' ancestors, and the only ancestor to be named here, probably flourished in the fourth century, as evidenced by the title of 'patrician', a rank introduced by the emperor Constantine I (Jones (1973), I, 106); see also MacGeorge [2002], 5–6). (The poet's mode of addressing him does not of course imply that he was still living, nor does the fact that S. calls him 'severe' in *c.* 24.92–3 imply acquaintance; the word equates to 'studious': he owned a library). He was probably either the grandfather or great grandfather of Avitus. See PLRE 1.693 (Philagrius 4), 2.36 (Agricola 1) and 2.1317/8 (with stemmas 14 and 15). Nothing is known of him besides what S. says here, unless perhaps he is the same as Philagrius 2 in PLRE 1.693, who was *notarius* ('notary') in 361–3 (Amm. 21.4.2) and *comes* ('companion') in the East in 382; an origin in Gaul is not ruled out. A birth-date for him might be *ca.* 330, which is also likely for Philagrius 4.

47 If such holders of consulships and prefectures existed, they have not been detected; and at the time few if any listeners would know otherwise. It is unusual in a panegyric for a person to be said to have made ancestors distinguished, as if, in the words of Anderson (p. 130, note 3), 'their distinctions came to them because it was ordained that a descendant should be Emperor'. In other words, they would not be famous but for Avitus.

he exposed his tiny limbs to snow, and told his infant son
to break ice with his feet and laugh at frost when he ground it down.
His growing mind was shaped by the Muses, and by Cicero,
with whose rhetoric you, Rome, are now thundering;[48] also   175
he learnt the deeds of your former generals; he learnt of battles,
studying in books what he might do on the battlefield. Scarcely
had he left infancy for boyhood, when, as it chanced, he slew
a wolf, raging with bloodstained jaws and seeking food for her young
and not just them, with ravening mouth; with the fallen rock he had seized 180
(there were pieces nearby) her head, crushed by the boulder, was
split into fragments, and the rock held fast within the wound.
Just so did my son Alcides, while wandering in the glens
of Nemea, meet a monster while unarmed, not carrying
club or quiver; with angry shout, he bravely held his ground,   185
and though surprised, with the beast so close, relied on his strong arms.[49]
Some feats are small, but must be told. Who was quicker than he
to lower to the scent a chained Molossian hound's tensed neck
and from its expert nostrils, not by sight, to locate beasts
lurking deep in their dens, and to sniff out their tracks in the air,   190
and if by chance his Umbrian hunting dog should terrify
a boar with its relentless barking, it was his delight
to break open the white crescents under its black throat,[50] and
with straining arm to thrust his massive spear through his victim.
How fine a sight it was, when, coming home from the wilds he appeared 195
all splendid in a boar's rough skin, and his bashful courage
betrayed after such brave feats an unwilling modesty![51]

48 Cicero is seen as the creator of the rhetorical expertise shown by educated Romans in general (including, of course, S. himself, when he writes in prose, as in the *Letters*), which influenced not only public speaking but the style of laws and other official documents that Rome thundered forth.

49 This refers to the labour of the Nemean lion, in which, according to some versions of the myth, Hercules's bow and arrows proved useless but his muscle prevailed.

50 The cartilaginous crescents or 'moons' indicate places in the animal's throat where the windpipe might be severed.

51 Though sometimes thought verbose, S. here expresses complex meaning most concisely, as may be seen by comparing the paraphrase of Semple (1930), 92, acute as it is: 'the veritable picture of a gawky lad! His valour was reluctant to praise itself: his modesty was therefore apparent: but his modesty in turn was unwilling to appear because of his brave exploits which deserved display.'

Just so in the Pandionian fields of the chaste Tritonis
did Hippolytus beam brightness from his rose-coloured visage
at the time when the woman of Crete, ablaze with double fury   200
surpassed all mothers in desire, all stepmothers in guile.[52]
What should I say of his passion for the birds of prey that nature
creates to harry almost cognate species? Who more adept
than he to teach them to make varied raids in the clouds? With a bird
he conquered birds, and as they swiftly swooped through the air no bird's 205
talons fought better for a master than theirs did for him.

Amidst all this, with no less zeal he followed civil law,[53]
and was first choice, although a youth, to go, alone, and bind
the wounds of his afflicted fatherland and seek relief
from a monstrous tax. At the time the strongest of the nobles there   210
was Constantius, later emperor;[54] he granted everything,
astonished by such talent and amazed to see such flair
at a young age and hear from the mouth of the young petitioner

52 The young Hippolytus, son of Theseus, king of Athens (Pandion too was a king of Athens) was an enthusiastic hunter who rebuffed the amorous advances of his stepmother Phaedra, daughter of Minos of Crete. She gained revenge by falsely accusing him of rape, before killing herself and causing him to die an awful death.

53 In this section S. moves from illustrating Avitus's early years, with their evidence of courage and endurance, to narrating his contribution to public and political life, in which qualities of wisdom and learning are apparent, as foreshadowed in the preface to this poem.

54 Constantius was emperor for a few months in 421 (details in *PLRE* 2.324) and in the ten or so years before that held three consulships and was continuously master of services; he received the title of 'patrician' (*PLRE* 2.321–5) by 415. His period of supremacy in Gaul is illuminatingly studied in McEvoy (2013), 187–220. His eminence in this region, which surely refers to southern Gaul (Ravenna, mentioned by Anderson, is not likely), enhances the prestige of the young Avitus, who impressed him when perhaps still in his teens. (Avitus was probably born *ca.* 400 or just before). The meeting took place before February 421, when Constantius became emperor, and its date was perhaps 418; Loyen (1960), 183 and (1942), 37 relates the episode to the re-establishment of the assembly of Gallic provinces at Arles in 418. He suggests that the tax was a fine imposed because of help given to the usurper Jovinus, Augustus in the years 411–13; but the tax, although vigorously denounced by S. as 'monstrous', need not have been punitive, but was rather (supposing exaggeration here) a smaller matter such as a levy made for the pay and provisioning of the army (Anderson, note 4, pp. 134–6). Whatever the issue, it would be surprising if at such an important event the young Avitus had been the only representative of Arvernum, even with his powerful connexions. Similar precocity is ascribed to the young Procopius, father of Anthemius (*c.* 2.75–85), and, in a different sphere, to Majorian (*c.* 5.524).

an elder statesman's words. Now, Rome, I will relate with pleasure
our leader's battles and treaties with kings. Struck down by varied   215
tempests of war your Gaul was charged to give the Gothic king[55]
pledges of peace. Among them you, Theodorus,[56] went, a noble
hostage, whom you, Avitus, out of loyalty to kin
actively sought out at the heart of the skin-clad monarch's court,
safe through your loyalty. Theoderic soon approved of this   220
example of commitment. It is marvellous, and worthy
of record, that by personal charm you could please a violent king.
From then on in his deepest thoughts he enjoys a foretaste of you
and deeply wishes you to be his; but you disdained to play
the friend rather than the Roman.[57] Though amazed by this rebuff   225
he liked you even more. Just so did you, Pyrrhus, once find
Fabricius resolute, when he, a poor man rich in soul,
shunned the wealth offered him, scorning the king, who employed his wealth
as advocate, and with cheap gold begged for a pledge of friendship.[58]

Then you followed Aetius, expert in Scythian warfare,[59]   230
who, albeit a supreme general, without your assistance

55 The Gothic king is Theoderic I (418–51: *PLRE* 2.1070–1), who succeeded Wallia late
in 418. In line 219 he is the 'skin-clad monarch', a mild paradox, but one in which, in this
context, neither word is pejorative.
56 Little is known of Theodorus (Theodorus 12 in *PLRE* 2.1087), presumably a young
man of high rank. Loyen's date of 418 for the demand for hostages gives good sense to the
phrase 'varied tempests of war' of lines 215–16, for the years before that date were indeed
turbulent in Gaul, and certainly 'varied', with the invasion of Vandals, Alans and Sueves and
other wars of the years 414–16, not to mention risings of usurpers and other matters (Loyen
[1934], 409). Alternatively (*PLRE* 2.1087), this episode could come after the resolution of the
wars of 425/6 mentioned by Prosper (s.a. 425), though these seem to have been less vivid or
varied.
57 These words of concise comment make clear that Avitus could be expected to take a
robust position with the Vandals too, and not, for example, show the friendliness ascribed to
Eudoxia, widow of Valentinian III, who invited Geiseric to be emperor (*PLRE* 2.411: John of
Antioch, fragment 201.6).
58 For Fabricius see n. 22 on lines 69/70, and for this famous meeting with Pyrrhus, the
king of Epirus who invaded Italy, Plutarch, *Pyrrhus* 20. This episode is set after the first of
his wars against Rome, in 280 BC; a later situation is used in c. 5.424–30.
59 Aetius was the obvious choice of commanding officer for an ambitious young soldier
like Avitus. Probably some ten years older than Avitus, he was for a long time the most
powerful person in the Western Empire. There is a full and detailed narrative of his life
and exploits in PLRE 2.21–9 (Fl. Aetius 7), a brief synopsis in Anderson, xv–xx, and the

achieved nothing, while you achieved, without him, a great deal.
For after dealing with the Iuthungi and the Noric wars,
having vanquished the Vindelicians, he freed the Belgae,
whom the fierce Burgundian had overwhelmed, together with you.[60]   235
There the Herul was surpassed in running, the Hun in throwing spears,
the Frank in swimming, the Sarmatian in shieldcraft, the Salian
in footwork, the Gelonian in swordplay;[61] in bearing wounds
were surpassed any for whom wailing means self-harm, gashing of cheeks,
and grubbing out of bloody scars upon their frightful faces.[62]   240
He gained, as early as this, the title of 'illustrious'.[63]

comprehensive monograph of Stickler (2002). The statement that Aetius was an expert in Scythian warfare (the word 'Scythian' here as often indicates 'Hun', as in lines 246, 280, 304), is not immediately clear, but it is surely Aetius's long experience of fighting with them, not against them, that is meant. Harries (1994), 67–75 brings out how the relationship of Aetius and Avitus is presented by S.

60 The Iuthungi (a tribe north of the Danube that threatened the province of Raetia; described in Amm. 17.6.1 as a branch of the Alemanni) were defeated in 430 (*Chron. Gall. 452*, item 106). Avitus presumably fought in this campaign and in one or both of the wars in Noricum (roughly, the eastern Alps) against the Nori, mentioned by Hydatius 83 [93] and 85 [95] (years 430 and 431). He alone is mentioned by S. as victor in the war against the Vindelici (near modern Augsburg) soon afterwards; and he fought in the war which freed the province of *Belgica Prima* from Burgundian occupation in 436 (or perhaps 435), fighting together with Aetius, as S. explicitly states; this point may be intended to reduce or remove from Avitus the suspicion of blame arising from this war. Nothing is said by S. about its sequel in 437, when the Burgundians were crushed even more, with the help of Aetius's Huns; Hydatius 99 [108]and 102 [110], and Thompson (1996), 72.

61 These lines (236–8) describe very manneristically the warfare of Aetius and Avitus and their auxiliaries, in which the Romans,or at least their two leaders, surpass their numerous tribal detachments, surely auxiliaries rather than enemies, even in their special skills. The style of this passage was imitated by Jordanes, *Getica* 261, in his description of the battle of the Nedao in 454: he specifies seven tribes, each fighting with a different weapon or tactic.

62 The final, less compressed, detail about bravery in bearing wounds recalls explanations of the Huns' habit of tearing their cheeks when mourning. Maenchen-Helfen (1973), 360–1 points out the inadequacy of Ammianus's explanation at 31.2.2 (that it is done to check the growth of hair) but is wrong to attribute the same misinterpretation to S. Claudian mentions the custom (*c.* 3.327–8), with no explanation, and Jordanes (*Getica* 255) describes it in the context of the mourning for the dead Attila.

63 The title *illustris* was the highest of the three grades of senators, awarded to those who had held certain high offices of state (specified in Jones [1973], 528–9), including some that were military. Avitus is not known to have held any of these, and so this award might be honorary, as Anderson inferred; but S.'s policy in his narrative is to select salient events rather than detail every step of his honorand's rise, and he may have passed over episodes that could not be presented with vivid detail. In line 462 (where Avitus looks back over

In armour scaled, the bruises from his bright helmet still showing,
scarcely had he conveyed his stained equipment home from camp
when, once again, a treacherous enemy stirred up new wars
and picked a fight beneath the very walls of his own city.[64]   245
Just then Litorius, mighty with the Aremorici subdued,
was speeding with his Scythian horsemen against the Gothic army,[65]
Arvernian, through your territory; here everything in range,
by raiding, burning, fighting, rioting, and pillaging,
they laid to waste, and made a travesty of the name of peace.   250
By one of them, one fiercer than the rest (but soon himself
to be struck down) a servant of Avitus was wounded;
the poor man fell, commending his sad fate to his master,
and, dying, took down to the Styx the hope of revenge to come.
And now news of this villainy reaches Avitus, guarding   255
the towers and gates and anxious for the fearful populace.
He starts, he stops; he pales, he reddens; he is cold, he is hot;
anger, varying in a single face takes many different forms
and, as is usual in one who mourns, he loves the one
that he has lost even more deeply.[66] At last he bursts forward   260

his career) three offices that preceded his prefecture are mentioned without elaboration.
Anderson (p. 139 n. 6) declares that the title of *illustris* must have been bestowed as an
honorary distinction, but this explanation is not necessary. Nor is it certain that S. has
'antedated' the award; Anderson is surprised that a Gallo-Roman should reach that dignity'
at such an early stage in his career, but gives no reason.

64 The latest, it appears (line 244), of a succession of enemies is a Hun whose treachery
is to attack Arvernum, the home town of Avitus. This man was one of a troop of Huns in the
army of the Roman general Litorius, who had just put down a rising by the Aremoricans in
north-western Gaul, perhaps allied to the Bacaudae (these were local brigands: Thompson
[1996], 137–9), and was speeding via the Auvergne, doubtless avoiding the Gothic territory
of Aquitaine, towards Narbonne, which was under siege from the Goths.

65 Litorius was Roman military commander in Gaul in the years 435–7, and by 439 was
according to Prosper second in power to Aetius, perhaps 'master of soldiers' in Gaul (*PLRE*
2.684–5). The date of his victory is given as 436 by Prosper.

66 The Huns had evidently lost all their discipline and given themselves to plunder and
worse. Avitus, guarding the walls and gates of his fellow-citizens (no mention is made of
any official position), was enraged when he heard that a servant of his was fatally wounded;
Avitus sought out the culprit and killed him in single combat. S. has developed this episode
into a picture of Avitus's intense anger (but nevertheless he makes a quick decision, unlike
Aetius in lines 334–5) and his strong devotion to one of his own fellow citizens. Schindler
(2009), 182–98 expertly brings out the centrality of the episode and its epic features, but
unnecessarily adopts the idea that the engagement was an 'everyday experience', which it

and shouts for his arms, his arms! he is brought his breastplate thick with blood,
his pike blunted by wounds inflicted on barbarians,
and his sword indented and made rough with incessant slaughter.
He sheathes his legs with greaves, and then places upon his head
a shining helm, which with its golden apex rising high   265
hurls like a weapon angry flashes from his head.[67] And now
he mounts his horse and tearing gates from their hinges shoots forth.
Courage, Anguish and Shame attend their champion. Unwearied,
with his pike he attacks armed troops, and by fighting seeks his real fight,
and among the panicking enemy ranks makes many pay with death   270
because a single man made himself scarce. Just so, while with
Emathian spear he sought the conquering Trojan champion,
did the grandson of Aeacus keep in check his mourning for
his slaughtered friend, content to rush through piles of Trojan corpses
(whole companies being worth nothing to him) and wield his sword   275
among the numerous hordes; the land flooded, o'er whelmed with blood,
and as the falling multitude makes blunt his heavy weapon
the absent Hector, to his mind, falls dead with every blow.
When finally the man responsible for such mayhem
showed up, Avitus addressed him: "Come on, you crazy man,   280
you foster-child of the Scythian Bear[68] who pride yourself only
in slaying an unarmed man, engage with one who is armed. Already
my wrath has made you a great gift: I have granted to you
a duel, but resist you must. I want to kill a fighter."
With that he leaps into the plain; his wild enemy comes also.   285
As soon as they bring close their chests and faces, one man trembles
with rage, the other with fear. The rest of the multitude now shudder

surely was not. In all the excitement of chase and combat the reader should not forget the
fact that the Hun is serving under a Roman general, so that in what follows Avitus was 'in
the position, technically, of a local leader attacking detachments of the official Roman army'
(Harries [1994], 75). S. has nothing to say about this; Litorius, the commander of the Huns,
may have been unaware for some time, as he sped on.

67 Avitus sallies out on horseback, his greaves as necessary as for any Homeric fighter on
foot. As for his helmet, 'Hector of the flashing helmet' was a common description in Homer's
Iliad. His awesome qualities as a fighter are glorified by recollection of Homer's scenes of
Achilles putting on his armour to avenge his friend Patroclus and slay Hector (*Iliad* 22.131–61),
and by hints of Vergil, notably *A*. 2.668 and 7.460–2, as Avitus calls for his arms (261).

68 The Bear (a constellation), also known as the Plough, is a pointer to the north pole, and
so not unsuited to a Scythian, insulted by Avitus as a denizen of the frozen north.

with their competing prayers and as they watch blow exchanged for blow
they hang upon the outcome. But after first and second bouts
and then a third have taken place, behold! from on high his spear   290
comes down and transfixes the bloodied foe. As the area of
his back is pierced, his corselet falls apart, burst open twice,
and as the bubbling blood drains through the double hole, as if
in rivalry the separate wounds consume his wavering life.[69]

After these feats (and, gloomy Styx, I call you to witness),   295
without unfairness he, as my prefect, applied the laws.[70]
When it accepted him as her leader, exhausted by
habitual destruction, Gaul was shocked by Gothic rage
Aetius was broken, getting nowhere, whether by prayer
or bribes or war,[71] Litorius captive, loss of land loomed large;[72]   300

---

69 Avitus's blow 'from on high' seems to have run right through his enemy. The nature of
Hunnic armour has been carefully studied by Maenchen-Helfen (1973), 241–53, who declares
it unlikely that Huns fought without the protection of armour; in this case the 'corselet' (line
292) will have been 'a metal shirt', which offered less protection from behind (p. 249, quoting
Procopius, *Wars* 7.2.22). In Ovid *M.* 9.129 a single poisoned dart creates a wound back and
front, as S. could well have recalled.

70 Avitus was praetorian prefect of the Gauls in 439, with responsibilities to administer
the laws (mentioned again in lines 312–15), and remained so probably until summer 440
(*PLRE* 2.197–8). The mention of this elevated office – and with it a guarantee, with the
strongest oath known to the ancients (by the river Styx in Hades) that he discharged it
incorruptibly (were there suspicions?) – is made to pave the way for what is presented as a
great feat of diplomacy (308–11) in difficult circumstances.

71 In the following episode S. gives the whole credit for restoring peace to Avitus's
document (308–11), not even mentioning the arrangements made by Aetius in Gaul (*PLRE*
2.26). His strong condemnation of the ineffectiveness of Aetius is very different from the
praise of Aetius by Merobaudes in his partly extant panegyrics; conversely Merobaudes
had nothing to say about Avitus' role in his *Panegyric* 2.14–22, where it might have been
expected. The difference is very eloquent; each panegyrist has his own patron (see further
Harries [1994], 73). Aetius actually did good (if indirect) service in Gaul with his roving
army, and was honoured by the senate and people of Rome with a statue in probably 439
(*PLRE* 2.25) for assuring the safety of Italy against Burgundians and Goths. Another factor
ignored by S. is the losses inflicted on the Goths by Litorius, albeit temporarily, which could,
in the opinion of Anderson (144 n. 1), have 'persuaded the king to come to terms with the
Romans ... as much as the diplomacy of Avitus [did]'.

72 Litorius had been wounded and captured after a rashly undertaken battle near Toulouse
in 439 (*PLRE* 2.685). The chroniclers who mention this (Prosper, Hydatius, Cassiodorus, all
under the year 439) suggest that he was soon put to death; but according to Salvian (*On the*

To extend his boundaries to the Rhone was the firm policy
of king Theoderic; there was no need for the Goths to fight,
but just migrate. The fierce victor redoubled his mad rage,
blaming people that he had seen the Scythian foe before
his walls.[73] There is nothing more dangerous than an anxious man   305
should he ever win a victory. Since there was no support
anywhere, and nothing, Rome, left for your generals, you renewed
the treaty, Avitus; when the text was read, the king relented;
for you it is enough to have ordained what the whole world seeks.
Will future races, future peoples, ever believe this thing?   310
A Roman's letter quashed your victories, barbarian.[74]
Here, then, he applied the laws; it was entirely apt that one
who will be maker of laws should then have been their champion,
so that the one given to the world, its leader, head and emperor,
its Caesar and Augustus, should know more than just fierce battles.[75]   315
Having discharged the most elevated office of prefect,
he had turned to the country at last (though rest or unwarlike
leisure was no concern of his, and his eagerness and care
for armed conflict remained), when the barbarian lands, bursting
explosively, discharged the whole of northern Europe into   320
you, Gaul.[76] The fierce Gepid, along with the Gelonian,

Governance of God 7.39–43), perhaps less credible, but not necessarily contradictory, he wasted away in a barbarian prison for some time. In line 300–1 S. mentions his capture but not his death.

73 King Theoderic blames all and sundry for the fact that he had witnessed Huns (probably troops of Litorius) so close to Toulouse, the Gothic capital. His uncontrollable indignation – directed at no-one in particular – shows the implacable mutual hatred of Goths and Huns, explained in contemporary sources by the Huns' treatment of conquered Goths as slaves. See Thompson (1996), 182–3.

74 A written document, even (or especially) unread, works wonders (cf. line 400). But this action of Avitus is also unverifiable, and in answer to the rhetorical question of line 310 – a common ploy of poets and orators (cf. *c.* 2.24; Pacatus in *Pan. Lat.* 2(12).12.3) – posterity has been less ready to believe in this case.

75 In *c.* 5.295–8 S. notes the value of a similar pause, or variation, within Majorian's career.

76 The invaders led by Attila (line 327), 'all kinds of peoples, a fierce and infinite multitude', in the words of our best source, Jordanes, invaded Gaul in 451. After much devastation they were confronted by a mixed Roman army led by Aetius at a location known as the Catalaunian Plains (or 'Fields'), or *locus Mauriacus* (the former term denotes a large area roughly bounded by modern Troyes, Reims and Châlons-en-Champagne; the latter

follows the warlike Rugian, and behind the Scirian
the Burgundian presses; Hun, Bellonotian, Neurian
Bastarnian, Thuringian, Bructerian and the Frank
bathed by the Neckar's sedgy stream rush forth.[77] The Hercynian   325
forest, hewn by the axe, is felled for ships, and cover the Rhine
with alder-wood. Now Attila with his fearsome hordes had spread
into your plains, Belgian.[78] Aetius had just left the Alps,
leading a thin and straggling force, of mere auxiliaries,
not legionaries, wrongly confident and presuming   330
that the army of the Goths would come to his own camp.[79] But when
the stunning message reached him, as leader, that now the Goths
were awaiting the Huns – a foe they now almost despised –
in their own territories, he in perplexity reviews
all his plans and subjects his mind to swirling waves of worry.[80]   335
At last, uncertainly, he resolves to entreat the mighty man,

location has not been identified with any certainty). S. says nothing about the course of the
battle itself – that is not his aim – or its outcome, which was a crucial Roman victory and the
repulse of the Huns; what concerns him is the preliminaries involving negotiation between
Avitus and Aetius.

77 According to Heather (2005), 337 (and the helpful map on p. 331), six of the twelve –
the first five, plus the Thuringian (Rugian, Gepid, Burgundian, Scirian, Thuringian, Frank)
– are likely to have accompanied the Huns, as 'real subjects'; the others, he adds confidently,
'had nothing to do with the Hunnic empire'. Of these five – Gelonian, Bellonotian, Neurian,
Bastarnian, Bructerian – the last two may well have been suggested by Claudian c. 8.450–1 (that
is a short list of German tribes, in which the last word is significantly followed by a reference
to the Hercynian forest, as in S. [326]). The name Geloni is found often in Claudian, some nine
times, and in classical writers. The Neuri, a Danubian tribe, are attested by the geographers
Pliny (*NH* 4.68) and the geographer Pomponius Mela 2.14, and perhaps by Amm. (31.2.14). The
Ballonoti/Bellonoti raise interesting questions, discussed in Extended note (ii).

78 This loosely refers to the territory of the two provinces, Belgica I and Belgica II, that
occupied large swathes of northern Gaul.

79 The aim of S. in treating this episode is to show how Avitus rescued the combined
Roman forces from grave trouble in a situation where Aetius had risked letting them down.
His criticisms are that Aetius had a force that was small and straggling when he left the
Alps, weakened by its reliance on auxiliaries, and that he was late – a point also made by
Jordanes. As S. explains, Aetius wrongly expected that the Goths would come to his own
camp, whereas they presumably stationed themselves where they could best protect their
homeland of Aquitaine from the Huns if need be. Both Prosper and Jordanes praise Aetius's
foresight in particular, but this misjudgement evidently threw Aetius into despair.

80 S. emphasises this perplexity with two pivotal passages from Vergil's *Aeneid* which
capture the painfulness of decision making (*A.* 8.19–21 and 11.551).

and when he has collected all his chiefs, in their presence
he comes to him as suppliant and speaks the following words:[81]
"Avitus, saviour of the world, for you it is no new
boast that Aetius entreats you, for when you so wished,   340
the foe does no harm; wish, and he helps us.[82] You lead so many
thousands of men, checked by your merest nod, and your favour
is the only limit for the Gothic peoples;[83] though always
our foes, they keep the peace with you. Greatest of heroes, show
your conquering eagles; may the Huns, whose earlier flight once shook us, 345
again suffer defeat, and so help me."[84] So he pleaded, and
Avitus, promising, makes his plea a hope. He rushed away
at once, and roused the tractable anger of the Goths for battle.[85]
The skin-clad hordes followed the Roman trumpets, as the Goths,
hearing his name, rushed to enrol, afraid of being humbled   350
by the name 'pay-stopped', fearing shame, not loss of pay.[86] Avitus,
even then the hope of the world, leads them to war, though now (or rather,

81 The point that after deciding on this he collected 'all his chiefs' (337) may be meant
to suggest weakness; he needs support. A significant change in roles is further indicated
by the description of Avitus as 'mighty' (line 336); the word had been applied to Aetius in
line 231. Aetius is now presented as a suppliant to Avitus, albeit one showing residual pride
(339–40).

82 The immediate efficacy of Avitus' authority (cf. 306–10) is underlined by the snappy
syntax (340–1), using short words, in English as in the Latin, and by the neat switch from
past tense to a generalising present tense, which gives the tone of a regular happening.

83 The approval shown them by Avitus, and their concern about losing it, is a powerful
constraint on the Goths' wishes to expand (cf. lines 301–2). This short speech (= 339–46)
highlights Avitus's qualities of authority and leadership, especially in dealing with the
Goths.

84 The Huns' first defeat was at Toulouse in 439 (300–1), with Litorius; Aetius was absent
in Rome (PLRE 2.25–6), but his power (he actually speaks of 'us') was weakened thereby.
The second defeat could be hoped for in the coming battle.

85 This plea, or at least Avitus's initiative, bore fruit: besides local contacts, to which
he now 'rushed away', there is possible evidence that Avitus used the envoy Hesychius (see
PLRE 2.554 (Hesychius 10)), showing the channel of communication with Theoderic II in
Spain). In line 548 the king seems to refer back, in similar language, to this rousing of Gothic
anger.

86 A strong motive is the fear of being marked out, and being made to join the dishonourable category of the 'pay-stopped' (for which S. uses the Latin technical term). The
narrative of their enrolment is broadly reminiscent of a passage in Pacatus's speech in Pan.
Lat. 2 (12). 32.4, on the smooth combination of Huns and Alans in the army of Theodosius.

as yet) a private citizen.[87] Just so does Phoebus' bird[88]
bring cinnamon to its pyre on the Erythraean hill[89] and rouse
the whole community of birds; in obedient crowds they hasten   355
and the overcrowded air impedes the unfurling of their wings.

The Fates had now come close to fulfilling the twelve ages
forecast by the vultures,[90] (but you know your woes, Rome, how you do!)
when the mad eunuch Placidus[91] murdered Aetius;
the diadem had hardly settled on your head, Petronius,[92]   360
immediately there came a deluge of barbarians;[93] Rome

87 This refers to his future elevation: being (currently, in 451) not in office, he is a 'private'
citizen; when emperor he will not be. Jordanes *Gothic matters*, 187 confirms that he led them
in the war (line 352).
88 This bird is the famous Phoenix, a favourite theme of S.; he describes it also in
c. 2.416–17 and *c.* 9.325–6, 11.125 and briefly 22.50–1. In each passage except the last he
focuses on the cinnamon, a highly valued spice which, as various sources mention, was
essential for its funeral pyre. The point of this simile is not the common topic of the rarity of
the Phoenix, or its rebirth, but the obedient eagerness and density of the throng of birds. S.
takes up this point from a simile in Claudian (*c.* 22.414–20) where the focus is the admiration
of the Phoenix by all kinds of bird (even eagles), but does not use Claudian's short poem on
the Phoenix (*Shorter Poems* 27), in which the description of the innumerable birds occupies
three lines (76–8). On the Phoenix in general, see Van der Broek (1972).
89 The word Erythraean (also in *c.* 5.497, see notes) refers vaguely to the large region
surrounding the Persian Gulf and Red Sea, based on the commoner noun Erythrae (a
place-name, no less vague, as used in *c.* 2.447).
90 For this forecast see note 25, on lines 55–6. The words 'but you know' carry the weight
of 'you know only too well'). This line and those that follow present the changed and charged
atmosphere of the years 455/6; the potential and integrity of Avitus stand out in contrast and
show him a more capable emperor.
91 The name Placidus denotes the emperor Valentinian III, who had reigned since 425
(Humphries [2012]). His description as 'mad eunuch' is surprising, for he married and had
two daughters (*PLRE* 2.1138/9); perhaps S. has confused or merged him with his assassin,
Heraclius (*PLRE* 2.541), who is described as a eunuch in various sources, among them
Prosper 454 and Hydatius 152 [160]. For relations between Valentinian III and Aetius before
that, see McEvoy (2014), 251–72 and 296–8.
92 Petronius Maximus (*PLRE* 2.749–51) was emperor for less than three months
(mid-March to May 455).
93 This 'deluge' is perhaps more striking in the Latin, where there are just two stark words
(literally translated, 'immediately barbarism'). In fact the gravity of the situation is difficult
to assess. Loyen (note 66, referring to Loyen [1942], 53) speaks of a 'triple invasion', but the
particular dangers (about to be described) of 369–75 are otherwise unattested, and may well
have been exaggerated, even invented. They seem to disappear very quickly (388–91), and

seemed to the Goths captured and the earth about to yield to their rage.
Just as marauding wolves, when to their keen nostrils is revealed
a rich aroma from enclosed sheepfolds, rouse and inflame
their hunger, carrying in their eyes a picture of their prey,   365
cheating their appetite, with jaws wide open; already,
in their expectant hopes a tender lamb is crushed, already
the imagined prey is being crunched on their voracious palates.
Besides, the region of Aremorica was expecting
the Saxon pirate, who delights to sail the British waters   370
in a hide and cleave the green-grey sea in a sewn-together skiff.[94]
The Frank was laying waste the first German and second Belgian
provinces,[95] and you, fierce Alaman, were from the Roman side
drinking the Rhine, and lording it over both territories,
whether still as citizen or as conqueror.[96] But Maximus,   375
now emperor, seeing masses of land lost did the only thing
that was left, and as his master of infantry and cavalry[97]
chose you, Avitus. News of the office conferred found him
down at the farm, plying the teeth of an inward bending mattock,
or stooping over his curved plough and turning upside down   380
the unexhausted lumps of earth in his rich acreage.[98]
Just so in days gone by did you, an impoverished ploughman, come,

without trace. If the Goths were not peaceful, as the simile in lines 363–8 suggests, that is
more evidence of the value of Avitus.

94 The Saxons had occupied part of Britain (Salway [1981], *passim*) and, pirates or not,
they could well be expected in Aremorica. (For the Aremoricans, see line 247 and note 64,
and line 548 below). Saxons were already established in certain maritime regions of Gaul
(Loyen [1942], 53). S. draws attention to their boats, which may have been like seaworthy
Irish currachs (larger than coracles) today.

95 The provinces are the First German and the Second Belgic, which, conveniently, fit the
metre in that order. The Franks had been present in northern Gaul for many years, and to
judge from *c.* 5.213–20 were well settled in the area of the Atrobates (Artois); Loyen (1942),
53–4.

96 The Alamans if on the west of the Rhine would be conquerors, otherwise they were
ordinary members of the tribe. Cf. *c.* 2.241 for the description 'citizen'.

97 This is the full name for the office; see introduction. The picture of Maximus so soon
after his death is broadly favourable, unlike that of Valentinian III, or at least not antago-
nistic; no doubt the reason in the mind of S. is this recent promotion of Avitus, and perhaps
the fact that they had both been prefects in 439.

98 Unexhausted because of their great intrinsic fertility, a common theme in such
contexts.

Cincinnatus,[99] to assist your broken fatherland, when your wife
in front of the oxen clothed you with the *trabea*, and doors
of willow welcomed a dictator, as he brought back home   385
whatever he had not sown, and as his triumphal purple
weighed down by a muddy burden held cheap common or garden seed.
As soon as he had assumed the weight of office thrust upon him
you sent envoys, Alaman, to ask pardon for your madness,
the incursions of the Saxons ceased, and the Elbe's marshy waters   390
contained the Chattian.[100] Scarcely had a third moon seen all this[101]
when Avitus made his way to the peoples and lands occupied
by the fierce Goth, where the Ocean, driven by the tide, disperses
the ebbing Garonne over the cultivated fields, and where,
as sea collides with river, its bitter liquid sweeps over   395
the streams that are sweeter, and the saline water, pushed along
the river-bed passes through reaches unfamiliar to it.[102]

99 Lucius Quinctius Cincinnatus, in the traditional story, was called from the plough to
be dictator in times of crisis (458 and 439 BC). This exemplum is also used in *c.* 2.527, and,
implicitly, in *c.* 5.300–4; the theme of retirement to a farm is developed by Pacatus in his
panegyric of Theodosius (*Pan. Lat.* 2(12).9.5–7). The dictator's formal clothing (like the
consul's), as S. imagines it – the *trabea* or 'consular robe' (see note 15 on line 13 above,
and *c.* 2.2) and the purple toga, here called 'triumphal' (it had been part of the insignia of a
triumphing general) – is contrasted with early Roman simplicity, symbolised by the doors
of willow-wood (perhaps wickerwork), typifying resourceful poverty (cf. Ovid *M.* 8.659, a
simple bed).
100 There is no corroborative evidence of an embassy from the Alamans, or of the
cessation of Saxon incursions at this point, and if the Chatti were beyond the river Elbe they
remained there. Such things might well have happened in the new situation as a result of
Avitus' appointment, but are not recorded. Chattians are mentioned in Claudian *c.* 26.420 and
Gregory of Tours, *History of the Franks* 2.9 (quoting the lost historian Sulpicius Alexander).
The name *Albin/Albis* is found in Claudian *c.* 8.452 and 10.278. Suggestions that this was not
the Elbe were reviewed and rightly rejected by Loyen (1933), 203–11 and 321–4.
101 That is, within three months; typical poetic embroidery.
102 S. alludes to this tidal phenomenon, where the Garonne joins the Durance, in
c. 22.18–19 and 105–13, and briefly in *Ep.* 8.12.5 ('the back-flowing flood'). There is no
need to suppose, as some have done, that on this visit Avitus went to or through Bordeaux;
no doubt he had seen the tidal phenomenon at some other time, or at least heard of it, and
adds it to his picture. His journey was to Toulouse, many miles up the Garonne river, where
the Gothic capital was. (On the Severn estuary in England, the 'bore' can reach nearly two
metres in height and travel fast for twenty miles, as a strong high tide thrusts water into the
funnel-shaped estuary).

Here, as the Visigothic chiefs gave free rein to their war-plans,[103]
their anger was restrained by the rumour that Avitus,
equipped with an official document,[104] was now entering   400
the homes of the Goths, having cast off for a while a magistrate's
high status, and taken the role of an ambassador.[105]
Amazement seized the leaders and the Scythian senators[106]
alike; they dreaded that he might perhaps withhold his peace.[107]
Just so, when lightweight Phaethon in the fiery chariot   405
was snatched off course and daylight paled with fear[108] and the harmony
of the elements, disturbed by the blazing world became mad rage,

103 The Goths are called by their name *Vesi* (whence 'Visigoths') here and in 431, and
c. 5.476; the variation of S.'s normal *Geta* or *Gothus* has no particular significance. Their
fighting was about to begin, or perhaps already had begun; the metaphor of 'giving rein' is
imprecise. Kulikowski (2008), 335–52, following Anderson, speaks of their 'letting loose
the war they had planned', and assumes from this that a war had begun; a war which, he
speculates, was a civil war between the brothers Theoderic and Frideric. There is very little
positive evidence for this, at least until the warlike ambitions of Thorismod in 451–3 (*PLRE*
2.1113–14). On the other hand, the warlike moves of the Goths would fit very well into the
pattern of Gothic rage or fury against Rome that seems to be always near the surface, to be
unleashed by crisis or opportunity – or a leader's skills – as in lines 298–306, 348, 360–8. It
is an important part of S.'s presentation of Avitus that he alone (cf. 403–4) can control and
manage this rage. The simile of lines 437–40, adduced by Kulikowski (2008), is discussed
below.
104 The meaning here of the Latin word *diploma* ('official document'), which S. uses
nowhere else, is not clear. It indicates something more than a certificate authorising travel by
public post, its commonest connotation, and certainly conveys the notion that his presence
was authorised by another, presumably the emperor, and this is of course the main point.
105 Though an envoy was a person of some rank (Jones [1964], 572–5, on 'notaries')
Avitus's relative informality and humility are emphasised by elements of this rumour.
Doubtless he or his agents would have canvassed allies before a formal meeting was held.
106 In this line the words 'Scythian senators' denote the Gothic senate, or rather assembly;
the Visigothic chiefs of line 398. The various meanings of the word' Scythian' as used by S.
are analysed in the main introduction, section 9.
107 The interpreter of this passage has to choose between 'their' peace and 'his' peace;
the reflexive Latin word *suam* used like this may mean either. According to Anderson they
feared 'lest he should deny their peaceful intent' (and so were concerned that he might wage
war to put them down), but there is no sign or previous mention of a 'peaceful intent' as such
among the Goths. In the interpretation preferred here, they were afraid of being denied peace
by Avitus, called 'his' peace because Avitus had unique power to impose it.
108 There are two shades to the Latin word used here: it could mean 'pale' in the sense of
dimness (so Anderson: but can one envisage 'dim daylight' in this situation?) or 'pale with
fear', a conceit more typical of S.

and the surging heat, so close, raged over dried up lakes, and the mud
was parched in the seabed, now a dust bowl, then the pitying flame
of Phoebus by itself expunged the unprecedented heat.[109]   410
At this point it so chanced that one of the Goths, having reforged
a pruning-hook, was beating out a sword,[110] and with a rock
sharpening its point, a man whom war-trumpets always inflamed,
only too eager to bury the earth with mass slaughter, with his
enemies unburied; when he learnt that Avitus was coming,   415
he exclaimed,[111] "War's finished; give us back our ploughs. If I recall
the well-known idleness of earlier peacetime, more than once
this man has taken away my sword from me. For shame! Ye gods!
Can loyal friendship have such force? Why do you, loyal to me,
even to my disadvantage, threaten time-wasting treaties?   420
You bid us both to ensure for you a shortened road to peace
and to owe it to you. Who could ever credit this? See how
the Gothic kings, wanting to obey, belittle their regal power![112]
Nor can I even say that you avoid battle to hide
lethargy; though a strong man, you love peace. Already Avitus   425

109 The classic narrative of Phaethon's wild ride is that of Ovid (*M.* 1.750–2.328); S.
also knows the brief treatment in Claudian *c.* 8.62–9, likewise in a simile, with the poet
highlighting the orderly return to normality. There, as here, it is Phoebus that puts matters
right, not Jupiter as in Ovid.

110 This is the opposite of the biblical trope of 'beating swords to plowshares' (Isaiah 2.4
and Micah 4.3: a sign of peace), as in Joel 3.10. In his *Oration* 16.211b the philosopher and
orator Themistius speaks of Goths turning swords into agricultural implements.

111 In this speech (416–30) S. purports to give the musings of a typical Gothic farmer-cum-
warrior, showing what might be in his thoughts at this juncture (though they are remarkable
for one of 'rough mind' [431])· they include in particular the respect he had for Avitus, the
perceived 'loyalty' and trustworthiness of Avitus, and the complexity of the situation. As
often in epic speeches, the need for compression requires quick transitions from one point
to another. The speech is notably full of paradox: for example, in 420, 'to my disadvantage'
and 'time-wasting treaties', which are used as a threat; in 421–2, where the Goths' tasks are
'to ensure peace, and owe it to you' (almost a complaint that Avitus gets the credit?); in 423,
where the kings are said to make light of their own power in favour of Avitus. This imaginary
Goth, though usually eager for war, puts a strong case for peace under Avitus's terms and
reaches an apparently good compromise for himself by deciding to become an auxiliary in
Avitus' army, ready to fight and so without total commitment to the 'idleness' of peace.

112 Unless 'kings' is a generalising plural, or one looking back in time, the Gothic kings
meant are Theoderic II and either his brother Frederic (not formally a king) or the late
Theoderic I; the former is more likely, as relevant to the current situation (435–6).

breaks down the factions; and Messianus, sent on ahead,
curbs Gothic rage.[113] As yet you have given orders: we put down
our arms. What is there left for you to wish to achieve? That we
are not foes is a minor point; if I know you from the past
I'll be an auxiliary. Then at least I'll be allowed to fight."   430
While the Visigoth turned over such matters in his rough mind
the two parties had come into view. The king and the master
halted near each other, the latter erect with steady gaze,
the former reddening with joy, with blushes that craved pardon.[114]
Then all three, with joined hands, the king's brother on one side and   435
on the other side the king, strode into Palladian Toulouse.[115]
Just so, clasping their hands by the cushioned couches of the gods,
did Romulus and Tatius once arrange a treaty, when
between the swords of fathers and husbands enraged in battle
on Pallas' hill Hersilia had plunged the Sabine women.[116]   440
Then, Rome, the Vandal captured you by stealth, when off your guard,
and the Burgundian, with treacherous guidance, wrung from you

113 Messianus – not mentioned anywhere else by S. – was subsequently made a patrician
by Avitus, and died in 456 fighting as his commander-in-chief at the battle of Placentia. The
'factions' (or 'parties') that he curbs are those of the Goths, reflecting either their generally
fissile nature ('Gothic rage') or recent strife of some kind. There is no sign of a full civil
war.

114 Pardon, that is, for the aggressive preparations for war (lines 398–9); he would not
need pardon for his role in a feud with his brother, or a minor discord (see note 103).

115 The description of this important and carefully choreographed event is embellished by
describing the capital city as 'Palladian' i.e. 'city of Pallas (Athena)', recalling the opening
word of the preface to this panegyric. The word was used by the earlier authors and epigram-
matists Martial (9.99.3) and Ausonius (X. 3.11, XI.17.7 Green) in praise of Toulouse's cultural
attainments, and its presence here continues the praise of Avitus as a man of culture as well
as prowess in warfare and statecraft.

116 The description in this simile telescopes two passages of Livy's history on the
aftermath of the 'Rape of Sabines': 1.11 (the mediation of Hersilia, wife of Romulus) and
1.13 (the battle of kinsfolk: Sabine fathers versus Roman sons-in-law). The couch of the gods
(437), or pulvinar, strictly speaking an anachronism, adds to the solemnity of the scene. The
'hill of Pallas' is Pallanteum, founded by Evander's ancestor Pallas, where the city of Rome
would later be founded (Vergil, A. 8.54). This simile is unusual for S. in that there are three
parties, rather than one or two; given the choreography of this grande entrée at Toulouse,
this might be a hint of earlier discord between the brothers, but hardly of civil war. In terms
of S's poetics it is an unusual simile, but the treatment of it by Kulikowski (see n. 103) is
over-elaborate (and the simile is certainly not 'botched').

enough alarm and rage to massacre the emperor.[117]
What an outrage! The faithless trumpets of Elissa's Byrsa
once more screech out the cue for war, and for a fourth ordeal.[118]   445
What evil, Fates, have you been fomenting? The Massylian
phalanx had scaled Evander's citadel, Marmarican feet
walked on the hills of Quirinus, and Barce took away
the tribute that, when in captivity, she had once paid.[119]
Exile for senators, evils for the people, the emperor slain,   450
the empire captive – all this rumour carried to Gothic ears.

Next morning, in the Gothic way, a conference of elders
is brought together; they stand there, august in years but alive
with advice; their clothes are filthy, and dirty linen garments
on their emaciated backs become matted with grease;   455
their skin coats, hitched up, cannot reach their calves, their knees are bare,
and a vulgar knot holds up their boots, which are made from horse's hide.[120]

117 Various chronicles describe the assassination of the emperor Petronius Maximus
in some detail (and with considerable variation), but there is no mention in them of a
Burgundian or Burgundians (as in lines 234 and 322, metre necessitates use of the singular
form where a plural may be meant). The detail is not likely to have been invented, and he
or they may have instigated or furthered the murder, whether by stoning (Loyen [1960],
ad loc.), or perhaps by falsely offering protection or safe conduct. The text reads as if the
Burgundian(s) took advantage of the city's capture and the attendant mayhem, but there is
a multiplicity of sources for the invasion. According to *PLRE* 2.751, which is not free from
confusion, he was killed while in flight, after the Vandals attacked.

118 The preceding ordeals were the Punic Wars, which resulted in the placing of three
yokes (note 34, on lines 72–3) on Carthage, again called Byrsa (cf. *c.* 2.351, 5.600), and
denounced as faithless (cf. line 73), with the epithet poetically transferred to the trumpets.
Dido, queen of Carthage, was also called Elissa by Vergil.

119 The poetic adjectives *Massylus* (Vergil *A.* 4.132; used again *c.* 5.346) and *Marmaricus*
(Lucan 3.293, used by S. again at *c.* 11.103, used in line 4 of this poem) are each starkly
contrasted with the name of a Roman progenitor: firstly, Evander, the founder of the earliest
settlement at Rome, and then Quirinus (that is, Romulus, cf. line 36 above). The language
serves to bring out the ignominy now being suffered by Rome. *Barce*, mentioned in Vergil
(*A.* 4.43), which was several hundred miles away from Carthage, here denotes the Roman
province of Africa; she now takes back what she paid.

120 Cf. Amm. 31.2.5–6, part of his description of the Huns, who have faded garments
that remain on their bodies until they fall off in rags, and goatskin boots that make poor
footwear.

When these elders, respected for their poverty,[121] had entered
the council, and the king, at once, had called for words of peace,[122]
the general said, "I would have wished,[123] I admit, to have enjoyed,   460
untroubled in my ancestral fields, the quiet of retirement
for ever, now that having held three public offices
I have a fourth honour, the prefecture's crowning glory.[124]

121 The Gothic elders, old and wise but to a Gallo-Roman deplorably clothed and poor, are implicitly compared to the traditionally poor and frugal leaders and senators of early Rome, often idealised, as in the picture of early Rome by Propertius 4.1.12: 'skin-clad senators, rustic souls' and other such evocations. In line 58 of this poem the king Romulus himself was described as 'poor'.

122 The 'words of peace' required by the Gothic king are not necessarily 'proposals' (Anderson), for the amity of lines 435–6 above suggests that the issues had in effect been decided. Loyen's 'conditions' also seems inappropriate: Avitus in his speech does not set conditions, and the one 'condition' set by Theoderic in lines 500–4 is not one for the rank and file, or anyone else, to debate. The point of the council is to implement plans.

123 In this speech of Avitus (notes on details follow, below) S. is speaking in his own words, but may have known at least the gist of what Avitus said, or realised what Avitus wished him to say in the senate. The speech begins more or less conventionally with a mention of his public offices and a kind of 'recusatio', declining the opportunity of holding power (see c. 5.12 n.) and preferring a quiet life. He goes on to state that he took on the task required by the emperor (Maximus), which others had declined to undertake, buoyed by the chance of coming to the Goths. That possibility was crucial, and its mention shows a ploy calculated to win his listeners' goodwill. His main point (line 469) is that he required a renewal or reaffirmation of the treaty between them and the new emperor, necessary because of the dangers newly affecting the state (lines 361–3), and with the recent accession of a new king of the Goths (this happened in the year 453). The elder Theoderic, he argues, would have agreed with a new treaty if he were alive (lines 475–80). Avitus takes the opportunity to praise the former king's help and affability, but also (it seems) to correct impressions created in the brutal siege of Narbonne in 436/7, stating that it was he, Avitus, who had advised Theoderic to lift the siege. Turning to the present king, Avitus recalls how he had known him as a babe in arms, and had assisted domestically. There is strong emotion behind these passages; S. was a knowing orator. The speech ends on a powerful note, where Avitus asks for a guarantee of their old love (this is almost amatory language) and emotively tells the young king that he can take it or not, but if not, they will be refusing his peace.

124 What all these three offices were is not known; as noted on line 241, S. does not mention every step in the rise of Avitus. One or more was probably military (see lines 233–5, where his warfare in the armies of Aetius is mentioned, though not his rank; in Arvernum he may have held military office, so PLRE 2.197); civil office is not ruled out by line 315, which makes but a broad distinction between Avitus' legal and military experience, nor is it incompatible with the Latin word *militia* used here, which regularly means 'public office', not military service. The fourth honour, his 'crowning glory', was the praetorian prefecture, held in 439 (line 296 and 316).

But seeing that Maximus, till recently our world's ruler,
after countless rebuffs by leaders,[125] called on me, unaware   465
and far away, to attend to wars after the laws,[126] and wished me
to exchange the usher for the trumpeter, I eagerly
clutched at a duty by which I could come to you as envoy.
I seek from you the old treaty which, if perchance I had
so ordered, that old friend of mine, for whom to attend to Avitus   470
was always to increase his power,[127] would now be holding fast.
I used to manage Gothic matters in the past; you know
that often you knew nothing of my schemes till they were applied.
But fortune has removed my former soulmate,[128] and whatever
credit I won expired with your father. He had encircled   475
Narbonne (you were small then), a city enfeebled by disease;
his siege had compelled thousands, in despair, to eat foul things;
he had already grimly reckoned that it would detract
from his own plunder if by chance any of the besieged should die,[129]

125 It is not known what leading figures Maximus had unsuccessfully sought; it seems
that only Avitus was prepared and able to fill the breach (as he was uniquely able, earlier, to
cope with foreign attacks [lines 375–8], and the problem faced by Aetius [lines 336–46]).
The Latin word *repulsa* in line 465, which referred originally to defeat in formal elections, is
here, by a kind of reversal, applied to the emperor. In the context it cannot refer to military
defeats (which had not occurred), as suggested by Semple (98–9), or 'candidatures', as
Loyen suggests; the leaders had not been applying for the post. Modest hesitation was often
considered a fitting preliminary to holding office (c. 5.10–12 n.), but clearly the rebuffs were
more than that.
126 That is, after the prefecture. The usher is a minor member of the legal staff (cf. c. 5.563).
127 The old friend is Theoderic I, king of the Goths from 418 to 451; see lines 220–6.
S. claims that Avitus had contributed to his success, a sweeping statement not supported
by anything in this panegyric except perhaps lines 475–80, but that intervention hardly
increased his power.
128 Theoderic I is here described as almost an *alter ego*. S.'s use of the word *genius*, used
here ('soulmate'), is very varied, and sometimes very vague (as in c. 5.556): it is unlikely to
have its commoner meaning of 'patron' or 'divine guardian' here, for that would contradict
the tenor of the speech. The word 'former' may hint that Avitus was offering a similar
relationship to the younger Theoderic, perhaps twenty years old at this point (Kulikowski
[2008], 351), building on the details given in lines 481–3.
129 Anderson (p. 158 n.; also in his introduction, at xvi) speculates that the arrival of
Litorius (lines 246; 300) at the walls of Narbo (436–7), not mentioned by S., inclined
Theoderic to make a temporary peace, one negotiated by Avitus; but Loyen (p. 186 n. 85)
describes the contribution of Avitus as 'no doubt minimal'. Yet Avitus may have done more
than to help dissuade the elder Theoderic from his grim purpose and crude reckoning of

when, accepting my advice, he freed the city walls from war.   480
And as for you yourself (there are old men here to attest it),
this chest has cherished you, these hands have held you, if you cried
as your nurse took you from me against your will, to give you milk.
Look, I am here, and ask you now for a pledge of our old love.
But if you have no loyalty, no reverence for your father,   485
go on, be unyielding, say no to peace." Then there burst forth
yelling and shouts from the entire council; denouncing war,
the unruly throng stirred up a concordant tumult.[130] Then the king
spoke out, "Renowned leader, I have for a long time complained
that you seek peace when you are well able to impose on us   490
even slavery,[131] or drag to war our tractable people.
Do not, I pray, shame me by mentioning my father's name;
how can I merit that, if you give no orders?[132] What in
his day you could have urged it is now enough simply to wish;
the sole delay is the Goths not knowing your desires. Through you   495
have I long rejoiced in Roman laws; as a small boy, my father
told me, in keeping with your words, to learn Vergil, so that
his ancient page could with its measures calm my Scythian ways.[133]

possible spoil, though S. is silent. For the horrors of the siege, compare *c.* 23.59–68, where S. describes its severe physical effects.

130 There is strong verbal paradox here: tumults are by definition not harmonious, and this throng is not obviously unruly or seditious. S. revels in the irony, as the Goths are acting contrary to their nature (or their reputation). Semple (1930), 99 suggested that the implied attack on Roman territory by the Goths with Avitus at their head was 'technically sedition', but even if that is 'literally true', as he claims, that is not a suitable point for S. to make here, as they are 'denouncing warfare'.

131 Taking them to war is as unlikely as imposing slavery – which is unthinkable.

132 Without orders he cannot deserve to achieve anything worthy of his father. The point is made that his followers need, in general, the orders of Avitus.

133 As well as developing a delight in Roman laws and (503) a respect for the Roman senate, he claims that he was introduced by Avitus to Vergil (who would be studied by reading aloud). The date of his Vergilian studies, or their duration, can only be guessed; Theoderic was a small boy in the year 437 (lines 474–6 n.) – he might not have been born at the time of Avitus's visit described in lines 215–29 – and Avitus was prefect soon after that, in 439, and unlikely to be available then. Boys learn Vergil at many different ages, and indeed Avitus's contribution could well be overstated. The use of the word 'Scythian' of his own character indicates a feeling of humility and awe towards Roman culture in one who is a mere Scyth (see earlier note in *c.* 2.165, where it is used literally: on Scyths in general

Even then you taught me to love peace. But learn what are the terms
of our allegiance; such a pact you will perhaps accept. 500
I call to witness, Rome, your name, so venerable to us,
and Mars, our common ancestor,[134] (in all its time the world
has had nothing better than Rome, and Rome nothing than the senate).
I swear that I wish to keep peace with you and obliterate
the wrongdoing of my grandfather, who was stained by one thing, 505
the fact that he captured you, Rome.[135] But, should the gods favour
our prayers, the guilt of the former sack can be purged by the avenging
of the present one[136] – only if you, illustrious general,
take on the name Augustus. Why avert your eyes? Reluctance
commends you all the more. We do not compel you, or insist, 510
but solemnly appeal. With you as commander, I am
Rome's friend; with you as emperor, I am her soldier.[137] You
are robbing no-one of the sovereignty; no emperor holds
the Latin heights;[138] the court, where it lies open, is yours.[139] It is,
I swear, not enough for me to refrain from harm, and, when you bear 515
the diadem, may it happen that I can help. My task
is just to exhort, but if Gaul, as it can rightly do,[140] forced you,

see the general introduction, section 9). The love of Roman culture exemplified here would
help to commend Theoderic's advocacy of Avitus to those who heard and those who read
the panegyric.

134 Mars, traditionally reckoned the father of Romulus, is described by Jordanes (*Getica*
41) as born in Thrace, among the Goths, evidently deducing this from Vergil, *A.* 3.35.

135 This is the famous sack of Rome by Alaric, his grandfather, in 410; it is meant also in
the following line by 'the former sack'.

136 The 'present one' is Geiseric's capture of Rome in 455 (lines 441–3). Avenging this
would require a resounding victory over Geiseric, and that fact demands that Avitus let
himself be proclaimed emperor.

137 There is a similar spirit in the panegyric of Pacatus on Theodosius (*Pan.
Lat.* 2(12).32.3–5), where the treaty of 382 between Romans and barbarians is praised.
Enemies have become potential allies.

138 The reference is to the city of Rome itself, with the word 'Latin' used as often to mean
'Roman'. No fighting with a rival claimant would be necessary.

139 This observation is almost a plea to be one of the inner circle when Avitus is emperor.
The court (he claims) is open to be filled.

140 Two bold statements end the speech. To say the Goths can force Avitus 'by right' or
'with justice' of course raises a very important question; and the 'obedience of the world'
could not be counted upon, as events quickly proved.

the world would obey you, to keep ruin at bay."[141] He spoke, and with
his brother gave solemn assent to the words proposed.[142] Avitus,
you left in sadness, for you knew it would not escape the Gauls   520
that with you as emperor they might be subject to the Goths.[143]
But when the fearful citizens realised that you were bringing
a treaty,[144] they ran quickly to you, and before you knew it
set up a platform. When it seemed to them that enough nobles
had gathered – men on whom the snowy crags of the Cottian Alps   525
look down, or men coming from the lands skirted at various points
by the Tyrrhenian sea's waters or those of the river Rhine,
or men from the lee of the Pyrenees, not under Spanish sway,[145]
Avitus, sad with his burden of cares, is approached by
a rejoicing throng. Then the leader of the nobles, their oldest,   530
a man worthy to be his country's mouthpiece, made this speech:[146]

141 The inelegant assonance of two similar sounds ('obey', 'bay') corresponds to wordplay
in the Latin between the words *pareat* and *pereat* ('obey' and 'perish').

142 For Theoderic's brother Frideric, see lines 435–6.

143 In line 521 the above translation takes *Getae* as dative singular, a move which, as argued
by Green (2016), remedies the unacceptable sense of previous readings. Avitus was surely
sad because he realised that the Gauls would fear subordination to the Goth (or worse) if the
Goths were to make Avitus emperor and so win influence, and not because (this rendering is
typical, but mainly Anderson's) they saw 'that the Goths could be at their service if you were
emperor'. That could not be the meaning. Other examples of the generalising singular ('the
Goth') are in lines 350 and 393 of this poem.

144 The 'citizens' are the Gauls (or 'Gallo-Romans'), their fears quickly assuaged once it
was known that Avitus was bringing peace, in a treaty that was no longer (cf. line 400) just
a rumour.

145 The boundaries of Gaul are indicated by the Cottian Alps, west of modern Turin, by
the Rhine and by the Tyrrhenian, or Tuscan, sea (the wordplay of the Latin words *Tyrrhenus*
and *Rhenus* cannot be reproduced in English), and, roughly speaking, by the Pyrenees.
Line 528 apparently refers to people from the lee of the Pyrenees who were outside Spanish
jurisdiction; perhaps a barbarian enclave, quite possibly of Sueves. Whoever they were, the
point seems a touch pedantic in the context.

146 The speaker has been plausibly identified as Tonantius Ferreolus, a Gallic nobleman
who was praetorian prefect of Gaul from 451 to 452 or 453 (*PLRE* 2.465–6). There is no
intention to obscure the person's identity or his role in this event; this would be well known.
He both then and later performed various services on Gaul's behalf; these are listed in (the
somewhat later) *Ep.* 7.12.1–4, where S., a relative through marriage, pays a sensitive tribute.
Anderson, in note * in volume 2, p. 362, outlines his career and connections, and also who
he is not, in case of confusion.

"That harsh Fortune through various trials for many a year
afflicted us under a young emperor in ruinous times[147]
it might be tedious to complain, great leader; you yourself
were a major part of those aggrieved, mourning our country's wounds 535
and unsettled by overmastering solicitudes.[148]
For us to live with these catastrophes and the world's demise
was death. But while in accordance with the words of our parents
we revered weak laws and thought our bounden duty was to follow
the old order, with all its failings, we endured a wraith 540
of empire, satisfied to bear even the old family's faults,
and a dynasty accustomed to the purple robe by habit,
rather than right.[149] There recently emerged a marvellous
state of affairs by which Gaul could assert her own armed might,
when Maximus was taking over the terrified city;[150] 545
she could well have taken the world, if with you as master she
had remade for herself the whole empire.[151] Who it was that revived
the Belgic lands, and Armorica's coast, who roused the Gothic rage

147 Valentinian III (emperor 425–55, *PLRE* 2.1138–9), briefly mentioned in line 359. He acceded at the age of seven. For his rule see Humphries (2012) and, briefly, McEvoy (2013), 303–4.

148 This hexameter line consists of three long words, something which is relatively rare in Latin; it is used here to provide weight and emphasis as well as ornament. The Latin word *sollicitudinibus* invited such games, and indeed enabled the early fifth-century poet Rutilius Namatianus to write a line consisting of just two words (1.450).

149 The current year was the first in sixty years – or indeed ninety, if Valentinian I is included – without that dynasty in place. The uncle of Valentinian III, Honorius (emperor 393–423), had acceded at the age of eight; in the East, Theodosius II (402–50) had been proclaimed Augustus in his first year, and ruled from 408, and his father Arcadius (Augustus 383–408) was probably five when his rule began. Dissatisfaction with the dynasty in this period has also been seen in the compiler of the *Chronicle of 452*, as noted by Muhlberger (1992), 28–37.

150 Gaul could have exploited the situation of chaos and terror after the coming of the Vandals (and even defeated them at the same time), though a different picture is given in lines 441–3, where Vandal stealth and Roman unpreparedness are the key words.

151 Gaul might have taken the opportunity to assert her power and take over the city – indeed, the 'world' – that is, the western empire. He uses the common jingle of *urbs* and *orbis* to some effect: taking care of the city helps take care of the world. It is far from clear how Gaul might have 'remade the whole empire'; interpretations differ. Anderson thinks of Gaul regaining 'all her rightful lands' (are these more than those mentioned in lines 547–8?) while for Loyen it refers unspecifically to Gaul recovering her powers.

is no secret;[152] in these great wars, hero, we yielded to you.
Now supreme power calls you; in crises an empire cannot   550
be governed by the faint-hearted. All rivalry comes second
when a crisis needs great men; after the defeats of Ticinus
and Trebia the fearful state quickly resorted to
Fabius;[153] the shame of Cannae, infamous for Varro's flight,
and Punic gloating in the Scipios' deaths was overturned   555
by the election of Livius.[154] In the city a captive world
(they say) lies prostrate,[155] the emperor has died; and now the empire
has its entire existence here in Gaul.[156] We implore you,
mount this tribunal, cheer all who are weak; the present time
does not require that another man show greater love for Rome.[157] 560
And do not think yourself unequal to the task of ruling:
when the standards of Brennus were harassing the Capitol,
our state, as you know, was just Camillus, who, his fatherland's
destined avenger, hid the smoking ash with slaughtered foes.[158]
No centuries have been bought for you by gold distributed   565
among the people, and no more do venal tribes, won over
by abundant cash, run to the vote.[159] The world's vote is not bought.

152 Though not named, Avitus is clearly the one credited with protecting the Belgae
against the Burgundians (lines 234–5), with activity of some kind to help the population of
the Armoricans (cf. lines 246–7: perhaps, as elsewhere, Litorius is forgotten), and with the
inspiring of the Goths to oppose the invading Huns before the Catalaunian Plains (lines 346–8).
153 After these defeats (218 BC), the Romans chose as dictator Quintus Fabius Maximus
in 217.
154 The crushing defeat at the battle of Cannae, often blamed on the flight of the consul
Terentius Varro, occurred in 216 BC; the deaths in battle against the Cathaginians of the
brothers Scipio occurred in 211 BC; Livius Salinator, consul, defeated Hasdrubal at the
battle of the Metaurus in 208 BC.
155 People say that the world, in Rome, is captive; you must take over, like the other
worthies. There is just a hint of the jingle made above in line 546; the point is important.
156 Everything now depends on Gaul, and Avitus – who with no further ado is summoned
to what will become a coronation.
157 In other words, 'this is no time for an election'.
158 These exhortations take up the longing of Rome for a Camillus (line 68) and Jupiter's
encouraging reminder of the flight of Brennus (line 129); they answer fears expressed by
Rome early in the poem, and Jupiter's reply. The piles of ashes here credited to Camillus
might be replicated by conquest of the Vandals.
159 In the Republic the voting units of Rome were the centuries and the tribes, both
notoriously open to bribery. There is a similar comment on the (former) tedious paraphernalia
of canvassing in Ausonius' panegyric of (the emperor) Gratian at XXI. 13.

Though poor, you are our choice: in achievements you are rich, and that
is enough. Why do you obstruct your country's wish, which commands you
to command? All share a single voice: "if you become our lord,   570
I will be free."
        Shouts of applause fill the halls of Ugernum,[160]
the place to which (it so happened)[161] the senate's devoted throng
had brought their weight, wishes and prayers. The place, the hour, and the day
are judged auspicious for his rule[162] at once the rejoicing nobles
wisely ordered a guard to be stationed. On the third day   575
thereafter, when Hyperion's light had dimmed the fleeing stars,[163]
the leaders come together, and on a quickly erected mound
ring Avitus with armed guards and deck him with a victor's torc,[164]
and honour him – still sad, for as yet he had put on only
an emperor's worries – with the insignia of sovereignty.   580
With just such an expression did the Tirynthian hero once
take up the burden of the sky (and those of his step-mother)
when the giant played truant away from his Libyan pinnacle
and the world's frame, more safely, rested on Hercules' back.[165]

160 Ugernum (modern Beaucaire) is nine miles north of the Gallic capital of Arles, on the river Rhone, and situated where roads from Arles, Glanum (St Rémy) and Nîmes intersect. Arles itself may have been avoided for fear of causing apprehension in a city that had often attacked by Goths and others; there had been a recent march on Arles by Throsimund (Kulikowski (2008), 350 n. 52) *Chron. Gall. 511*, 621. The form of the place-name is certain from inscriptions, whereas the manuscript readings *Viernum* and *Tiernum* (or *Thiernum*) – of which the first has sometimes been accepted in texts and reference works – both lack support. See note on the text used.

161 The word *forte* (literally 'by chance'), so common in poetic and other narratives, should not be taken to imply that the presence of the senate was just a happy coincidence. Unless secrecy was deemed paramount the meeting may have been arranged as a special meeting of the council of the Seven Provinces.

162 The Latin *imperio felix* (574) could equally mean 'happy for the empire'.

163 Hyperion is the sun, as in 2.406; in this suitably aptly elevated description of 'sunlight'. Two dates are given in the various sources, July 9 or 10 (that is, seven and six days before the Ides of July); according to Hydatius (156 [163]) Avitus was proclaimed *Augustus* first at Toulouse, then at Arles.

164 The military torc (or 'collar') was originally an important part of military awards and insignia, discussed by MacCormack (1981), 241–2.

165 In the eleventh of his twelve labours Hercules sought out the apples of the Hesperides and sent Atlas to get them; meanwhile, he took on the burden of Atlas, traditional upholder of the firmament. Claudian had used this tale for panegyrical purposes at 21.143–7 (praising Stilicho), likewise claiming that Hercules did the job better.

Rome, I have given you this man, while Gaul in her broad plains   585
applauds him thunderously as Augustus and while, now stronger,
Boreas carries the auspicious cries towards the pale Auster.[166]
He will restore Libya to you, in a fourth captivity,[167]
and it is now easy to believe what will be achieved in wars
by one whose journey alone has after centuries restored   590
Pannonia's lost lands.[168] What nations, stunned by his eagles
will be placed beneath your yoke by an emperor who in private life
shrugged off momentous omens of his rule, when in his travels
by chance the wing of a startled bird dislodged his common cloak.[169]
But now, Rome, the ancient parent of gods, overjoyed to have   595
such a great emperor, lift up your eyes and throw off sloth;[170]
behold an emperor, who will restore your youthful vigour,
one more mature than those boy-emperors who made you old".[171]
Hardly had the father of the gods ended; the gods applauded,
their cheers rippling through the council. The Fates spun for your reign   600
a happy span, Augustus, and for this your consular year[172]
with wool on spindles whirling fast they wove a golden age.[173]

166 Boreas, the North wind, no longer a symbol of the uncivilised north, but now
strengthened by the alliance of Avitus and the Goths, carries the applause to Rome and
Africa, home of Rome's recent captors. Auster, the south wind, and the south generally, here
signifies the lands held by the Vandals, now pale with fear. Compare lines 14/15 of the poem;
Auster is not to be feared.

167 After the first three wars against Carthage, there will be a fourth captivity, especially
for Geiseric. Cf. line 444.

168 A sweeping claim, which no evidence supports. It seems unlikely; for the condition of
Pannonia, see Mócsy (1974), 339–58, esp. 351. Perhaps there was a small skirmish involving a
subordinate, or a piece of Roman diplomacy, or even a Hunnic pretence of obeisance.

169 Birds are notably prescient according to ancient lore, but this omen, contrasting with
the army's eagles or standards, is not a usual one; it might even be based on autopsy.

170 The Latin word veternum ('sloth', 'sluggishness') encapsulates all the privations of old
age and recalls the unkempt figure that had entered the council of the gods (lines 45–50).

171 This re-emphasises the complaint that the immaturity of recent emperors (lines 532–3
above), has made drastic renewal necessary.

172 The ceremony was basically the celebration of a consulship (lines 12–13).

173 The operations of the Fates match the twofold process of spinning and weaving in
Antiquity. Wool, provided in raw bundles (pensa: originally, daily allocations to a slave; not,
as Anderson's rendering might suggest, the spindles themselves), was drawn out with the
help of fast-moving spindles and then woven as necessary.

Extended notes

(i) (on 80–2). This sentence corresponds to three elaborately constructed lines of Latin, of which the first gives a list of victors, the second lists, in the same order, their five opponents, and the third lists very summarily the five kinds of loss that the opponents were made to suffer. The arrangement is in metrical terms impressive, but not historically exact; had metre allowed, Sulla and Pompey might have changed places to produce a better correspondence. Sulla had little to do with Tigranes II of Armenia, who was actually defeated by Pompey at Artaxata in 66 BC, and forced to make peace and cede much territory. Pompey did conquer Mithradates VI, but in a less spectacular victory than that won by Sulla in the First Mithridatic War (89–85 BC). Pompey may have forced him to take poison, but Sulla had tried that too (only to find Mithradates immune). As for the others, Scipio Asiagenes defeated Antiochus III at Magnesia in 190 or 189 BC (here, though the translation 'flight' is possible, the extensive cession of territory, effectively 'banishment', is more pertinent); Curius Dentatus defeated Pyrrhus of Epirus in 275 BC, the last of several wars, and Pyrrhus may have been required to pay tribute; Lucius Aemilius Paul(l)us defeated Perseus, king of Macedonia, at Pydna in 168 BC, consigning Perseus to prison for the rest of his life.

(ii) (on 321–5, especially 323; applies also to *c.* 5.476) The Bellonoti/Ballonoti raise interesting questions, in particular whether S. could have read the poem *Argonautica* of Valerius Flaccus, where it appears at *c.* 6.161, with very small variations of the spelling in the manuscripts. Did S. know of this passage? Valerius was a little known author at the time, though signs of possible imitation have been suggested by the literary scholars Manitius (1889), 248–54, at 253 and Zissos (2006), 165–85, at 253; Maenchen-Helfen (1973) references him a number of times on p. 161 [*sic*], in note 810, observing various similarities between S. and Valerius, though as commoner words these have no probative value. In his commentary on *Argonautica* Book 6 Wijsman (2000), 72 ff. postulates a common source for the reading Bellonoti/Balloniti, and indeed Toryni/ Toringi (Valerius 6.145), without being specific about this common source. That S. used Valerius cannot be ruled out; the suggestion may invite scepticism, but is not ridiculous, especially as S. mentions the southern coast of the Black Sea, as far as Phasis, a number of times. See also Thompson (1996), 149 for a brief comment.

Poem 8
To Priscus Valerianus, of praetorian rank

INTRODUCTION

Priscus Valerianus (*PLRE* 2.1142–3) included a patrician among his ancestors; how exactly he was related to Avitus (lines 1–2), and whether the fall of Avitus affected his subsequent career, is not known. In a letter to one Sapaudus (*Ep.* 5.10.2), of uncertain date, S. describes him as highly eloquent and expresses admiration for his choice of son-in-law and his later opportunity to use him as judicial assessor when prefect of the Gauls.

The verses mentioned here – they are hastening away to be appraised by Priscus – are unlikely to include, or consist of, the Panegyric of Avitus and its preface, as assumed in PLRE; it is hard to imagine that the panegyric, or even a part of it, could even jokingly be thought a candidate for burning, as suggested in the poem's final line. The tone of the poem suggests that Priscus had been asked to comment on poetic offerings from S. before; the present set know where to go, and are keen to do so. The poem, modestly and wittily dedicating them to Priscus, must have been written in the short period between Avitus's accession in July 455 and his military defeat (October 456). As he tells his reader, he was awarded a statue in the forum of Trajan (a fact repeated much later in *Ep.* 9.16.3, verses 21–8); this was a very considerable honour, though he seems to appreciate the statue less than the honour done him by enthusiastic senate and people.

In the Edinburgh Companion Kelly (167–70) speculates that this poem was originally a prefatory poem for the Avitus panegyric, but moved to its present position to round off the section of panegyrics and related poems (which are tabulated by him on p. 168). The metre is elegiac couplets.

TRANSLATION

Priscus, ever my pride and joy,[1] whose house, with Avitus
emperor, the imperial purple connects to itself,
as my trifles dash off to you to be appraised, I say,
"stay here, runaways, where are you going? He loves me.
A man who loves is always one who gives censorious verdicts;   5
soft-hearted friendship reads a work with furrowed brow.
There is no value in the esteem added to my repute –[2]
that the Ulpian portico shines bright with my statue[3]
or that with populace and senate still applauding me
the vales of hollow Rome re-echo their 'bravos'.[4]   10
They answer, "yes, we will dash off, we will go, and you cannot
stop us: from such a judge even censure is a joy.
There is no better judge than he; he examines poems well,
slow with disparagement, acute with criticism."
And since I could not stop my injudicious words, I ask,   15
once read, don't hesitate to assign them to the flames.[5]

1 The Latin word here, often translated 'glory', was used by Horace of (his patron) Maecenas at the head of his *Odes* (1.1.2) and elsewhere.

2 The public esteem already gained will not affect Sidonius' readiness to accept the opinion of Priscus.

3 The statue was in the Forum of Trajan (cf. *c.* 1.544 for 'Ulpian'; and again in *c.* 7.114–16, where Ulpius is Trajan). On the significance of this location, see Chenault (2012), who describes it as 'the most important public venue for the honorific statues of senators in the city of Rome in the fourth and fifth centuries'.

4 Latin adjectives for 'hollow' are applied to towns and cities in a valley, or in this case a part of Rome. For 'bravos', see *c.* 1.4 (shouted by gods), also *c.* 5.8 (those of Europe).

5 A common point of modest poets. In his preface to the *Griphus* (XV Green), 11–13, Ausonius cites the supposed example of Plato, who burnt his tragedies, and leaves it open that this work of his own be relieved of infamy 'with the help of Vulcan'.

Poem 9
To Felix

INTRODUCTION

This most unusual poem is addressed to a friend and former fellow-student of S., Magnus Felix (*PLRE* 2.463–4: Magnus Felix 21), or simply Felix, as in the usual title. He will be regularly referred to as Felix also in the notes, partly to avoid any confusion with his father Magnus (Magnus 2 in *PLRE* 2.700–1). There is no indication of date within this poem, and its placing in the whole collection, discussed in my main introduction (section 6), does not help.

'To Felix' is a reply to a poem in which Felix had apparently requested poems from S., a request that he construes as a demand for a *libellus* or small book (line 11) of trifles written in his youth. S. does not refuse outright, and warns Felix of his unconventional solution. Felix will surely have been surprised at the form the response took, which was to put together a poem listing an enormous number of topics that S. says he will *not* deal with. Out of modesty, or more probably as a piece of erudite fun, he chose to defeat expectations. The poem is not, though, informal, but well crafted and often witty.

Its positive qualities should not be disparaged: they include, clearly, his skill in manipulating the hendecasyllablic metre throughout, and the construction and control within it of fluent long sentences (for example, on the death of Cyrus); he even manages the rare feat of presenting slices of Roman Republican history, in terms of disasters, within his section on Lucan. In places he writes with notable sensibility (for example, on the life of the young Achilles or the love of Alphaeus for Arethusa); elsewhere (as when describing the physiognomy of the mythological giants), he gives rein to wit and humour.

Some of the topics (though all of them are here categorically spurned or discarded) are favourites of S., such as the labours of Hercules or the engineering work of Xerxes, which he had used or would use in the near future, but many are new to his poetry, whether from mythology, history or literature. Broadly speaking, he proceeds from east to west, treating themes from the history of the Middle East and then the Persian invasions of Greece and Alexander's successes in Asia. He turns (in line 65) to mythology, which is represented by the Argonauts, the Giants, Hercules, the house of Tantalus, Paris and others. From the Trojan War there are contrasting accounts at some length of Achilles and Odysseus. The focus then changes (168) to religion, with a miscellaneous section – marred by a hiatus in the manuscripts, creating a small lacuna after line 197 – on various divine beings and on a selection of cults and practices.

The section on classical literature runs from 211 to 273: on the Greek side (211–16) are Hesiod, Pindar, Stesichorus and a few others, but no Aristophanes or Sophocles. On the Latin side there are, among others, Vergil, Horace, Statius, Seneca, Lucan; the long list includes some, such as Gaetulicus, of whom almost nothing, then as now, was extant. Coming nearer to his own time, S. mentions Claudian and three more poets, of whom one is anonymous, and one, Quintianus, almost unknown. The other is Merobaudes, honoured with a statue by the cherished emperor (an unexpected reference to Valentinian III) and the senate. There follow favourable assessments of friends and various luminaries. At the end of the poem (318–46) a surprise of a different kind meets the reader; the statement that he rarely entrusted his writings to anything but small sheets of paper, better used for fish suppers (an old poet's joke) – which some have taken seriously. Finally he hopes, as he regularly does, that his work for all its apparent demerits will have the support of its reader or readers against any carping or contemptuous critics. There are detailed studies of aspects of the poem by Consolino (2008) and Hernández Lobato (2015; see pp. 425–7).

TRANSLATION

Herewith profuse greetings from Sollius
Sidonius Apollinaris to
Felix, master and to his kind brother.[1]
Tell me, please tell me this, Felix Magnus[2]
happy by name, in mind, fame, honour, body,   5

---

1 The words 'profuse' and 'greetings' are in the Latin first and last (respectively) in this neat salutation.

2 Along with the clear pun on the name Felix, there is a lesser one in Magnus ('great').

happy in sons, wife, siblings,[3] and parents,
in the brothers of your mother and father
and in the greatest of cousins, Camillus[4] –
why do you order reckless trifles[5] of
your friend, scattered in fun as a childish youth,   10
to be assembled in the form of a book,
and all at once a load of ill-will roused
and masses of good paper thrown away?[6]
Your orders I obey, but first I announce
what a bumpy ride the reader – you – will have.   15
I do not here pass down the old highway,
nor will you find a place where my Thalia[7]
runs in the ancient tracks of earlier poets.[8]
Not here the Antipodes and the Red Sea,[9]
not here will I sing of Memnon's Indians[10]   20
scorched by the fire of nearby Aurora,[11]
nor will I sing Artaxata[12] or Susa[13]

3 The family members cannot be identified except for the brother (Probus 4 in *PLRE* 2.910–11: also in line 333 below, and *c*. 24.94) and his sister Araneola (*PLRE* 2.126 and *c*. 14); the wife of Magnus Felix was Attica (*PLRE* 2.181–2), at least at a later date.

4 For Camillus see *PLRE* 2.255, and *Ep*. 1.11.10.

5 Trifles they may be; but of course this word cannot be meant to describe S.'s subsequent publications, as has been suggested, or assumed.

6 The (potential) waste of paper was a conventional criticism made of writers of light verse. Of course, as S. realises, much more paper would be used up for the finished poem.

7 Thalia, seen as the Muse of light verse, is the favourite Muse of S., who mentions her six times in all. Other Muses are used much less: Erato and Calliope twice each, Terpsichore and Clio once each.

8 As S. surely knew, the metaphor of poet as a rider or charioteer who shunned the main, well-travelled, paths was developed by Greek poets of Alexandria, notably Calllimachus, and used by Roman poets to claim originality. He shows little or no sign of the writing poets themselves, and is unlikely to be satirising them here.

9 A droll comment, for almost nothing was known about the Antipodes. The east–west movement of the poem then begins with mention of the Red Sea, which in his other verse he never mentions as such.

10 Memnon (often called king of the Ethiopians in ancient sources) was leader of a military force at Troy; cf. *c*. 2.521, with references there.

11 Aurora, usually regarded as his mother, is here just a fellow-citizen of the Indians.

12 Artaxata was 'a royal city' (OCD[4]) of Armenia. Cf. *c*. 2.445.

13 Susa was a Persian capital (mentioned by S. in moods of zealous patriotism, *c*. 2.50, 6.502), like Bactra.

or Bactra, Carrhae, or brick-baked Babylon,[14]
which, open to the river that fosters it
drinks amply from both banks the enclosed Tigris.   25
Here's nought on Ninus, Assyria's first king,[15]
nor will I voice the Medes' king Arbaces[16]
or the richness of ashes from the pyre
of Sardanapal, built to escape his foes,[17]
or mention Cyrus, Astyages' grandson[18]   30
who, so they say, was fed by a canine teat;
that Cyrus, whose greed was not slaked even
by the treasures of Lydian Croesus,[19] and whose
blood-lust was not sated until, having made
a massacre of two hundred thousands,   35
trapped in a Scythian valley, he met his end
in the bag of Tomyris, bereaved by him.[20]
You'll not read here the feats of Cecrops' race[21]
nor any wars in bloodstained Marathon[22]
or of Xerxes, spurring thousand thousands,   40
vainglorious with their multitudinousness,
who though his armies drank deep rivers dry
in a trice, still suffered thirst, and who then rode

14 Bactra: the word can denote the city of Bactra (*c.* 2.448, *c.* 5.603) or the whole country of Bactria (also in *c.* 23.249), much of it in what is now Turkestan. Carrhae is the town in Mesopotamia where Crassus and his son (cf. line 251 below) were defeated in 53 BC (*c.* 2.455). The city of Babylon was in modern Iraq, and not on the Tigris, as S. says (25), but the Euphrates. Its walls of brick were sometimes described as 'cooked', as in Ovid. *M.* 4.58, Justin 1.2.7.

15 Ninus was the first known king of Assyria, and legendary founder of Nineveh.

16 Arbaces was a military leader and king of the Medes in the seventh century BC.

17 Sardanapallus: the last king of Assyria (ninth century BC); for a narrative of his luxurious life, see Justin 3.1–5.

18 The daughter of Astyages, king of Media, had married Cyrus's father Cambyses: cf. *c.* 2.117–18.

19 Croesus, king of Lydia (mid-sixth century BC), was defeated by Cyrus: Herodotus 1.82–4.

20 This story of Cyrus's end and this tale of Tomyris are narrated by Herodotus 1.214.

21 A common poetic description of Athenians, based on the supposition that Cecrops was ancestor or first king of Athens.

22 Marathon, in Attica, the site of a battle of 490 BC against the Persians, but also used by S. for Athens and Attica in general, as in *c.* 6.3, *c.* 23.237; for its adjective, *c.* 5.193, *c.* 15.35.

with his mad battalions through Thermopylae[23]
and the waves of Helle, spurning obstacles   45
of land and sea, and then with the sea which raged
up to the summit of the leafy peak,
admitted into the Athos headland,
he with his fleets passed through the hewn out canyon.[24]
Nor shall I tell how the Garamantic god's   50
offspring, who ruled whole realms and their rulers,
animated by his father's thunderbolts,
tornadoed through the widespread lands of Asia[25]
and overpowered first the panic-stricken
prefects and satraps of king Darius,   55
then the king himself, proud on his fathers' throne,
prattling about the gods (his relatives),
but who with wife, children, mother, captured[26]
was ordered to resume the human state;
who having roused the greatest of all wars   60
and brought from far and wide the entire army
of Persia to a single battlefield,
is said to have achieved but a single thing:
that his enemy would enjoy a longer sleep.[27]
Of the Minyae's voyage, with their speaking plank,   65

23 At the pass of Thermopylae the army of Xerxes (but not Xerxes, who sailed, as stated
in 46–9) forced its way through the thin but fearless Greek defences, in 480 BC.

24 King Xerxes drove a canal through the Athos peninsula (Herodotus 7.22–3), through
which the fleet duly sailed (7.122). Another famous detail from the progress of Xerxes – his
bridge of boats over the Hellespont – is used in a comparison at *c.* 5.451–5.

25 This refers to Alexander the Great, who claimed to be the son of Ammon (or Zeus
Ammon), who had the power of hurling thunderbolts. For stories involving this god in
Alexander's birth, see Plutarch, *Alexander* 2–3 and Justin 3.11.11. S. refers to such claims by
Alexander in *c.* 2.121–4; in *c.* 5.202 he makes a short, dismissive comparison with Majorian.

26 His mother, wife and two daughters were captured at the battle of Issus (Plutarch,
Alexander 21).

27 Not the same point as Plutarch makes in *Alexander* 32, which is that the enemy had,
conveniently for him, gathered in one place, and did not need to be rounded up. Here the point
seems to be that his enemy, or Darius's enemy (Alexander himself), could sleep for longer.
Alexander could afford to be facetious. The battle, which he won, is that of Gaugamela,
331 BC.

I will not speak, nor of how they came to Phasis[28]
when, struck by the Pelasgian leader's charm
the heroic maiden calmed the maddened bulls
without fear, even when her farmer-friend,
having sown the molars of the vanquished snake,   70
stood trembling amongst the armour-plated grasses,
amazed to see there bloom a hostile harvest
and, as what had been corn ears came to blows,
to see the brothers, just now stems and stalks,
drenching the warlike earth with blood – green blood.   75
I'll not speak here of the earth-born company[29]
lent vigour by the poison in their veins,
who, to say nothing of their limitless shape,
had snakes whose bodies writhed in sinuous coils;
they stretched aloft their scaly legs, which ended   80
with feet that served as jaws and mouths and throats.
So did these wanton youths of threefold shape,
wearing away the earth with gluttonous feet,
run on their heads, amazing to behold,
and when the trumpets of the gods resounded   85
in immediate answer to the thunderclaps
they dared with hissing feet to enrage the gods.
Nor do you read here Phlegra's lands, enlarged
as mountains hurled as missiles fly through the air,
Pindus, Pelion, Ossa, Olympus, Othrys,   90
complete with forests, flocks, beasts, and glaciers,
their rocks, their springs, their rivers, and their towns,
all grasped and flung by hands more vast than they.
Nor will I adorn the labours of Hercules[30]

28 Minyae is a term applied to the Argonauts (e.g. by Ovid *M.* 7.1 in his version); for
the talking plank, see Apollonius of Rhodes 1.526–7, Valerius Flaccus 1.301–5. Phasis here
denotes not, as elsewhere, the river or the town, but the region around the river mouth. The
full story of Medea and Jason, and the help she gave him in this (68–75) and other ordeals, is
given by the poets named above.
29 The battle of the giants with the gods at Phlegra (line 88) is alluded to in *c.* 6.15–29. For
the Gigantomachy in S., see *c.* 6.21–8, *c.* 15.17–29, with some differences of detail.
30 The labours of Hercules,which were more numerous than the canonical twelve, are
represented here with extreme compression. The following notes reference other treatments
of the labours by S. For further details the reader is referred to March (2008).

for whom the boar, hind, lion, giant, Amazon,[31]   95
the host, bull, Eryx, birds, Lycus, thief, Nessus,[32]
the Libyan, mountains, apples, maiden, serpent,[33]
Oete, the horses of Thrace, and cows from Spain[34]
the wrestling river, the three-headed dog,[35]
the carrying of the heavens, won life in heaven.[36]   100
Not here will I set forth Elis, famed for
its chariots,[37] nor will I relate in my verse
the one celebrated for a river's love,
when through the depths of the sea Alpheus passed
and foreign water in bliss embraced her waves.[38]   105
Not here the tale of the house of Tantalus,
how Pelopea, raped by her father,
became her children's sister, and her father

31 These labours are: the search for the Erymanthian boar (c. 13.7–8, c. 15.141); the capture
of the Kerynitian hind (c. 13.11, 15.141); the killing of the Nemean lion (c. 13.3–4, 15.141); the
killing of the giant Cacus (c. 13.9–10, 15.141); the fetching of the belt of Hippolyte (c. 13.11,
c. 15.142. The giant here is not Antaeus or Lycus (both occur below) or Typhoeus, whose
defeat (cf. c. 6.27) was not one of the labours.

32 These are: the killing of Busiris (c. 13.11, 15.142); the conquest of Achelous, the
river-god who took the form of a bull (c. 13.11, c. 15.143); the conquest and death of Eryx
(c. 13.11, c. 15.142); the driving away of the Stymphalian birds (c. 15.142); the defeat of Lycus
(c. 15.143) – a rare tale, mentioned in the list of Hyginus, Fables 31 and 32 and in Seneca's
tragedy Hercules in Fury, 274); the punishment of the thief (Geryon: c. 13.13–14); the killing
of Nessus (c. 15.142).

33 These are: the crushing of the Libyan Antaeus (c. 13.11, c. 15.141, 'the giant'); the
erection of the 'Pillars of Hercules' (the mountains Calpe and Abyla); the picking of the
apples of the Hesperides (c. 13.12, c. 15.143), the saving of the maiden Hesione (c. 15.143); the
killing of the Hydra of Lerna; (c. 13.7–8, c. 15.141).

34 These are: death on Mount Oeta (c. 15.143); the capturing of the horses of Diomede
(c. 15.142 [Thrax]); the fetching of the cows of Geryon (c. 13.9–10, c. 15.141).

35 The wrestling with the river (Achelous: in its true form; cf. c. 2 408–9) (c. 13.11,
c. 15.143); the fetching of Cerberus from the underworld (c. 13.12, 15.141).

36 The carrying of the world (c. 15.143), placed here in simple antithesis with 'heaven', as
in c. 13.1–2.

37 Elis, in south-western Greece, was famed for horse-breeding. Olympia, home of the
Olympic games, was not far away.

38 Arethusa was a Greek nymph seen and pursued by the river Alphaeus, changed into
a fountain by Diana and later removed to Sicily. Alphaeus followed her, and their waters
mingled. This amatory myth is alluded to in Vergil, E. 10.4–5 and A. 3.694–6, and by Statius,
Silvae 1.2.201–8.

in a new outrage begat an evil grandson.[39]
Here are no sad tales: I do not depict   110
Thyestes' grief, when, at the sumptuous feast
by his brother's wickedness, he devoured (poor wretch)
his children, and became their living tomb.[40]
After this feast Titan, of a sudden
turned round his chariot, went west to east,   115
fleeing the guest, putting the day to flight.
Nor will you have to read the Phrygian shepherd,
for whom diminished Dindymum is said
(her summits shorn of trees) to have made a fleet
when at the behest of Venus, lust's patron,   120
that rapist stripped the lands of Oebalus,
slighting Amyclae's hospitality,
as he wooed across the sea a yielding prey.[41]
I will not speak of Pergamum, and its
ten-year war, or Agamemnon's cruel troops   125
or Sinon's lying tale by which the city
sanctified by the statue of Pallas
prised open by the traitor's wiles, took in
the horse that carried enemy infantry.[42]
Not here do I tell, in the Maeonian style,   130
the Thessalian's pluck and the Dulichian's
sagacity:[43] of these the former, thought
to have been trained in a cave on Pelion
in hunting, music, wrestling, herbal drugs,
by Saturn's elderly son, as he frequented,   135

39 Tantalus was father of Pelops, who was father of Atreus and Thyestes. Pelopea was the daughter of Thyestes, and the mother by him of Aegisthus.

40 Thyestes was deceived into eating his children at a feast prepared by his brother Atreus in a family feud.

41 Oebalus was an earlier king of Sparta. Paris's abduction of Helen, wife of Menelaus, is usually presented as a greater grievance than the plunder of Spartan land, but not here. For the theme of building a fleet (lines 118–19) and its effect on the landscape, cf. *c.* 5.441–4.

42 The Palladium (127) was an image of Pallas Athena that was believed to make a city impregnable; its seizure from Troy was effected by the artifice of the Wooden Horse, deceitfully explained by Sinon (Vergil, *A.* 2.108–94).

43 The carefully written, and relatively long, stories of Achilles and Odysseus that follow (130–66) focus on the youth of Achilles and the problems of Odysseus' s homecoming.

a mere boy, the lairs of wild animals,
sometimes took a rest in snowy Pholoe,
or sometimes, lying in the much loved stable,
slumbered more softly on his master's mane.[44]
Then, given to the father of the maids   140
of Scyria, he bore the false name 'Pyrrha',
and though enrolled in stern Minerva's classes
whirled secret wands in honour of Venus too.[45]
Lastly, to the sound of Phrygian pillage
the glory of dragging captured Hector drew him.[46]   145
But as for the other hero, lucky enough
to return after sixteen years to Ithaca,
not even Smyrna's tome[47] reveals it all:
for who could make a full account of all
the labours that he bore by land and sea,   150
seizing the Palladium, finding Achilles,
capturing Dolon, swift of foot though he was,
stealing from Rhesus the snow-white horses
before they could imbibe Xanthus's waters,
snatching the quiver too, which, Philoctetes,   155
your patron god gave you; outdoing Ajax,[48]

44 This account of the education of Achilles by the centaur Chiron (son of Saturn and
Philyra) broadly follows Statius's poem *Achilleid*, an unfinished epic, from which lines
1.116–17 (on learning about herbs) and 1.196–7 (sleeping on the centaur's shoulders) are
especially influential.

45 In this picture of the young man using embroidery classes to honour Venus the 'wands'
are the thyrsi (cf. *c.* 4.596) more often linked with Bacchus (as in Statius, *Achilleid* 1.827–40).

46 The anticipation of the glory of dragging the dead Hector around Troy, the climax
of Homer's *Iliad*, amidst the hurly-burly of war and pillage – imagined, perhaps, but not
literally heard by him at this stage, and helped by much persuasion from the Greeks until
Troy filled his heart and mind (Statius, *Achilleid* 1.857) – seems to have been devised by S.
himself, in compressed language. (The afterthought of Anderson [182 n. 1], followed here, is
more correct than his first main version.)

47 It is uncertain whether S. knew the two Homeric epic poems in the original Greek or
in a sufficiently detailed Latin version, if there was one; this line certainly does not attest
acquaintance. But he may well have known which themes were not covered, as shown in line
151. Lines 152–6 and 160–7 follow the Homeric narratives (though he locates Scylla and
Charybdis less precisely) of *Odyssey* 12.58–110.

48 Lines 156–9 are inspired by the treatment of this contest in Book 13 of Ovid's
Metamorphoses (1–390), especially perhaps line 159, which is verbally close to 13.383.

the son of Telamon, enraged when he,
pleading his own case by the ships, won the prize
of the great warrior's arms, through fine speaking;
escaping Polyphemus, Circe, and   160
the king of Laestrygonia's appetite,
and then the rich man's orchards and Calypso,
and Sirens who charmed men to their deaths; fleeing
the darkness round the torch of Nauplius[49]
and the rabid loins of greedy Scylla, and   165
the rocks which Tauromenian Charybdis
breaks into holes when belching up the deep.[50]
Those gods who show particular favour to
certain lands, cities, isles, I do not sing;[51]
Saturn to Latium; Jupiter to Crete;   170
Juno to Samos; the sun-god to Rhodes;
Persephone to Henna, Minerva to Hymettus;
Vulcan to Lipara, Dione to Paphos;
Perseus to Argos; Priapus to Lampsacus
Euhius to Thebes, and Vesta to Ilium,   175
the Delian to Thymbra, to Lycaeus Pan;
Mars to the Thracians, to the Scyths Diana;
all these the temples honouring them made gods
by incense, salt, spelt, meal, by worshippers'
observance of unnecessary rites.[52]   180
I will not sing awesome Eleusis, with[53]
Triptolemus, who gave the very first

---

49 Nauplius caused the Greek fleet returning from Troy to be wrecked by lighting false beacons at Cape Caphaereus (cf. *c.* 5.195–7, *c.* 15.1). Vergil named the cape at *A.* 11.260.

50 Scylla and Charybdis were normally located near Taormina in eastern Sicily: Homer, *Odyssey* 12.73–126. Homer's Scylla is more ravenous for large fish than for sexual gratification; his Charybdis belches great water-spouts, but without breaking rocks.

51 Not all these need comment; only the less familiar place-names are mentioned. Phoebus equates to Helios the sun-god of Rhodes; Henna, in central Sicily, was associated with Proserpina; Hymettus denotes Athens; Lipara, an island of Sicily, was the home and workplace of Vulcan; Thymbra was an important shrine of Apollo near Troy; the Scyths (in general introduction, section 9) are here the Taurians of the Crimea, worshippers of Diana.

52 A trenchant comment from (probably, but not necessarily) a Christian viewpoint.

53 Eleusis in Attica was the home of awesome mysteries, observed in an annual festival.

wheat-ears to the peoples fed by Chaonia's oaks,[54]
nor Apis of the Mareotic lake
roused by the sound of Memphis's rattles.[55]   185
I'll not say how the youth of Lacedaemon
dedicated oily combats to the sons
of Tyndareus, instructed in Therapne,
who alarmed the wrestlers on Bebrycia's sand;[56]
or cite the Lycian lots or those of Caere[57]   190
or the pre-Delphic responses of Themis[58]
or those gods which the Etruscan, to expiate
a lightning strike, seeks in a fenced *bidental*[59]
or those gods which upon Antenor's hill,
by Euganean Timavus, the augur saw   195
stirring a war in Thessaly,[60] or those
that Amphiaraus and Melampus....[61]
              LACUNA (at least one line is lost)
[Metellus]...from the very ashes ...(who) snatched the gods
as the flames ran riot through the sanctuary,
Metellus, happy though he lost his sight.[62]   200

54 Triptolemus was the giver to mankind of corn, which replaced acorns; these were associated with the oaks at the oracle at Dodona (Vergil, *G.* 1.7–8 and 147–9).

55 Apis was the sacred bull worshipped by Egyptians.

56 The sons of Tyndareus are Castor and Pollux, part of the Argonautic expedition. Made to fight with king Amycus of the Bebrycians, Pollux skilfully defeated him (*c.* 5.162–3).

57 The lots of Lycia, mentioned by Vergil *A.* 4.346 and 377, located in the city of Patara in Asia Minor. Caere, one of Etruria's oldest and wealthiest cities, stands for its religious traditions.

58 Themis, a primordial goddess associated with justice and order, was supposed to have been the owner of the Delphic oracle before Apollo.

59 The *bidental* was a place struck by lightning, which was then walled off and sacrifices performed there. The implication that gods were sought may be S.'s addition.

60 Derived from his civil war narrative in Lucan 7.192–200; Lucan discusses possible causes, but without ascribing it to a god or gods, as S. does.

61 It is clear that line 198 does not cohere with 197 in sense or syntax; a line (or more) has been lost. Amphiaraus and Melampus were famous seers in Greek mythology; what else, if anything, they had in common is not known.

62 Lucius Caecilius Metellus is said to have saved the Palladium in the year 241 BC when the temple of Vesta was burnt, and in some accounts to have lost his sight thereby. In translating this sentence I have added the name present in line 200 to line 198 to give some sense to the damaged text.

Not here will (the) Cinyphian Hammon be sung,
the god who lifts his mitred head from the sands,
though loth even when a hecatomb is offered
to reveal himself from his Syrtean chasm.[63]
Not here will I describe mount Dindyma[64]   205
nor Curetes, lauding the Berecyntian
with flutes of boxwood,[65] nor Bacchus, mounting
triennial rites and coming with fury
amongst the trembling Bassarids, or whirling
his devotees round the incense-burning altar.[66]   210

Here you could not view Hesiodic poems
from fertile Ascra,[67] or Pindar's music;[68]
not here the wit of sock-wearing Menander,[69]
not the wild iambs of hurt Archilochus,
nor the more staid verses of Stesichorus,[70]   215
nor what the Lesbian lass put into verse;[71]
nor what proud Mantua, not yielding to Homer,
added to Latin letters, though she became
jealous that with the tomb of Maro there

63 Hammon or Ammon is the Egyptian god Amun (OCD[4]); cf. the Alexander legend in
Arrian *Anabasis* 3.3–4. Ammon certainly did not court publicity (Lucan 9.518–20). See also
Parke (1967), chapter 9; and Pliny, *NH* 35.140.
64 Dindyma (also Didyma) was a famous oracular shrine in Asia Minor.
65 The Curetes were young men who worshipped and honoured Zeus and by extension
Cybele (honoured at Mount Berecynthus).
66 There is a longer but no less vigorous description of imagined Bacchic ritual in
c. 5.490–8.
67 Hesiod, the oldest known Greek poet with the possible exception of Homer, wrote a
variety of poems in about 700. Ascra in central Greece was his birthplace and home.
68 This description of the lyric poet Pindar, of the early fifth century BC, seems to allude
in particular to his metrical richness, evident to eye and ear.
69 Menander wrote his comedies in the fourth and early third centuries BC. Roman
references to comedy focus on the 'sock' worn by actors (actors in tragedy had a buskin): cf.
c. 23.125–30.
70 Stesichorus will not have been known directly to S.; his epithet is probably distilled
from the comment of Quintilian (10.1.62) that he gives due dignity to his characters; if so, S.
ignores the point that his style is inflated.
71 Sappho, the lyric poet, was born near the end of the seventh century. S. has nothing to
say of her quality or content, having probably little information about her.

Parthenope gained equal fame to hers.[72]   220
Nor what, after the mixtures of the Letters
and the witty Satires, and the new Epodes,
the books of Odes and the Art of Poetry,
when writing the praises of Phoebus and
wandering Diana, Flaccus wished to express;[73]   225
nor what Papinius, joy to you and me
voices amidst the rage of the Labdacid house
or when in shorter metres and rhythms
paints in his short *Silvae* bejewelled meadows.[74]
Do not expect to find here the eloquence   230
that Cordoba, great in her sons, produced:[75]
one of whom respected rough old Plato, and
offered advice in vain to his Nero,[76]
while the other pounds the Euripidean stage
following Aeschylus, smeared with wine-lees,   235
or sonorous plays of Thespis staged on carts.[77]
These, having worn down with buskins many

72 In fact Vergil is said to have had great respect for Homer. The 'pride' of Mantua, his birthplace, and its imagined jealousy of Parthenope (Naples), where he died, could be S.'s own conceit, an expression of their predominance as poets.

73 The titles of the works of Horace (Flaccus) – a favourite of S. – are largely self-explanatory. The *Epodes* are a form that Horace claimed to have introduced into Latin (*Ep.* 1.19.23–5), hence 'new'. The last-mentioned item, best known by its Latin title of *Carmen Saeculare* ('Song for the Secular Games') is identified by its praise of Phoebus and Diana (as goddess of woodlands, where she roamed, or is she here the moon?) in the opening line.

74 Papinius Statius wrote an epic on the wars against the city of Thebes (the Labdacids, or descendants of king Labdacus, were the royal house), and five books of shorter *Silvae* (occasional poems better described in the exquisite two words 'bejeweled meadows' of line 229 than in a literal translation such as 'woods'). He also began an epic poem on Achilles, used elsewhere in this poem, but not mentioned here.

75 Seneca – whom S. surprisingly but perhaps understandably considers to be two men, one a philosopher and one a dramatist (cf. *c.* 23.162) – and Lucan were born in Cordoba in Spain.

76 Plato here stands for Greek philosophy in general. For discussion of Seneca's advice and help to Nero, see Griffin (1976), 67–128.

77 In other words, Seneca developed the Greek drama of Euripides (late fifth century BC) and Aeschylus (first half of the fifth century BC), and that of Thespis, a shadowy figure of the previus century mentioned by Horace, *Art of Poetry* 276–7. The description of Aeschylus's appearance is derived from what Horace said about actors in the time of Thespis in line 277.

a stage, secured a smelly she-goat's mate.[78]
The third of these described Caesar's battle
(Caesar of Gaul), how father- and son-in-law   240
drove Rome into a conflict between kin;[79]
he gave such rein to grief in his Philippi[80]
that he considered Cremera's ruin slight[81]
and thought that Allia's rout and Jove's ransom
in the scales of Brennus, were less to be mourned,[82]   245
dismissed disastrous Cannae and Trebia[83]
ignored the carnage at Trasimene,[84]
reckoned the brothers Scipio, interred
in lands of Tartessus, needed no comment,[85]
was quiet about the march to the Euphrates   250
and Carrhae soaked with the blood of the Crassi,[86]
and the consuls' swords which you, O Spartacus,
supreme with daggers, routed time and again,[87]

---

78 These actors competed for what Horace at *Art of Poetry*, 220 calls a 'common he-goat'.
The Latin could also imply that the dramatists themselves had trodden the boards.

79 The second of these two (or as S. would have it, three) Corduban writers is Lucan,
who wrote an epic on the civil war between Caesar and his father-in-law Pompey, and often
laments conflicts between kin.

80 Lucan is certainly given to high-flown lamentation, but makes no remarks that justify
the claims in the next sixteen lines that, by omission, he made light of the great disasters
of Roman history, or missed their importance. In line 242 S. seems to confuse the names
of Philippi – which was not the topic he needed – and Pharsalia. Hasty reading or false
recollection of Vergil *G.* 1.490 ('Philippi has again seen a battle', as if they were geograph-
ically close) might underlie this. Lucan's epic was and is sometimes known as the *Pharsalia*
rather than *On the Civil War*.

81 Cremera, a river in Etruria, by which the Fabian clan were wiped out by the men of Veii
in 477 BC.

82 The Allia, a tributary of the Tiber where the Romans suffered defeat in 390 BC; this
may have been followed by the capture of Rome by Brennus. For the story underlying the
disputed weights and Jove's ransom, see Livy, 5.48.8–9.

83 Cannae (216 BC) and the Trebia (218 BC) were battles won by Hannibal.

84 The Romans were also defeated at Trasimene in 217 BC.

85 These were Publius and Cnaeus Cornelius Scipio, defeated in Spain by Hasdrubal in
211 BC.

86 The reference is to Licinius Crassus and his son Publius Crassus, who both fell at
Carrhae. S. refers to both at once here, as Lucan often does.

87 Spartacus (cf. *c.* 2.238), a gladiator, headed a revolt, mainly of slaves (note 'daggers',
contrasting with 'swords') in 73 BC, and was long undefeated.

nor did he shed more tears over the war
which, drunk with Cimbric triumphs and the capture   255
of Jugurtha the Nasamonian,
seeking a Mithridatic triumph, Marius
the Arpinate chose to wage against Sulla.[88]
No Gaetulicus is here for you to read[89]
No Marsus,[90] Pedo,[91] Silius or Tibullus,   260
or what the humour of Sulpicia's Muse
composed cajolingly for her Calenus,[92]
nor Persius' harshness,[93] or Propertius' charm,
or Terentianus of the hundred metres;[94]
Lucilius[95] and Lucretius are not here,   265
nor Turnus,[96] Memor,[97] Ennius,[98] or Catullus,
not Stella,[99] Septimius,[100] Petronius
or Martial, fiercely snapping without end,
nor he who at the time of the second Caesar
eternally unpardoned, lived at Tomi.[101]   270

88 The same episodes are treated in *c.* 2.227–31. Marius defeated Jugurtha in Africa in 104 BC, then the Cimbrians who invaded Gaul, and then Mithridates, before taking on Sulla.
89 In what follows notes will not be given for well-known Latin authors who are extant. S. begins with some who are now virtually unknown, and probably were in his time too. Gaetulicus, listed among erotic poets by Martial, was consul in AD 26, and died in AD 39. S. mentions him again in *Ep.* 2.10.6 (along with his girlfriend Caesennia).
90 Marsus: a writer of epigrams, patronised by Maecenas.
91 Albinovanus Pedo is known from Martial's preface and from the small part of an epic poem quoted by Seneca (*Suasoriae* – these are rhetorical exercises – 1.15).
92 Sulpicia wrote love poems to her husband Calenus at the end of the first century AD.
93 The contrasting tones of the well-known poets Persius and Propertius are set together with alliteration.
94 Terentianus Maurus, of the late second and third centuries AD, wrote – in verse – a treatise on metres. S. here alludes to its title.
95 The satirist Lucilius, now known only from fragments, wrote in the second century BC.
96 Turnus was a satirist of the late first century AD.
97 Memor, brother of Turnus, was a tragedian who wrote in the late first century AD.
98 Ennius (239–169 BC) was a writer of epic and various other genres of poetry.
99 Stella, poet and patron of Martial and Statius, was consul early in the second century AD.
100 Septimius Serenus, who seems to have flourished in the early third century, wrote two books on 'country matters', in many different metres. The name is mentioned in the prose preface of *c.* 14, section 3.
101 The 'second Caesar' is Augustus, who exiled Ovid, Julius Caesar being reckoned the first.

nor he who later, with a similar fate
was exiled at the whim of an angry actor
who met the clamouring people's fickle taste,[102]
nor he sprung from Pelusian Canopus,
who sang the dark seducer's wooing and   275
the inhabitants of Hell, with heavenly Muse.[103]
Nor those who already in their earliest days
were the very best of friends to our fathers;[104]
of these one, following after Boniface
and also foolhardy Sebastian,[105]   280
shunned as a boy his birthplace of Cahors,
enamoured more of Pandion's Athens;
if you should read his many-splendoured poem
you'd think that Phoebus and the Hyantian girls,
soaked with their draughts of Hippocrene's fountain,   285
and also Amphion and Maia's son
and the bard of Rhodope were in concert
blending their melodies and songs in one.
Nor are you and your thunderings read here,
most worthy Quintianus (the second one),[106]   290
who, abandoning your home, Liguria,
in a new abode began to love the Gauls.[107]

102 For the various versions of this story, see Courtney (1980), 5–8.
103 This is Claudian, who originated in Egypt and came to Italy near the end of the fourth century. S. is quite terse (though the single word 'heavenly' is certainly a word of praise, even in the trite contrast): he picks out Claudian's unfinished epic *De Raptu Proserpinae (On the rape of Persephone)*, but there is nothing on Claudian's many panegyrics, which had some influence on his own (general introduction, section 6).
104 The first of these is not given a name (and there is no other kind of evidence); he is Anonymus 120 in *PLRE* 2.1237, which rightly questions whether he literally visited the city of Athens. The praise of this unnamed poet is unusually full, but one can only guess at the nature of his work from lines 283–8 here.
105 For Boniface see *PLRE* 2.237–40 (after a distinguished career, he died in battle in 432), and for Sebastianus (his son-in-law), who had what Anderson rightly calls 'an adventurous career', *PLRE* 2.983–4. Having been declared an enemy of the Romans, he travelled to the Eastern court (Hydatius 95 [104]), but this move was short-lived; he fled to king Theoderic (Hydatius 121 [129]), but eventually took refuge with the Vandals, only to die there soon, probably *ca.* 450.
106 Quintianus, a panegyrist of Aetius, is not otherwise known (*PLRE* 2.932–3).
107 Here 'Gauls' refers to various parts of Gaul, not the people as such.

Among the trumpets, standards, spears, and squadrons
you praised Aetius, taking time for a book,
with ivy adorned in a camp with laurels crowned.[108]   295
But neither now will the third of these be read,[109]
who left his native Baetis once for all
for damp Ravenna (albeit a place of thirst),[110]
for whom the applauding Romans, and the emperor
adored for his obliging openness   300
in Trajan's forum placed a shining statue.[111]
But do not seek to compare me with those
whom I, myself much younger, admire the more,
Paulinus[112] and Ampelius,[113] Symmachus,[114]
Messalla with his searching intellect,[115]   305

108 The laurels denote the military victories of Aetius; the ivy is part of poetic garlands.

109 This is (Flavius) Merobaudes (*PLRE* 2.756–8), important parts of whose poems are preserved (MGH AA 14, 3–20). If in line 296 S. meant 'not even read', that would be a trenchant comment from a rival; but his meaning is surely '(not) be present in this poem'. On Merobaudes, and his version of events, see Harries (1994), 70–5, and *c*. 5.

110 An old joke, or gibe, that goes back to Martial, as Anderson's note shows; Sidonius recycles it here and twice in letters. In *Ep*. 1.5.6 he admires its aptness for trade while deploring the marshes; in *Ep*. 1.8.2 (to an acquaintance who lived there) he is most uncomplimentary about the din of mosquitoes and frogs. There are no comments in S. on Ravenna's suitability as a capital, as it was for some time. The chariot race of *c*. 23.307–427 probably took place in Rome, not Ravenna (see note 81 of that poem).

111 The statue was awarded in 435 by emperor Valentinian III and the senate (*PLRE* 2.757). The tribute in line 300 is an important indication of S.'s own attitude to that emperor. See also *c*. 8.7, and for Trajan's forum Chenault (2012), 103–32.

112 This Paulinus (the name was not uncommon) is perhaps Paulinus of Nola (*PLRE* 1.681–3), a correspondent of Ausonius when he lived near Bordeaux, before his move to Italy, and a prolific poet. There is no suggestion that the Pontius Paulinus of *Ep*. 8.12.5 (cf. *c*. 22; son of the castle's owner) had literary inclinations, but that cannot be ruled out.

113 Ampelius is perhaps Publius Ampelius, who held several high offices in the mid- and later fourth century, though evidence of an interest in poetry or cultivated letter-writing is lacking (*PLRE* 1.56–7).

114 In all probability this is the famous Q. Aurelius Symmachus (*PLRE* 1.865–71), well known for speeches and letters written over the later fourth century, and distinguished for his learning.

115 This may be (Valerius) Messalla Avienus of *PLRE* 2.760–1, a correspondent of Symmachus and a character in the *Saturnalia* of Macrobius, and also perhaps the poet Messalla mentioned in Rutilius Namatianus, *On his return* 1.267–8.

and Martius,[116] in our time surpassed by none
and Petrus, in a new style, yet equal
to the ancients, when he speaks so enthralling,[117] or
the manager whom the senate rightly prefers
to the poets of the municipal towns,[118]   310
or the eloquent men retained by our own land,
charming Anthedius and Hoenius
my teacher, graced with awe-inspiring Muses,[119]
clever Lampridius,[120] and the astute Leo,[121]
Severianus, supreme in the high style   315
and no less able with the writer's pen,
just as Quintilian used to recommend.[122]

These measures of my really sterile Muse
seldom do I entrust even to a shred
of paper that might wrap pepper and mackerel.[123]   320

---

116 Martius has not been convincingly identified; a Martius Myro is mentioned in
c. 23.444, owner of a large house, and may be the person meant here (*PLRE* 2.731).

117 For Petrus, praised in *c.* 3.5–10 as a patron of S., and extolled in *c.* 5.564–73 as an
outstanding member of Majorian's staff, see *PLRE* 2.866.

118 A prefect of the city may be meant, as Anderson, citing a passage in the satirist Juvenal
(4.77), suggests; Loyen identifies him with the author of an extant treatise on agriculture, of
uncertain date, with one book in verse, but his multiple identification is unstable.

119 Nothing is known of Anthedius (*PLRE* 2.93), except the little that Sidonius provides:
in the prose introduction of *c.* 22 he is praised for his poetry (as the head of the 'Apolline
college') and his expertise in various branches of erudite learning. Hoenius presumably
taught at Lyon or Arles (so PLRE 2.566).

120 Lampridius (*PLRE* 2.656–7) is complimented in a letter that S. wrote to him (*Ep.* 8.9) as
'the glory of Thalia' ('light poetry'), and elsewhere praised for his grandeur in both prose and
verse (*Ep.* 9.13.2, vv. 21–3); he taught at Bordeaux. In *Ep.* 8.11.3–14, S. laments his murder.

121 Leo (*PLRE* 2.662–3) received from Sidonius *Ep.* 4.22 and *Ep.* 8.3 in the 470s, and was
warmly praised in the latter for his accomplishment in both prose and verse; in *c.* 23.446–54
he is praised as a jurist, and also as a writer of epic. He was eminent in many technical
subjects, as shown by the prose introduction to *c.* 14.2. His career perhaps extended into the
480s.

122 Severianus (*PLRE* 2.999–1000) is praised as a *rhetor* (teacher of oratory) in *Ep.* 9.13.4
(he was a guest at the party with Domnulus, Lampridius, Sidonius and Majorian), and
praised in passing in *Ep.* 9.15.1 *c.* 37. His work collecting rhetorical precepts (see Halm
[1860]) is extant, and gives some point to the comparison with Quintilian.

123 An old joke about the possible fates of paper that had contained bad poetry: what could
they be used for later when rejected? The reference to mackerel goes back to Catullus and

For what god will allow my thrown away sheets
to enjoy fine scents, to hold nard-oil, or touch
alabaster boxes fragrant with perfumes
like those devised by famous Niceros,[124]
or cinnamon derived from the Indian pyre   325
that makes the Phoenix young again through death,[125]
costum, malobathron, amomum, roses,
myrrh, or incense, or balm of Gilead?[126]
Therefore stand up for what I have done, defend
what though unwise was just good manners from   330
a school-friend who was simply obeying you.
But first remember to summon that pillar
of learning, brother Probus;[127] he surely,
a kindly man, knows well how to attach
a forthright theta to this kind of scribbles.[128]   335
But I know well; I don't dispute my guilt;
the learned do not like a shameless poet.
But I'll not greatly fear the pompous words
of a reproachful reader, should there be
one who, fancying himself as stern and strict   340
and spoiling the fun of my Terpsichore,[129]
like a third Cato[130] corrugates his lips
and trains on me his rhinocerotian nose.[131]

Persius, the reference to pepper to Horace. This passage has no relevance to the question of
how S.'s work was published, as Anderson (introduction, lv, n. 1) and others have supposed.
Line 321 makes it clear that the subsequent fate of the paper once used is the issue.
    124 Niceros was an expert maker of perfume in the time (late first century) of the epigram-
matist Martial (6.55.3, 10.38.8, 12.65.4).
    125 The death of the Phoenix is a favourite topic of S. (c. 2.417, 7.354, 11.125, 22.50).
    126 See the remarks on the longer list of fragrances at c. 2.413–15.
    127 Probus 4 (*PLRE* 2.910–11) was a pupil at the school of Eusebius (in Arles or Lyon); S.
speaks very highly of him in *Ep.* 4.1.2–3.
    128 Theta signifies 'death' (from the Greek word *thanatos*), and is used playfully by
Martial and Ausonius in their light verse as a mark of disgrace.
    129 S. uses the name of the Muse Terpsichore (Muse of dancing) only here in his verse,
perhaps for its self-belittling suggestion of 'dancing about' or frivolity; his preferred Muse is
Thalia (c. 9.18). In *Ep.* 8.16.2 he refers to using a 'fictitious Terpsichore' in earlier work.
    130 The phrase 'third Cato' may derive from the satirist Juvenal (2.40); it refers to a critic
of morality or (in this case) Latinity in the tradition of the elder and younger Catos.
    131 Cf. *c.* 3.8. n.

Don't be afraid of such a learned man;
But if you wish to know the truth, no-one,   345
believe me, knows as much as he does not know.[132]

---

132 However knowledgeable a person may be, there is much more that they do not know.

Poem 10
Preface to the Epithalamium
for Ruricius and Hiberia

INTRODUCTION

Hiberia was the daughter of Ommatius, to whom Sidonius sent an invitation to attend a sixteenth birthday celebration at his home (poem 17). The families were no doubt friends, with status and interests in common. There is a detailed account of Ruricius in *PLRE* 2.960, but the information belongs to a later date; he was a cleric by 477, and a bishop (of Limoges) eight years later. A letter to him from S. (*Ep.* 8.10), from this much later context, is taken up with the exchange of eulogies. One of the five children of the pair married Agricola, brother of Sidonius' wife Papianilla and son of the deceased emperor Avitus (*PLRE* 2.1319, stemma 16). There is no detail in this epithalamium by which a date for this poem could be fixed or even suggested, and it would probably be wrong to see a chronological progression in the poems of this section.

Sidonius has composed a colourful and playful prelude, as each god enacts a relaxed parody of his or her specialism, with more or less ability. Epithalamia (without preludes), some much longer than this poem, had been composed by Catullus (poem 64: its description of the setting, in Thessaly, in lines 31–48 seems influential on S.), by Statius (*Silvae* 1.2) and by Claudian (poem 10 and *Shorter Poems*, 25). Claudian also wrote Fescennines, suitably dignified, for the marriage of the emperor Honorius and Maria (*ca.* 12–14). Numerous adaptations of the epithalamium were composed by Christian writers, including Paulinus of Nola, Dracontius and Venantius Fortunatus; this one follows older types of expression. On epithalamia in general there is a brief but helpful notice in OCD[4]. This prelude is in elegiac couplets; the main poem (*c.* 11) is in hexameters. The more ambitious epithalamium of S. (*c.* 15) is introduced by a short preface in hendecasyllables (*c.* 14), as well as a letter in prose.

TRANSLATION

When Pelion revealed the marriage-feast in Pagase's caves
for the young sea-goddess beneath Emathian crags,[1]
the abundant luggage of the gods made the area too confined;[2]
on one side heaven, on the other, sea, vied with their wealth.
Well nigh hidden in green attire, the father-in-law, himself   5
matching his sea-green cloak,[3] directed choruses;
the nymph also, who came from the waves naked to her wedding,
began to fear the members of her clothed husband.
All the gods who attended set aside their fearsomeness
and joked about their functions, each one's special power.   10
Jupiter hurled a tepid thunderbolt, lacking in weight,
and said, 'much better now, with Cytherea's heat!'[4]
Then Pollux, praised for boxing, Castor for his horsemanship,
Pallas for her plumed helmet, Delia for her quivers,[5]
did a bit; Alcides played the fool with his club, Mars with his spear,   15
then Arcas with his staff, Bromius with his fawnskin.[6]
Here too peerless Orpheus had introduced the Pipliades
to delight with strings, with voice, by hand, in songs, with pipes.
Pretentious Hymen[7] brought together all the arts; any who
did not please by their skill perhaps did so in spirit.   20

---

1 Pelion is a mountain in Thessaly, and Pagasa a nearby town, a suitable venue for the gods of Olympus and other participants. The same area is evoked at the beginning of Catullus *c*. 64.

2 This detail was inspired perhaps by Catullus, *c*. 64.32–4.

3 Nereus, father of Thetis, is here in three shades of green.

4 A full-strength thunderbolt would have been dangerous; the heat of Venus (Cytherea, named from the island sacred to her) would compensate for the tepid one, and be more pleasant.

5 For Pollux and Castor, twin sons of Leda, see *c*. 5.183, 287, *c*. 7.35. Pallas, as warrior goddess, has a helmet with distinctive plumes; Delia (Diana) was the goddess of hunting.

6 Arcas (meaning 'born in Arcadia') is Mercury, whose staff, used for special purposes, was distinctive. For Bacchus and the fawnskin he wore, cf. *c*. 5.497.

7 Hymen, the god of marriage, is here presented as an ostentatious impresario, making a parade of the divine skills.

Fescennine songs,[8] however, did not gain entry, till our
Apollo's well-known lyre had rung out with this song.[9]

8 Fescennines, supposedly songs of ribald abuse sung at weddings, are mentioned, but
rarely exemplified, in the ancient evidence; they usually remain in the background of formal
epithalamia. Here Fescennines are said to be postponed, so that Apollo (see next note) may
sing his larger offering.

9 Like other poets, S. regularly sees Apollo as a personal patron of verse. The song or
poem that follows is of course his own work ('our' in line 21) and his style 'well-known', and
there is probably a joking reference to the fact that he was nicknamed 'Apollo' or Phoebus by
his friends (*Ep.* 8.11.3, and in lines 2 and 30 of the poem within it).

Poem 11
Epithalamium of Ruricius and Hiberia

INTRODUCTION

The poem begins by describing a temple, wherever it was, one exquisitely constructed and decorated by the god Vulcan (1–33); meanwhile Triton (one of the minor sea-gods), the nymph Galatea and the Loves assemble and play together (34–46). The Love-god visits Venus to tell her the good news that Ruricius has fallen in love, and praises Ruricius (61–71); Venus replies, eulogising the beauty of Hiberia, said by her to surpass the loveliest women of mythology (72–92). In lines 93–134 the guests and officiants all travel – Venus in her remarkably splendid chariot – to the ceremony, and the wedding takes place, in the setting briefly given by the preface (*c.* 10), with suitably brief words from the goddess. On epithalamia in general, see the introduction to the preface (*c.* 10), and for the possible influence of Claudian, Gualandri (2020).

It is most unfortunate that the opening lines, especially line 5, that help to portray the setting of the temple of Venus and its background are so textually corrupt as to be unintelligible. The rather drastic remedies suggested by Loyen (1960), xlix and 96 do not improve the situation.

Between the Dark Blue rocks, the Ephyrean summits,[1] where
Above Idalium skyward ascends Orithyion[2]
with salt-scoured mountain summit, where, as it chanced, the alarmed Tiphys

---

1 The 'Dark Blue rocks', as they were often called in Greek and Latin writers, are the Symplegades (line 4) at the entrance to the Black Sea. Ephyra is an old name for Corinth, and the phrase here refers to its citadel or mountains close by. These places are far from each other, and from Malea in line 5; they could all be part of a journey by Jason, perhaps from Pelion to Delphi (cf. Herodotus 4.179), as Anderson noted, but such a journey would have no relevance to the location of the wedding.
2 Idalium is a town in Cyprus, sacred to Venus. Orithyion might be one of its two hills.

made his escape, and so made fast, the errant Symplegades[3]
(*corrupt*) and ...?belched forth... ?running back...Malea ?to raucous noise,[4] 5
there emerges into the Isthmian sea[5] encased in wings of rock,
from beneath the towering cliffs a bay; often in this recess,
as if gathered somehow from all the light of the whole sky,
the assembled daylight is compressed and through the trembling waves
penetrates the secrets of the bay; while the water, suffused   10
by this deep radiance, passes on, and – marvellous to describe –
the water drinks the sun, but added to the delicate stream
the light pierces the liquid with unwetted rays, quite dry.
This spot favoured their enterprise; for there the Lemnian
built for Venus a mock-temple, while, thunderbolts set aside,   15
Pyragmon, blackened by his fire, made smoke assiduously.[6]
Here there is marble from five regions, giving five colours
– Ethiopian, Phrygian, Parian, Punic, Lacedaemonian –
their tinctures purple, green, mottled, ivory-like, and white.[7]
On the doorposts coruscates the yellow radiance of topaz;   20
fluorite, sardonyx, Iberan amethyst, Indian jasper,[8]
Chalcidic gems, and Scythian emeralds, beryl, agates[9] –
all these ennoble double doors, on silver hinges hung,
through which the light pours from the dark emeralds that are within.
Onyx thickly encrusts the threshold, and, nearby, sapphires   25

---

3 The Symplegades were literally 'clashing' rocks', fixed according to myth after the passage of the ship Argo, steered by Tiphys.

4 Cape Malea is the southernmost promontory of the Peloponnese, a notorious hazard for shipping. To the acute geographical uncertainty of these lines is added a very severe one of grammar and sense. The word 'running back' seems to describe Malea or the disturbed water around it; the remainder is quite uncertain. The text of the line seems beyond repair, as noted above, and how a line, or a passage, written by S. reached this state is incomprehensible.

5 The Isthmian sea is one of the two seas close to Corinth (cf. *c.* 2.476). The point of 'emerges' is to show how the bay appears to the viewer, perhaps looking from a height.

6 Pyragmon: a Cyclops (a giant) who worked in Vulcan's smithy.

7 The list of their colours does not exactly co-ordinate with the list of marbles, as S. might have wished, if it were possible: Ethiopian is purple (*c.* 5.35), Phrygian is mottled (cf. *c.* 5.37), Parian white; Punic ivory-like (cf. *c.* 5.37), and Lacedaemonian green (*c.* 5.38–9).

8 Iberan amethyst (the Iberans, not to be confused with Iberians, lived in the Caucasus region) is not known; 'Indian' is a rare epithet for *iaspis* (jasper) (Pliny *NH* 37.114–18).

9 The Chalcidic gems have been identified with *chalcitis* (Pliny *NH* 37.191, Isidore, *Etymologies*, 16.15.9 and 20.11). Scythian gems were of high quality, as no doubt all these stones would be.

project their well-matched colouring onto the bluish lake.
The exterior is not made of dressed stone, but a thick layer
of pumice roughened by the incessant impact of the waves.
In the interior Mulciber[10] copied in gold the boulders
which jut out everywhere, and with his skill in full control   30
mimicked with consummate polish the unpolished works of nature,
committed to the job in hand, for as yet he knew not
the trickery which he would later scold with Lemnian chains.[11]

Here scaly Triton, in the join between his double backs,
just where the convolutions of his twisting tail combine,[12]   35
his heart enflamed even amidst the waters, bore Dione.
But Galatea, applying pressure with her twinkling shell,[13]
tickles the half-wild creature's bottom, and with stiffened thumb
gives it a pinch, pledging with secret touch the joys of marriage.
Then he – her lover – amused by this tormenting joke, smiles archly   40
at the cheeky wound, and gently smacks her with his fishy tail.
Behind there comes a host of Loves in amorous companies;
one steers a dolphin using roses, another, mounted on
a green sea-calf, rejects such reins, spreadeagled on its horns.
Others, who stand (though teetering when they move), with soaking feet   45
slither around, but fortify their footsteps with their wings.

Venus had let her soft cheek rest upon her bended arm;
her violets were withering, and, heavier with sleep,
her neck had started drooping with the chafing of the flowers.
Absent alone from the brothers' group was the one most beautiful,   50
the Love-god: he was planning for the Gauls an exquisite feast,
which father-in-law Ommatius, noblest of a noble race,
descendant of a patrician line,[14] laid on for his daughter
and her bridegroom, with fine omens.

---

10 Another Latin name for Vulcan. He is also called the Lemnian, from his birthplace on
the island of Lemnos (line 33).
11 The story about Ares and Aphrodite secretly lying together is told in Homer, *Odyssey*
8.268–366.
12 That is, where the tail joins his body.
13 Galatea, like Venus, often travelled in a shell.
14 For Ommatius see the introductions to *c.* 10 and *c.* 17.

But when the appointed day
duly shone forth, with rapid flight he visited his mother,   55
his torch, his bow, his quiver dangling from his body. Then,
dropping his head and resting on the edge of his left hand,
he beat his wings against his feet, well balanced in the air,[15]
and snatching kisses from his mother, as she returned from sleep,
he tapped her eyes, but half awake, with a lightly touching feather.   60
Then in excitement he spoke first: "mother, I bring to you
new joys, news of a wondrous spoil: haughty Ruricius[16]
is warmed by our love torches, and, enticed by your sweet poison,
gives heartfelt sighs for the anguish long desired by him – and us.
If their ages were present now, the Lemnian maid would be   65
awarding him her power,[17] the Cretan girl, the labyrinth's thread,[18]
Alceste her own life,[19] Circe her herbs,[20] Calypso apples[21]
Scylla the fateful lock,[22] Atalanta her feet,[23] Medea her rages,[24]
Hippodame her wax,[25] Jove's offspring by a swan, her crown;[26]
for him Dido would have braved the sword,[27] and Phyllis used her noose,[28] 70

15 The wings, flapping hard to keep him stationary, appear to beat against his feet. For
this subtle picture S. draws on the poet Statius for a choice word (at *Thebaid* 9.686).

16 The word 'haughty' hints at reserve on the part of Ruricius, seen through Love's eyes.

17 Hypsipyle, queen of Lemnos, welcomed Jason when he came with the Argonauts to her
island, and shared her authority with him.

18 Ariadne gave Theseus the thread that enabled him to escape from the Cretan labyrinth.

19 Alceste (cf. *c.* 15.165; the name is usually Alcestis) gave her own life for her husband
Admetus.

20 On the island of the witch Circe turned Odysseus's followers into pigs with a magic
herb (*Odyssey*, 10.235–43); while he was there Odysseus was given a magic herb by Hermes
(10.287–93).

21 For Calypso, see *Odyssey* 5.1–200. She would have feasted Ruricius as she did
Odysseus, over many years.

22 Scylla had cut off the tress of her father Nisus's hair on which his life depended, and
offered it to Minos, the invader, with whom she had fallen in love (Ovid *M.* 8.81–95).

23 For swift-footed Atalanta, cf. *c.* 2.495–7, *c.* 5.167–8.

24 Rage is a less estimable quality, but certainly useful.

25 Hippodame (also Hippodamia) provided the wax with which her lover Pelops disabled
the chariot of his rival and won the race (cf. *c.* 2.490–2). Also in *c.* 14.12 and *c.* 23.392.

26 Helen crowned Menelaus with a garland (Hyginus [the mythographer], 78).

27 Dido, queen of Carthage, killed herself out of love for the departing Aeneas.

28 Phyllis longed in vain for the promised return of Demophoon, and took her own life.

Evadne would have faced the flames,[29] the Sestian maid the waves."[30]
To this she replied: "We are pleased, my son, that you have overpowered
this rebel, and that you praise him; but such is the girl's beauty
that if in times past Stheneboia's hero had looked on her
he would not, following his scorn, have quelled the dire Chimaera,[31]   75
and though the man who, proud of his Thermodontian mother,
despised the audacious prayers of his Cnossian step-mother,[32]
had he seen her, he would have died (I grant), but rightly accused;
and if by chance she had been a fourth contender in the contest,[33]
the shepherd on Rhoetaean Ida would have damned me too;   80
or if he had said "if you must win, give her to me; I prefer her",
then I would have awarded him, in return for beauty's prize,[34]
this beauty. What grace and spirit glow in her face! Her colour
makes purple inconspicuous; outshone by her bright face
the twinkling of the pearls circling her neck is so much blackness.   85
By various deeds, Hiberia, would men have sought your hand:
Pelops with chariot,[35] Hippomenes in races,[36] in wrestling
Achelous,[37] in war great Aeneas,[38] Perseus with Gorgon;[39]

29 Evadne burnt herself on the funeral pyre of her husband Capaneus.
30 Hero, a priestess at Sestos, drowned herself when her beloved Leander failed to swim across the Hellespont.
31 The scorn of Bellerophon for Stheneboea (Homer, *Iliad* 6.160–1) led indirectly to her father's demand that he kill the Chimaera, which he did. Cf. *c.* 5.178, 184.
32 If Hippolytus (*c.* 7.199, *Ep.* 7.2.8), son of an Amazon mother, had known Hiberia, he would have met his death for passionately assaulting her, but not after a false accusation, as happened to Hippolytus.
33 The beauty contest on Mount Ida, in which Paris had to judge between Venus, Juno and Minerva.
34 Had Hiberia been a candidate in the beauty contest, Paris might have preferred her to Venus but bargained that he should take Hiberia yet not claim the prize.
35 This refers to the expertise of Pelops in chariot racing, not the foul play on his behalf mentioned in *c.* 2.490–2.
36 For Hippomenes compare *c.* 2.496, *c.* 5.168 and *c.* 14.14–15.
37 Achelous is the 'wrestling river' of *c.* 9.99 and 'the river' of *c.* 15.143, which only Hercules could overcome.
38 Aeneas fought in Troy and in particular in Italy, as related in Vergil's *Aeneid*.
39 Perseus is mentioned briefly in *c.* 7.35 and *c.* 23.296, with the scimitar in the latter passage. The fatal Gorgon which he wielded is mentioned in *c.* 15.7 and 23, the latter passage showing how the sight of it brought instant death. In *c.* 9.174 his worship at Argos is briefly alluded to.

Nor is her beauty less than that which so often led Jove
to be Delia, or a bull, swan, satyr, serpent, thunder, or gold.[40]   90
So come, let them be joined; their wealth, beauty and ancestry
are equal: your arrow has found no inequality.
But why do I delay the marriage?"

                                                 So she spoke and sought
her chariot, with its yoke of crystal, which in early winter,
when the ice of the young world began to enlarge the Caucasus,   95
were crushed by a slab of Tanais with Hyperborean frosts,
taking the nature of a gem, having lost its watery nature.[41]
Coupling the chariot is a yokebeam shaped in yellow gold;
a river had sent this, the one in whose whirlpools the Nymphs
cherished Mygdonian Midas, who, a pauper amidst gold,   100
enriched the river Pactolus, when his lust for gold backfired.[42]
The wheels, which glitter, with pellucid rims joining the spokes,
are made from the jaws of a Marmaric beast; the creature moans
that with its curving tusks torn out its mouth had been disarmed.[43]
This, also a gift, was sent by one who vexes warm Erythrae[44]   105
– naked, with an Ethiopian's colour, and hair well greased –
a flabby Indian, leading odoriferous safaris.[45]
Her swans, accustomed to take food in Cyprus, Venus steers
with myrtle reins bound with ribbons; their bodies otherwise taut,
their milk-white necks are curved into a circlet of bright coral.   110
So like this they set out; floating, the wheels furrow their way

---

40 With typical compression S. packs into a single line many of the disguises adopted by
Jupiter. In the form of Delia/Diana he came to Cynosoura, nurse of Zeus; he came to Europa
as a bull; to Leda as a swan; to Antiope as a satyr; to Mnemosyne as a snake; to Semele as
a thunderbolt; to Danae as a shower of gold. There is a similar list in c. 15.175–6, where five
cases are mentioned and the victims named. A passage of Ovid (M. 6.110–14) underlies both.
41 On the genesis of crystal Sidonius follows, in his poetic terms, the explanation
generally current in antiquity (for example in Pliny NH 37.23–9). Among others Claudian
wrote epigrams (Shorter poems, 33–9) on the topic.
42 The 'golden touch' of Midas famously got the better of him.
43 There is qualified sympathy for the mutilated beast, as in c. 2.54–5.
44 On the town or region of Erythrae see also c. 2.447, c. 5.285, c. 22.22.
45 The dressing used on his hair lends its aroma to the whole trip.

through the empty air, and in this clear expanse no track is left.[46]
Here the threefold Graces with single impulse join with her,
here Plenty from her ample horn diffuses its fragrance,[47]
here Flora strews the earth with flowers, but flowers that never fade,   115
here Pharian Osiris joins Sicilian Ceres,
here in her robe Pomona brings abundant fruit in season,
here Pallas comes with oil-mills overflowing among the presses[48]
here a Bacchante, her body embellished by a dappled fawn-skin,
whirls the Indian emblems of Bromius with Echionian wand.   120
Here too the now sexless Corybant who in Sigeum's caves
dances on Dindymon warms up again; from his hoarse throat
the hollowed flute groans forth his lust through double cavities.[49]

So they come to the wedding; incense, nard, balsam, and myrrh
are here; the Phoenix offers cinnamon from his living pyre.[50]   125
Indeed, the coming winter, quickened by the festive warmth,
already is less cold, and offering the feel of spring
the wedding gives this place what the seasons do not give the world.
Then the Paphian, joining the right hands of the bride and groom,
intoned the customary prayers, but not in many words,   130
lest even words should cause delay: "may you lead your lives as one,
happy and prosperous; may you have children and grandchildren,
and may great-grandchildren discern in you what they should wish for."

---

46 In a very different situation Ovid makes much of the absence of clear markings for
Phaethon as he rode in the sky (cf. *M.* 2.133, modified by *M.* 2.170).
47 The fabled goat's horn of Amaltheia, or horn of plenty (cornucopia).
48 The presses were smaller, but the mills overflowed too, such was the fertility brought
by Athena and her olives.
49 The Corybants were priests responsible for the worship of Cybele; S. imagines one
living in a cave near Dindymon, where her worship took place.
50 For the Phoenix see the note on *c.* 2.417, and Van der Broek (1972).

Poem 12
To Catullinus, senator of high rank

INTRODUCTION

This poem, placed between the two epithalamia, but of a very different nature, is a reply in hendecasyllables to a request from Catullinus for an epithalamium, whether for himself or someone in his family. Catullinus (*PLRE* 2.272–3) was a native of Auvergne, like Sidonius, and a close friend of his, as emerges very clearly from *Ep.* 1.11.3. Along with S., he had held office, identified as that of *tribunus et notarius* ('tribune and notary'), at some time between 458 and 461 (*PLRE* 2.117). The designation *v. c.* (probably added by Sidonius himself) – that is, *vir clarissimus* – indicates the senatorial grade that they attained from the office.

The precise details of the troublesome situation that S. describes are not clear. (Catullinus, of course, may well have known something of them; he would certainly be amused as well as disappointed). The poet's immediate problem is his close proximity to a group of Burgundians, with their Germanic words, their awful songs and their bad breath. A kitchen scene is indicated by lines 13–19 (the reference to Homer in line 19 would otherwise have no point); perhaps S. found himself in charge of feeding them, but how that happened we can only speculate. This predicament may have happened in Lyon, where Burgundians were (or had been) numerous at the time of Majorian's arrival there (*c.* 5.567–73 might refer, though the picture is not clear). For discussion of the episode and its context see Stevens (1979), 91 n. 3, and Kelly (2020), 171, n. 33, who references numerous scholars and concludes that the date is 461 or a little later.

TRANSLATION

Why do you order me to write a poem
(as if I could) , for Fescennine Dione,[1]
placed as I am among these hairy hordes,
obliged to put up with Germanic words
and praise continually – with scowling face –   5
whatever is crooned by a fat Burgundian[2]
as he saturates his locks in rancid butter.[3]
Would you like me to tell you what wrecks a poem?
Repelled by barbarous strumming, my Thalia[4]
has jettisoned the style of six-foot verse   10
since glimpsing my patrons – all seven feet tall.[5]
Happy, one may say, are your eyes and ears,
happy, indeed, your nose, if it avoids
the reek of garlic and filthy onions
belched out at you each morning by ten saucepans;[6]   15
happy too not to be sought, like a father's
old parent or your nurse's husband,[7] by
so many and such large giants at daybreak
as even Homer's kitchens could scarcely feed.[8]

1 Dione (Venus) is expected to enjoy Fescennines, described above on *c.* 10.21 n. Like most poets who mention them, S. did not produce any Fescennines of his own, even in happy circumstances. In the preface to poem 11 they disappear from consideration (see *c.* 10.21 and note).

2 The Burgundians were a Germanic tribe active in Gaul; S. will have recognised at least some German words, if he cared. On the Burgundians in general, see Wood (2021).

3 Butter was not a feature of Roman upper class diet or coiffure.

4 The Muse Thalia stands for light verse, as in *c.* 9.18 (see note) and *c.* 23.435.

5 As in English, the Latin word for 'foot' is applied both to metre and to anatomy. If S. had written an epithalamium for Catullinus, it would probably have been mainly in the hexameter, but here of course the wordplay is the main thing. 'Patrons' is sarcastic.

6 Anderson is helpful with his 'breakfasts'; the smells must, however, come from some kind of cookware, or perhaps platters (the Latin word here is *apparatus*).

7 This complaint – the third part of the mock 'makarismos' ('happy are you if ...') – refers, as earlier Roman writers often do, to the tedium of the *salutatio*, the formal morning call on patrons. S. imagines types of elderly caller or 'client' (as they were called), but these giant Burgundians, whatever the actual relationship was, are far worse.

8 The reference is to *Odyssey* 7.103–5, where Homer speaks of the fifty maids employed by Alcinous, whose kitchen garden is described in 7.112–32. There was a lavish supply of food and wine there (7.175–7).

But now my Muse is dumb and after jesting   20
with these few hendecasyllables reins me in,
lest anyone call even these lines satire.[9]

9 Catullinus would have recognised the reference here, now amusing but on a previous
occasion less so. When an anonymous and treasonable satire, directed against various
citizens, appeared in Arles in 461, Paeonius, an enemy of S., sought to implicate him on the
basis of his close friendship with Catullinus during a dinner in the presence of the emperor
Majorian. Some quick-witted repartee saved S., who protested his ignorance and innocence
and won the day. This story is related by him at length in *Ep.* 1.11 and discussed by Stevens
(1979), 51–6 and Harries (1994), 14–15 and 93–5. In this line he is not, of course, admitting
guilt, but mockingly referring to his enemy's ill-advised accusation.

Poem 13
To the Emperor Majorian

INTRODUCTION

Poem 13 is a neat and in some ways witty poem, but also a very serious one, addressed to the emperor Majorian, now in Lyon, on what Sidonius calls a matter of life and death. It begins by speaking eulogistically of the many labours of Hercules, with whom the emperor identified; but S. focuses on one particular labour, the killing of the three-headed monster Geryon, and semi-facetiously asks Majorian to imagine his suppliants to be Geryons and cut out three 'heads' in each case. (What the 'headings' or perhaps demands of this tribute or tax that had been imposed or threatened exactly were is unclear: the joke is not affected.) The poet continues, in the second half, in a different metre (hendecasyllables replace elegiacs) to beg the emperor to restore his shattered fatherland and his own very life, and, in language that resembles that of lines of the panegyric (*c.* 5.574–85), to save ruined Lyon. If Majorian grants the boon he seeks, may the Sidonian purple he wears (there is at least a hint of an cheeky pun on the poet's name in line 26: 'Sidonius' also means 'purple') clothe him for many years; may he in due course celebrate a quinquennial celebration; and may he pacify Rome's enemies in North Germany and the Low Countries. He reminds the emperor of one of the traditional functions of poets, which is to immortalise the achievements of the great. But now his Muse has fallen silent and, instead of polishing his poetic craft, he has to look for money. Whether the plea succeeded is not known – the episode is discussed by Stevens (1979), 52–86 and Harries (1994), 84–6 – but he was probably not literally impoverished, and relations may have been amicable thereafter, as before.

It is assumed in what follows that poem 13 followed the panegyric (*c.* 5); if it had preceded, and that had became known, Sidonius might have been embarrassed, to say the least, by an apparent attempt to put himself first, and by the facetious elements.

TRANSLATION

Amphitryon's descendant Hercules earned life in heaven,
(so says revered antiquity) for freeing the Earth.[1]
But though with terrible demeanour, using his bare arms
he crushed the hoarsely bellowing throat of Cleonae's beast[2]
and though even with his flesh-searing sword, he hardly slew   5
the hydra, as death drew from each wound an extra life;[3]
and though when bringing from the Erymanthian wood his captive prey
he ridiculed the monstrous wild boar's crippled snout;[4]
and though bursting open the flame-born thief's smoke-belching throat
at last he bade the cows go straight ahead once more,[5]   10
and although bull, hind, giant, wrestler, host, and Amazon,[6]
the Cretan beast, the dog, the Hesperides extol him,[7]
no accomplishment of his outshone the rout of Geryon,
whose one and only trunk he stripped of its three heads.[8]

1 Roman poets often called Hercules the son of Amphitryon, preferring a sonorous word to a biologically exact one. After his many labours on earth Hercules was taken up to Olympus to be immortal and live the luxurious life of the gods.

2 Cleonae was a village in the district of Nemea in southern Greece; the beast is also called the Nemean lion.

3 The Hydra took a long time to die, two heads being produced when one was chopped off. The problem was solved by searing each wound as it occurred.

4 The Erymanthian boar roamed and ravaged in a mountainous part of Arcadia, in southern Greece.

5 The giant Cacus, son of Vulcan, stole from Hercules, when he came to Rome, several of the cattle of Geryon that he had brought from Spain, disguising their hiding place by pulling them backwards into a cave. Hercules, deceived by this but then alerted by mooing, tore open the cave and strangled him.

6 In this line and the next Sidonius presents these and other labours and feats in the tersest possible way, as he liked to do (cf. c. 9.94–100, with the main note, and c. 15.141–3). The Amazon was Hippolyte, whose girdle Hercules was ordered to obtain; she and her Amazon army were defeated.

7 Here the reference is to the beautiful bull that Hercules was to bring back from Crete. After subduing it he rode it back to Greece, before freeing it. The dog is Cerberus, the fierce guard of the Underworld, which Hercules was ordered to overcome without weapons and then take to earth. The Hesperides were nymphs that dwelt in the far west, from whom Hercules took their golden apples after overcoming a serpent.

8 The three-headed (in some accounts triple-bodied) giant Geryon was destroyed by Hercules, who, as commanded, took away his marvellous cattle (cf. above, lines 13–14).

So much for Alcides; but you, second Tirynthian,[9]   15
an emperor, indeed our great God's greatest care,[10]
whose arrows dragon, deer and boar alike experienced
when neither tooth nor poison nor retreat availed,[11]
imagine we are Geryon,[12] and this tri-bute a monster:
relieve me of three heads, and so keep me alive.   20
(new para) These pleas your suppliant subject has addressed to you
and awaits a reply that is kind and beneficent –
that you restore our country, and so our life as well,
delivering Lyon after its catastrophe[13] –
this is the entreaty that your own Sidonius makes.   25
So may the purple (treated with Sidonian dye)[14]
be your official dress for many years to come;
so, with five years of your eternal power discharged
may a quinquennial festival honour your rule;[15]
so, with the double bank's o'erflowing swell subdued   30
may the Sygambrian drink the Waal shorn of his locks.[16]

9 Another poetic name for Hercules, the most famous inhabitant of the Greek city of Tiryns.

10 The last three words recall a passage in which the goddess Venus so refers to her beloved Iulus, son of Aeneas at Vergil, *A.* 1.678. The broad similarity of the allusion is noteworthy, and the reference to a prominent context in Vergil's epic has especial point. For Sidonius the reference is to the Christian God (the supreme power), not the goddess Venus, and the change of context from Iulus to Majorian is pointed, a strong sign of his commitment to the new emperor: a good example of what is known to critics as *Kontrastimitation.*

11 Cf. *c.* 5.153–4.

12 An exquisite joke involving Geryon. The reading of the manuscripts and all conjectures offered are far less apt. See note on the text used.

13 S. surely refers to the closing lines of his panegyric of Majorian, *c.* 5.574–603.

14 This is a clear reference to S.'s own name, which is also a poetic word for 'purple', as used in imperial regalia. The poet is in earnest but capable of humour; his name may come to show its significance in the future, to his and Majorian's political advantage. The point of repeated 'so' is 'if you do this'.

15 S. wishes Majorian at least five more years in power, something that was relatively unusual. In the event Majorian ruled for a slightly shorter period, and in less happy circumstances than S. expects here.

16 Sidonius wishes peace, or easy victories over peoples of the Rhineland (proud like the river, by implication) and the Sygambri, by the Waal, famed in literature for their blond hair, which the Romans (here) would remove; for this custom cf. *Ep.* 8.9.28–30. The Vandals occupying Africa – a more dangerous enemy – are not mentioned.

If you bestow upon your poet this benefit,
I will commit to history's eternal page
whatever feats you celebrate with glorious triumphs.[17]
But now my garrulous Muse is mute, faced with the tax:[18]   35
rather than study her Vergil and her Terence.
she counts the shillings and pence owed to the treasury
and dreads the hand and rope that punished Marsyas[19]
who with his long-held hate of Phoebus Apollo
now threatens Apollo's poets with death by public hanging.   40

17 The emperor's exploits, which would (it is assumed) earn triumphs, would be written up by S. in prose or verse – as poets often promised to their patrons.

18 S. wishes to be relieved of any heading in the law that applied to him and his countrymen, or any financial contribution required of them. He himself pretends to be a pauper, unable to find the funds owed to the Treasury.

19 Moreover, as one devoted to Apollo, the poet fears that Marsyas will take revenge for his famous flogging at the hands of Phoebus Apollo (March [2008], 83–4). Marsyas, the former satyr, had become, with symbols of hand and rope, a figure symbolising 'Italian rights', and so liberty, such as many cities (including Lyon) possessed in prominent places. Statues of him were common: see Platner and Ashby (1929), *Statua Marsyae*.

Poem 14 (Prose letter)
Greetings to his friend Polemius

INTRODUCTION

This letter is clearly related to the epithalamium (*c.* 15), which is preceded also by a preface with a strong mythological element, a feature found elsewhere in Sidonius though in a different metre (elegiac couplets, not hendecasyllables as here). As in the editions of Lüetjohann, Loyen and Anderson, and in early testimonies, the preface follows the letter immediately and then leads into the main epithalamium. Presumably this arrangement goes back to the original organisation of the poems, whether this was performed by the author himself or perhaps a close contact (on this question see introduction, section 6). The arrangement of preface and the epithalamium written by Claudian in *ca.* 9 and 10 is formally similar, though there is no letter, formal or informal (one can hardly imagine Claudian being informal or intimate), and the same is true of the *Praefatio* of eight lines before Claudian's epithalamium in *c.m.* 25. The date of the Epithalamium of Sidonius is unclear, but is more likely to be in the 460s than the 470s.

In *PLRE* 2.895 there is information (from *Ep.* 4.14, written to Polemius) about his supposed descent from the historian Tacitus, and perhaps from the poet and statesman Ausonius too, as well as on the career of Polemius after 470 – at which time both S. and Polemius evidently had a strong commitment to Christianity. Having conveyed his greetings, S. quickly turns to his main concern, which is to defend his use of certain technical words in the main poem that are taken from the Greek, a feature that might offend some linguistic purists. As for the point at issue in this letter, S. assembles an interesting group to defend his own linguistic preferences. Not obvious thoughts on the morning of a wedding, perhaps, but S. appears to have had reservations about the conventional jollities of the wedding ceremony and finds philosophy preferable – he and Polemius share an interest here – or at least of equal importance.

Greetings From Sidonius To His Friend Polemius

1. After your departure, Polemius, my dear brother, I was pondering at length to what extent I should sing Fescennines[1] at the wedding of a philosopher, such as you are. A topic occurred to me, which now that it has been worked out can make clear that I took more account of your learning than your situation. So setting aside the tenderness of an epithalamium, I drove my pen through the harshest and most rugged rules of philosophy, the nature of which is such that without many new words – I say this with apologies to all other men of eloquence – which are known particularly to you and your fellow Platonists even trifles such as these could not be expounded. 2. You must consider whether the ears of some people, out of unfamiliarity, are over-hasty to regard the use of *centrum, proportio, diastemata, climata, myrae* as not useful in an epithalamium.[2] This much I can certainly affirm with confidence: that according to Magnus, a man of consular rank, who is indeed great, Domnulus, a man of quaestorian rank, and the eminent Leo,[3] music and astronomy, branches of philosophy which are next to arithmetic in importance, can in no way be clarified without these words; if any despise them as Greek (which they are) and foreign, they should be aware that they will either have to renounce once and for all any reference to this sort of knowledge or else be unable to discuss it at all – certainly not in precise detail, anyway – on that basis. 3. If any suggest that the truth of the matter is not as I declare it to be, I surrender in my absence to these criticisms; but let those who feel differently be sure that my position cannot be condemned without also condemning Marcus Varro,[4] Serenus (I mean Sammonicus, not Septimius),[5] and Censorinus, who wrote a splendid book about birthdays.[6] 4. Here you will also read a new word, namely

---

1 For Fescennines, see note on *c.* 10.21; given their supposed character, S. exaggerates his dilemma.

2 The references are respectively to lines 78; 69; 64; 66; 66.

3 For Magnus, see *PLRE* 2.700–1; for Domnulus (who may be the quaestor of *c.* 5.570) *PLRE* 2.374; for Leo *PLRE* 2.662–3 and *c.* 9.314, *c.* 23.446–54. They all find such words necessary.

4 For Varro, see *c.* 2.190, *c.* 23.150–1.

5 Serenus Sammonicus, an antiquarian scholar, was author of a long work (entitled 'Recondite Things'); Septimius Serenus wrote books of poetry on rural matters. The latter is mentioned in *c.* 9.267 in the same line as Petronius and Martial.

6 Censorinus, a Roman grammarian of the third century AD, wrote a work 'On Birthdays'.

essentia; but you should be aware that Cicero himself used that word, for he cited *essentia*, and also *indoloria*, commenting – quite rightly – that 'it is permissible to give new names to new ideas'.[7] For just as from the words (for example) *sapere* and *intellegere* we form the nouns *sapientia* and *intelligentia*,[8] so, following the rules, we do not avoid *essentia* which is from *esse*. Therefore since, I, a man of Gaul,[9] led by devotion to your love, have introduced the subject-matter of a sophistic circle, I look to you in particular to intercede for what I have done. Let Venus and the fabricated depictions of gods of love be bestowed on a person who cannot be eulogised in these terms.[10] Farewell.

7 Cicero was used as an authority for the word *essentia* by the philosopher Seneca in *Ep.* 58.6, but the word has not been found in his extant works. He discusses the legitimacy of Grecisms in general in *Academic Questions*, 1.7.

8 These words mean respectively 'wisdom' and 'understanding'.

9 He mentions his Gallic identity to validate his claim to be a speaker of good Latin.

10 If they (people who disagree with me) cannot be praised in the way that I am praising you, they need not expect more than love's conventional fictions.

Poem 14
Preface to the Epithalamium addressed
to Polemius and Araneola

INTRODUCTION

In this preface S. addresses the Muse Calliope and assures readers that in this wedding there is nothing unholy, with a quick reference to a few unhappy unions from mythology (a theme he also uses in *c.* 2.487–99). Then in three lines (21–3) the learned groom and his bride are introduced to the reader and S. calls on Calliope again for her help. If even the centaur Chiron could take part in the music (as he claims he did at the marriage of Peleus and Thetis famous from Catullus [*c.* 64]), then so can he. For Araneola, daughter of Magnus and sister of Felix (*c.* 9), see *PLRE* 2.126 (Magnus 2); for Polemius, see the above letter and *PLRE* 2.895. There is a helpful though short commentary on the epithalamium, the accompanying letter and the preface, by Ravenna (1990). The metre of this poem is hendecasyllabics.

TRANSLATION

Benignly shines the day arranged for this marriage;
May kindly Clotho grace it with her snow-white threads,[1]
May the white stones of the dark-skinned Indians mark it,[2]
and the ever flourishing and verdant olive-tree,
symbol of peace and youthfuness, ennoble it.   5
Calliope, come with your hand so glittering,
grant me the eloquence of the holy fountain[3]

---

1 Clotho is one of the three Fates. For their joint operations in different contexts from this one, see *c.* 5.312–13, *c.* 7.600–2.
2 The imagery used by S. combines Horace and Martial, as Anderson usefully explains.
3 Calliope was the chief of the Muses.

that Pegasus with flying hooves dug from the ground,
his mane dripping with poison from his mother's neck.[4]
Here there is no impiety; the maiden is   10
not dowered by the deaths of competing suitors,
nor does a Pelops here listen to the bloody
transactions of Oenomaus about a race;[5]
no pale Hippomanes slows down Schoeneus' maid
at the turning point of the race by dropping three apples;   15
not here does Calydon watch from her Aeolian height[6]
in wonder at the wrestling of Hercules, as
he bore down on the horn of the blustering river
continually refreshing his exhausted body
from the billowing waters of his enemy.   20
No: a learned young man and a modest young woman,
both holding from their birth the highest rank in Gaul,
are being married; so, goddess, instantly string
the heavenly lyre, and just because a greater Muse
has thundered forth, do not make my poor voice be quiet.[7]   25
When Thetis married, with Phoebus giving assent
even Chiron with his inferior plectrum played
without his bumpkin style arousing ridicule
from the good-natured crowd, although (it must be said)
the monster by his frequent neighing wrecked his song.   30

4 The poison is that of the Gorgon Medusa, beheaded by Perseus.
5 For the Pelops myth, see *c*. 490–1, and *c*. 11.87; for Hippomanes, *c*. 5.168, *c*. 11.87; for the contest with Achelous over Deianira, *c*. 2.497–9. These examples are used before S. in Claudian, *Shorter Poems* 30 (*Praise of Serena*), at lines 166–75; the wording of S. is largely his own.
6 The town of Calydon gave a grandstand view of Hercules's wrestling contest with the river Achelous, mentioned but briefly in *c*. 11.99 and *c*. 15.143.
7 According to Ravenna ([1990], 52) this 'greater Muse' refers to the poet Claudian, on the strength of the similarity noted above (n. 5), but this is an unlikely basis for such an identification, let alone a personal statement from S. More probable is a reference to another participant in the festivities, whom S. wishes to compliment.

Poem 15
Epithalamium of Polemius and Araneola

INTRODUCTION

The epithalamium itself begins with Athena returning from her vengeful mission at Caphareus, and making her way, via Africa, to Athens. Here, presumably on the acropolis, we are to imagine two temples, one the home of philosophers and the Seven Sages, the other devoted to Minerva, the goddess of weaving (Minerva is another name of Athena). Chief among the philosophers described are Pythagoras (51–78), Thales and various of his pupils (83–96) and Socrates, Plato and later philosophers – Stoics and Cynics, but emphatically not Epicureans (96–125). The breadth of interest of S. in philosophy may seem extensive, though it must be said that at times he is out of his depth. In the temple of Minerva we are shown embroidered likenesses of Jupiter, Glaucus and Hercules (126–45). Araneola is at work there, shining out among the others so engaged, women from Athens and Corinth. She copies the cloaks (*trabeae*) of an ancestor (great-grandfather: [150–3)] and makes imitations of the cloaks he wore in office (154–7); less seriously, she adds episodes from famous marriages of old, and the loves of Jupiter are not forgotten (158–78). Noticing that Athena has turned to look at the philosophers, Araneola's attention suddenly turns to the depiction of Lais, a courtesan, famous as the conqueror of the Cynic philosopher Diogenes (182–95), which leads Athena to offer witty but relevant advice to both parties (186–92). The ceremony is briefly described, and the Fates concur (196–201).

For details of the situation see also poem 14 and the letter that precedes it; on the genre epithalamium, see poems 10 and 11. The metre of 15 is the hexameter.

TRANSLATION

By chance, as she returned from the stormy height of Caphaereus,
having avenged the rape of Phoebus's Trojan priestess,[1]
Pallas was going from Xanthus to Erechthean Hymettus.[2]
Her head shimmered with gilded bronze; she took on greater calm
without her fearsomeness, though with her thunderbolt set aside   5
she had not yet cooled her rough limbs in Cinyphian Trito.[3]
Gorgo[4] occupies the middle of her chest, with power, albeit
detached, to halt beholders in their tracks. The perilous form
shines haughtily; its attraction lives on, though the life has gone.
A towering mass of snakes adds horror to her grisly head;   10
the biting dreadlocks twist their spotted coils and furiously
the swarm of raging ringlets gives vent to hideous hisses.
Her scaly corselet does not reach the mid-point of the waist;
where the steel finishes, her hanging cloak covers with its
encircling hem her feet, which as they move beneath her clothes   15
set up a rustling in the stiff folds of her puckered robe.
Her left hand holds a shield brimful of Phlegra's violence:[5]
Enceladus wields the uprooted Pindus and whirls it starwards,
while Ossa is made a missile by the raging mad Typhoeus.
Porphyrion seizes Pangaea, Damastor Rhodope   20
along with the springs of Strymon, and as the hot thunderbolt
descends he hurls the river like a missile to quench it.
Elsewhere one Pallas seeks the other Pallas, but he had seen
the Gorgon, so her spear met a corpse solidified already.

---

1 On the rock Caphaereus Pallas Athena avenged the rape of her priestess Cassandra by Ajax son of Oileus in the Trojan war by leading the Greek fleet to shipwreck (Vergil, *A.* 1.41–5 and 11.260). S. gives his own graphic description in *c.* 5.195–7.

2 For Xanthus cf. *c.* 9.15; for Hymettus *c.* 9.172.

3 The lake or river Trito(n), from which her name *Tritonis* (line 179 below and *c.* 7.198) derives.

4 The paralysing motif of the Gorgon is on her corselet (not, as often, on her shield, as in lines 17–31 below), and fully enabled. In *c.* 11.88 Perseus is called famous for his use of it.

5 Phlegra, pictured on her shield, was the scene of the Gigantomachy (the battle of gods and giants): see *c.* 6.15–28, *c.* 7.134 and, vigorously described, in *c.* 9.88–93.

Here Mimas shielding his brother throws Lemnos at her aegis;[6]   25
the weaponised island convulses heaven with its impact.
Here multiplex Briareus with a body of many people
fights bearing his army of relatives; from this one being
you could discern the hands that sprouted from his branch-like arms.[7]
Nor had Vulcan given, by his skill, the monsters just their forms,   30
but frenzy, too; indeed he feared the passions he had made.
Her right hand holds a spear, which lately in Aracynthus' vale
Pallas had plucked from an olive she herself had planted there.
This grew in such a promising place, that it was there, in her
footsteps, that the berry of Marathon would feed the rolling mills.[8]   35

There shine two temples here;[9] a single place pre-eminent
for human scholarship as for location; this houses
some who with probing thought study what is the sky's structure,
what the earth is, the groove that is the sea, the stormy air,
what do the successions of night and day, the moon's monthly   40
increases mean, and why equal decreases follow on.
Here live ensconsed, supreme, the seven wisest men, the sages:[10]
the first beginnings of philosophers beyond number.
Thales, born in Miletus, damns the giving of sureties;
You, Lindian Cleobulus, urge moderation as the ideal;   45
You, Periander, adorn Corinth, with your 'care for the whole;'
Solon from Attica uniquely approves 'nothing to excess';[11]
You say, Bias of Priene, that 'the masses are spiteful'.

---

6 Lemnos, a large Greek island in the Aegean sea, is hurled at her aegis – which was 'a large all-round bib with scales, normally decorated with the Gorgon' (OCD[4]), used for defensive and offensive purposes – often thought in Antiquity also to be a garment, shield or breastplate.

7 Briareus, one of the giants known as the 'hundred-handers'; he is also called Aegaeon.

8 Olives were grown and intensively developed in the countryside around Athens. For the description 'of Marathon' or 'Marathonian' to signify 'Athenian' cf. *c*. 6.3 and note.

9 The two imaginary temples (almost research centres, but open to people of all epochs) are in Athens, probably on the Acropolis. The second one is described in lines 126–201.

10 For the Seven Sages and their teachings cf. *c*. 2.156–63 and the more compressed *c*. 23.101–10.

11 In *c*. 2.160 Solon is noted as stressing the need to look to life's end, not, as here, as dwelling on the ubiquitous saying 'nothing in excess'.

You, Pittacus, in Mitylene born, taught us to learn
'the proper time', and you, Spartan Chilon, to know ourselves.   50

Here Samian Pythagoras asserts after five years
of learned silence, that the prime mover of the solid world
is music, which transmits a harmony from the certain stars,
and that the thrice four signs which the circle of the zodiac holds[12]
in highest heaven do not turn with a motion that is theirs   55
but rather are positioned with equal spaces between them,
and, fixed in the sign-bearing belt, are, like it, carried downwards;
and that the seven wandering stars produce outstanding music[13]
for this reason: the numbers in each case are deemed perfect.
He asserts that by this number, in this order, all things turn: 60
The old sickle-bearer's zone[14] crosses the highest parts of the sky;
and then (with Jupiter between) the adjacent star of Mars
proceeds, and then, on a fourth track, the Sun directs its course;
so too the placid Paphian holds the fifth diastema,[15]
the Arcadian the sixth,[16] and, in the last circle, the moon   65
runs on through almost thirty degrees within the tropic clime.[17]
So all tones which have been produced by lyre, harp, flute, and voice
(with the pitch of the sounds assigned after this pattern, complying
with the requirements of proportionality),[18] accord,
as he declares, with the intervals between the seven planets.   70
By harmony he means also that the four elements
are so placed that for those of great weight there exists a place
in the centre of the earth (it is clear that what in a round shape

---

12 There is a useful note on the zodiac in Ravenna (1990), 69, quoting the comment of Cicero in his *Aratea* (a study of the astronomy of Aratus), which contrasts Greek and Latin names for it. The word 'sign-bearing' (used in line 57 below) was commonly preferred by Latin writers thereafter.

13 The seven wandering stars are the planets.

14 Saturn; he is described in this way by various classical poets.

15 This word is one of those mentioned in the introductory letter to this poem.

16 Mercury, named as often from the region of his birth (e.g. *c.* 1.7).

17 Semple (1930), 109 and Anderson agree that there must be a confusion here between the thirty degrees (*myrai*) of the zodiacal circle which the sun traverses in about a month and the thirty days of the moon's monthly revolution (S. may have misunderstood the word *myrae* that he mentioned in his introduction).

18 It is not clear what S. means by 'pattern' here; compare the vagueness in *c.* 5.319–20.

is absolutely the middle must be the lowest part);[19]
so it is that water, being lighter, springs up above the land   75
and that higher than both is air, of greater purity,
and that sky, with its unsurpassed lightness, bounds everything,
and that the whole system owes its balance to the centre.
Here too Thales studies, through calculations and the stars
how he can announce the sun's eclipses and the moon's labours   80
in advance.[20] But he posits a vain first principle for things,
believing that the universe originates with water.
The idea of his disciple[21] is a different one: he asserts
that all things are made from their own peculiar beginnings
and states that each particular thing has some kind of fountains   85
that are eternally flowing and full of the seeds of things.
He was followed by one who holds that our air produced all things,
and he says that the gods originate in the same way.[22]
Fourth, Anaxagoras retains the doctrines of Thales
while feeling that it is a divine mind that produced the world.[23]   90
A younger colleague sits by him, but he, believing air
to be the substance from which all created things derive,
supposes that God took from it the means to make all things.[24]

19 As expressed by Semple (1930), 110, 'that which is the perfect centre is clearly equidistant from any point on the circumference of a sphere'; he cites the astronomical poet Manilius, 1.168–70 and Cicero, *Tusculan Disputations* 5.24.69.

20 Thales is mentioned in Augustine, *City of God* 8.2, an influential passage at this point, where S. is presenting the pre-Socratic philosophers, beginning with Thales, one of the Seven Sages. For S., as well as Augustine, the ability to predict eclipses, thanks to his grasp of astronomical calculation, is the major achievement of Thales. The following list of philosophers closely follows this passage of Augustine (or an excerptor of Augustine).

21 This is certainly Anaximander, successor of Thales, who held that every thing has its own special source (very different from the basic principle of water posited by Thales).

22 The unnamed third philosopher is Anaximenes; here S. is close to Augustine's short account.

23 Fourth is Anaxagoras, implicitly a successor to Thales. His universe is controlled by a supreme Intelligence. Anderson (232 n. 2) is surprised by the assertion (89) that he held to the teachings of Thales, but gives no reason.

24 Probably a reference to Diogenes of Apollonia, mentioned in Augustine after Anaximenes; he believed that all things were created from air, which participates in divine Reason. For whatever reason, S. diverges here from Augustine somewhat (cf. Anderson 232 n. 3); perhaps there were doctrines of Thales that he upheld.

Following these Arcesilas[25] figures that this great world
was fashioned by the divine mind, composed of those parts which   95
he himself calls light atoms. Then shines forth the Socratic school
which, moving onwards from the weighty questions of nature,
transferred its interest to the improvement of human conduct.
This school, it is said, the unequalled Plato cultivated, but
configured it in three sections, being the most expert   100
in joining physics to logic, and logic to ethics.[26]
He was the first to ascertain how much the first essence
differs from the highest good, that is, the sixth.[27] Since rocks are rocks
alone, and proved to be nothing at all except being;
and after that come things which clearly both exist and live   105
but to which you could add on nothing more (such as trees and grass);
and the third essence is that of cattle, whose being and life
is not without movement and sensation; the fourth creation
relates to his own fellow mortals, who are given being,
movement, life with sensation, and that paramount gift, wisdom   110
and the capacity to distinguish falsehood from truth;
the fifth substance reveals created beings dwelling in heaven;[28]

25 This is not Arcesilas, but Archelaus, as is clear from Augustine, and also from the fact
that Socrates, supposedly a pupil of Archelaus, comes next. S. may have garbled Augustine,
or even, as Ravenna (1990) suggested, had a faulty text. Cameron (1970), 323 n. 2, here
suggested, surprisingly and unnecessarily, in criticism of Courcelle (1948), 240–1, that there
is no corruption of the text here but that 'obviously' S. deliberately shortened the name. This
would be quite untypical of Sidonius.
   26 Cf. c. 2.172–3 on this point. According to Augustine the author of this triple division
was Plato (City of God 8.4); Anderson, seeing no good reason for this, suggests Xenocrates,
a pupil of Plato. The division later became standard in Stoicism with Zeno.
   27 In section 6 of Book 8 Augustine turns to examine the Platonist conception of natural
philosophy, and in what follows S. shows clearly that he used this, at least in his analysis
of the material world: he instances trees, which live, animals, which in addition have
sensibility, and human beings, which have intelligence also, and finally angels, which are not
unlike the beings of lines 112–15. S. talks in terms of substances, or essences, and claims to
have demonstrated by how much the 'first essence' (line 102) differs from the highest god,
the sixth, the discovery of which he attributes to Plato (in lines 102–3). The argument has a
neo-Platonic veneer, and it is weak both on Plato and on Augustine. According to Courcelle
(1948), 179–81 and 241 n. 4, S. derived it from a manual of Celsinus, a writer on philosophy,
available in a Latin translation.
   28 Hernández Lobato (2015), ad loc. (p. 559) speaks of spirits and daemones (supernatural
beings), and refers to the work of the philosopher Apuleius On the God of Socrates 9–11.

which some authorities have called gods since they take bodies
for humans to observe, though shortly they abandon them
and then revert to their own form, one of the very finest.   115
So it emerges clearly that the sixth substance, the highest,
is the creator, with nothing above, but all beneath.[29]
In this school Wisdom cultivates the life of Polemius
and herself cherishes the one attached to her son Plato;[30]
and though the Academy raises objections to all schools,   120
denying that truth exists, it adorns him with wholehearted praise.
After them, but in reciprocal agreement, Chrysippus
and Zeno instil adherence to their Stoic principles.[31]
By now the Cynics are almost shut out, but wait upon
the threshold; but virtue expels Epicureans entirely.[32]   125

But elsewhere, in Minerva's weaving room, Jupiter's robe,
the first of three being made, glows bright, its silken threads tinctured
by purple of Sidon, twice-boiled in the cauldron. Not only
does the deep-dyed garment breathe out sumptuous vermilion:
it includes some interwoven lightning, and on the rigid threads,   130
laden with a piece of splintered thunderbolt, the purple gleamed.[33]
Here hung a green-eyed Glaucus, in voluminous drapery,[34]
its billowing folds artistically set forth, and feigned turmoil
in which the embroidered storm was inundating hollow ships.
The third garment to be seen was for Amphitryon's descendant;[35]   135
the infant, encircled by his stepmother's two snakes,[36] unaware
smiles at the monsters, and thinking the trap to be a game
in ignorance loves them and with sorrowing face laments
the extinction of the snakes that he himself was murdering.

29 Cf. 102/3. But nothing clearly emerges as claimed.
30 The philosopher Plato is Wisdom's favourite; naturally she fosters one attached to him.
31 Chrysippus and Zeno are regarded as the founders of Stoicism.
32 There were strong and widespread objections to Epicureans, and not only among Christians: they held that humans are mortal; that the cosmos was the result of chance; that there is no providential god; that pleasure is essential to the good life.
33 This pictures the special threads as they were drawn out and applied to the loom.
34 For Glaucus, cf. *c.* 7.27.
35 This is Hercules, as explained in *c.* 13.1.
36 Juno, as in *c.* 7.31 and *c.* 7.582.

Also presented, in their different shapes, are these subjects:[37]   140
boar, lion, deer, giant, bull, yoke, Cerberus, the hydra,
the host, Nessus, Eryx, birds,Thracian, Cacus, Amazon
Cretan, river, Libs, apples, Lycus, virgin, sky, Oeta.
This work, and any other garments fit for the gods, maidens'
hands have produced; but among the whole array of women from   145
Cecropian Athens and Ephyreiadan Corinth[38]
Araneola stands out; Minerva herself struggles to match
her work, and when, defeated, she retires from the work-baskets,
when her rival holds the web Minerva prefers to hold weapons.
Here, then, copying her great-grandfather's *trabeae*[39] she makes   150
a palm-decked robe for her father, by which, himself consul,
he may match Agricola his grandfather and teach his grandsons
to link their grandfather's honour to that of their great-grandsire.[40]
She had also woven the cloaks in which he had shone out
as Master in high esteem throughout the Tartessian cities,   155
and in which during the prefecture that was conferred on him
high on his official seat, he interpreted our sacred laws.[41]
But she had also, less seriously, on the *trabea*
portrayed, on a raised strip, famed episodes in marriages
of old. First, Ithaca's tale and the Dulichian's home; she even   160
wove in Penelope herself undoing her slow work;[42]

---

37 See also *c.* 9.95–8, in the hendecasyllabic metre, with the explanations there.

38 S. has slightly remoulded a line of Claudian (*c.* 26.629), from a different context – a tirade against Alaric and his demanding wife – using words connoting Athens instead of Claudian's 'Argive' but keeping the choice epithet for Corinth from Statius.

39 For the word *trabea*, denoting a consul's official robe, here and in line 158, cf. *c.* 2.2 n., and *c.* 7.13.

40 Her great-grandfather was Agricola (*PLRE* 2.36–7 and stemmata 14 and 15), praetorian prefect of the Gauls (this included Spain) twice (both times in 418), and consul in 421. Her father is Magnus 2, consul 460 (*PLRE* 2.700–1) – this was perhaps not yet taken up at the time of this poem, as Loyen (1960), 191, suggested. The grandsons are the children of Araneola; they will learn to link his, Magnus's, honour with that of their great grandfather, and so rejoice both in their remote consular and in the recent consul, and thus appreciate the family's continuing distinction.

41 This sentence refers to the praetorian prefecture of 'the Gauls' – the sphere of such a prefect included Spain – that he held in 418. The word 'Master' here does not indicate a military position, as it often does elsewhere.

42 This would not be easy to portray in weaving (as is true of many of these themes), but the story was well known from the *Odyssey*.

Here Thracian Orpheus beats in vain with his strings on Taenarus
for his wife, twice seized after he breached the law of Avernus,
not this time looking back for her, thinking that this would help him.
Here Alcestis, putting her husband's life first, vows to end   165
her own life; you could see this in the actual wool of the Fates –
not fully woven, while her life (through Fate) remained to her.[43]
Here brightly shone in gold that night of Danaus' daughters,[44]
on whom their villainous father is fastening fifty swords
and, ordering discord, creates concordant lunacy.   170
Only Lynceus, saved by the kindness of Hypermestra,
escapes; you could see her fearing but little for herself
but pale and anxious only for the husband spared by her.
Now she was changing Jove into the shapes in which he embraced
Mnemosyne, Europa, Semele, Leda, Cynosoura;   175
that is to say, serpent, bull, lightning, swan, and Dictynna.[45]
Her work now turned to Danae's tower, and the rain of metal;
here Jupiter was dripping with another kind of gold,[46]
when the girl saw that the eyes of Tritonis were turned away,[47]
looking with greater pleasure at the arts that give learning;   180
upset, she changes theme, and with her dexterous thumb began
to represent Lais, conqueror of the philosopher,[48]
who all over the boorish Cynic's chin and wrinkled neck
barbered his odorous beard with fragrantly perfumed scissors.
Pallas laughed, and with decorous lips added these words, "No more   185
will you make fun of our philosophies, my dear, who are
about to marry my philosopher; rather, taking
the wedding veil, allow your mother to produce this work.
Arise, Polemius, great glory of philosophers, and now
at last put away your Stoic pride, and copying Cynic lovers   190
you shall begin to make for me again a small Plato."

43 For Alcestis, see *c.* 11.67.

44 In gold perhaps because of the heroism of one of the fifty.

45 Following the order of the nouns, he was a serpent when with Mnemosyne, and
Dictynna (Diana) when with Cynosoura (who was a nurse of Jupiter). Mnemosyne became
the mother of the Muses.

46 That is, the golden thread(s) in the weaving, as well as that in the actual myth.

47 On Tritonis see line 6 above; and *c.* 7.198.

48 This explained by Semple (1930), 111: '(she was) vindicating her own work by
portraying the confusion of the Cynic philosopher at the jest of Lais'.

As he demurred, the Master[49] addressed him thus: "Come willingly,
and do not think to disapprove marriage,
as bidden by the old teacher who swiftly quaffed the poison
with his eyes and thoughts fixed on the gods, while Anytus' cheek grew pale".[50]   195
The master had spoken; he rises, and with modest mien
commends the austere cloak to the keeping of the knotted staff.[51]
The goddess then binds each one's hair with green olive, emblem
of peace, then joins their hands, and solemnizes the contract
for grandfather Nymphidius to see.[52] Then Atropos[53]   200
approves the omen, and the Fates unite their golden threads.

49 The philosopher Plato speaks through a senior member of those present at the wedding (Ravenna [1990], 89), who is active in lines 196 and 197; Loyen (1960), opting for the real Plato, ignores this.

50 If Anytus, influential in the trial and condemnation of Socrates, had been present in the prison, he would have been terrified by what he had done.

51 The cloak and thick staff both mark the philosopher (*Ep.* 4.11.1, 9.9.14), but here the clothes woven by Araneola after the turn just described are commended to Polemius – who is indicated by the staff: their union is thus sealed. Just as Venus joins the hands of the lovers in *c.* 11.129–30, so here the 'Master' (see on line 192) links the happy couple through their interests in philosophy.

52 Nymphidius was grandfather of either the bride or the groom; of which is uncertain.

53 Atropos is the name of one of three Fates, which S. uses only here.

Poem 16
Thanksgiving to Bishop Faustus

INTRODUCTION

In the manuscripts this poem is signalled as a *Euchariston* (i.e. *Eucharistikon*) – that is, a giving of thanks. These thanks are for various kindnesses rendered to S. and a young brother in the past. Faustus was bishop of Riez (Latin Reii, near Aix-en Provence and Fréjus), and the poem has a very different flavour from the remainder of S.'s works. It owes this, first, to the reverence of Sidonius, and also to his frank dismissal of the Muses, Orpheus and related myths, which are replaced by praises of the Holy Spirit, still in the 'you-style' of aretalogies (formal praises of gods and heroes) in elevated classical verse. The poem ranges over the Old Testament (6–39) and then (40–64) turns more briefly to the New. References to the Old Testament relate to Miriam at the Red Sea, to Judith, who killed Holofernes, to Gideon, David, the children in the furnace, Jonah in the whale's belly and Elisha. From the New Testament the narrative and exposition focuses on Christ, in particular his birth and death, and the achievement of pardon and life for the sinners and resurrection for all.

After this lengthy invocation, S. thanks Faustus for his care of his young brother on one occasion (71–7), and then for the thoughtful care of Faustus when he himself visited Riez in the heat of summer one year (78–82). Even better, S. was enabled, to his great delight, to see the church there, the one perhaps in which he had been baptised. In his long formal farewell to Faustus (91–128) S. imagines, poetically, where Faustus the ascetic might be: whether among deserted mountains or in the monastery at Lérins or among his flock in Riez. He seems well informed of developments in these places, and is also aware of the demands on a dedicated pastor.

The date of this poem is quite uncertain (Kelly [2020], 172). It need not be assumed that the poem marks a major transformation in his religious allegiance at this time, but from the literary point of view it is an interesting experiment in presenting stories of the Old Testament in the high style and august metre of classical poetry (the hexameter), while keeping various of his small-scale stylistic characteristics. The metre is the hexameter.

TRANSLATION

Phoebus and thrice three Muses, along with Pallas, and Orpheus
and legendary water of the horse's spring,[1] and lute
Ogygian,[2] which inspiring the rocks that followed it
erected through its tuneful strains the keenly listening walls –
despise all this, my strings; rather, Spirit divine, come now,   5
I pray, to me as I address your bishop, you who once
entered the heart of ancient Mary[3] when Israel, quite dry,
shaking its tambourines proceeded through the hollow trench,
in the middle of the waves, walled in by bulwarks of water,
a multitude covered in dust, acclaiming your triumph.   10
And you who assisted Judith's hand to strike Holofernes[4]
when, with his neck cut through, the torso lay prostrate on the floor,
and the weaker sex belied itself well in the mighty blow;
you, who filling the basin with water squeezed from the fleece
and after that moistening the earth with the fleece remaining dry,[5]   15
comforted Gideon; O spirit imparted to loud trumpets
with victory coming from their blast alone;[6] you who also
inspired the king called from the flock of Jesse, rich in sheep[7]
when the enemy, placing on the cart the ark of the covenant
with no ploughman in charge to steady it, exposed to view   20

1 These two words render its title Hippocrene, for which see *c.* 9.285 and *c.* 23.20, and verse 96 within *Ep.* 9.13.

2 On the word 'Ogygian', cf. *c.* 5.491; for Amphion, builder of Thebes through his music, *c.* 23.120.

3 Not the New Testament Mary, but Miriam of Exodus 15.20–1; she sang God's praises to the Hebrews. The typological assimilation of two persons is not unusual in Christian thought.

4 Judith 13.8–10. S. pictures the torso before she wrapped it up, taking away the head separately.

5 See Judges 6.36–40, for the story of the fleeces; the agency of the Spirit in this is assumed.

6 See Judges 7.16–21. Victory came with the sounding of the trumpets, aided by the Spirit, as (literally) 'breath'.

7 In 1 Samuel 16.11–13 Samuel chooses David, a lowly shepherd from among the sons of Jesse.

by infected swelling in the anus the awful disease;[8]
you who once did make music in the mouths of those three boys,
who, placed inside the fiery furnace of the Chaldaean king
were wetted by a dewy flame while the oven itself was burnt;[9]
you who as he walked about in the belly's spinning spaces[10]   20
fed Jonah while the innards of the monster resonated
with singing of the Psalms within by the food he had ingested,
and raw hunger spewed up the load of a stomach full but hungry
with no harm to the prophet, whom from his heaving entrails
the famished behemoth threw up without making a bite;   30
you who once passed into Elisha's breast in double measure
as the flaming chariot was taking up the old Tishbite
and, leaving as a gift his sundered coat of skin, the unkempt
driver entered the fiery chariot and assumed the reins.[11]
You also, when about to send the second Elijah,[12]   35
being placated, tied the tongue of just Zachariah, when
the wrinkled mother made him an elderly father; this showed
that in ordering the prophet's silence great things were portended:

8 Two stories about the ark of the covenant, neither involving David, from different books of the Old Testament. S. combines material from two separate contexts; this need not be dismissed as confusion, but follows a common expository or homiletic practice whereby one passage is combined with another to enrich the teaching. The tale of the tumours (which were punishment for the Philistines, who held the ark) at 1 Samuel 5.9–11 is combined with the narrative of the cart that held the ark slipping (the cart nearly falls, when the oxen faltered) in the much later 2 Samuel 6.3–7. The absence of a ploughman (line 20) is given as the reason by S. For the general contexts of this see Barton and Muddiman (2001), 203.

9 For this story see the book of Daniel, chapter 3. The claim of line 24 is based on verses 50–1 in a passage found in Latin Bibles only, as helpfully explained by Anderson (244 n. 1). On the word 'Chaldaean' in S., see c. 2.85, c. 5.42 and 260.

10 The well-known story of Jonah and the whale in chapters 1 and 2 of Jonah was frequently retold in graphic terms in Late Antiquity, by poets as well as preachers. S. is no less vivid and adventurous in his six lines.

11 Elisha received a double share of the spirit of Elijah when Elijah was taken into heaven (2 Kings 2.9–15). Elijah is regularly referred to throughout the biblical narrative as the 'Tishbite' (from the area in which he had lived). His coat was not a gift to Elisha, but fell apparently by accident; nor was it torn or divided (2 Kings 2.13). Elisha tore his own clothes in two, but respected the mantle of Elijah. S. assumes that Elijah took the reins; this is not mentioned in 2 Kings 2.11.

12 Jesus Christ, often referred to in the gospels as Elias (Elijah); the references are given in Anderson (245 n. 4).

that when grace came the law should know that it must be silent.[13]
You, who were to be born without seed of a pure virgin,   40
being God ere the existence of any time, then Christ in time,
as far as body is concerned, you did create yourself;[14]
who accustomed to restore sight to the blind, movement to the lame,
hearing to the deaf, speech to the dumb, loosening their tongues, came with
this purpose also in mind, that the limbs of lifeless bodies might   45
arise from a bed, a pauper's bier, and a tomb;[15] who also bore
punishment in the flesh that you had taken on yourself,
enduring buffetings, derision, chastisement and thorns,
the casting of lots, your bonds, the cross, nails, gall, spear, vinegar,
and finally confronted death, but so as to rise again,   50
taking away all that had passed into the old enemy's
dominion by our own wrongdoing when the first woman,
disobeying the instruction, bound us with perpetual guilt.
The enemy, attacking you with death and finding nothing
in you that he could prove his own, lost everything that Eve   55
had given him by her fall. That bond by which mankind became
the property of a thief was cancelled by this recompense.[16]
Lacking all sin, you became an ample ransom for sinners,
and, a new Adam, as if paying the interest on a debt[17]
by dying, rescue the old Adam from death. So death is dead,   60
so death deceived itself by the ambush of its own making;
for by attacking innocent and guilty indifferently

13 An allegorical interpretation of the angel's silencing of Christ's earthly father, who had
expressed surprise and doubt, before Christ was born (Luke 1.19–20). This interpretation,
based on the opposing concepts of 'grace' and 'law', was not unusual.

14 As members of the eternal godhead, Christ and Spirit were, along with God the Father,
Creator.

15 Examples of healing and resurrecting mortals from the New Testament are given
in S.'s characteristic quickfire style, as are the elements of suffering in Christ's passion
(line 49).

16 Explanations of the working of the atonement have often depended on a passage in
Paul's letter to the Colossians (2.14) and its exegesis: in one translation, this reads '(God) ...
having cancelled the bond which stood against us with its legal demands; this he set aside ...'
(Revised Standard Version).

17 The idea that Christ somehow paid the required ransom for sinful humans was a
common one; likewise the idea that Christ is a 'new Adam', redeeming the 'old' Adam of
Genesis, bound by sin, which goes back at least to the letters of Paul (later first century AD).

he brought it about that even those enslaved by sin could be freed.[18]
You also ordered the ashes of the just to rise with you
in the fulness of time, when to those long ago interred   65
sudden salvation forced its way and life at once poured in
and shook out of the tombs their ashes, back in human form.[19]

Grant me to celebrate your Faustus, grant me to offer thanks
which even afterwards it is a joy to owe. Great priest,
my lyre extols you, albeit with a plectrum quite unequal.   70
This then is the first reason, the first subject of my praise,
that while youth's unsure age rolled on my brother's virtue was
with your help safeguarded,[20] through the blessings of the Lord, and proved,
with no uncertainty surrounding his good name. This gift
with all its goodness, points to you; the reward will be owed to him,   75
but he to you. If he chose not to fall, let his be the praise,
but the fact that he was not even able redounds to you.
I praise you as well, because when I once came to Riez,[21] when
Procyon was on the rampage, when the sweltering fire of the sun
was inscribing the thirsty fields with convoluted cracks,   80
with you as host our labours were promptly relieved and eased
by peace, a home, shade, water, blessing, and a meal and bed.
But much greater than these things is the fact that you wished me
also to go to the threshold of our holy mother.[22] There
I stiffened up with fear, I admit, feeling quite unworthy,   85
and suddenly a thrill of awe suffused my adoring face;
I trembled just as if Israel somehow were bringing me
to Rebecca, or long-haired Samuel taking me to Hannah.[23]

---

18 With the statement that 'Death is dead', and the more imaginative notion of a misguided 'ambush', the exposition of Christ's achievement (with the Spirit) ends. Death has overreached itself.

19 The ashes of each and every dead person were literally (following the Latin of S.) 'solidified'. Much ingenuity was shown in expounding the idea of bodily resurrection.

20 The details of this situation and its problems are unknown.

21 The Latin name was Reii.

22 Probably 'Mother Church', not an individual. His joyful reaction suggests that he was recalling his baptism.

23 In this simile S. envisages being taken to meet biblical mothers: to Rebecca by her son Jacob (whose name became Israel: Genesis 33.28), or to Hannah by her son Samuel (whose hair was left uncut as she had vowed: 1. Samuel 1.11–20]).

For all these things, honouring you incessantly with prayers
we avow our great affection in these small and simple verses.   90
Whether you live by the fiery Syrtes,[24] and in some barren
desert, or in some marsh made green with slime, or rather dwell
unkempt among black rocks in depths where, with the sun unknown,
hollow caverns keep guard over their age-old gloominess,
or whether the Alpine range, extending with precipitous crags   95
tremble before you, anchorite, as you take quick slumbers
on the icy turf (which though it holds the freezing cold, never
subdues the warmth of Christ which is conceived within your heart)
heeding ways urged on you now by Elias, now by John[25]
now the two Macarii, now also the hero Paphnutius,   100
now Or, now Ammon, now Sarmata, now Hilarion;[26]
now Antonius, lightly clad in the tunic woven by
the kind hand of his master out of fronds of palm, calls you;
or whether Lérins has embraced its former parent,[27] where
though now worn out, instead of taking a long rest, often   105
you come to wait on your disciples, scarcely enjoying
the relaxation of slumber, or the eating of cooked food
you lead a frugal life, and make fasts rich by adding psalms,
and make known to the brethren what great eminences have
been sent into the sky from that flat island,[28] or what kind   110

24 Possible domiciles are used to commend and perhaps exaggerate the ascetic's
toughness and devotion. An anchorite (line 96) (literally 'one who withdraws') is one who
has retired into such places; S. expresses great admiration.

25 These names may refer to the prophet Elijah and to John the evangelist or to John the
author of the book Revelation, as sources of inspiration, or alternatively to contemporaries
who spurred him on; the names will not have been uncommon.

26 Of the ten persons named in lines 101–2, Hilarion, Antonius (and his master Paulus)
and (one) Macarius are mentioned by S. in *Ep.* 7.9.9 as outstanding monks. An Egyptian
monk named Paphnuntius was known in the fourth century, and others may have taken
the name out of reverence. The names Ammon and Sarmata suggest earlier allegiance or
ethnicity, and may have been common. Nothing is known of Or, or anyone similarly named.
The name Antonius (102) recalls that of the well-known St Antony of Egypt, the well-known
ascetic and hermit. His 'master' may have been Paulus of Thebes, an older monk whom
Antony revered.

27 Lérins (*Lirinus* in Latin), the island monastery to which many of them belonged, had,
it seems, been reconciled to Faustus, clearly identified as a previous abbot.

28 The 'eminences', literally 'mountains' (that is, outstanding monks), contrast with the
'flat island' of Lérins.

of holy lives the old Caprasius lived, and young Lupus,
what grace awaited father Honoratus, who Maximus[29]
was, he whose city and monks you rule as bishop and abbot,
twice his successor; and also in these praises you acclaim
the arrival of Eucherius, the return of Hilarius;[30]   115
or whether the people in your trust have you, and the lesser ones
with you in their midst dare to despise the proud ways of the great;
or whether you give anxious thought to food to nourish the sick,
for food that the stranger may have, and what food may sustain
one whose crippled limbs are worn down by shackles of a prison,   120
or whether, with your busy mind fixed on burying the dead,
if the bruised bones of a dead pauper should go green and livid,
you carry it yourself without disgust to a burial place,
or whether on the prominent steps of the sacred altar
the devoted multitude surrounds you as you come to preach   125
so that their ears may absorb the medicine of the law explained.
Whatever you do, wherever you are, may you, I pray, be always
Faustus, always Honoratus, and always Maximus.[31]

---

29 Honoratus was a founder of the Lérins monastery, with the help of Caprasius. Maximus and Lupus (later to be bishop of Troyes) are held up as models by S. in *Ep.* 8.14.

30 Eucherius, ascetic and writer on Christian topics, was later bishop of Lyons until his death in 449; Hilary/Hilarius was archbishop of Arles and before that a monk at Lérins.

31 As well as being names, the words mean respectively 'fortunate', 'honoured' and 'greatest'.

Poem 17
To Ommatius, a senator of high rank

INTRODUCTION

Ommatius was the father of Hiberia, and his daughter Hiberia's wedding to Ruricius is celebrated in *c.* 11.52–4; there S. pays a laudatory tribute to him as descendant of one who was a patrician (for an explanation of this term see main introduction, section 10). The common abbreviation *v. c.* in his title (also in the title of Catullinus, recipient of *c.* 12) stands for *vir clarissimus*, which denoted 'a man of the highest standing in the senate' (Jones [1966], 272). It is clear that the two men shared a Christian faith.

Like many Latin poems from Antiquity, this poem presents an invitation but stresses the frugality of the host when compared with the luxury of those with richer tastes. Hernández Lobato ([2015], 602) instances poems of Catullus, Horace and Martial in particular, but perhaps goes too far to call this poem a series of echoes of all the poems that he cites. An echo of a different kind is apparent in line 9, from Ovid (see note). The date of the celebration is given: 29 July, but the year is unknown. The metre is elegiac couplets.

TRANSLATION

Four days before the first daylight of scorching August shows
its countenance bedecked with spikes of corn to the world,[1]
a sixteenth birthday will be celebrated by our family,
a day which begs to be gladdened by your presence.
Your meals will not be set out on tables inlaid with gems,   5
nor will Assyrian purple dignify your couch;
nor from the nooks and crannies of a glittering sideboard

---

1 29 July: note the parody (or avoidance) of the normal kind of dating, which would be 'on the fourth day before the Kalends of August' (with inclusive reckoning).

will I dig out piles of age-blackened silverplate,
nor will you here be offered a cup of which the entwined handles[2]
grasp sides encrusted with a glistening of gold.   10
My dishes are moderate in size, not made in such a way
that the artistry offsets the lack of large portions.[3]
Your Gallic friend's rustic table will not hold loaves of bread
such as paint yellow fields in Libya's Syrtes.[4]
My wines are not from Gaza, or Chios, or Falernum,   15
or of the sort you might drink from Sarepta's vines.[5]
My cups are not distinguished by the names of the village
which the triumvir himself set up in our country.[6]
But please do come, we beg. Christ will provide all things, Christ who
provided for me, through your love, a new homeland.[7]   20

2 S. surely recalls Ovid, *Letters of Heroines*, 15.254, using the same two unusual Latin words.

3 In plain language, the artistry makes large portions not possible, but (this is perhaps ironical) seeks to compensate for that.

4 The fertile corn makes the fields bright yellow; cf. *c.* 24.22, describing the river Triober.

5 Chios, the Greek island, and Falernum, an area close to Rome, had long been famous for wine in poetry; Gaza, a fertile area on the route from Egypt to Asia, and Sarepta, on the coast between Tyre and Sidon, were less renowned for their wine in the classical period.

6 This is Lepidus, later a triumvir, who, according to the historian Cassius Dio (46.50), founded Lugdunum (Lyon) and may well, as S. states, have set up a village in this vine-rich region.

7 S. alludes to the Arvernian property called Avitacum that came to him with his marriage and which he evidently preferred to his estate at Lyon (Stevens [1979], 20, quoting *Ep.* 2.2.3, and Mratschek in Kelly and van Waarden [2020], 248–50). It seems that Ommatius arranged or encouraged this new life for S., with the help of Christ.

Poem 18
On the baths of his country house

INTRODUCTION

A neat comparison of Avitacum (see n. 7 on Poem 17) with the architectural and other kinds of grandeur and beauty offered by the region of Baiae and the Lucrine lake. The sea urchins are a remarkable addition to what one might expect, and add amusement. Mratschek (2020) presents the sociological aspects of such a comparison, and further reading. The metre is elegiac couplets.

TRANSLATION

If you (or anyone) think fit to see my Avitacum,
may it please you; so may your own house please you always.
Its roof rises up high, contending with the cone at Baiae;[1]
likewise its peak shines out, with elevated crest.
The water falling from the brow of a neighbouring hill murmurs   5
more clamorously than all the streams of mount Gaurus.[2]
Wealthy Campania would repudiate the Lucrine lake,[3]
if she could see the unruffled waters of my lake.
That other shore is ornamented by red sea-urchins:[4]
in our fish, dear stranger, you can see both aspects.[5]   10

---

1 The cone is also mentioned by S. in his *Ep.* 2.2.5, in a letter that describes Avitacum in detail.

2 Gaurus: a Campanian mountain, famous for its wine, often part of such descriptions.

3 The Lucrine lake, a lagoon close to Baiae, was famous for its oysters.

4 In *Ep.* 2.2.17, the description of Avitacum, S. mentions fish with red flesh (which he explains as due to obesity) and white stomachs; these are the supposed sea urchins.

5 These aspects are probably, as Anderson suggests, both redness and prickliness (the latter due, as Loyen suggests, to their many bones). Neither Campania nor Avitacum is given preference.

If you so wish, and if you share our joys with a quiet heart
whoever you are, you make a Baiae in your mind.

Poem 19
On his Swimming Pool

The point of this poem, which has sometimes been misunderstood and unnecessarily corrected (see Anderson's note on p. 257), turns on the (tacit) contrast between the water of the baths at Avitacum and those of a nearby lake (this is probably the lake d'Aydat), visible to swimmers from the baths. The same point was made by Pliny the Younger less teasingly in his *Ep.* 2.17.11, where he says that from the villa swimmers can look at the sea beyond.

After the sweltering baths, come into the cold pool, so that
the water by its chill may strengthen your warmed skin;
and though you are immersing your limbs in this water alone
it is on our lake that your eyes will be floating.

Poem 20
To Ecdicius, his Brother-in-Law

S. invites his brother-in-law Ecdicius (brother of his wife Papianilla: see *PLRE* 2.383–4) to join his birthday celebrations on 5 November, which, according to the Roman reckoning, are the Nones of that month. The identity of his wife is unknown, and nothing is known of the expected addition. The *genius* is much involved in the discussion and celebration of birthdays, and makes a neat beginning to the poem.

My genius reminds me that the Nones of November
are near. I do not ask you to come – I order you!
Bring your wife with you; hurry, the two of you; we hope, however,
that in a year's time you will be the third of three.

Poem 21
On Fish Caught at Night

A short poem to accompany a present of fish. The recipient is not named, but might well be Ecdicius again. The sharing of the catch is calibrated by the poet's affection, with the very common trope of unanimity as the sharing of souls. A contemporary and closely similar group of words comes from the contemporary poet Rutilius Namatianus, *On His Return* 1.426.

Last night, for the first time, four fish were fastened to my hooks;
I have kept two of them; take two for yourself too.
These that I send you are larger ones – a very fair division:
you have always been the greater portion of my soul.

Poem 22
The Burgus of Pontius Leontius

The poem is preceded by a letter in prose (22A) and followed by a prose epilogue (22B)

22a Sidonius to his Friend Pontius Leontius, Greetings

TRANSLATION

1. While I was killing time in Narbo, the city named after Mars but which now has really become a city of Mars,[1] it occurred to me to concoct some hexameters out of affection for you so that when you read them, you would know for sure that even though our respective household gods[2] dwell in places further apart than is right, that does not mean that our hearts are as far apart as our homes are. 2. Here, then, you have Dionysus, worse for wear, among the delights of his Indian triumph;[3] you have Phoebus too, who, it is agreed, was made, by a poet's right, a lodger with you after being a god, the Phoebus, that is, who is very intimate with my friend Anthedius,[4] of whose college he, the principal, excels not only all musicians but also geometers, arithmeticians, and astrologers in the art of exposition; for I would think that no-one knows in more detail what are the special influences of the oblique stars of the zodiac, of the wandering of the planets, and of the scattered stars outwith the zodiac.[5]

---

1 Narbonne (Narbo Martius was its full name) was taken by Theoderic I in 436; cf. *c.* 7.475–80, *c.* 23.69–72. Its occupation by Theoderic II in 462, though effected by betrayal, was essentially peaceful (Hydatius 212 [217]).

2 The gods of each household, or *Lares*.

3 On the Indian triumph of Bacchus cf. line 20 and note.

4 Anthedius is described as a poet in *c.* 9.311–12; he is known only from this passage and *Ep.* 8.11.2. The college here is probably a college of poets (Loyen).

5 On the zodiac, see *c.* 15.52–66; on the 'scattered stars' see the learned note of Delhey (1993), 55.

3. For he is so distinguished in these limbs of philosophy (if I can call them that) that he seems to me to have understood Julius Firmicus, Julianus Vertacus, and Fullonius Spartacus, very expert authors on the science of astrology,[6] without a guide and with the aid of his intellect alone. Following the footsteps of such learning I acknowledge myself to be a raucous goose before a melodious swan.[7] Why do I detain you longer? I have made your home, the Burgus[8] my own, with the privilege appropriate to a friend, knowing well that my topic will please, even if as a whole the poem does not.

6 The first of these writers wrote in the mid-fourth century AD, the others perhaps in the third century AD; the last two are mentioned again by S. in *Ep.* 8.11.10 (Delhey [1993], 66–7).

7 This metaphorical comparison goes back to Vergil, *E.* 9.

8 For the name Burgus, see line 17 and note, and lines 126, 229 and 235.

Poem 22
The Burgus of Pontius Leontius

INTRODUCTION

The link of this estate with the modern town of Bourg sur Gironde is not exact, but the name Burgus has been retained as more informative than Anderson's 'castle'; in the Latin it is used four times, and with some apparent affection, by the poet. It deserves the attention and praise of visitors, as S. argues in a strong opening passage; they should remove themselves if not full of praise for it. The muse Erato (by this time in poetry something of an all-purpose Muse) is invoked to tell of its origins, its position and its many-sided amenity. The setting is provided by one of S.'s favourite topics, the clashing of rivers (here the Gironde and Dordogne) and the periodical conflict of the Garonne with the incoming tides (lines 18–21; also 105–10). He even mentioned it in *c.* 7.393–7, although it was some way out of the journey to Toulouse that he is describing. Here, in a flight of fancy, he imagines the presence of poetic nymphs, and asks here the Nereids from the sea to teach local Dryads and other nymphs their graceful dances (15–19).

Bacchus and Apollo meet in their respective journeys, obviously in mid-air (they are, of course, gods). Bacchus (22–63) is leading a triumphal procession of defeated enemies from India; they include the river Ganges, Aurora, Phoenix, an ugly band of elephants and many other new subjects; Apollo (64–85) approaches from Mount Helicon and is, like Bacchus, en route for Thebes. But he is tired of the disrespect and gross immorality there, and makes a suggestion (99–100). At a junction of two rivers (he says), on a prominent hill, there is, or rather will be, in Roman times, a fortified stronghold. Its description will occupy most of the poem from now on (111–220). S. gives a very detailed report (and on the whole it is very clear) of the Burgus, where he had recently enjoyed the hospitality of its owner, Pontius Leontius (*PLRE* 2.674–5). The poem is more than a polite 'thank-you', nor is it a minute description for its own sake. He carefully describes its rural setting, the problems of living there in various seasons and, for Bacchus, a useful room in which to store wine. In its own way, it is a challenge to descriptions of country houses in classical literature, notably those of Statius (some of these are mentioned in the letter that follows the poem). It is precise, sometimes amusing and a neat tribute to the noble owner and his wife; the gods can imagine themselves occupying it at some stage. The poem is one of the longest of S.'s poems apart from the political panegyrics and the panegyric to Consentius (c. 23); whether it was written during the same visit to Narbo as c. 23 is uncertain, but quite possible.

Synopsis

1–11 Address to the visitor
12–21 Invocation of Erato and various nymphs
22–40 Description of the triumphal procession of Bacchus
41–63 Ganges, Aurora, Phoenix, the elephants
64–100 Bacchus and Apollo (who is also on a journey) meet and talk
101–25 The position of the Burgus
126–41 The baths erected on the river Dordogne
143–68 The entrance to the villa; the peristyle; the pictures
169–86 The granaries; the villa's rear quarters
187–220 The western part of the villa: colonnade, dining-room
221–30 Discussion of the two gods on how they will share and use the
         dwelling; they bid farewell to their previous cult centres.

TRANSLATION

Stranger, go and see the stalls of the Bistonian king,[1] the altars
of Busiris,[2] Antiphates's tables,[3] and the Tauric
realms of Thoas,[4] and Cyclops reft of sight by the Ithacan's guile[5]
and who, dwelling within the hollow mountain's cave, bears on
his huge forehead a vast, dark hole, where his eye was quarried out –   5

---

1 Diomede was a Thracian king supposed to feed his horses on human flesh.
2 Busiris was a legendary king of Egypt famous for his cruelty, who sacrificed strangers on his altars.
3 Antiphates was king of the cannibal Laestrygonians; he is linked with Cyclops in Homer, *Odyssey* 10.199–200 and Ovid, *M.* 14.249.
4 The Taurians and their king sacrificed visitors to Diana; cf. *c.* 5.249, *c.* 9.177.
5 The tale of the Cyclops (Polyphemus) who imprisoned the Greeks in his cave, but was blinded in a clever ruse of Odysseus to secure their escape, is told in Homer, *Odyssey*, book 9.

if you have come to this castle meaning to keep silent;[6]
for though Phoebus does not loosen the reins of song at random
nor does he unfurl for everyone the sails of pleasant speech,[7]
whoever you are who observe this great home without praising it,
you are yourself observed; your choice, albeit unvoiced, sounds forth: 10
your silence cries aloud that you are secretly envious.

So come, Erato,[8] pluck Pierian strings for me: Satyrs,[9]
may you respond, and play your part, moving fingers and feet
but not so as to wreck our songs with uncontrolled dancing.[10]
All festive dances that Dryads or Hamadryads, joined with   15
Napaean nymphs,[11] have ever danced, may they now offer you,
great Burgus; and, kind chorus of Nereids, teach Naiads here[12]
when, as happens from time to time, the Garonne returning hither,
you come and plough the sea when it is engulfed by the river.
So reveal the house's origins, Erato, disclose what is   20
its *genius*; so great a home must have its deity.[13]

Euan, having sacked Erythrae[14] with its skilful archers,
was yoking to his chariot tigers bridled with vines,
where a yoke-beam bearing grapes went under the yoke's double arch.
He himself, dead beat, sits in the chariot; his towering neck   25

---

6 Visitors who say nothing are directed to go away and see, or at least read about, the aforementioned horrors.

7 Phoebus (Apollo) does not give eloquence or poetic gifts to everyone, but there is no excuse for indifference.

8 Erato, a Muse sometimes invoked in epic (Vergil, *A.* 7.37); cf. line 20 below.

9 Satyrs were wild and often uncouth demigods; the hint of the Muses in 'Pierian' is ironic.

10 As elsewhere, S. is playfully aware of the effect of poor dancing (*c.* 14.25–30).

11 Dryads and Hamadryads are wood nymphs; Napaeae, nymphs of wooded valleys.

12 With a neat twist to a favourite topic (the clash of tidal waters and river flow, cf. *c.* 7.393–7), S. asks Nereids (sea nymphs) to teach the Naiads (river nymphs) to dance whenever there is such an event. There is a longer description of the dancing and revelling of various nymphs and other beings in Ausonius, imagined in quieter circumstances, at *Mosella*, 169–88.

13 The ancient Roman idea of *genius* encompassed that of tutelary deity or spirit; a *genius* assisted not only men and women but also cities, such as Rome itself.

14 Erythrae: not an exact location, nor perhaps equivalent to India as a whole; cf. *c.* 2.447, *c.* 5.285 and *c.* 11.105. Here it is imagined to be a capital city. The conquest of India by Bacchus is alluded to by Statius (at *Thebaid* 4.652–63) and Claudian (*c.* 8.602–10), and forms the climax of the *Description of the World* by the fourth-century AD poet Avienius.

is wet from overflowing wine, on his head the golden horns
bulk large, and shoot forth the inborn fire, (the lightning first received
when long ago, at his birth, he was transferred from his mother
into his father's thigh).[15] His temples both carry the wealth
of spring; bright flowers interlaced with the harvested vintage.   30
His right hand grips a winebowl, his left hand holds a thyrsus,[16]
and his cloak does not cover his naked arms, just touches them.
His eyes swim sweetly and, should he turn them on the enemy
by his look alone he makes the astonished Indians merry.
Then, whenever the chariot is shaken by a pothole,   35
the wheel is inundated with a shower of new wine.
Silenus, full already of the deity he had nursed,[17]
was teaching Bassarids and Satyrs, Pans and Fauns to play;[18]
his hair was trim and well turned out, for on his balding pate
he took great care to make amends for his hairloss with garlands.   40

Horned Ganges is the next display in this novel triumph.
He stood, his head hanging, with face bedraggled, mouth dripping
and with his shimmering tears helped to refill his dried-up river.
His hands, shackled behind his back, were tied with a vine-branch.
Refreshed by this captive[19] moisture the vine-shoot gradually   45
by itself grows green again so as to envelop his moist arms.
There also in chains passes the wife of a stolen husband,[20]
Aurora; her saffron-coloured face was downcast, but her light
could not be hidden, and she glowed when tinted by the sun.
Present here too was the Phoenix, without its cinnamon,   50
dreading that there might be no second death in store for it.[21]

15 This myth is related by Ovid. *M.* 3.256–315.
16 The *thyrsus* was a wand 'tipped with a fir-cone, tuft of ivy or vine-leaves' (OLD),
carried by Bacchus and others in celebrations.
17 Silenus, the elderly attendant and tutor of Bacchus, is, as usual, quite drunk.
18 Pans and Fauns were seen as half-human beings of the countryside.
19 The water of the tears is itself a captive.
20 The wife is Aurora (Dawn), and the 'stolen husband' Tithonus; she once carried him
off, according to the Homeric *Hymn to Aphrodite*. Her home is described in *c.* 2.407 (where
she comes over as more demure) as being close to the Indians.
21 For the Phoenix and its cinnamon see *c.* 2.417, *c.* 7.353–4, *c.* 9.326, *c.* 11.125 and in
general van der Broek (1972). If the Phoenix had any idea of its future, it might have feared
that it would never live to see another death.

There followed a cohort of captives, who were carrying trays
heaped with their treasures. Here are ivory, ebony, and gold,
and snow-white pearls purloined from black bosoms, are brought. Whoever
has nothing to transport is placed in fragrant bonds; you could see   55
that even punishments like this gave pleasure, you could smell
the fresh green fetters that exhaled the scents of violets.
Last in the cavalcade of plunder came dark elephants,[22]
a shapeless herd: the skin upon their backs, shaggy and coarse,
would hardly admit a sword, nor is the network of their bones   60
punctured even by volleyed spears; the backs of the animals
   as they alternately contract and stretch, crack audibly;   61
with long experience of self-protection they resist
the offensive missile by a shaking out of their wrinkles.

The victor now was pressing on to Thebes through the endless air,
raising the bacchanals to the topmost clouds, when he espied   65
the Delian god approaching from the height of Aonia.[23]
What he steered was griffins: jagged curbs of woody laurel
tie up their curving beaks; the pendulous reins with ivy entwined
are green too. Gently do these winged creatures glide through the air
and over land, lest by some sudden agitation of   70
their wings they cause, perhaps, the woody reins to snap asunder.
The god himself as ever gleams, his forehead emphasised
by clusters; and his locks, which match, brush his gilt chariot.
In his left hand he holds a resounding lyre of the utmost charm,
with Python engraved on it;[24] his right hand clutches arrows,   75
and strings resounding with their own particular twang. With him
go the Pipliades; surrounding him they give shadow
to the centre of the chariot with their nine sweeping robes.

22 S. mentions elephants elsewhere (in *c.* 2.55, *c.* 11.103–4), with sympathy for their
exploitation, and in *c.* 2.374 (part of a triumphal display). Here he admires their imperme-
ability, mentioned by Pliny (*NH* 8.30), which could be his source; this and other possibilities
are discussed by Delhey (1993), 92. Could the young S. have seen one, perhaps in captivity
in Arles or Rome?
23 Apollo had been on Mount Helicon, in central Greece; the meeting is located close
by, but seemingly in mid-air; they have the panorama of Aonia (Boeotia in central Greece)
beneath them, and one of Delphi too.
24 For Python cf. *c.* 2.154, *c.* 2.311.

Stretched over the smooth tripods, the snake of Epidaurus hangs,
disseminating sacred poison through its health-giving neck.[25]   80
Here too Pegasus brought hair-born wings, wings from the Gorgon's hair;[26]
he carried Croton, articulate through the skill of his dancing feet.[27]

When the two companies joined up, each of the gods arose
to embrace his brother, but Euan rose somewhat more slowly,
wary that in so doing he might betray his tottering feet.   85
Then Phoebus said, "Where are you going? You're not, are you, Bacchus,
perhaps making for guilty Thebes? Echion's son, it is true,
denies that you are a god.[28] But leave them their city, I beg you;
just leave them, and join me, turning your wheels around.[29] Agave
scorned your worship,[30] Niobe mine; she is now a pillar,   90
suffering as many wounds as she beholds her offspring suffer.[31]
Longing to die, she is more painfully distressed by mercy;
To spare is often a punishment: to grief it adds anguish.
Will not the mother of Pentheus, having murdered her son,[32]

25 The snake of Epidaurus was renowned for its healing powers, transmitted by the
practice of incubation, in the name of Asclepius, whose symbol it was. The holy tripods here
must have been in Apollo's chariot, along with the serpent.

26 The adjective 'hair-born', a literal translation of the Latin word here, is a unique
word, and a problem. In the stories of Ovid, *Fasti* [The Roman calendar] 3.450 and Hesiod
before him, the horse Pegasus, wings and all, was born from the neck of the Gorgon Medusa
(cf. *c.* 14.9) and his mane was spattered with her blood. The suggestion by K. Wulf (TLL
4.1205.38ff.) that S. alludes to the Greek word *krene* ('fountain'), making an audacious
compound of Greek and Latin words ('fountain-born'), as Ausonius did on occasion, is
rejected by Delhay (1993), 107 as outside the parameters of this myth. Pegasus sprang from
the fountain *in toto*. Loyen (1960), 194 assumes that the Gorgon's head of hair was used for
the horse's wings, as perhaps one must do.

27 Crotos was son of Euphemia, the nurse of the Muses; his father was Pan (Hyginus
Fables 224.3: and see *RE* 11.2.2008). He is said to have indicated with his feet and hands the
various metres of poetry sung by the Muses as they danced.

28 Echion's son was Pentheus, who succeeded him as king of Thebes.

29 The speakers are still, it seems, airborne, elephants and all; but the poor balance of
Bacchus in lines 83–5 above is not due to altitude.

30 Agave, mother of Pentheus, refused to recognise Bacchus as son of Jupiter.

31 Niobe, daughter of Tantalus, boasted that she had borne more children than Leto, who
had but two (Artemis and Apollo); she sent them to kill Niobe's more numerous brood. Cf.
c. 2.310–13.

32 Maddened during a Bacchic celebration, Agave unknowingly killed Pentheus.

become sane only so that she may rage more furiously?   95
And can we bear to dwell in Aonia's hills, when in the future
an adulterer gains the bride of the father whom he murdered
and will be deemed his sons' brother, the husband of his mother,
and his own stepfather?[33] If it is your wish to go with me
I'll tell you where we two together should locate our home.   100

There is a place where you, Garonne, rolling from watery cliffs,
and you, mossy Dordogne, who rush to the plain with similar course
and flow from a curve in the river bed strewn with gravel and sand,
unite and gradually blend your now abating streams.[34]
Here the sea races into them, and with much to-ing and fro-ing   105
both spurns and seeks the waters which the rivers roll along.[35]
But when, after being driven back by the lunar increments,
the Garonne gathers on its back once more its own waters,
it rushes violently back in headlong spate, and seems
to move towards its source, not backwards but rather downwards.[36]   110
Then the Dordogne, although as the lesser it takes less water
from its flooding brother river, is likewise swollen itself
by the Ocean, and transforms its river banks into sea shores.
Between these rivers, though closer to one of them, is a
mountain that bursts into the sky, impressive with high summit,   115
destined to have mightier masters, indeed its own senators.[37]
One day Paulinus Pontius, the family's founder,
when Romans rule over his fatherland,[38] will surround it
with high ramparts, and soaring towers that penetrate the sky,

33 These relationships all apply to Oedipus, who in ignorance killed his father and married his mother.

34 The location of the villa, which gave its name to the town of Bourg-sur-Gironde, is discussed by Delhey (1993), 8; at p. 60 he raises grammatical points about its name.

35 After the confluence of the two rivers there is a clash of tide and river, for which the scientific term is 'bore'; for fuller description see cf. *c.* 7.393–7.

36 'downwards' is hyperbolic. The river travels with the speed of something descending or falling.

37 Cf. Ausonius, *Moselle* 402: the Moselle region has its own senate, or 'breeding-ground' (Loyen) of senators.

38 The divine speaker looks forward to the epoch of Roman rule and Gallo-Roman ascendancy. For details of Paulinus (whose name here is chosen for metrical convenience, rather than 'Leontius'), see PLRE 2.674–5.

so that on their summits, shining together, may settle   120
Magnificence and Assistance.[39] These walls no siege-engine,
no battering-ram, no high-piled structure, no earthwork at the walls,
no whistling boulders launched by catapult, no tortoise-like
array of soldiers' shields, no mantlet,[40] no wheeled vehicle
with ready-placed ladders, shall ever have the strength to shake.   125
Already I seem to see, Burgus, (that is what you will be called)
what awaits you in years to come.

　　　　　　　　　　　　　　Buildings rise from the river's edge;
within your circling battlements sit brightly sparkling baths.
Here whenever the swell is ruffled by the dark north winds,
the jagged rock begins to snarl from the rough embankment,   130
but then a torrent leaping up from out of the broken rocks
is thrown up to the skies, to descend like rain onto the roofs;
it hoists people in boats, and frequently makes fun of them
with a pretend shipwreck; when the storm is over, the waters
recede and leave marooned the fleets they have driven into the baths.   135
But how many, how notable are the columns that support them!
Admit defeat,[41] marble of purple hue from Synna's cave,
and you, marble like ivory, found in Numidia's hills;
and you, marble verdant as spring, with grassy veins of green.
No more do I prize white marble from Paros or Carystus;   140
meaner, for me, is the purple that hangs in the crimsoned rock.[42]

And, lest posterity should wonder who the builder was,
a stone fixed at the entrance registers the founders' names.

---

39 Magnificence and Assistance: a neat and eloquent encapsulation of what a landed family should provide; 'the two lights', as Anderson has it. The owners will thus express their wealth, high nobility and magnificence, and also have the ability and readiness to provide economic, military and social protection.

40 Soldiers advancing on a walled city used as protection an array of shields carried on their backs that took its name from its likeness to a domed tortoise shell. What is here called 'mantlet' was a movable outhouse or, in an older sense of the word, penthouse.

41 A vigorous version of a favourite rhetorical device to express preference. Cf. c. 2.299, an appeal to antiquity when comparing two modes of punishment for enemies of Rome.

42 For a list of types of marble and their origins, see c. 5.34–9, adding the marble of Paros from c. 11.18. Paros and Carystus (in the Cyclades and the island of Euboea respectively) are both mentioned in Ep. 2.2.7: S. says proudly that they are absent from his own house. The sentiment of line 140 is pure rhetoric.

Nearby there is some water which expunges all footprints
and wipes away all mud and dirt with its cascading stream.   145
The house-wall, decorated with panels of cut marble,
reaches the golden ceiling, which is copiously covered
by the tawny metal; for a household's rich fortune lets not
its wealth be a secret, but reveals it thus, hiding its roof.
Behind this rises, passing high above a double suite[43]   150
a colonnade, itself double, but to the double Wain
unknown.[44] This, with its gently sloping roof, can be seen from
its curving wings, rather like horns that turn slightly inwards.
From its right curve the colonnade beholds the newborn day,
from its front it sees the midday sun, from its left the setting sun.   155
It misses nothing at all from these three quarters of the sky
and keeps the whole day's sunlight, thanks to the crescent moon-shaped hall.
Here[45] sacred herds of trident-wielding Jupiter are plunged
beneath the waves by the father of Pharnaces;[46] you would think
the horses' bodies really had been struck by an axe, and that   160
the wounds were red from spurting blood. The true horror of carnage
is there, and the picture of slaughtered horses is alive.
Here, on one side, the king's huge forces invest Cyzicus;
on the other, consul Lucullus brings help to his allies,[47]
and the Mithridatic soldiers, compelled now to suffer   165
extremes of hunger, envy the enemy being besieged.
Here a fired up Roman soldier swims landward through the sea,

43 See the note on the text used for the reading followed here, preferable to an emendation
of Anderson. Delhey (1993), 142–6 gives a very full vindication of the manuscript text. In
general, as Anderson declares (272 n. 3), S. is writing to one who knew the house; but the
writing is not 'desperately obscure'.
44 This constellation is also known as the Great Bear and Little Bear.
45 These pictures, hanging in the peristyle as pictures relating to the family regularly did
(Delhey [1993], 151, with references), refer to events in the Third Mithridatic War and the siege
of Cyzicus in 73–72 BC. The subject may have appealed to Pontius Leontius, the owner, as the
words 'king of Pontus' (Pontus was a Roman province) suggests (unless it is mere wordplay). S.
also describes this episode in c. 2.511–14: for historical detail, see Magie (1950).
46 The father of Pharnaces II bore the name Mithridates, a name difficult to express in the
metre; hence the periphrasis (note the solution in line 165, using an adjective).
47 Licinius Lucullus was consul in 74 BC; his subsequent raising of the siege of Cyzicus
was a major Roman success.

conveying on his wet body a scroll completely dry.[48]
Above, the granaries with their far-reaching buildings loom,
and with the abundant harvests make the house seem congested.   170
To them will come as much as Africa gleans from warm fields,
as much as the Calabrian reaps, or the lively Apulian,
as big a harvest as swells in the stores of Leontini,
as much as Gargara entrusts to its Mygdonian furrows,[49]
as much as Attic Eleusis, which worshipped Ceres with dances   175
in secret, used to store for her citizen Triptolemus[50]
when in days past, as the human race abandoned the acorn
when given golden corn, the golden ages were dying.[51]
Then, on one side, a summer portico faces the freezing
north, on the other, a gentle heat comes from the winter baths   180
and softens the air as is required. For cooling purposes
this is more suitable; for what avoids the Lion's mouth
is ill equipped to endure the rage of the Lycaonian Bear.[52]
But into the building's warm baths there comes a stream from above;
it falls into the mountain,[53] and funnelled through wide channels   185
spreads round through hollow passages its confined river-water.
Towards the setting sun, beyond the darkened granaries,
there stands a winter home for the occupants; here there crackles
a welcome flame, feasting off logs ready to hand, winding

48 There are various versions of the episode and its background: in Florus (1.40 [3.5] 16),
in Plutarch, *Lucullus* 10.1, and in Frontinus, *Stratagems* 3.13.6 (where it is said that the man
swam seven miles). According to Florus (who does not mention the scroll) he proceeded 'on
an inflated skin, steering with his feet, presenting to distant observers the appearance of
some sea-monster', and raised the morale of the townspeople.

49 Such types of comparison are favoured in panegyrical writing; there is a closely
repeated exemplar in *Pan. Lat.* 2.(12).4–5 (on Spain; it is the best of places and countries).
Delhey (1993), 158 draws attention here to the notion of 'purple patch' mentioned in the
prose epilogue to this poem.

50 Triptolemus was a hero of Eleusis in early mythical times, and the giver of arts of
agriculture to mankind.

51 The mythical Golden Age (singular, as in the standard account in Ovid *M.* 1.89, though
S. prefers the plural) saw the adoption of corn in place of the acorn, to which Vergil alludes
in *G.* 1.8 and 148–9.

52 Lycaon, father of Callisto, became the Great Bear constellation. This hall is a relief
from very hot ('the Lion's mouth', also a reference to the constellation) or very cold weather.

53 This phrase is a deliberate paradox, and not necessarily 'feeble' (Anderson). This
sentence is resumptive, explaining the uses of the water.

its way from the stove, a current of warm cloud, its force now spent,   190
dwindles and radiates thinned vapour through the whole building.

Next you could see, joined on to this, the weaving chambers, which
the architect boldly designed to rival Athena's temples.
Here one day the respected wife of great Leontius,[54]
than whom no other wife of the Pontian house has gloried more   195
in the high rank of an illustrious husband,[55] will be acclaimed
for stripping her Syrian distaffs or twisting silken threads
along the delicate reeds, or for the use of golden threads
on the ever-swelling spindle, weaving the softened metal.
Next to them, with a common wall, stands a bright edifice,   200
which illustrates the early days of the Jews, the circumcised.[56]
This gleams unceasingly, nor does fading of its colours
over the length of time devaluate its appearance.
As you turn left, an ample colonnade now welcomes you,
curving but with straight passageways. At its furthest margin   205
perches a forest of stone, composed of tightly packed columns.
Here opens up a very tall dining room with swing doors.
Nearby is a conduit cast in metal; water falls into
an artificial pool before the door, and following
the flow, the swimming fish end up in a dining room with waves.[57]   210
Close by is the first (and also last) tower; here it will be
the custom of the occupants to place their winter couches.
Sitting on its conspicuous roof often will I look at
the mountain which delights our Muses – and the goats as well;
Among yon boughs and leafy laurels will I walk, and here   215
I will believe that timid Daphne has belief in me.[58]

---

54 The wife is not named, and unknown: *Anonyma* 18 in *PLRE* 2.1239.
55 The text implies that he held the rank of *illustris* (*PLRE* 2.674–5); whether this honour
was honorary or not (cf. *c.* 7.241, the case of Avitus) is not clear. His wife would use up the
threads on a spindle with outstanding speed.
56 Which experiences of the Old Testament Jews were displayed is not known; perhaps
the institution of circumcision itself (Genesis 17), or aspects of the story of Abraham.
57 Diners and fish each have their place for dining; the fish will entertain the guests.
58 Apollo (the speaker since line 86) here speaks of his love for Daphne before her
metamorphosis (Ovid *M.* 1.452–567).

Now if by chance you turn your steps towards the Arctic Bears
to reach the temple of that god who is the greatest God,[59]
the store-room and repository give scents of various charms;
you will be frequently there, brother.[60] Now share with me   220
this domicile, leaving to me this spring, which as it flows
down from the mountain, in the extensive shade of the hollowed vault,
is not without embellishment: nature has given it grace.
It pleases me that nothing man-made has pleased them; no pomp
through art; no hammer with its ringing beats will ornament   225
the rocks, nor will dressed marble supplement the worn tufa.
The fountain here is enough for me, my own Castalia.
For the rest, keep and enjoy; may the hills tremble at your dominion;
release your captives here, and let their loosened chains become
prolific and happy vineyards throughout the braes of Burgus."   230
Silenus, now almost sober, confirmed these words; in concert
sang the approving bands of revellers: "Nysa, farewell
from Bromius;[61] twin-peaked Parnassus, farewell from Phoebus.
Let not Naxos search for the one, or Cirrha for the other,[62]
but rather let Burgus, which will ever please us, be our home."   235

59 The god of the Christians is meant, even in the mouth of Apollo, who might have had
reservations.
60 Bacchus, hitherto portrayed as enjoying his drink, will be attracted to the storeroom;
Apollo, on the other hand, seeks a wider aspect.
61 Nysa was the birthplace of Bacchus/Dionysus; mount Parnassus a favourite haunt of
Apollo.
62 The island of Naxos (in the Aegean sea) will no longer see Bacchus (who found
Ariadne there), nor will Cirrha (near Delphi) see Apollo.

22b
Prose Epilogue to Pontius Leontius

INTRODUCTION

If he undergoes judgement, S. says, Bacchus may suffer for this (he means too, perhaps, that his own reputation might), and so jokingly enjoins secrecy. Then he changes the subject, imagining criticism for excessive length. The style is typical of the wordy and orotund style regularly found in the letters of Sidonius.

TRANSLATION

See, I have sent you something that you can read among your cups and sconces whenever you wish to brighten a feast with fuller vessels.[1] You will relieve my modesty if it does not reach sober ears. This request is not unlawful, nor inconsistent with equity, since a tribunal, I fear, is being set up prematurely for my friend Bacchus, who might suffer a judgement of decemviral severity.[2] If someone should think that a longish poem should be criticised because it has exceeded the conciseness of an epigram, it is quite clear that he has not read the "Baths of Etruscus" or the "Hercules of Sorrento" or the "Tresses of Flavius Earinus" or the "Tibur, home of Vopiscus", or anything at all from the little *Silvae* of our Statius; that highly reputed man does not confine all these descriptive poems[3] within the limits of distichs or tetrastichs, but rather, as Horace in his volume "The Art of Poetry" counsels,[4] tastefully develops matters that have been broached by adding stock purple patches consisting of commonplaces.

---

1 S. uses a very choice word from Horace here (*Odes* 1.36.14).
2 Exceptional rigour, in other words. For the decemvirs, see *c.* 23.477–9.
3 The references are to *Silvae* 1.5, 3.1, 3.4 and 1.3, two of which are considerably shorter than *c.* 22.
4 *Art of Poetry*, 15. There is an interesting discussion of this passage and other uses of it in Pelttari (2016).

Let this suffice as an example of my defence, lest this plea in mitigation of prolixity should itself seem over long. Farewell.

Poem 23
To Consentius

INTRODUCTION

Consentius was a close friend of Sidonius, one of many who regularly exchanged letters and poetry with him. Here S. has received a letter–poem to which, although (so he claims) it had at first disconcerted him by its polymetry and elevation of style, he responds and tries to repay the debt. This reply, in the hendecasyllablic metre, has 512 lines, which at the end of the poem beg their addressee's pardon for their loquacity. The letter quickly takes the form of a formal panegyric – though it is not a parody: S. is doing what comes most naturally – and deals first with his friend's fatherland, which was Narbo, and then at some length with his father (also named Consentius), mentioning his education, marriage and the birth of Consentius the younger (at some time between 415 and 425). This is followed by an account of the son's accomplishments and his varied imperial service; this included a praetorian prefecture (*PLRE* 2.308–9), from which, S. remarks, he refused to make money, and from time to time work as interpreter in Rome and Constantinople for the emperor (presumably Valentinian III).

A good half of the long section praising his correspondent is taken up with the description of a chariot race in the presence of the emperor, probably in Rome and perhaps in honour of the emperor Valentinian's consulship (see note 82). This description is an example of what I have elsewhere called a 'tableau' or vivid description of the kind that is included in the panegyrics. The race as it is described has excitement and pace that perhaps make it more thrilling than the race portrayed in Statius, *Thebaid* 6.389–453; in its empathy and animation it could be compared with the Vergilian boat race and shipwreck in *A*. 5.114–285, or the race passionately and emotively reported (it is actually fake news) in Sophocles, *Electra*, 701–63.

The poem's date is uncertain; it is often linked with *c*. 22 by reason of the visit to Narbo, but this link cannot be pressed (Kelly [2020], 173): why not a separate visit? The date may be sometime between the panegyric to Majorian and that to Anthemius, in the early or middle sixties. See Loyen (1960), 160–1 for a thumbnail sketch of Consentius's possible career and note 100 below.

Synopsis

1–31 acknowledgement of the letter
32–96 praise of the city of Narbo
97–177 praise of Consentius's father, in particular his wealth of learned
    reading
178–303 praise of Consentius the younger, including his leisure activities
304–427 the chariot race staged by the emperor, won by Consentius
428–33 the later career of Consentius
434–506 happy recollections of meetings with Sidonius and friends in
    their homes.

TRANSLATION

Consentius, summit and glory of manners,
when, as your excellence deserves, I was planning
to devote the music of my poor little reed pipe
to singing praises of your hospitality,
unbidden you brought out for poetry your trumpet   5
changing our normal practice,[1] and in verse challenged
your friend, who is more used to lighter kinds of verse.
My Muse obeys you, but will ply her impudent pen
with much more care, and this is why: when calling for
poems from me so eloquently, you persuade me   10
to want to write poems, but make me keep silent.

---

1 The letter/poem from Consentius was weighty, but not necessarily epic in nature, though the common trope of 'trumpet' might suggest that. In any case, S. pleads his case for their normal practice of exchanging light verse.

Recently, when, speeding on horseback,[2] you were going
to Phocis[3] and the Sextian watering places,[4]
cities renowned in titles and records of battles[5]
by virtue of the triumphs won by two consuls[6]   15
(the one endured the army of Julius Caesar
and faced the fury of the fleet under Brutus,
the other, smeared with blood, bore battles with Teutons,
and Marius, still standing upright as Cimbrians fell)[7] –
you sent me a many-splendoured poem, replete   20
with learning, noblesse, cogency, and elegance.
In it hexameters paraded with great pride;
elegiacs made footprints that were comparable
but smaller, being restricted to five feet per line;[8]
you sent the metre of the triple trochee too,   25
accompanied by spondee and dactyl (in a word,
tuneful hendecasyllables),[9] and you obliged
your Sollius[10] with a captivating kind of debt.
I am asked for the interest on that, and now pay it,
though what I now pay in respect of your poem   30

2 Dictation on horseback, even of poetry, to a friend or scribe may not be impossible, but probably this was written in one of the towns mentioned.

3 Like certain other Latin writers, notably the epic poet Lucan, S. uses Phocis as a name of Massilia (Marseilles).

4 This is now Aix, in Latin named *Aquae Sextiae* after a Sextus who founded the spa in 123 BC.

5 By 'records' he might be thinking of annalistic history and perhaps biography, or assuming that such formal records existed; 'titles' suggests victories perpetuated in a general's nomenclature.

6 The consuls are respectively Pompey, who is claimed here to have helped Marseilles withstand Julius Caesar and Decimus Brutus in 49 BC, and Caius Marius, who defeated the Teutons and Cimbri, invaders from northern Gaul, in 102 and 101 BC. These victories of Marius are commemorated elsewhere by S. (*c.* 2.230 and *c.* 9.255–8).

7 The contrast of 'stood'and 'fell' is typical (cf. *c.* 5.72).

8 He means that the elegiac couplet combines a hexameter line, partly identical to the hexameter metre, with a line equivalent to five feet (known as a pentameter).

9 By 'triple trochees' Sidonius means the hendecasyllabic metre, in which the three trochees are preceded by a spondee and a dactyl.

10 The name Sollius is also used in the first line of Poem 9.

is but a mere hundredth of the praises due to you.[11]
To what in you should I pay homage first, and give
my reverence?[12] To your fatherland, surely, and then
your father; although he could rightly claim the first
place for himself, it is essential nonetheless   35
that the land which gave birth to your parents should precede.

Hail, Narbo, mighty in your healthfulness, in town
and countryside a pleasing prospect, with your walls
encompassing your citizens; equipped with shops,
with gates, with porticoes, with theatre and forum,   40
with shrines of the gods, with stately capitols,[13] with mints,
bath-houses, arches, granaries, marketplaces,
with meadows, and fountains, with islands and salt-pans,
your pools, your river, your commerce, your bridge and brine;[14]
you have a unique right to be the worshippers   45
of the gods Lenaeus, Ceres, Pales and Minerva
for corn and vines, for pastures and for olive-mills.[15]
You trust solely in fighting men, without seeking
the help of nature: leaving mountains far beneath
you thrust into the skies an even higher mass.[16]   50
You are protected by no gaping moat, no mound
of earth crowned high with bristling stakes is your defence;[17]
you do not fasten marble blocks onto your walls,[18]

11 This equates to 12 per cent per annum, 1 per cent per month, but the point is that
Consentius deserves far more than S. can give.
12 Like many a panegyrist before and after, S. pretends to be baffled by the choice of
material; in fact he follows the normal arrangement.
13 The word for 'shrines' in line 41 does not exclude Christian churches. By 'capitols' tall
and imposing buildings, not necessarily on the scale of Rome's, are meant.
14 The alliterative 'bridge and brine' (Anderson) captures well the striking wordplay in
the Latin words *ponte ponto*.
15 By its fertility and economic advantages Narbo is said to have deserved the attention
of these gods (Lenaeus is another name of Bacchus; Pales cared for flocks and herds).
16 An exaggeration, though from certain viewpoints mountains in the background can
appear smaller.
17 As will appear, Narbonne had walls, and strong ones, rather than the fortifications of
traditional camps, which are implied here to enhance the contrast.
18 The poet turns to the common theme of excessive luxury, often castigated in the
context of individual homes and mansions.

or gilt or glass, there is no gleam of Indian
tortoise-shell, no ivory torn from the faces   55
of elephants from Marmarica;[19] nor do you adorn
any golden gates with pieces of mosaic stone
spread in the 'unswept' style.[20] But standing proud among
your strongholds, half-demolished though they be, showing
the glories that you won in conflicts of old time,   60
you bear enormous stones, smashed down by others' blows,
for which praiseworthy ruins you enjoy the more esteem.[21]
Let other cities boast more menace thanks to their
position, having been built high by weaker men;[22]
let cities placed by nature on abrupt summits   65
brag that they never have been stormed; but you impress
because you have been buffeted, and the assault
on you has made renowned your valiant loyalty.[23]
Because of this Theoderic, the warrior king,
greater than his great father, glory of the Goths,   70
the pillar and salvation of the Roman race,
esteems you for your previous loyalty to him
in dangerous disturbances, and values you.
But you should not be judged dishonourable because
so many siege-works bored their passages through you,   75
for on the bodies of the greatest warriors
the greater be the scar, the greater is the glory.

19 S. shows apparent sympathy with elephants elsewhere too (c. 2.54–5 and c. 22.58–63).

20 The 'unswept style' (Greek and Latin *asarotum*) used assorted pieces of mosaic to mimic the floor of a room where crumbs and other droppings had not been swept up. S. knew the word probably not from contemporary life but from the poet Statius, *Silvae* 1.3.56.

21 These words recall the violent attack on Narbo made by Theoderic I in 436/7, alluded to in c. 7.475–80, where S. in the mouth of Avitus depicts a situation of extreme pressure, and less openly in the preface to c. 22. Theoderic II occupied Narbonne in 462, but apparently gained it through betrayal and without conflict (Hydatius 212 [217]; *PLRE* 2.1072).

22 In panegyrical mode the poet mentions apparently similar situations, but gives reasons why the comparisons are not valid. Cities that are perched higher on rocks may have less impressive manpower than Narbo (line 48); cities never stormed may owe this to nature alone.

23 The assault of 436/7, horrific as it was, is claimed to have had a permanent good outcome: Narbo is highly esteemed for its loyalty then and, according to S., earned its gentle treatment in the year 461 (note 21).

For a warrior in the Marathonian campaign[24]
it was a great reproach to be without a wound;
among the Publicolae, renowned for their brave hands,   80
Mucius was prominent for his disabled arm;[25]
when Pompey was demolishing Caesar's rampart
among so many faces untouched by the foe
the face of Scaeva, now one-eyed, was the most noble.[26]
The glory of withstanding misfortune is hard   85
to achieve; inactive courage is often a thing
feigned by the indolent, the coward, the untested.

And what is more, in the formation of emperors
happy in your heroic progeny, you made
sons who were emperors together with their father.   90
For who will leave unsaid the campaign against Persia
or the successful war of the emperor Carus,[27]
and the achievement of Roman legions, who marched
unhurried all over the mountain Niphates,[28]
at the time when the emperor was struck down by lightning,   95
so ending a life that was itself like a thunderbolt.

So blessed in citizens, city and countryside
you fathered (kind Narbo!) the sire of Consentius,
in whom there was, with Attic grace, a sparkling wit
but also a Roman's gravity. On hearing him[29]   100

---

24 Probably a reference to the famous battle of Marathon (490 BC), when the Persians
were defeated by the Athenians (cf. *c*. 6.3); this assertion may be invented by S. to help his
present argument. A reference to practice in the Athenian army generally is less likely, and
has no parallel.

25 They all bore wounds, but Mucius's wound was greater.

26 Scaeva's endurance was outstanding: see Lucan 6.140–262; Caesar, *Civil War* 3.53.4
(noting 120 wounds), Suetonius, *Julius* 68.4.

27 In his Persian expedition of 283 Carus (*PLRE* 1.183) and his army advanced as far as
Ctesiphon; further advance was ruled out by his death from lightning.

28 The Niphates mountains were a branch of the Taurus range in Armenia, near the
source of the river Araxes.

29 The following list of the 'seven sages' has similarities to the passages at *c*. 2.157–68
and *c*. 15.44–50, which present their famous sayings, or sum up their wisdom; here S.
imagines what would have been their reactions if they had actually heard Consentius senior

Milesian Thales could have been struck dumb, likewise
Cleobulus, famed among the hills and citadels
of high-soaring Lindos and you, Periander, who
originated in Corinth and you, Bias,
whom Priene gave to the world and you, sophist   105
of Lesbos, Pittacus, and you, Solon, a man
of power in dour Athens and you, who overshadow
the disputations of Socratic schools, and you,
Chilon, of Tyndarean Therapnae, rated
more outstanding than Lycurgus the lawgiver.   110
This person,[30] if, when duties permitted, he wished
to note what were the courses of the stars in heaven,
did not use ways distinct from those of Aratus;
and when he put his mind to the art of geometry
even Euclid, though so conversant with the vault   115
of heaven, would not have been able to follow him;
nor, should he want to build rhythmical periods,
could Chrysippus have hindered him in any way
by practising his new method of *sorites*.[31]
When concentrating on the art of Amphion   120
with plectrum, with his thumb, his voice, and flute, he made
the poet of Thrace, Arcadia's god, and Phoebus seem
but second rate in every kind of song;[32] and you
would not have reckoned even the Muses themselves
so musical. And if in long robe and buskin   125
he had entered the Attic theatre just once
Euripides and Sophocles would have given way;
or if wearing the comic slipper[33] he had wished

---

speak. There are some slight changes: Cleobulus of Lindos is described a little more; Solon
has moved down in the list, after Periander and Bias, and here his political power and skill in
debate are mentioned. Chilon is now compared with Lycurgus (for whom *c.* 2.163 and 166).

30 This is still Consentius senior.

31 Aratus was outstanding for his versification of astronomical discoveries; Euclid
excelled in geometry; the philosopher Chrysippus was famous, or notorious, for his *sorites*,
which has been described as 'a logical trick in which a proposition is added to or whittled
away bit by bit' (OLD).

32 Respectively Orpheus, Pan and Phoebus Apollo.

33 For the 'slipper', a defining feature of comic actors, cf. *c.* 9.213, again of Menander.

to make the stage resound, Menander, you would have
signalled with a finger that you were giving him the palm.[34]   130
When he was polishing the six-footed style taught
in the traditional ways of the Smyrnaean school,[35]
or when he gave himself to serious history,
the primacy of torrent-like Herodotus[36]
and thundering Homer could hardly have been maintained.   135
No grander a speaker would have been that orator
who once in Pandion's city with peerless skill
used fractiously to arouse the audience of the courts,
whether by laying into one-eyed Philip, or
persistently pleading the cause of Ctesiphon[37] –   140
an orator who sought incessantly the people's
favour, and using it to advance, one rightly deemed
to occupy the topmost peak of eloquence;
a blacksmith's son, he preferred to sharpen his tongue's edge.
Why should I speak of you, exemplars of Latin   145
eloquence from Arpinum, Padua, and Mantua,[38]
or you, Terence, writer of comedies, or you,
Plautus, who, though born in forbidding times, surpass
Greek wit with your humour, and you, Varro, revered
for the multifarious profuseness of your books,   150
and you, Crispus, outstanding for your conciseness,
and, finally, as for you, Cornelius Tacitus,[39]
because of your flow of creativeness, no tongue
should ever taciturnly disregard your work;[40]
and you, the Arbiter, in your *Massilian*   155
Gardens, a worshipper of the sanctified tree-stump,

---

34 Menander would have conceded immediately.

35 S. imagines (not altogether implausibly) a school devoted to writing Greek hexameter verse in Smyrna, Homer's supposed birthplace.

36 Herodotus, the famous historian of the wars of Greece and Persia.

37 The speeches of Demosthenes against Philip of Macedon and the one defending Ctesiphon were particularly praised.

38 These are respectively, Cicero, Livy (cf. *c.* 2.189) and Vergil.

39 Varro was a prolific polymath of the first century BC; Sallust and Tacitus were historians who wrote on Republican and Imperial themes respectively.

40 There is a different pun on the name Tacitus in *c.* 2.192.

the equal of the Hellespontine Priapus,[41]
and you, known through your voluptuous poems, tender
Ovidius Naso, sent into exile at Tomi,
once in subjection to the daughter of Caesar,   160
to whom you gave the invented name of Corinna?[42]
Why should I speak of the great Senecas,[43] or of
Martial, the product of high-towering Bilbilis,
all of them natives of Hispanic provinces?[44]
Why speak of the poets whom Argentaria   165
Polla, joined in marriage to each of them, revealed?[45]
But why retrace so many writers and their styles?
Whether tender, tuneful, witty or homourless,
in the presence of Consentius, all were eclipsed.

To this man, of supreme ability and also   170
supreme nobility and handsomeness, was joined
a lady, who, transferring to her husband's home
the decorations of the veteran Jovinus,[46]
filled with his consul's robes[47] the abode of a scholar.

41 This is Petronius, known as the Arbiter, author of the novel *Satyricon*. S. seems to
consider *The Gardens of Massilia* as a title of the work, or of a portion of it. As Loyen (1960),
150 explains, Petronius through his main character Encolpius may be seen as a worshipper
of Priapus, of whom there was an ithyphallic statue near the Hellespont, and his equal in
devotion. See also the reconstruction of Jensson (2004), 108–22 (a reference which I owe to
Professor Panayotakis).

42 S. jumped to a wrong conclusion here; Ovid indeed wrote in his love poetry about
a woman that he called Corinna, but this Corinna was not the daughter of the emperor
Augustus. He may have confused her with the emperor's daughter Julia, who was disgraced
and sent into exile. The exact causes of Ovid's own exile, to Tomi on the Black Sea, are not
known.

43 As it emerges from *c.* 9.230–40, S. thought that the philosopher Seneca and the
tragedian Seneca were different people, which is certainly not the case.

44 Martial's birthplace is suitably described: see Howell (1980), 216–17.

45 These poets, Lucan and Statius, were according to S. each married to Argentaria Polla.
That Lucan married her is stated by Martial (7.21); she may have married a patron of Statius,
but not Statius himself. See Hardie (1983), 4 and n., and Nisbet (1978), 1–11.

46 Jovinus was consul in 367 (Amm. 27.2.10: *PLRE* 1.462); the word 'veteran' implies
that at the time in question S. considered him elderly. The lady's name is not known (*PLRE*
2.1239; *Anonyma* 11).

47 The words 'consul' and 'scholar' are here in contrast.

So inside the domicile that is yours, Consentius,   175
proud glory of your fatherland, your grandfather
lives on through his honours, your father through his books.
Yourself, a man of influence through your descent
but even more through the excellence of your conduct,
I could not celebrate with the praise that you deserve,   180
even if, singing in his Odrysian cavern,
where Hebrus with his scurrying waters resounds
among the craggy mountains of the Cicones,
that famous chief of poets had instructed me,[48]
when his sweet strings brought down the animated rocks   185
from Rhodope's slopes by the power of his music,
and switching their accustomed roles bound the fountains
and forced the lands around to run, gasping for breath,[49]
and as mount Ismarus became open to the sun
and the forest, listening with new ears, sought his lyre   190
and snows which no amount of heat had ever dissolved
came rushing madly down from sloping Ossa's heights;
or when the Bistones glimpsed Strymon standing still,
its hurried water thirsting after song, nor even,
if given to Pelion's bi-formed inhabitant,   195
I had taken my place beside the Centaur's lyre
dreading a negative neigh from my two-bodied tutor[50]
nor if I had been taught in music by the god
who was ordered to feed the flock of his servant
by the Amphrysus – when a god became a farmhand –   200
because he had with his bow struck down the grime-coloured
Cyclopes in the furnaces of Lipara,
shooting from his bowstring a thunderbolt more dire.[51]

Now when you were still warm after your placid birth
the nine sisters cradled you in their arms, and took you,   205
a wailing infant, from your mother, to dip you

---

48 Orpheus; the description of his music continues down to line 194 (cf. *c.* 6.4–28).
49 For this unwonted athleticism of trees and rocks cf. *c.* 6.4.
50 For Chiron's inappropriate neighing, cf. *c.* 14.30.
51 Apollo, god of music, was punished by being made a herdsman for killing the Cyclopes
working in the forge at Lipara, his bow being more potent than their thunderbolts.

in the glassy water of the pool of Hippocrene;
immersed in this, it was letters that you imbibed
instead of rivulets of chattering water.
Then, already a boy more able than a teacher   210
you gobbled up all aspects of the rhetor's art
and all the parts of grammar (including debates),
sating yourself, just as when younger you had sipped.
The court soon claimed you, and the sacred emperor
placed you at once in the eminent ranks of tribunes   215
included in the imperial consistory;[52]
then the empurpled emperor, at the empire's head,
used to be present[53] at your councils, an honour
which your virtue deserved for its nobility.
Such elevation and astounding distinction   220
is clear from lists of honours set down in chronicles.[54]
From here you assumed a great responsibility;[55]
you should have added to your salary from this
office by unofficial rulings (no less just),[56]
but you refrained from this widespread exploitation,   225
and came back home richer in repute, considering
as yours only what you had given away to others.
Next, if there were any issues that the emperor
desired to reach the ears of his father-in-law[57]
in the East from a trusty and trained interpreter[58]   230

52 He was tribune and notary (*tribunus et notarius*) under Valentinian III from 437,
according to *PLRE* 2.308–9. For an explanation of consistories, see Jones (1973), 1, 333–41.
53 The meaning is not entirely clear: 'used to take charge of' is also possible. However,
this would be less commendatory to Consentius; S. wishes to put in high relief his contribution and authority, the point being that he had caught the emperor's eye.
54 It is not clear what chronicles are implied; S. sometimes refers to annals or other
sources of information that may or may not have existed and would be difficult to check or
gainsay (cf. *c.* 5.112–14).
55 This line, with 226, suggests that he was praetorian prefect, possibly for the East,
though this is not otherwise attested.
56 Exploiting his services, S. claims, was no less just than making official rulings without
favour. *PLRE* 2.309 mentions 'legitimate perquisites'.
57 This is Theodosius II; Valentinian III became his son-in-law when he married Eudoxia,
his daughter, in 437.
58 There was a corps of interpreters (Jones [1973], 1, 584); their help may have been
employed as necessary.

he would without delay choose you, a learned person,
to hold negotiations in both languages.
O tell me, pray, how many times, as you spoke Latin,
did listeners in Byzantine realms give you 'bravos'[59]
and how often, whether you sounded to them like   235
a Roman born in Rome's Subura,[60] or whether
you flowed with the rich smoothness of the Argolic tongue
just like one born in Marathon,[61] did the Bosphorans,[62]
dumbfounded as they applauded you, think less highly
of native speakers of Attica's own language!   240
So if the treaties of the whole world were destroyed,
peace would, with you as mediator, be granted
by wild and warlike peoples: Hun, Sarmatian, Goth,
Gelonian;[63] you could reach the Tungrian,[64] the rivers
Waal, Weser and Elbe, the farthest marshes of   245
the Franks, with the respect of the Sygambrians,
kept safe in the midst of arms by character alone.
Constant and fearless you would approach Maeotis
and the Caspian Gates and Bactra,[65] where the cavalry
of the ever changing Parthian rides,[66] so that, casting   250
aside the pomp and swagger of his arrogant court,
the tyrant who, seated above his satraps, boasts
of his relationship with demigods, would bend
in deference to you his crescent-shaped tiara.[67]

59 Cf. *c*. 5.8 n. The word is no less suitable in the present context than it was there.

60 The Subura, a well-populated valley in the centre of Rome, was 'notorious for bustle and noise' (OCD[4]).

61 On Marathon, cf. *c*. 6.3. Probably the city of Athens is meant here, and not the deme Marathon, site of the famous battle (cf. *c*. 23.78).

62 The cultivated citizens of Constantinople.

63 A handful of formidable tribes; the Geloni are prominent with the Huns in *c*. 7.321, and like those just mentioned part of the Hunnic empire.

64 The Tungrians were a tribe in north-west Germany; the rivers mentioned add to the picture of danger and inaccessibility.

65 Maeotis is now the sea of Azov, in the Black Sea; the Caspian Gates are south of the Caspian sea, in the Caucasus range; Bactra/ia (cf. *c*. 2.448; *c*. 5.603, *c*. 9.22), a symbol of remoteness, is well to the east of the Caspian sea.

66 The meaning could be 'roving' or 'inconsistent', or could even refer to their flowing clothing.

67 For this kind of tiara cf. *c*. 2.51.

If Rome's fortunes were not preventing you from going   255
to Byrsa and meeting the Tanais-born rebel,
insurgent in the provinces of Africa,[68]
the fury of war would come to an immediate end,
and after all his losses due to buccaneers
the trader would be sending out ships full of goods,   260
and with the re-establishment of peace through you,
no more, I know, would warfare be ruling the waves.

But when you finished serious things, from time to time,
and the shows of the theatre were gripping you,
the whole body of actors went quite pale, as if   265
the Bow-bearer himself and the nine Muses were
sitting beside the stage ready to judge. In your
presence a Caramallus or a Phabaton[69]
with tightly fastened jaws and eloquent gestures,
with nodding head, with leg, knee, hand, and bodily twirl,   270
will be ignored for once throughout the performance,
whether the daughter of Aeetes and her Jason[70]
are being staged there with wild Phasis, which dreaded
the teeth broadcast over the fields of Colchis when
a pullulating army of men came into view   275
and spearheads grew, mingled with waving ears of corn;[71]
or whether someone represents the banquet of
Thyestes,[72] or your wailing, grim Philomela,
or the young boy who was butchered and given as food
for your husband, who now became the less guilty,[73]   280

---

68 Gaiseric, now in Carthage, was born in Scythia, perhaps somewhere in the Tanais valley.

69 Nothing is known of these two mime-actors. The names are very rare; Caramallus is attested as an oustanding dancer in sixth-century Byzantium, much later: see Cameron (1976), 19 (from the historian Malalas).

70 Medea and Jason, in Phasis the region around the river of that name, which is here personified. Cf. *c* 9.66–75.

71 These warriors grew up in the fields from the dragon's teeth which Jason had to sow.

72 The suffering of Thyestes is narrated also in *c*. 9.106–16.

73 After raping Philomela, Tereus had cut out her tongue, incurring further guilt, but killing and eating Itys was not his fault.

or enacts the abduction from Tyre, and Jove the bull,[74]
who left behind his thunderbolt and caused more fear
with his horns; or if Danae's tower is being shown,[75]
at the point when it is being drenched with a shower of wealth,
giving joys, stolen joys, more golden even than gold;   285
or whether someone plays Leda,[76] or Ganymede,[77]
and setting him to be cupbearer makes the lad
from Troy sweeter to the Thunderer than wine itself;
or whether someone is portraying Mars just caught
in the Lemnian's chains,[78] or gives to Mars, as spurned lover,   290
the appearance of a boar, roughening his head and back
with bristles, and upwards, away from his shaggy jaws,
curving the smooth ivory, or perhaps the actor
might be burlesquing such a hairy-backed monster,
sharpening his up-bent weapons with sustained rubbing;   295
or whether the theme portrayed is Perseus and his maiden,
delivered by her lover's scimitar;[79] or whether
something is mimed from the realms of song and story that
the ten years' war around blockaded Troy supplies.
Why should I tell how the players of lyre and flute,   300
and mime actors, rope-walkers and laughter makers
cringe when they nervously show off in your presence
reed-pipes and plectrums, banter, wrestling, and rope-tricks?[80]

But it is right for my Muse joyfully to record
what you achieved as victor in the circus-games   305

74 The thunderbolt of Jove, S. reckons, caused less terror than his horns did on this occasion.

75 Danae was imprisoned in a tower for her safety; but Jove approached this as a shower of gold.

76 Leda's role is not developed here (in some versions Jove was hiding in a swan): cf. *c.* 15.175–6.

77 Ganymede was taken to the home of the gods to be Jove's cupbearer.

78 For Homer's story of Mars and Venus caught in bed together, cf. *c.* 11.32–3. In the fuller tale, Vulcan was jealous of Venus's devotion to Adonis, which is related in Ovid *M.* 10.503–59.

79 Perseus saved Andromeda from a monster, killing it with his weapon (scimitar or sickle).

80 A vivid picture of minor entertainments which S. might have noticed in the city.

when the city of Rome[81] echoed with thunderous applause.
With Phoebus wheeling round through the seasons of the year
Janus of the two faces brought round his Kalends,[82]
the time when magistrates take up their curule chairs.[83]
It is the emperor's custom to arrange for games   310
(described as private games)[84] twice in a single day.
At these a company of young men, all from the court,

---

81 The games about to be described almost certainly took place in Rome, not Ravenna as sometimes assumed. Anderson stated firmly that the word 'Rome' in lines 304–6 is not to be taken literally, and that Valentinian III (425–55) resided in Ravenna; he was followed, it seems, by Cameron (1976), 51–2, whose work influenced others (including Humphrey [1986], 632–4). But a very different picture of the political roles of Ravenna and Rome is now indicated, in particular by Gillett (2001), whose thorough analysis of laws and other evidence from the fifth century shows the importance to each emperor of varying circumstances and personal preference. (See also McEvoy [2014], *passim*). Whatever the reasons, it seems that Valentinian III was only an occasional visitor in Ravenna, unlike, for example, the previous emperor Honorius, who spent thirty years there (393–423) (but that period is too early for the present passage). Moreover, in a long note ([2001], 160, table 33, Gillettt also showed that the evidence for a circus in Ravenna in both literary and artistic depictions before the mid-sixth century is weak. Judith Herrin, who carefully describes the visits to Ravenna that S. mentions in a few letters ([2020]), 52) is led to assume that a circus near the imperial palace had ceased to exist by the mid-ninth century. (There was one later, according to Herrin [2020], 414 n. 17, who comments that the evidence for one is 'very confused'). I am also told (by Tom Brown, in an email) that there seems to be no evidence at Ravenna of suitable buildings or a circus in the fifth century.

It is possible, and tempting, to suggest that these games were held by the short-lived emperor Avitus at the beginning of his inaugural year 456, when Sidonius, his son-in-law and supporter, was close to events and could have been responsible for the inclusion of the Gallic Consentius in the programme of celebrations. His descriptions of the arena and the underground preliminaries to a race (lines 315–20) go beyond what is provided by earlier literary descriptions, such as they are, and suggest close knowledge. The date implied by this is not impossible. If Consentius was born *ca.* 420, within the dates favoured by Loyen (1960), 160–1 n., in fact 415–20 – a date which allows for the political career sketched by S., and a race in 440 – he might still be able to compete successfully with the high degree of skill, energy and physical fitness that S. describes. The silence of Sidonius about the wider context of the games might be explained by his discretion or so-called 'prudence' in public matters, especially as they concerned the role of his deceased father-in-law (Mathisen [1979a], 165–72).

82 For Janus, and his connection with the consular celebrations, when new magistrates generally took up their offices ('their curule chairs'), see *c.* 1.8–12 and *c.*7.9–13.

83 In *c.* 7.9–10 the senators are told they are pleased to have granted Avitus a curule chair (the consulship) but that the gift of a (triumphal) chariot lay in the future.

84 That was their title (the comment of S. is in no way sceptical).

gives a ferocious imitation of the games
once held at Elis with prancing four horse chariots.[85]
Now you are summoned by the lot, and called out by   315
the screaming acclamation of the raucous crowd.
Then, at the place where the door is, and the consuls' seats,
 (this is surrounded by a wall, with on each side
six vaulted chambers, which contain the starting-pens),[86]
you take by lot one chariot from the four, gripping   320
the sinuous reins, and go into the arena itself.
Your colleague did the same, and likewise the rival team.
There is a burst of bright colour, with white, blue, green
and red, the emblems of your team and of
the team opposing you.[87] The hands of assistants   325
control the mouths and reins of each, and with their stiff
brushes they force the twisted manes to disappear,
at the same time giving their own encouragement,
fondling the horses with affectionate touches
and implanting in them a rapturous frenzy.   330
They rage against the barriers, and throw themselves
at all restraints, and breathe right through the boards that block
their progress, and before the race begins the field,
though as yet not entered, fills with panting and puffing.
They push, they pull, they bustle, they struggle, raging   335
and jumping, fearful and creating fear; their feet
cannot keep still, but dash against the barricades
of hardened timber. At long last there comes the blare
of the resounding trumpet, and the trumpeter,
having assembled the impatient four-horse teams,   340
lets loose into the field the rapid chariots.
No devastating strike of threefold thunderbolt,

---

85 The games at Elis, which became the Olympic games, are mentioned in *c.* 9.101; the town of Pisa there is brought into a simile in lines 392–3.

86 The starting pens were known as *carceres*, 'prisons'. S. describes these semi-underground arrangements in some detail; he may well have visited this area at some stage, for whatever reason.

87 The order of the colours is largely dictated here by metre; the pair 'white and blue' must stand where they are, and shed no light on the question of the choice of colour as discussed by Cameron (1976), 66.

no arrow from the bowstring of a Scythian,
no trail described by any swiftly-falling star,
no hurricane of leaden projectiles, even   345
whirled and propelled from Balearic slings,[88] ever
burst through the limpid highways of the sky like this.
The earth yields to the wheels, the air is blackened by
the dust thrown up in their tracks; the drivers hurtle on,
all governing their horses with the lash; already   350
they stretch out with their bodies from the chariots
over the breasts of the horses, as they speed along.
They strike their horses' withers, not touching their backs,
nor could you quickly see whether the chariot poles
or the wheels supported them more as they lean forward.   355
Now you, as if on wings flying out of sight, having
by now devoured the more open part of the course,
were limited by the space, made artificially tight,[89]
through which the central barrier had extended
its low, long structure enclosed by a double wall.   360
When the later turning post freed all of you from checks,
your colleague found himself ahead of the other two,
who had passed you, so that you were then in fourth place
in keeping with the arrangement of the curving course.[90]
Those in the middle took note that the first rider,   365
forced by his horses' momentum too much to the right
might leave unoccupied the channel on the left

88 Slingers from the Balearic islands (Majorca and Minorca) were an important adjunct
to the Roman army.
89 The word translated 'central barrier' is *euripus*, originally a short stretch of water
or a trench, notably the one made by Julius Caesar (Suetonius, *Julius* 39.2; also Dionysius
of Halicarnassus, *Antiquities*, 3.68 [this was ten feet wide], and Pliny, *NH* 8.2). In this
racecourse its function is, like that of the *spina* (a low wall), sometimes mentioned, to add
complexity to the racing.
90 With the turning post (safely) passed, and a clear way ahead, Consentius found himself
in fourth position, behind his two rivals, who were chasing his colleague. Anderson's 'law'
seems to suggest a formal regulation that bound him in the fourth position, but there is
nothing to indicate a regulation of that kind; S. in fact refers to the 'condition' of the curving
course similar to that familiar today from running or cycling races (*mutatis mutandis*). He
seemed to have no option, given the built-in camber.

by going at full pelt for the arena wall[91]
and could be passed by a chariot driven on the inside.
But you, bent almost double by your exertions,   370
constrain your team and with the greatest skill wisely
save up their energies for the seventh and final lap.
The others pressed on desperately with hands and voices,
and in a waterfall of spray onto the course
the sweat of riders and horses ran everywhere.   375
The raucous shouting of supporters stirs their hearts,
and the heat of the race and the chill of fear affect the steeds
and the men themselves in equal measure. In this way
they go round once, and then a second time; there is
a third circuit, then a fourth, both of them just the same;   380
on the fifth circuit the leader, being unable
to handle the pressure of those pursuing him
withdraws his team, because with his demands on them
he had realised that they were exhausted; now with
the sixth lap entirely completed, and the crowd   385
already calling for the announcement of the prizes
the opposing side, in front and not at all fearing
your dynamism, were happily scouring their wheels[92]
when suddenly, tightening the reins, and tightening
the muscles of your chest, with front foot firmly fixed   390
you increased the pressure on your swift horses, as much
as that famed charioteer who swept Oenomaus
along with him and startled the city of Pisa.[93]
Here one from the other team, hugging the shortest route,
which wheeled around the turning-post, constrained by you,   395
had not the strength to pivot his team in unison
as they were swept along by their great impetus.
Since he had crossed over in disarray, you passed him
holding your position, expertly slowing down.

---

91 The arena wall or 'podium' formed the base of the raised seating for spectators; its
lower portion is where the emperors used to sit (Cameron [1976], 176–8), and so drew
competitors, as happens in a small way in line 400.

92 The notion of 'scouring' wheels may be sarcastic for a now useless action, or is perhaps
a technical term of the sport.

93 For Oenomaus and Pisa, cf. *c.* 2.490–2; *c.* 14.12–13.

The second man, delighting in the crowd's applause,   400
ran too much to the right, towards the spectators.
Then as he turned sideways, too long indifferent,
and much too late applied the whip to his horses,
you passed your swerving rival, taking a straight course.
Then the enemy incautiously caught up with you, and   405
thinking the first man had already gone ahead,
shamelessly clashes with your wheel, athwart his own.[94]
His horses were brought down, a violent mass of legs
fouled up the wheels, and all twelve spokes were squashed, until
the spaces in between them gave a loud crack, and   410
the madly spinning rims shattered the horses' feet.
Then he, a fifth victim (after the four horses),[95]
thrown headlong from his chariot, which buried him,
creates a mountain of all kinds of destruction,
disfiguring his face with blood as he lay prostrate.   415
A new outburst of shouting makes confusion worse:
noise such as neither cypress-bearing Lycaeus,
nor mount Ossa, shrouded with forests, generates
when it is pounded by incessant hurricanes;
noise such as neither the Trinacrian sea, whipped by   420
the south wind, ever creates, nor the Propontis with
voraginous deeps, a wall of sea to the Bosphorus.[96]
Then the just emperor[97] ordains that silken ribands
be added to the palms, and crowns to their necklets,[98]
and that their merits be duly rewarded; but   425

---

94 According to Anderson Consentius could not have won after such an impact (as 'dashed against' would suggest); he prefers 'made for your wheel', which leaves the obvious scale of the accident unexplained. We must assume that it would have been even worse but for Consentius's alertness and skill.

95 That is, his opponents' four.

96 The Propontis, the smaller sea that joins the Aegean sea and the Black Sea (Euxine), is not mentioned as such elsewhere by S.; nor is the word *Trinacria* ('three-cornered') for the island of Sicily and its seas. For the Bosphorus cf. *c.* 2.55.

97 Perhaps Avitus, as argued earlier; or Valentinian III: cf. the praise of him in *c.* 9.300.

98 The palms of the victors are decorated with ribands, their collars (or wreaths?) with crowns of some suitable kind. It is unlikely that a 'torc' (worn round the neck) was offered, given its imperial connexions (cf. *c.* 7.578). Little is known about the prizes or awards at such events.

that rugs of many-coloured hair be awarded to
the vanquished in their obvious ignominy.[99]

But as for the man you were when a young man's years were over,[100]
the man you showed yourself to be in later times
when summoned to the court of my father-in-law,   430
(you ran the office of Controller of the Palace)[101] –
these things I will describe in subsequent writings,
supposing I have more leisure in the future.[102]

But now, in brief, let my obedient Thalia
sing out the hospitality that I have mentioned.[103]   435
O sweet abode, O sacred household gods, that are
by both freedom and mutual respect adorned,
in a blend so difficult to achieve and then maintain!
O what banquets, what anecdotes, what books are ours!
The laughter, and the seriousness, the badinage;   440
the gatherings, the ever true companionship,
whether we were worshipping in the temple of God,
* (*misplaced in the mss.*) or making a visit to Livius' glorious home[104]

99 The word here translated 'rugs' might also refer to tapestries or hangings of some kind. Though relatively trivial and not objects to be prized, these awards are not in essence demeaning.

100 In this line the strenuous victory just described might seem to be classed with youthful games, street entertainments and other pursuits enabling him to relax after the demands of office (lines 214–303). The contrast that seems to be made here is not the same as that in lines 304–6, where there is a strong rhetorical comparison between street games, on the one hand, and the serious matter of the chariot racing, on the other. In the present passage the emphasis is on the political service of the mature man (for the varied implications of the word *iuvenis* see the introduction to Panegyric of Majorian).

101 A highly prestigious change is brought by his appointment to the Care of the Palace, an office whose importance can be seen from references to notable holders of it in the historian Ammianus, collected in Jones (1973), II, 1148). It is not known how long the appointment of Consentius lasted, as it might have done even after the death of Avitus.

102 There is no further reference to a memoir of Consentius; perhaps, for whatever reason, it was perhaps never written; such a promise is easily made.

103 S. cites Thalia since lighter verse is now indicated, suited to the relatively relaxed finale.

104 Of Livius (*PLRE* 2.685) nothing else is known, though he could be the poet mentioned in the anonymous *Life of Hilary of Arles* (line 11).

or directing our steps to the home of the bishop[105]
or to the tall dwelling of Martius Myro,[106]   445
or to the residence of well-spoken Leo[107]
(had Leo expounded the Twelve Tables of the law
Appius Claudius would happily have shunned
the public eye and been a minor figure in
that great decemvirate;[108] or if he wrote an epic   450
or with his ringing lyre changed to a metre of
short lines, he would have made the trenchant Horace dumb,
even though after his satires and his lyric odes
Horace aspired to soar on high like Pindar's swan).[109]
Such was the atmosphere if we were entertained   455
by your kindness, Magnus, a man possessed of many
of a male's good qualities – good looks, high birth, judgement,[110]
and wealth. Were I to count his many accomplishments
I would wear out a hundred mouths, yes, iron mouths,
in praising them;[111] he was steady, clever, able,   460
a wise arbiter, a first-rate relative, one who
deprived neither himself nor anyone of fun,
and who took note of persons, places, circumstances.[112]
Such was the atmosphere, too, if it was your halls

105 Anderson suggests that this is Bishop Hermes, who became bishop of Narbonne in 462.

106 No secure identification can be made.

107 Leo: see *PLRE* 2.662–3; his poetic gifts emerge from *c.* 9.314 (this identification has not been challenged), and various letters of S. Later he was adviser to the Gothic king Euric for several years.

108 Appius Claudius was a member of the first decemvirate, which in 450 BC drew up the law of the Twelve Tables, before falling into disagreement when a second set of laws was necessary.

109 Notwithstanding Horace's emulation of the swan-like Pindar in book four of his *Odes* (by 'lyric odes' he means his *Odes*, books 1–3), he would be stuck dumb by Leo, unable to criticise his writing either of epic or of lyric. Cf. *c.* 9.221–5 for a different schema of Horace's verse output.

110 Magnus (*PLRE* 2.700–1), father of Magnus Felix (cf. *c.* 9, lines 1–2).

111 For this trope see Vergil, *G.* 2.43 and *A.* 6.625; in both cases the expression 'a voice of iron' immediately follows.

112 He was interested in persons, their origins and their circumstances, and was fair in his opinions.

my Marcellinus, expert in the law,[113] that held us,   465
a man who, very forthright and very austere,
considered stern by those not acquainted with you,
though one who has appraised you well appreciates
a power of judgement which they'd like to be their own:
you never fear to say what is right, nor would you, even   470
if Sulla or savage Carbo were menacing you,[114]
or the likes of sullen Marius or cruel Cinna,[115]
or if somehow triumviral swords had gathered round[116]
your head and body. Such was the atmosphere when we
were received at home by Limpidius,[117] magnificent   475
citizen and outstanding character, who closely follows
his brother's standards; such was the atmosphere when we
were entertained together by the agreeable
attentiveness of the outstanding Marinus,
a man whose conscientiousness and comradeship   480
deserve my ceaseless praise; or if two of us chose[118]
to pay a visit to see others of the brethren –
to have leisure for visiting such people is
to my mind a commendable activity.
Their names, if only metre did not rule it out,   485
I would like dearly to record in my verses.

Then you would summon us to your own residence,
when the early morning had finished, and the hot sun
offered a second hour that was convenient,[119]

113 Marcellinus, if it is the same man, is mentioned in *Ep.* 2.13.1, where calls him 'a man of tried wisdom and of many friends'.

114 Sulla and Carbo are notorious in the turbulent times at Rome in the early first century BC.

115 This is another side of the successful general Marius (*c.* 23.19 above, *c.* 2.230, *c.* 9.258). Sulla's opponent Cornelius Cinna is not mentioned otherwise by S.

116 The triumvirs meant here are Mark Antony, Octavian and Lepidus, from the end of the Republic.

117 Limpidius seems to be unknown, like Marinus (479), whom *PLRE* 2.725 naturally sees as a citizen of Narbo like the others in this section.

118 Presumably S. and a friend; perhaps a Christian pair, whence the stress on visiting.

119 There is a play with the word *secundus* not unlike that in *c.* 2.1: 'favourable' as well as 'second'.

then, bringing out small balls and hoops, and then the dice   490
in their rattling dice-boxes, which made us ready for
the competition of throwing, just like the son
of Nauplius, who was the inventor of this art,[120]
you enjoyed encouraging a frolicsome quarrel.
Then to the baths – not of the Neronian kind – or like   495
those given by Agrippa,[121] or the emperor
whose tomb is visible to Dalmatian Salonae,[122]
but it was a pleasure to avail ourselves of baths
that catered well for privacy and modesty.
Then drinking from your cups, and lying on couches   500
in the company of your Muses would divert us;
such statues and such likenesses were never produced
in bronze or coloured marble by Praxiteles
or Mentor, or Scopas, nor did Polyclitus
himself make anything so great, nor did such forms   505
come from the chisels in the workshop of Phidias.[123]

But now your pardon for such babbling is implored
by five hundred hendecasyllables. So long
a poem, even if it pleases, is too long.
Enough now! You yourself are inconvenienced   510
reading your tedious friend in this poem, a man
more lethargic than people who really are asleep.

120 Palamides (son of Nauplius) was credited with the invention of draughts and dice.
121 The baths of Agrippa, dating from *circa* 20 BC, 'set new standards of luxury and (architectural) elaboration' according to OCD[4]. S. may have regarded the baths of Nero as extravagant and in bad taste, for whatever reason.
122 Diocletian's baths in Rome are meant. For a modern account of Salona (Split, in Croatia), see MacGeorge (2002), 19–23.
123 These were all sculptors, except for Mentor, a silversmith.

Poem 24 Envoi

INTRODUCTION

This short and lively poem in hendecasyllables presents a most attractive itinerary, taking the reader through a picturesque region of southern Gaul and shedding varied light on an area between Clermont and Narbonne and mostly on the western flank of the Cévennes. From Avitacum to Narbo it traces a zigzag route (Demougeot, quoted in the excellent short commentary by Santelia [1999], 20). Some locations cannot be identified for certain, but in a few lines for each of ten locations the poem provides fascinating detail, even about local fish or quickly changing microclimates. A harsher world is represented by the mountains of Lozère, the peaks of Aigoual and the river Tarn. In lines 56–68 S. evokes the exquisite gardens of his friend Apollinaris in one of his finest *tableaux*.

One manuscript only tries to classify the poem, making it a *propemptikon* – that is, a 'send-off' of a kind not infrequent in classical Latin poets. Classical versions of this genre tend to worry about the safety on the outward or return journey of the person concerned; but Sidonius pretends to be sending away his small book into safe hands (for perusal or copying, presumably) and with no reluctance and without any foreboding of danger. I have preferred to retain the very suitable title used by Anderson (*L'envoi*), which implies that S. is saying farewell to the reader and to some of his less well-known friends. S. expresses no regret for the amount of walking involved, and the 'little book' does not object to terrain too steep for mortals (in *c.* 8 the verses are given a mind of their own). Perhaps the poem is dedicated to the last person named, Magnus Felix (who has access to a good library). In that respect, there is a similarity to *c.* 9, clearly a high tribute sent to Magnus Felix, but one which (as argued in the general introduction, section 6) surely does not make of the diverse poems (9–24) a unit of their own. The date of this poem cannot be pinned down: see note 38 below, and Kelly (2020), 173 with his note 48.

The book is represented as proceeding through the countryside, not on the road and not shirking some steep climbs. Most places have been identified, and they are recorded as far as possible in the useful commentary of Santelia (1999). As a whole, the poem gives an impression of S.'s family and social life with a general tone not unlike that which ends poem 23 (lines 436–506).

Synopsis, of places and people to be visited

10–15 to the Clermont area, to see Domitius
16–19 to Brioude (see note 4, and the map); here his father-in-law Avitus
     was buried
20–2 towards the river Triober, now the Truyère (no person is mentioned)
23–5 past the Gabales, who lived in the territory of Gévaudan (no person
     is named)
26–30 to the Justin brothers' home; its location is not known
31–43 to Trevidos (which may now be St Laurent de Trèves); here the
     book will see Tonantius senior
44–52 to Vorocingus, where Apollinaris lives, modern Brocem; the
     mountain is today's Lozère
75–9 to Cottium, of which the location is not certainly known
80–3 to the home of Fidulus, location unknown
84–9 to the Three Villas, perhaps now S. Matthieu de Tréviers, to meet
     Thaumastus
90–8 to see Magnus father and son, at their villa near Narbonne

TRANSLATION

My little book, when you have left my house
remember to stick to this route, which follows;
it leads conveniently to friends of mine,
whose names I have assiduously included.
Don't labour down the old, familiar, highway   5
along whose length, on very ancient columns,
shines Caesar's name conspicuous in green,[1]

---

1 Which Caesar was responsible for the milestones on this road is not known. Green is an unexpected colour for them, unless it refers to vegetation or decay. Stevens (1979), 75, sees this comment as critical of the delay since the last repair of the road.

but walk unhurriedly; slowing the pace
makes for a ready welcome from our friends.

First you shall visit (this will alarm my Muse)   10
the home of stern Domitius;[2] not so harsh
was the man who laughed (according to reports)
on only one occasion in his life;[3]
but you may well be glad of his strict learning:
if he commends you, then you'll please them all.   15
Next you'll be welcomed by kindly Brioude,[4]
that cherishes the bones of saint Julian,[5]
which are deemed dead by those already dead,
yet from that tomb sparkles a living power.[6]
Now here, with a sharp right turn, you go through fields,   20
and having crossed a ridge (all in one day)
you'll see next day Triober's flaxen stream.[7]
Then you'll see the deep snow of the Gabales,[8]
and, as the locals wish us to believe,
you'll see a towering city in a well.[9]   25

2 Domitius (*PLRE* 2.371), the recipient of *Ep.* 2.2, was a *grammaticus* (teacher of basic texts).
3 This was supposedly Marcus Crassus, a praetor in the second century BC. The joke, ascribed to his contemporary the satirist Lucilius, was often repeated, and was known in the fourth century as well as it had been to Cicero and the Elder Pliny.
4 Brioude (Latin *Brivas*) is in Haute-Loire some thirty miles south of Clermont.
5 St Julian was probably beheaded under the emperor Decius, or else Diocletian. After the death of Avitus (the emperor, and father-in-law of S.) his body was buried at the foot of Saint Julian, according to Gregory of Tours, *History* 2.11. This saint is called 'our Julian' in *Ep.* 7.1.7, where S. mentions that Mamertus bishop of Vienne had reburied the head. See also Santelia (1999), 17–18.
6 Unusually strong sentiments for S., at least in his verse; he is closely involved.
7 'Flaxen' is an epithet used by Vergil of the Tiber (*A.* 7.31) (where the colour is explained by sand) and other Augustan poets. This river is the modern Truyère, a tributary of the Lot.
8 Gabales (*Gabalitani* elsewhere in Sidonius) are in the mountainous territory of Gévaudan, north-west of the Cévennes.
9 The place is not named, and various explanations of the description have been attempted, without finding general acceptance. Textual emendation has not been fruitful. Perhaps the 'well' is a crater, such as one caused by volcanic action, filled with rainwater, in which the town, or part of it – not of course an actual city – is seen in an elongated image (Santelia [2002], 25–7).

From here push on to the Spartans of our day
(Castor and Pollux), Justin and his brother,
whose famous friendship, on the wide world's lips,
excels that of Pirithous and Theseus
and the mad Orestes with his staunch comrade.[10]   30
Then, after their welcome with open arms,
Go to Trevidon,[11] and the hill, alas,
too close to the Ruteni, slanderers all.[12]
Here you will find the father of the learned
Tonantius, the Gauls' linchpin and leader,   35
Ferreolus,[13] the peer of old Syagrius,[14]
whose wife, Papianilla, sharing his burdens,[15]
assists him with exemplary efforts,
a woman such as not even Tanaquil
nor your daughter, Tricipitinus, were,[16]   40
nor that priestess sacred to Trojan Vesta
who against the river Albula in full spate

10 Justin and his brother (we are not told where they live) are compared to Castor and
Pollux, twin sons of Leda in Greek mythology and faithful friends; so too Pirithous and
Theseus, and Pylades and Orestes (who in the story became mad at one point); see also
c. 5.288. Justin and his brother, Sacerdos, received a short letter from Sidonius (*Ep.* 5.21).
    11 Trevidon is near modern St Laurent de Trèves, where Tonantius Ferreolus (see below)
had a property. The Ruteni lived to the south of the Gabali (note 8), and their name survives
in French Rodez. The two tribes are mentioned together in Caesar, *Gallic War* 7.64.6.
    12 Why they should be condemned as slanderers is quite unclear; an ongoing dispute over
land, perhaps. S. seems not to favour the Ruteni.
    13 Tonantius Ferreolus (*PLRE* 2.465–6) was praetorian prefect of the Gauls in 451–3 and
a long-standing support to the Gauls and Gallo-Romans, not least through his strong support
for Avitus in 455 (assuming he is the speaker at *c.* 7.530–1). A compliment is paid here to
his son, also Tonantius, conceivably still in education and indeed still 'young' in 479 when
S. wrote *Ep.* 9.13.3 to him (*PLRE* 2.465–6). The father's name (line 34) is not known; but he
was 'not a person to be overlooked' (*Ep.* 7.12.1).
    14 This is Flavius Afranius Syagrius (*PLRE* 1.862 and 2.1320, stemma 17).
    15 For Papianilla, wife of Ferreolus (not Syagrius), see *PLRE* 2.830 (Papianilla 1). The
name suggests a close relation to the wife of S. (Harries [1994], 34).
    16 These *exempla* are Tanaquil the moral paragon, as in *Ep.* 5.7.7 and Ausonius,
Professores 30.5, and the famous Lucretia, daughter of Tricipitinus (cf. *c.* 7.62–3, where she
is likewise unnamed).

hauled with her virgin's locks that fateful ship.[17]
Next, overtopping Scythia's Caucasus
Lozère will glimpse you,[18] as will hurrying Tarn,[19]   45
which carries in its limpid stream a fish
mud-loving, and crammed full of solid flavour.[20]
Here take the wings of Zetus and Calais
to avoid the ridge covered in cloud[21] – take care,
for it abounds in unremitting gales.[22]   50
But, no matter how rapidly you travel,
Vorocingus will be your lodging when tired.[23]
Here will you find my own Apollinaris,[24]
whether against the raging lion's heat[25]
he clothes his house with the coolness of marble,   55
or whether he strolls in gardens tucked away –
gardens like those that thrive in honeyed Hybla,[26]
like those that charmed the old Corycian,
darkened by the waters of black Galaesus;[27]
or whether among violets, and thyme, and privet,   60
serpyllum, marjoram, saffron, marigolds,

17 The fullest description of this famous story is at Ovid, *Fasti* [the Roman calendar]
4.291–325. The detail that she used her hair probably derives from Claudian, *Shorter Poems*
30.16–18.
    18 The Lozère (Latin *Laesora*), the highest mountain in the Cévennes (1,702m). An
amusingly exaggerated comparison with Scythia's Caucasus.
    19 The Tarn rises in this part of the Cévennes, and flows into the Garonne near Toulouse.
    20 The long list of fish with their habitats and gastronomic qualities in Ausonius, *Moselle*
85–149 includes a mud-loving fish at 122–3, evidently sold mainly in takeaways.
    21 Zetus and Calais (cf. *c.* 5.546) were the sons of the North wind (Ovid, *M.* 6.711–18).
    22 The ridge is identified as the Aigoual by Santelia (2002), 49.
    23 Vorocingus: this estate, identified as modern Brocem (near Alès), is mentioned also in
Ep. 2.9.7.
    24 For this person see PLRE 2.113–14, and stemma 14. The description that follows is a
great compliment to S.'s uncle Apollinaris.
    25 The height of summer, when the sun is in the sign of Leo. Cf. *c.* 22.182.
    26 The bees of Hybla were famous (Vergil, *E.* 7.37).
    27 S. refers to a famous passage from Vergil's fourth *Georgic* (*G.* 4.125–48) which
describes an old man from Corycus in Cilicia, devoted to his gardens near Tarentum in
Italy. The name of the river, and the impression of its darkness, come from the same source
(*G.* 4.126).

narcissi, and flowering hyacinths,[28] he is spurning
a clod of earth brought by a man from Saba[29]
seeking a high price for his frankincense;
or whether he unwinds in a mock grotto   65
at the hill's margin, where the trees sweep back,
striving to make a natural portico
and from their trees create not a grove, but a cave.
Who could now choose to compare that Indian king's
orchard of old and the vines made of gold,   70
with neatly trimmed tendrils of lush electrum,
when Porus made a vineyard of metal
with treasure rustling on the yellow branches
and gems in bunches swinging on the vine?[30]

From here you'll go to Cottium,[31] and say   75
to our Avitus, 'hi', and then 'good-bye'.[32]
To him you owe obedience without end
(and may my kinsmen forgive me for this);
not even a parent comes before a friend.
From here now Fidulus,[33] glory of the good –   80
no mere second, even to Tetradius,[34]
in moral qualities and zeal for the right –
with caring hospitality receives you.
From there direct your steps to 'Three Villas'[35]
And seek Thaumastus (either of the two) –   85

---

28 Also inspired by Vergil, especially the list of flowers in lines 60–2 (Vergil, *E.* 2.18 and 45–50, *G.* 4.181–3). S. creates a similar scene in *c.* 2.412–16: the home of Aurora.

29 Saba (Sheba) is in the south-west of the Arabian peninsula.

30 Such extravagances of luxury created by King Porus, an opponent of Alexander the Great, are described in the pseudonymous *Letter of Alexander to his teacher Aristotle*. Typically, S. develops the descriptive possibilities of this romantic material while dismissing any comparison.

31 Cottium has not been identified.

32 Avitus: recipient of the effusive *Ep.* 3.1 and a relative and close friend of S. (*PLRE* 2.194–5, and stemma 14).

33 Fidulus is unknown; perhaps a lawyer, like Tetradius, who was a jurist from Arles.

34 Tetradius received the short commendatory *Ep.* 3.10.

35 Identified on linguistic grounds as St Matthew of Tréviers, between Nîmes and Narbonne.

the younger one is my good companion,
and colleague, and indeed my brother too –
but if by chance you find the older one,
bow low and greet him almost as an uncle.[36]
Thence go, my wee book, to the ample home   90
of consul Magnus,[37] and to your friend Felix,[38]
and where their father's library is, whose like
was never owned, even by stern Philagrius.[39]
Probus will prove, approve, and admit you.[40]
Here you will be often read by my Eulalia,[41]   95
whose nature, like Cecropian Athena's,
scared stern old men, and even her husband's
father when wearing the purple of his office.[42]

But that's enough! come now, leave my harbour
before I swamp the boat with heavy ballast.   100
Raise the anchor, with these verses as cargo!

36 The two Thaumasti are probably father and son, and so uncle and cousin of S. (*PLRE* 2.1062–3, stemma 14), rather than Thaumastus and Apollinaris (see *PLRE* 2.113–14), as maintained by Anderson. S. got on well with the younger man, but less so perhaps with the elder; he plays on the senses of the word for 'uncle' (*patruus*), which may also indicate a harsh or censorious person, with the words 'almost my uncle' conveying a certain coldness.

37 Magnus (*PLRE* 2.700–1) was consul in 460. He is mentioned in *c.* 5.558–61, *c.* 9.1–5, *c.* 15.154–7, *Ep.* 1.11.10.

38 Cf. *Ep.* 2.3.1 (congratulating Felix on elevation to the patriciate) and *c.* 9. He was praetorian prefect in 469, surely after the date of this poem; he could hardly mention the honour of Magnus but not that of Felix if it had already happened.

39 For Philagrius, ancestor of Eparchius Avitus, see *c.* 7.156–7 and *PLRE* 1.693.

40 For Probus cf. *c.* 9.6 and *c.* 9.333; *PLRE* 2.910–11 (Probus 4).

41 This is Eulalia, a cousin of S. (*PLRE* 2.418), addressed by him in *Ep.* 4.1.

42 Probus's father was Magnus: see note 40.

GLOSSARY

Abydus: a town on the Hellespont
Achaemenian, Achaemenid: (usually) Persian
Aeacides: Achilles (after his grandfather Aeacus)
Aetolia: district in western central Greece
Alans: a tribe settled within western Europe in late 406
Alcides: Hercules (descendant of Alceus)
Amyclae: a town near Sparta (town): Sparta (region)
Aquilo: the north wind
Arcadian: the god Mercury
Arpinas: from or born in Arpinum, town in central Italy
Arsacid: successors of Arsaces, the first Parthian king
Assyria: Assyria, in Mesopotamia (Iraq), or nearby lands
Athos: a rocky promontory in northern Greece
Auster: south wind
Avernus: the underworld
Babylon: city on river Euphates in Mesopotamia (Iraq)
Bacchantes: worshippers of Bacchus
Bassarids: worshippers of Bacchus
Bebrycian: of Bebrycia, a land on southern shore of the Black Sea
Berecyntian: an epithet of the goddess Cybele
Bistonian: Thracian
Boreas: the north wind
Bow-bearer: Apollo
Calpe: Gibraltar
Castalides: Muses
Ceres: goddess of corn
Chaldaeans: inhabitants of southern Assyria

Chalybes: inhabitants of the south shore of the Black Sea
Chaonia: related to Dodona (adjective)
Cicones: a people in southern Thrace
Cilicia: a region in south-east Asia Minor
Cinyphian: African
Colchis: a country to the south-east of the Black Sea
Cytherean: Venus
Dacia: a province north of the Danube
Dindymon, Dindymum: a mountain in Phrygia sacred to Cybele
Dione: Venus, or her mother
Dryads: wood-nymphs
Echionian: Theban
Emathian: Thessalian
Ephyra: Corinth
Ephyreiadan: Corinthian
Epidaurus: a city near Argos
Erechthean: Athenian
Euganean: related to the region of north-eastern Italy
Eurus: the east wind
Haemonian: Thessalian
Haemus: a mountain range in northern Thrace
Hebrus: a river of Thrace
Hyperborean: from/in the far North
Illyricum: region/province east of the Adriatic sea
Labdacids: the family of Labdacus, who ruled Thebes
Lacedaemon: Sparta
Lenaeus: Bacchus
Libya: north Africa
Lipara: Lipara, island north of Sicily
Lucina: goddess of childbirth
Lyaeus: Bacchus
Lycaonian: from/in Arcadia
Maenalus: a mountain range in Arcadia
Maeonian: Homeric

Mareotic: of Mareotis, an Egyptian lake
Mars: god of war; warfare
Mimalliones: Bacchantes
Mygdonian: people of Macedonia or Phrygia
Nabatean: from northern Arabia; Arabian
Nasamonians: a people of Libya
Noricum: a province in the Alps, south of the Danube
Odrysian: Thracian
Ogygian: Theban
Othrys: a mountain range in southern Thessaly
Paean: Apollo
Paeonian: (belonging to) a people living north of Thrace
Pandion: a king of Athens
Paphian: Venus
Parthenope: Naples
Pelasgians: (equivalent to) Greeks
Pelethronian: Thessalian
Phasis: town on the Black Sea, and its river
Pholoe: a district in Thessaly
Python: serpent (as slain by Apollo)
Rhodope: mountain range in Western Thrace
Riphaean: of mountains of the far north
Sarra: Tyre
Satyrs: demigods of wild places
Sigeum: a town in the region of Troy
Sithonian: a Thracian tribe
Susa: Persian city, capital of the Achaemenians
Syrtes: dangerous sands off the coast of north Africa; also fertile fields
Tanais: river Don
Tantalids: descendants of Tantalus
Tartesian: in/from the far west of Spain
Therapne: a village near Sparta
Thermodontian: from a river in the Black Sea region
Trinacrian: Sicilian

Tritonis: Athena (named from a lake in north Africa)
Tyrian: of the city of Tyre
Zephyrus: the west wind

NOTES ON THE TEXT USED

The text translated in this work is that of Anderson's/the Loeb edition, from which I have diverged in the following places:

c. 1. 25 *doctore*: *Victore* Loeb

c. 5. 385 *nuper post*: *ferus* Loeb

c. 7. 572 *Ugerni*: *Vierni* Loeb

c. 11. 89 *minor*: *minus* Loeb

c. 13. 19 *Geryonen*: *Eurysthea* Loeb; the word in the manuscripts, *histriones*, which means 'actors', is surely impossible

c. 22. 150 *aedem*: *aream* Loeb

c. 23. 157 *Priapi*: *Priapo* Loeb

c. 24. 81 *satis*: *latens* Loeb

BIBLIOGRAPHY

AMHERDT, D. (2001) *Sidoine Apollinaire, Le quatrième livre de la correspondance*, Bern.

ANDERSON, W. B. (1934) 'Notes on the *Carmina* of Apollinaris Sidonius', *Classical Quarterly* 28: 17–23.

ANDERSON, W. B. (1936) *Sidonius, Poems and Letters Translated, with Introduction and Notes*, Cambridge and London.

ANDERSON, W. B., ed. (1980 and 1965) *Sidonius: Poems and Letters*, in two volumes, Cambridge, MA and London.

BARTON, J. and MUDDIMAN, J. (2001), eds, *The Oxford Bible Commentary*, Oxford.

BEARD, M. (2007) *The Roman Triumph*, London.

BÉRANGER, J. (1948) 'Le Refus du pouvoir', *Musée Helvétique* 5: 178–96.

BLOCKLEY, R. C. (1983) *The Fragmentary Classicising Historians of the Later Roman Empire II*, Francis Cairns.

BROLLI, T. (2013) 'Writing Commentary on Sidonius' Panegyrics', in *New Approaches to Sidonius Apollinaris*, ed. J. van Waarden and G. Kelly, Leuven, 93–109.

CAMERON, Alan (1970) *Claudian: Poetry and Propaganda at the Court of Honorius*, Oxford.

CAMERON, Alan (1976) *Circus Factions: Blues and Greens at Rome and Byzantium*, Oxford.

CAMERON, Averil and GARNSEY, P., eds (1998) *The Cambridge Ancient History*, volume 13: *The Late Empire, A. D. 337–42*, Cambridge.

CAMERON, Averil, WARD-PERKINS, B. and WHITBY, M., eds (2000) *The Cambridge Ancient History*, volume 14: *Late Antiquity: Empire and Successors, A. D. 423–600*, Cambridge.

CARTLEDGE, P. (1993) *Ancient Greece: A Very Short Introduction*, Oxford.

CHASTAGNOL, A. (1960) *La Préfecture Urbaine à Rome sous le Bas Empire*, Paris.

CHENAULT, R. (2012) 'Statues of Senators in the Forum of Trajan and the Roman Forum in Late Antiquity', *Journal of Roman Studies* 102: 103–32.

CLOVER, F. M. (1971) 'Flavius Merobaudes', *Transactions of the American Philosophical Society* 61: 36–45.

CONSOLINO, F. E. (2020) 'Sidonius' Shorter Poems', in *The Edinburgh Companion to Sidonius Apollinaris*, ed. G. Kelly and J. van Waarden, Edinburgh, 341–72.

COURCELLE, P. (1948) *Les Lettres Grecques en Occident de Macrobe à Cassiodore*, Paris.

COURTNEY, E., ed. (1980) *A Commentary on the Satires of Juvenal*, London.

COURTOIS, C. (1955) *Les Vandales et l'Afrique*, Paris.

DELHEY, N. (1993) *Apollinaris Sidonius, Carm. 22: Burgus Pontii Leontii*, Berlin and New York.

DEWAR, M., ed., tr. and comm. (1996) *Claudian: Panegyricus de Sexto Consulatu Honorii Augusti*, Oxford.

DOLVECK, F. (2020) 'The Manuscript Tradition of Sidonius', in *The Edinburgh Companion to Sidonius Apollinaris*, ed. G. Kelly and J. van Waarden, Edinburgh, 479–512.

DRINKWATER, J. and ELTON, H., eds (1992) *Fifth Century Gaul: A Crisis of Identity?* Cambridge.

FRAENKEL, E. (1957) *Horace*, Oxford.

FRANZOI, A. (2016) 'Ancora sul vicus Helena', *Lexis* 34: 420–4.

FURBETTA, L. (2015) 'L'epitaffio di Sidonio Apollinare in un nuove testimonio manoscritto', *Euphrosyne* n.s. 43: 243–54.

FURBETTA, L. (2020) 'Sidonius Scholarship: 15th–19th Centuries', in *The Edinburgh Companion to Sidonius Apollinaris*, ed. G. Kelly and J. van Waarden, Edinburgh, 543–63.

GEISLER, E. (1887) *Loci Similes Auctorum Sidonio Anteriorum*, in *Monumenta Germaniae Historica, Auctorum Antiquissimorum Tomus* viii, *Apollinaris Sidonii Epistulae et Carmina*, ed. C. Luetjohann, Berlin, 351–416.

GIBBON, E. (1776–88) *The History of the Decline and Fall of the Roman Empire*, London.

GILLETT, A. (2001) 'Rome, Ravenna, and the Last Western Emperors', *Papers of the British School at Rome* 69: 131–67.

GILLETT, A. (2012) 'Epic Panegyric and Political Communication in the Fifth Century West', in *Two Romes: Rome and Constantinople in Late Antiquity*, ed. L. Grig and G. Kelly, Oxford, 265–90.

GNOLI, R. (1988) *Marmora Romana*, Rome.

GREEN, R. P. H. (1985) 'Still Waters Run Deep: A New Study of the *Professores* of Bordeaux', *Classical Quarterly* 35: 491–506.

GREEN, R. P. H. (1990) 'Greek in Late Roman Gaul: The Evidence of Ausonius', in *Owls to Athens: Essays Presented to Sir Kenneth Dover*, ed. E. M. Craik, Oxford, 311–19.

GREEN, R. P. H. (1991) *The Works of Ausonius*, Oxford.

GREEN, R. P. H. (2016) 'The Sadness of Eparchus Avitus', *Classical Quarterly* 66: 821–5.

GREEN, R. P. H. (2020) 'Translating Sidonius', in *The Edinburgh Companion to Sidonius Apollinaris*, ed. G. Kelly and J. van Waarden, Edinburgh, 618–27.

GRIFFIN, M. T. (1976) *Seneca: A Philosopher in Politics*, Oxford.

GRIG, L. and KELLY, G., eds (2012) *Two Romes: Rome and Constantinople in Late Antiquity*, Oxford.

GUALANDRI, I. (2020) 'Sidonius' Intertextuality', in *The Edinburgh Companion to Sidonius Apollinaris*, ed. G. Kelly and J. van Waarden, Edinburgh, 341–72.

HALM, R., ed. (1860) *Rhetores Minores*, Leipzig.

HARDIE, A. (1983) *Statius and the Silvae: Poets, Patrons and Epideixis in the Graeco-Roman World*, Liverpool.

HARRIES, J. (1994) *Sidonius Apolinaris and the Fall of Rome*, Oxford.

HEATHER, P. (1991) *Goths and Romans 332–489*, Oxford.

HEATHER, P. (2005) *The Fall of the Roman Empire: A New History*, London.

HERNÁNDEZ LOBATO, J. (2015) *Sidonio Apolinar, Poemas*, Madrid.

HERRIN, J. (2020) *Ravenna, Capital of Empire, Crucible of Europe*, London.

HOWELL, P. (1980) *A Commentary on Book One of the Epigrams of Martial*, London.

HUMPHREY, J. H. (1986) *Roman Circuses: Arenas for Chariot Racing*, London.

HUMPHRIES, M. (2012) 'Valentinian III and the City of Rome (425–55): Patronage, Politics, Power', in *Two Romes: Rome and Constantinople in Late Antiquity*, ed. L. Grig and G. Kelly, Oxford, 161–82.

HUTTNER, U. (2004) *Recusatio Imperii*, Hildesheim.

JENSSON, G. (2004) *The Recollections of Encolpius: The Satyrica of Petronius as Milesian Fiction*, Groningen, 108–22.

JONES, A. H. M. (1966) *The Decline of the Ancient World*, London and New York.

JONES, A. H. M. (1973) *The Later Roman Empire 284–602*, Oxford.

KELLY, G. (2013) 'Sidonius and Claudian', in *New Approaches to Sidonius Apollianaris*, ed. J. van Waarden and G. Kelly, Leuven, 171–9.

KELLY, G. (2018) *Erasing Victor: Sidonius, Manuscripts, and Prosopography* [blogpost] <http://research.shca.ed.ac.uk/sidonius/2018/02/18/erasing-victor-sidonius-manuscripts-and-prosopography/> Edinburgh.

KELLY, G. (2020) 'Dating the Works of Sidonius', in *The Edinburgh Companion to Sidonius Apollinaris*, ed. G. Kelly and J. van Waarden, Edinburgh, 166–94.

KELLY, G. and van WAARDEN, J. (2020) *The Edinburgh Companion to Sidonius Apollinaris*, Edinburgh.

KNEISSEL, P. (1969) *Die Siegestitulatur der römischen Kaiser*, Göttingen.

KULIKOWSKI, M. (2008) 'Carmen VII of Sidonius and a Hitherto Unknown Gothic Civil War', *Journal of Late Antiquity* 1.2: 335–52.

LENSKI, N. (1997) 'Initium Mali Romano imperio: Contemporary Reactions to the Battle of Adrianople', *Transactions of the American Philological Association* 127: 129–68.

LOYEN, A. (1933) 'Qu' est-que l'Albis?' *Revue des Études Latines* 11: 322–4.

LOYEN, A. (1934) 'Les Débuts du Royaume Visigothique de Toulouse', *Revue des Études Latines* 12: 406–15.

LOYEN, A. (1942) *Recherches Historiques sur les Panégyriques de Sidoine Apollinaire*, Paris.

LOYEN, A. (1960) *Sidoine Apollinaire Tome 1: Poèmes*, Paris.

LÜETJOHANN, C. (1887) in *Apollinaris Sidonii Epistulae et Carmina, Auctorum Antiquissimorum Tomus viii*, Berlin.

MACCORMACK, S. (1981) *Art and Ceremony in Late Antiquity*, Berkeley, CA.

MCEVOY, M. A. (2013) *Child Emperor Rule in the Late Roman West AD 367–455*, Oxford.

MACGEORGE, P. (2002) *Late Roman Warlords*, Oxford.

MAENCHEN-HELFEN, O. J. (1973) *The World of the Huns*, Berkeley, CA.

MAGIE, D. (1950) *Roman Rule in Asia Minor to the End of the Third Century after Christ*, Princeton, NJ.

MANITIUS, M. (1889) 'Vorbilder und Nachahmer des Valerius Flaccus', *Philologus* 48: 248–54.

MARCH, J. (2008) *The Penguin Book of Classical Myths*, London.

MARROU, H. I. (1956) *History of Education in Antiquity*, Paris.

MATHISEN, R. W. (1979a) 'Sidonius on the Reign of Avitus: A Study in Political Prudence', *Transactions of the American Philological Association* 109: 165–71.

MATHISEN, R. W. (1979b) 'Resistance and Reconciliation. Majorian and the Gallic Aristocracy after the Fall of Avitus', *Francia* 7, 597–627.

MATHISEN, R. W. (1991) *Studies in the History, Literature and Society of Late Antiquity*, Amsterdam.

MATHISEN, R. W. (2020) 'Sidonius' People', in *The Edinburgh Companion to Sidonius Apollinaris*, ed. G. Kelly and J. van Waarden, Edinburgh, 29–75.

MATTHEWS, J. (1975) *Western Aristocracies and Imperial Court A. D. 364–425*, Oxford.

MÓCSY, A. (1974) *Pannonia and Upper Moesia: A History of the Middle Danube Provinces of the Roman Empire*, London.

MOHR, P. (1895) *Caius Sollius Apollinaris Sidonius*, Leipzig.

MRATSCHEK. S. (2020) 'Creating Culture and Preserving the Self in Sidonius', in *The Edinburgh Companion to Sidonius Apollinaris*, ed. G. Kelly and J. van Waarden, Edinburgh, 237–260.

MUHLBERGER, S. (1992) 'Looking Back from Mid Century: The Gallic Chronciler of 452 and the Crisis of Honorius' reign', in *Fifth Century Gaul: A Crisis of Identity?* ed. J. Drinkwater and H. Elton, Cambridge, 28–37.

NISBET, R. G. M. (1978) 'Felicitas at Surrentum (Statius, *Silvae* II. 2)', *Journal of Roman Studies* 68: 1–11.

NIXON, C. E. V. and SAYLOR RODGERS, B. (1994) *In Praise of Later Roman Emperors: The Panegyrici Latini*, Berkeley, CA.

OOST, S. I. (1964) 'Aetius and Majorian', *Classical Philology* 59: 23–9.

PARKE, H. W. (1967) *The Oracles of Zeus: Dodona, Olympia, Ammon*, Oxford.

PELTTARI, A. (2016) 'Sidonius Apollinaris and Horace, *Ars Poetica* 14–23', *Philologus* 161: 322–36.

PIGANIOL, A. (1972) *L'Empire Chrétien*, Paris.

PLATNER, S. B. and ASHBY, T. (1929) *A Topographical Dictionary of Ancient Rome*, Oxford.

RAVENNA, G. (1990) *Le Nozze di Polemio e Araneola*, Bologna.

ROBERTS, M. (1992) 'Barbarians in Gaul: The Response of the Poets', in *Fifth-century Gaul: A Crisis of Identity?* ed. J. Drinkwater and H Elton, Cambridge, 97–106.

ROBERTS, M. (2001) 'Rome Personified, Rome Epitomized: Representations of Rome in the Poetry of the Early Fifth Century', *American Journal of Philology* 122: 533–65.

SALWAY, P. (1981) *Roman Britain*, Oxford.

SANTELIA, S. (1999) 'Note sul culto di san Giuliano di Brioude: Sidonio Apolinare Carm. 24, 16–19', *Vetera Christianorum* 36: 287–96.

SANTELIA, S. (2002) *Sidonio Apollinare: Carme 24 Propemptikon ad libellum*, Bari.

SCHETTER, W. (1994) *Kaiserzeit und Spätantike: Kleine Schriften 1957–1992*, Stuttgart.

SCHINDLER, C. (2009) *Per carmina laudes*, Berlin and New York.

SEMPLE, W. H. (1930) *Quaestiones Exegeticae Sidonianae*, Cambridge.

SHACKLETON BAILEY, D. R. (1976) 'Notes, Critical and Interpretative, on the Poems of Sidonius Apollinaris', *Phoenix* 30.3: 242–51.

STEIN, E. (1959) *Histoire du Bas-Empire*, tr. J. R. Palanque, Paris.

STEVENS, C. E. (1933 and 1979) *Sidonius Apollinaris and his Age*, Oxford.

STICKLER, T. (2002) *Aëtius: Gestaltungsspielräume eines Heermeisters*, Munich.

STROHEKER, K. F. (1948) *Der senatorische Adel in spätantiken Gallien*, Tübingen.

TAN, Z. E. (2014) 'Subversive Geography in Tacitus' *Germania*', *Journal of Roman Studies* 104: 181–204.

THOMPSON, E. A. (1996) *The Huns*, revised by P. Heather, Oxford.

VAN DER BROEK, R. (1972) *The Myth of the Phoenix*, Leiden.

VAN WAARDEN, J. and KELLY, G. (2013) *New Approaches to Sidonius Apollianaris*, Leuven.

WIJSMANN, H. J. W. (2000) *Valerius Flaccus Argonautica Book VI. A Commentary*, Leiden.

WOOD, I. (2021) 'The Making of the Burgundian Kingdom', *Reti Medievali Rivista* V. 22.2.

ZISSOS, A. (2006) 'Reception of Valerius Flaccus' *Argonautica*', *International Journal of the Classical Tradition* 13: 167–9.

INDEX